AF352479

EMPIRE
AND
POETIC
VOICE

SUNY series

EXPLORATIONS

in

POSTCOLONIAL STUDIES

Emmanuel C. Eze and Arif Dirlik, editors

EMPIRE
AND
POETIC
VOICE

*Cognitive and Cultural Studies
of Literary Tradition and Colonialism*

PATRICK COLM HOGAN

STATE UNIVERSITY OF NEW YORK PRESS

Published by
STATE UNIVERSITY OF NEW YORK PRESS, ALBANY

© 2004 State University of New York

All rights reserved

Printed in the United States of America

For information, address State University of New York Press,
90 State Street, Suite 700, Albany, NY 12207

Production by Christine L. Hamel
Marketing by Michael Campochiaro

Library of Congress Cataloging-in-Publication Data

Hogan, Patrick Colm.
   Empire and poetic voice : cognitive and cultural studies of literary tradition and
colonialism / by Patrick Colm Hogan.
       p. cm. — (SUNY series, explorations in postcolonial studies)
   Includes bibliographical references and index.
   ISBN 0-7914-5963-2 (alk. paper)
   1. Commonwealth literature (English)—History and criticism. 2. English literature—20th
century—History and criticism. 3. Postcolonialism—English-speaking countries. 4.
Influence (Literary, artistic, etc.) 5. Imperialism in literature. 6. Colonies in literature. I.
Title. II. Series.

PR9080.H646 2003
820.9'9171241—dc21

                                                                                        2003045838

10   9   8   7   6   5   4   3   2   1

In memory of
Agha Shahid Ali

4 February 1949 – 8 December 2001

Contents

ACKNOWLEDGMENTS

Parts of the introduction and chapter 5 were presented at the 2000 Modern Language Association convention in Washington, D.C. An earlier version of portions of chapter 1 was presented at the 1995 Modern Language Association convention in Chicago. A few paragraphs of chapter 2 appeared previously in "Historical Economies of Race and Gender in Bengal: Ray and Tagore on the Home and the World," *Journal of South Asian Literature* 28.1/2 (1993): 23–43. I am grateful to Professor Surjit Dulai for permission to reprint. An earlier version of part of chapter 4 appeared in "Understanding *The Palm-Wine Drinkard*," *Ariel: A Review of International English Literature* 31.4 (2000): 33–58. I am grateful to the Board of Governors, University of Calgary, Calgary, Alberta, for permission to reprint.

I am indebted to Paula Richman for information on variants of the Rāma story, to Tapan Roy for his invaluable help with the Bengali original of Tagore's novel, and to Lalita Pandit for cogent comments on one chapter and for suggesting the glossary of theoretical terms. Two anonymous readers for the State University of New York Press gave insightful comments that have improved the book substantively. Jane Bunker, my editor at SUNY, handled the manuscript expertly, just as I expected from working with her on *Colonialism and Cultural Identity*. Finally, I am grateful to Christine Hamel and all those involved in the production process for their fine work.

Decolonizing Literary Identity

Almost a quarter century ago, Chinweizu, Jemie, and Madubuike issued their famous call for the decolonization of African literature. They began by asserting that anyone "concerned for the health of African culture" should look at "the ways and means whereby Western imperialism has maintained its hegemony over African literature, and the effect of that hegemony upon the literary arts of contemporary Africa" (x). In short, they situated literary tradition and literary identity at the center of cultural imperialism and the struggle of colonized peoples to achieve genuine independence and autonomy.

Virtually everyone in a colonized society is faced with the problem of cultural identity. The "metropolitan" culture (that is, the culture of the colonizer) is dominant everywhere. It has authority, prestige, familiarity, and widespread currency. Indigenous practices in Africa or India are continually challenged by the hegemony of European practices. Indigenous laws or religious beliefs become questionable if they are contradicted by European laws or religious beliefs—or they become valued insofar as they appear to mirror or perhaps even anticipate European ideas and practices. Thus such simple decisions as how to conduct a birthday celebration become politicized in terms of their relation to colonialism. Consider, for example, one practice formerly common among economically stable families in some areas of India. The child's birthday would be marked by the family giving milk, sweets, food, clothing, or other presents to poor children. Such practices are associated with religious songs, such as one about the incarnate God, Kṛṣṇa, as a little boy. He loved butter so much that he would rub it all over his face. When giving butter to poor children, he would often rub it on their faces. His mother would chide him, saying: You rub the butter on your face because you can eat it whenever you want; let them eat the butter first. The question, then, is: Should a birthday celebration in India forego traditional practices and set aside traditional songs for a celebration in which the child of a well-off family receives toys from the children of other well-off families and everyone sings "Happy Birthday to You"? Should such a celebration mix the two traditions? If it does incorporate Western practices, does this enrich the custom, debase it, or neither? Is birthday cake a matter of "changing with the times," or is it a surrender to dubious practices that have achieved their value due to Western wealth and force of arms?

While these issues confront everyone, they face authors—as well as filmmakers and other artists—with particular force. Authors do not simply live in ordinary culture. It is their job to make culture. Literature itself is part of culture. Moreover, it is not just some isolated part. Literature is one of the primary means by which a culture represents to itself the ambient acts and ideas of daily life. Our actual experience of lived culture is limited to our own circle of family and friends. Moreover, it is radically incomplete. It is partial, biased, fragmentary. We hardly ever know an actual marriage in the broad and detailed way that we know a marriage described in a novel or portrayed in a play or film. Thus authors encounter the dilemmas of cultural identity at a number of different levels, and with perhaps unique urgency.

PRECOLONIAL PURITY, MULTICULTURALISM, AND HYBRIDITY

Chinweizu, Jemie, and Madubuike advocate one common response to these dilemmas—return to authentic indigenous traditions of literature and orature. Today, that position is not as popular among postcolonial critics as it once was. For example, Chinweizu et al. do not merit a single mention in Leela Gandhi's introduction to postcolonial theory. They appear only once in Ashcroft, Griffiths, and Tiffin's massive *Post-Colonial Studies Reader*, in a brief dismissal by Tiffin. Specifically, Tiffin writes that "the contradictions inherent in a project such as Chinweizu, Jemie, and Madubuike's *Toward the Decolonization of African Literature* demonstrate" that "pre-colonial cultural purity can never be fully recovered" (95).

For reasons that will become clear below, I believe that *Toward the Decolonization of African Literature* is a work of intellectual power and theoretical value. Nonetheless, I do have to agree that their argument is at times contradictory. A reader cannot always tell if these authors are arguing for genuine Africanness, or a synthesis of African and European. They suggest the former when they "begin by declaring the separate and autonomous status of African literature . . . from all others" (Chinweizu et al. 10). But they state the latter quite plainly when they "demand" a "deliberate and calculated process of syncretism" (239). Sometimes they imply that postcolonization literature is already synthetic, as when they write that "the African novel is a hybrid out of the African oral tradition and the imported literary forms of Europe" (8). At other times they indicate that most recent African literature has actually failed to incorporate African traditions. In consequence, they call on writers to undertake "an apprenticeship in the African oral tradition" (240). Then there are places where they say that at least some writers are fully African, as when they characterize "Tutuola's mythic imagination" as "completely within the Yoruba African tradition" (288).

But self-contradiction is not the only reason for the relative unpopularity of this call for a literary return to indigenous sources. More importantly, most critics writing today feel that an insistence on cultural identity risks fundamentalism; that, however opposed to cultural imperialism it may be, an appeal to authenticity is itself an assertion of cultural imperialism. Here too, despite my admiration for Chinweizu, Jemie, and Madubuike, I must agree. The problem is not at all confined to calls for authentic African literary identity. Judith Butler has put the general point concisely. Reflecting a common suspicion of any calls for self-definition in relation to some putatively genuine group identity, she writes that she is "permanently troubled by identity categories" (14) for she sees them as "instruments of regulatory regimes" (13).

But at least two significant questions arise here. First, there is the issue of just what identity categories are and how they operate. We will turn to this in the next section. Second, there is the issue of whether the alternatives to Chinweizu, Jemie, and Madubuike are less problematic.

An obvious alternative to the account of Chinweizu et al. is the celebration of diversity through multiculturalism. If the appeal to a single, unified, purified, indigenous tradition is implicitly hegemonic, then what could be better as a response than the advocacy of many distinct cultures? However, as Walter Benn Michaels has suggested, all appeals to cultural identity—even appeals to multicultural identities—tend to be strongly and persistently ethnicized (see 137–42). In this way, the problem of identity categories merely repeats itself for each segment of a plural culture. Now, instead of a hegemonic African culture, we have a hegemonic Igbo or Yoruba or Hausa culture. Instead of a hegemonic Indian culture, we have hegemonic Hindu, Muslim, Keralese, Tamil, and other cultures. What Judith Butler called "regulatory regimes" do not disappear. They are merely greater in number and lesser in extent (though not necessarily lesser in coercive force). (There is, of course, another use of "multiculturalism" which implies no ethnic linkage and which is not open to these objections. We will return to this in the afterword.)

Among postcolonial theorists, the most popular response to the dilemma of literary identity—and indeed to cultural identity generally—is "hybridity." The idea is associated with Homi Bhabha, though he hardly originated the notion. Hybridity is often seen as offering a genuine solution to dilemmas of colonialism and fundamentalism. In part this is the result of a common cognitive tendency to prefer whatever is perceived as the "middle" between two standard alternatives. It is an unfortunate tendency, for many reasons (the two alternatives may be wrong in precisely the same way, so that their averaging will only repeat the same error; the middle ground may combine the faults of each, producing a result that is worst of all). In any case, hybridity is widely valued in contemporary postcolonial theory. For example, even a writer such as Leela Gandhi, who is critical of the use of the concept, nonetheless calls for a "postnational ethics of hybridity" (137). It should be obvious from this that hybridity is not an evaluatively neutral concept. It has a very strong normative component. For theorists of hybridity, hybridity is good. As Terry Eagleton puts it, "hybridity" gives an "exhilarated sense of alternative possibilities" that "have the power to shake a post-imperial identity to its roots" (qtd. on i of Bhabha *Location;* for a more critical view of Bhabha, complementary to the following discussion, see Dharwadker 120–24).

Here we might ask first whether hybridity really is something good. Prima facie it would seem that it is sometimes good and sometimes bad. It depends on the particular case. A blanket valorization of hybridity would appear to entail strange conclusions. For example, it would seem to suggest that a rāga is *better* when written out note for note and played by a Western orchestra than when partially improvised on a sitar, and that it is better simply because it is played by a Western orchestra, since that makes it hybrid. In any given case, an orchestra version of a rāga may be better—but that would be due to the qualities of the piece, not due to its hybridity per se. Of course, no advocate of hybridity would claim that playing a rāga on an oboe automatically makes it better. But the point is that a celebration of hybridity as hybridity would appear to entail this, no matter what individual theorists might claim.

This brings up the more important issue of hegemony. One standard assumption in discussions of hybridity is that hybridity is opposed to identity categories. Thus to be hybrid is to reject identities; to celebrate hybridity is to cast off regulatory regimes. But this is not true. Hybridity is no less an identity category than "authentically indigenous" or "westernized." It has the same function in defining and opposing groups and in setting out norms. It simply defines groups differently and establishes different norms. Instead of adjuring us to be authentically African, Indian, Hindu, Igbo, Irish, or whatever, it adjures us to be hybrid.

In the introductory essay for his collection *The Location of Culture,* Bhabha discusses some of the horrible effects of binarism in world politics—

ethnic cleansing, slavery, and so on. He then goes on to oppose binarism to hybridity, for political activity today "requires a movement away from a world conceived in binary terms" (14). There are at least two problems here. The more obvious problem is that, for Bhabha, there are precisely two alternatives—bad binarism and good hybridity. But that makes his own view a form of binarism. More importantly, it is not clear that the political horrors isolated by Bhabha are problems of binarism anyway. The apartheid system of South Africa made distinctions among Africans, coloreds, and whites. Thus it was not binaristic. Was it, therefore, alright? Of course not. Conversely, it is highly binaristic to say that Nazi genocide or American slavery was bad and that opposition to these practices was good. Should we condemn people who make such statements because they are binaristic? Should we prefer hybrid, middle positions—for example, the view that Jews should have been confined to work camps, but not exterminated (arguably a hybrid position between Nazi extermination and an anti-Nazi advocacy of equal rights). Similarly, are we to celebrate the "in-betweenness" of colonial collaborationists or quislings? Of course, Bhabha would never support the "hybrid" option in these cases. My point is not to criticize Bhabha's own views or actions, but to indicate that the valorization of hybridity does not have the consequences it is widely believed to have. Identity categories need not be binaristic. Binaries need not be identity categories. Moreover, hybridity can be and has been recruited to the same brutal ends as other identity categories. Hasn't European and American violence against the Islamic world been underwritten by an ideology according to which "we" are plural and combinative while "they" are singular and exclusionary? Isn't this the defining opposition of the Cold War as well—and of the current "War on Terrorism"? In each case, our bombs are justified precisely by our hybridity.

Of course, it may seem that hybridity at least has the advantage of being open to everyone. Not everyone can be English or African. English colonialism defines "English" in such a way as to exclude Africans. African fundamentalism is no less a function of skin color and ancestry. Hybridity, in contrast, is available to all. But this argument has numerous problems. Christianity and Islam are open to all. That does not prevent them from operating quite coercively. Indeed, in Ireland, the openness of Christianity—the possibility of conversion—is what gave rise to some of the worst oppression. Conversely, even "Englishness" was not entirely closed to colonized people, despite widespread English racism. Moreover, if Chinweizu, Jemie, and Madubuike are taken to represent fundamentalism, it turns out that anticolonial fundamentalism is not necessarily exclusionary. They give two examples of people who have genuinely returned to African literary traditions through "apprenticeship," allowing them to "master the verbal art" of African orature. One of these is a Black man, Birago Diop. The other is a White woman, Minne Postma. They state explicitly that "You don't have to be an African to master an African . . . art" (53).

In contrast with this, we might consider Bhabha's characterization of hybridity. Bhabha certainly allows every man and woman his/her own hybridity. Yet he is entirely explicit that not everyone is equally hybrid. He stresses the importance of "the minority perspective" (2; note that this is not "minority perspectives," presumably because minorities share the definitive identity of hybridity). He points to the centrality of "postcolonial migration" and "narratives of cultural and political diaspora" (5). Most strikingly, he invokes Salman Rushdie "to remind us . . . that the truest eye may now belong to the migrant's double vision" (5). Bhabha is not unusual here. One expects this sort of thing for any identity category. For example, one expects rural Irish to consider themselves better specimens of Irishness than urban Irish, and vice versa. One expects Hindus to consider themselves better instances of Indianness than Muslims or Sikhs. So Bhabha considers members of his particular subgroup—minorities, migrants—to be better examples of hybridity. But this indicates once again that hybridity is an identity category of the usual sort, with all that this entails.

On the other hand, there is a tension here. In part, Bhabha is arguing that everyone is hybrid. That is just the condition of the world today. But how then can he point to a particular group as specially hybrid? And how can he valorize hybridity? How can other theorists derive a "postnational ethics of hybridity" from a universal condition? There is, in other words, a systematic ambiguity in Bhabha's use of the term "hybridity." He employs it both normatively and descriptively, as part of an evaluative theory and as part of a descriptive theory. The problem of systematic ambiguity in technical terms is not confined to Bhabha. It is relatively common in literary theory. Part of the self-contradiction in Chinweizu, Jemie, and Madubuike appears to have a similar source.

There are difficulties along these lines in Butler's writing as well. She calls for "a certain resistance to classification and to identity as such" (16), but she seeks this through identity categories defined as sites of "disruption, error, confusion, and trouble" (16). She insists that that the "use" of such categories as "lesbian" must be "such that the instrumental uses of 'identity' do not become regulatory imperatives" (16). But it is difficult to see how these categories could be specified as sites of disruption and so forth, without this constituting a regulatory regime. (After all, nondisruptive uses of "lesbian" are faulty by this definition.) In keeping with this insistence on disruption, Butler tries to undercut the fixity of identity categories—in this case, gender identities—by reference to gender as performance, specifically imitative performance. If all gender identities are performative, then gayness is not distinct. Indeed, neither heterosexuality nor homosexuality is an identity. Thus, she explains that "drag enacts the very structure of impersonation by which *any gender* is assumed" and, as such, "it implies that all gendering is a kind of impersonation" (21). Yet, she goes on to reassert a difference—a difference of identity—almost immediately, as she maintains that "gay identities . . . expose heterosexuality as an incessant and *panicked* imitation" (23). Gay identities are "parodic" (22) and "subversive" (23). Thus Butler makes the apparently anti-identitarian argument that all putative gender identities are marked by imitation (much as all cultural identities are hybrid, in Bhabha's account). Yet she argues simultaneously that some groups (gays and lesbians) have a privileged place with regard to this ubiquitous nonidentity. The latter argument leads to an identity category of the standard, hierarchizing sort. Thus, while both Bhabha and Butler argue against a form of "authentic" identity, they end up substituting another form of identity that has all the characteristics of authenticity—for it seems clear that the right sort of gay or lesbian is, for Butler, parodic, disruptive, and so on.

The situation becomes more complex when Butler writes "I do not mean to suggest that drag is a 'role' that can be taken on or taken off" (23), going so far as to claim that "there is no volitional subject behind the mime who decides, as it were, which gender it will be today" (24). Rather, the very "self"—what one might have thought engages in disruptive, parodic insubordination—is simply "the *constituted effect* of a discourse" (18). This argument is difficult to follow. Her contention that gender is performance appears to work only insofar as gender is open to choice and alteration. The title of her essay refers to "insubordination," which suggests will. She writes that "the negative constructions of lesbianism . . . can be *occupied* and *reworked* to *call into question* the claims of heterosexual priority" (17, emphasis added). Statements such as this seem to imply volition and agency, as does her insistence that one "plays" at being a lesbian (18). Interestingly, the allowance of choice in performativity would seem to leave disruptiveness open to heterosexuals as well—much as African authenticity is open to Europeans, according to Chinweizu, Jemie, and Madubuike. The disallowance of volition, in contrast, appears to fix the implicit hierarchy all the more fully and all the more rigidly, for it ties disruption irrevocably to a sexual identity that one cannot choose. On the other hand, this disallowance simultaneously undermines the normative aspect of Butler's argument. It makes no sense to favor disruptive and parodic performativity if one has no choice in the matter.

In short, the arguments of Bhabha and Butler are no less self-contradictory—and no less assertive of identity and hierarchy—than those of Chinweizu, Jemie, and Madubuike. Despite this, I find some of Butler's comments insightful, and I find many arguments by Chinweizu, Jemie, and Madubuike compelling. However, in order to isolate what is valuable in these writers, and in order to advance our understanding of the issues they are addressing, we need to draw some basic distinctions about identity, fundamentally that between practical and categorial identity.

PRACTICAL IDENTITY AND CATEGORIAL IDENTITY

Identity is not a simple thing. Indeed, the word "identity" is ambiguous in ways that are theoretically consequential. Perhaps the most important ambiguity is that between practical and categorial identity. Categorial identity (or "reflective" identity, as I called it in *Colonialism and Cultural Identity*) is one's self-reflective identity or self-concept. It is defined by a set of categories, prominently including gender, race, ethnicity, religion, and so on. Categorial identity produces in-group/out-group divisions, with all that they entail. In contrast, practical identity is one's set of habits, skills, and propensities. To use a Heideggerian phrase, it is one's way of being in the world. Or, in Wittgenstein's terminology, it is one's form of life. (On these ideas from Heidegger and Wittgenstein, see my *Philosophical Approaches* 119–26, 275–76, and citations.) It includes not only one's own competences, but also one's expectations of others, for one's practical identity must fit with the practical identities of people in one's community. Thus practical identity includes everything from greeting practices (what to say, to whom, in what circumstances) to driving a car to professional activities (e.g., teaching or submitting articles to journals). Note that a group of people may share practical identity involving extensive and complex mutual interdependence—as in, say, a village in India where different farming, craft, and other activities require one another. However, these same people may divide along lines of categorial identity (e.g., Hindu vs. Muslim), even to the point of mutual violence that is destructive of everyone's practical identity and thus well-being.

In the following pages, I will be drawing heavily on principles of cognitive science to present an "algorithmic" or step-by-step account of particular aspects and manifestations of these identities. In a preliminary way, we might say that categorial identity involves a hierarchy of categories in a person's internal, mental lexicon. These categories have two components. The first is a presumed extension, which is to say, the presupposition of a set of persons to whom the term applies—for example, the presupposition that there is a set of persons who are Catholic, Hindu, African, Igbo, or whatever. Obviously, individual lexicons do not include a complete list of these persons. The extension is open. It often includes some sort of identification criteria (e.g., ways of telling who is Catholic, Hindu, and so on). But these are not definitive. Perhaps what is most important here is that the mere fact of inclusion in an extension (e.g., the mere fact of falling under the category "Catholic,"

"Hindu," or whatever) is what produces in-group/out-group divisions, with their biases, antagonisms, and so on. Social psychological research indicates that these divisions are produced even by explicitly arbitrary assignment to different groups (see Duckitt 68–69). The rivalry between two high schools is not a matter of some supposed traits shared by students at each school. In my case, for example, antagonism between students at my Jesuit high school and those at the rival Christian Brothers high school—a rivalry that sometimes led to fisticuffs—had nothing to do with real or even imagined characteristics of those students. It was solely a matter of belonging to one group or the other. The same point holds for everything from street gangs to nations. Of course, in all these cases, the opposition may be *justified* by some appeal to supposed properties of group members—that "our" people are tougher, cleverer, more devout, more just, more chaste, or whatever. But in fact, the sole definitive property is group membership. The rest is propaganda.

This leads us to the second lexical component of categorial identity, definition—or, rather, a complex characterization that includes definitional elements, but also prototypical and even stereotypical properties, ideals, and so on. For example, this semantic component for the category "man" includes much more than a biological definition (male, adult, human). It includes expectations, ideals of manliness, and the like. While the extension of an identity category determines in-group/out-group division, the semantic element determines our evaluation of group members, including ourselves—and, as just suggested, it frequently serves as the ideological justification for antagonism between groups or for hierarchization of groups. Thus a man and a woman or a Hindu and a Muslim who show similar traits are not typically categorized together. Rather, they are assigned to opposed groups extensionally, then evaluated by reference to those groups (perhaps with opposed valences, when there is similarity in traits—as when a woman is criticized for having traits that are praised in a man, or vice versa). Note again that the group assignment is what produces in-group favoritism, in-group/out-group antagonism, and so on. However, the descriptive element of group characterization may be recruited subsequently to justify that favoritism, antagonism, and so on. For example, the male/female identity division creates in-group/out-group hierarchies on its own. However, men or women may subsequently invoke putative group properties ("Women are too emotional"; "Men are insensitive") to justify those hierarchies—which may be systematized institutionally, as in the case of patriarchy.

In cognitive terms, practical identity is a complex of interrelated "procedural schemas." Procedural schemas are, roughly, skills—cognitive structures that allow us to do certain things. For example, one complex of procedural schemas allows us to drive a car. We acquire procedural schemas largely by practice. We learn to drive a car by practicing aspects of driving a car, then practicing the coordination of those aspects (i.e., we acquire procedural schemas for turning, braking, etc.; then we acquire procedural schemas for the coordination of turning, braking, etc.). Practice itself involves repetition and correction. Specifically, it requires "cognitive monitoring," self-conscious self-observation and self-evaluation in comparison with an ideal. Once we acquire a procedural schema, we simply "run" the schema while thinking about larger goals. When driving, I think about getting over to the right lane. I do not think about how to check my rearview mirror, how to check the blind spot, how to turn the wheel, and so on. Rather, I think of the larger goal and then act on the procedural schemas necessary to achieve that goal. In acquiring procedural schemas, however, I concentrate on components—turning back to the blind spot, slightly turning the wheel, adjusting the speed relative to cars in the other lane.

Our practical identity comprises a vast number of procedural schemas. We chose and acquired some of these self-consciously. Others were chosen for us in childhood. In those cases, cognitive monitoring was simply a matter of paying attention to what other people said; Mom and Dad did the evaluating for us and we only had to listen and adjust our behavior when they said No or Yes or when they gave more specific instructions. These procedural schemas are impossible to change as a group. However, individually, these schemas are, in most cases, malleable through repetition and cognitive monitoring. Moreover, it is always possible to add new schemas, usually with no deleterious effect on schemas we already have (e.g., acquiring the schemas for driving a car does not cause us to lose the schemas for riding a bicycle).

The semantic part of identity categories includes category ideals. These provide ways of evaluating our behavior and thus they may guide us (sometimes via our parents, teachers, and so on) in cognitive monitoring and practice. Consider a banal example. Max comes to believe that men should be self-assertive. Though he tends to be shy, he monitors his behavior and begins to make small gestures of self-assertion. These develop into procedural schemas until he responds with self-assertion automatically. The same point holds for Krishna and properties of being a Hindu. In this way, categorial identity can have deep effects on one's practical identity. Of course, these effects are not simple, nor are they confined to the imitation of an ideal. In some cases, the ideal may be unattainable and give rise to despair. In other cases, a stereotype my give rise to aversive behavior (e.g., knowing the stereotype of Irish as drunkards, Seamus may avoid alcohol entirely). Moreover, one's categorial identity is shaped by many categories, which interact in complex ways. Gender is particularly important in this regard, for it invariably inflects other categories. In terms of ideals, stereotypes, and so forth, being an Igbo man is different from being an Igbo woman; being a Hindu man is different from being a Hindu woman. Indeed, identity categories are in part contextual. In one context, Azu may be "African"; in another, he may be "Igbo"; in another, "Catholic." Further complications arise from the fact that category meanings are idiolectal. They are not dictionary or encyclopedia entries, shared by everyone. They are the residue of an individual's experiences and understandings. While they partially overlap with other people's category meanings, they are necessarily in part idiosyncratic as well. No two people have precisely the same idea of "Igbo" or "African" or "Catholic."

Here we may clarify both Butler and Bhabha. When Butler speaks of performance, she is isolating something close to practical identity. Practical identity is a "compulsory" form of "mime" (24) in that it derives from a broad range of social practices that we learn through imitation and that are often chosen for us at an early age. Moreover, practical identity is largely determinate at any given moment. It is not something we can simply choose, at least not as a whole. At the same time, contrary to Butler's explicit assertions, there is an element of choice here. For at least many areas of practical identity, we may decide among possibilities. In some cases, the choice is simple. In some cases, it is complex and requires extensive practice. For example, it is possible to choose drag. Moreover, in choosing drag, one may highlight certain common semantic elements of gender categories. In highlighting those aspects (clothing, makeup, modes of prescriptively gender-appropriate behavior), one may indeed suggest their arbitrariness, as Butler maintains.

Thus we may to some degree reconcile the apparent contradiction between the normative account of imitation in Butler and her denial of subjective choice. On the other hand, our analysis also indicates more clearly some of the problems with her critique of identity categories. It is clear that the normative component of identity categories has powerful effects, effects that do foster homogenization, conformity to "gayness," "Africanness," or whatever. On the other hand, it is also clear that the harm of identity categories is not confined to ideals, nor to stereotypes, nor to the semantic component at all. The most powerful effects of identity categories result from the antagonism—ranging all the way to war—that results from semantically vacuous extension. Butler suggests something along these lines at the outset of her essay, and in her call for "resistance to classification and to identity as such" (16). However, she apparently retreats from this point in redefining identities as sites of insubordination, parody, and so on. The problem is that the mere extensional definition of identity groups produces all the pernicious effects of identity. It doesn't matter if the extension is then related to an insubordinate or parodic definition.

Thus, by the lights of the present analysis, Butler's arguments involve insights, but also contradictions and highly problematic forms of identity politics, despite her stance against identity politics. Bhabha's contentions involve similar difficulties. We have already seen that there are problems with

Bhabha's advocacy of hybridity. First, it is not at all clear that hybridity is a good in itself. Second, it appears to be another hegemonic identity category, with all the paraphernalia of a regulatory ideal, defining an elite group that establishes what genuine hybridity is, and so on. In addition, we noted that "hybridity" is ambiguous between a norm and a description. That leads to problems and apparent contradictions in his argument. On the other hand, it could allow us to separate out the "theoretical" part of Bhabha's discussion from the political advocacy or normative part. The political advocacy would be the celebration of hybridity, with the problems just mentioned. The theoretical or descriptive part, however, might avoid those problems.

Descriptively, "hybridity" may be understood either as a categorial identification or as a practical identity. Clearly, it is not a universal categorial identity. Some people identify themselves as hybrid. Others do not. Insofar as it is the common postcolonial condition, then, hybridity must have its descriptive application to practical identity. That makes sense. But the notion falls far short of a theory in this context. Indeed, it is in effect trivial to say that practical identity is hybrid. By some direct or indirect route every tradition in the world has been influenced by a range of other traditions. For example, Christianity influenced Indian thought and Hinduism and Buddhism influenced European ideas long before the advent of European colonialism. Simply to say that every tradition, thus every practical identity, is hybrid is to say almost nothing. A theory of hybridity needs to treat the varieties of influence, their degree, sources, nature, complexity, operation—what sorts of combination arise, how they arise, what their precedents are.

Followers of Bhabha might respond that at the very least the notion of hybridity disallows any talk about pure or genuine traditions. But even that is not accurate. When, say, Chinweizu, Jemie, and Madubuike call for a return to precolonial tradition, they need not be claiming that African traditions developed in absolute isolation from the rest of the world. They need only claim that there has been a particular sort of violence against precolonial traditions and that the beauty, the moral and practical value, of those traditions should not be lost simply because of such violence. It is all well and good if Indian traders brought ideas about medicine or yoga to Eastern Africa and some people were attracted to those ideas, incorporating them into their practical identities and thus into their traditions. But such noncoercive contact and interaction are not the same as Europeans taking virtually all the land in southern Africa, breaking up families with guns and a racist economic system, destroying any possibility for the continuation of traditional culture. One can reject changes of the latter sort—or even changes brought about by global economic domination and global domination of information technology—without in any way committing oneself to the position that African, Indian, or other societies were entirely insular before European colonialism.

On the other hand, it is true that noting the inevitable hybridity or syncretism of traditions does have one salutary consequence. Some writers not only wish to revive or preserve precolonial traditions. They see their goal as actually eliminating all foreign influences, not just those that were imposed through violence or economic domination. The stress on the inescapability of syncretism does indicate that the project of these writers and activists is impossible. Of course, a number of writers stressed this long before the current vogue of hybridity (see, for example, Tagore's 1917 book *Nationalism*, 27, on the inescapable syncretism of Indian tradition).

This last point brings us to a final issue that we should consider before returning to literary identity. There is not simply one way in which categorial identity operates. Thus an advocacy of "Africanness" may lead to a concern for lost practices and beliefs or to a rigid repudiation of anything that is identifiably foreign. Moreover, these differences are not simply multiple and random. There are patterns to the operation of categorial identity. I have discussed these at some length in *Colonialism and Cultural Identity*. Here I will simply outline them briefly. At a basic level, it is clear that categorial identification may refer to the home culture (again, contextually defined—African, Igbo, or whatever), the metropolitan culture (e.g., English culture), or some combination of the two.[1] But this division is not yet fine grained enough. We need to consider the relation between categorial identity and practical identity. The two may be coordinated or they may stand in contradiction with one another. Thus an assertion of indigenous identity (e.g., African identity or Igbo identity) may be connected with a genuine practical integration into African traditions or it may be practically disconnected from those traditions. Thus we have two sets of parameters. The first is indigenous tradition/metropolitan tradition/some combination of the two traditions. The second is practically integrated/practically disconnected. In combination, these parameters yield six possibilities. If the assertion of categorial identity is paired with a practical identity that is indeed integrated, then I refer to it as orthodoxy (for indigenous culture), assimilation (for metropolitan culture), or syncretism (for a combination of the two). For example, an Igbo who is fully conversant with Igbo traditions and who affirms Igbo categorial identity in relation to that fluency would be affirming orthodoxy, in my sense. In contrast, if there is a disconnection from practical identity, then I refer to the affirmation of categorial identity as reactionary traditionalism (for indigenous culture), mimeticism (for metropolitan culture), or alienating hybridity (for a combination of the two).

Though these categories appear to be encompassing, individuals need not simply fall into one category across all areas of culture. Someone who is orthodox in music or art may be a reactionary traditionalist in religion (e.g., an Indian Hindu may be fully conversant with, say, Indian musical traditions, but relatively ignorant of Hindu sacred texts, even while affirming his/her categorial identity as Indian and Hindu in both areas). In addition, there is no reason to believe that people are wholly consistent in their relation to tradition, even within one area of culture. The same person might shift among different attitudes toward theology or marriage practices. Indeed, there are some fairly consistent patterns to such shifts, such as the tendency of reactionary traditionalism to derive from a prior mimeticism (see my *Colonialism* 15–16 and citations).

But we still need to spell out this relation between categorial and practical identity a little more fully. Integration is fairly straightforward. Parts of tradition proceed from daily life and are shared by everyone who grew up in the culture. Others require consistent and extended practice or study. One has a certain familiarity with a culture's music simply by living in the culture. But a fuller integration into a musical tradition—integration of the sort that would be important for a composer or musician, or even a discerning listener—comes only from practice and study. Moreover, this sort of connectedness need not be singular or univocal. First, in any area of even slight social complexity, there will be different, changing traditions. Language is a good instance here. There are regional and other variations as well as historical changes in any given language. Every speaker of a language has greater practical integration with some dialects and less with others. The same holds for other aspects of tradition and practical identity. Moreover, one might have different attitudes toward change and diversity. One might be more incorporative, seeing a wide range of variations as legitimate parts of tradition, or one might be more exclusionary, seeing some variations as right and others as wrong. Turning again to language, one might accept different dialects or insist that one version of a language is correct and others are faulty. Similarly, one might stress popular customs, scholarly texts, or some other source of traditional knowledge. In cases of conflict, one might affirm one over the other (e.g., adjuring a reformation of popular customs in light of scholarship, or urging a change in some elite practice to bring it in line with popular custom). In general, then, there are many varieties of orthodoxy. In my usage, there is nothing that requires orthodoxy to be rigid or doctrinaire. Indeed, rigid and doctrinaire affirmations of tradition are more likely to be reactionary, and thus in some degree disconnected from the traditional practices they purport to affirm.

Disconnection may result from any number of factors. In a colonial or neocolonial situation, two are prominent. The first and more obvious is a lack of knowledge—scholarly knowledge or practiced familiarity. To adopt a term from Noam Chomsky (see *Aspects* 4), we might say that this is a matter of whether or not one is competent in the relevant tradition. The notion of competence, borrowed from linguistics, is particularly apt because language itself is one part of practical identity and competence in language is one part of being practically integrated into a culture. Disconnection due to lack of knowledge or competence most often involves judging the culture in question by stereotypes. Thus a mimeticist is notoriously someone who not only tries to imitate metropolitan culture, but who does so from a position of ignorance and thus ends up imitating a stereotype of that culture. The same sort of stereotyping often occurs in reactionary traditionalism as well, though in this case the stereotypes concern indigenous traditions. The second sort of disconnection (what I have elsewhere called "purgative") results not from ignorance, but from a defensive repudiation of some aspect of the tradition—commonly, the most hurtful or disempowering aspect. A mimeticist of this sort consciously or unconsciously rejects those elements of metropolitan culture that are reminiscent of indigenous culture. In other words, he/she maximizes the difference between the traditions. Mimeticism is, in this way, an escape from the denigrated culture. The reactionary traditionalist, in contrast, repudiates those aspects of indigenous culture that he/she sees as having allowed European domination to begin with (such as a putative undervaluing of military might in Hinduism). Reactionary traditionalism is, in these cases, an escape from the trauma of conquest and domination, for it seeks to establish a tradition that would never have been dominated and denigrated in the first place (e.g., a form of militant Hinduism that would have resisted conquest).[2]

Here we may return again to the theories of identity discussed earlier. Bhabha's views are fairly straightforward in this context. He affirms a combined identity, in effect denying other possibilities—except, by implication, reactionary traditionalism, the undesirable alternative to hybridity. However, lacking an account of competence, he cannot clearly distinguish these various categories—including reactionary traditionalism—and develop their implications, as we have already discussed. Indeed, it is not entirely clear how Bhabha could differentiate syncretism from alienating hybridity, though the valorization of combined identities clearly indicates that he primarily has syncretism in mind.

Though less immediately obvious, Butler's contentions fit here as well. Specifically, Butler's argument is, among other things, a criticism of appeals to authenticity. In our terms, her argument is against orthodoxy. Her implied antagonists contrast some authentic lesbianism, on the one hand, with the mere imitation of heterosexual gender forms, on the other. This is roughly the opposition between orthodoxy and mimeticism. Like Bhabha, she denies the possibility of genuine orthodoxy (though, also like Bhabha, she does not clearly isolate the category) and thus in effect indicates that all assertions of orthodoxy are reactionary. For Butler, the nonexistence of orthodoxy applies across the board—not only to gays and lesbians, but to heterosexuals as well. Butler's even-handed denial of orthodoxy leads her to the conclusion that all sexuality is imitation. Thus, just as Bhabha makes syncretism ("hybridity") ubiquitous, Butler makes mimeticism ubiquitous. Moreover, just as Bhabha in effect establishes the most apparently and self-consciously syncretistic group as the most definitive and valued, Butler in effect makes the most apparently and self-consciously mimetic group the most definitive and valued. In keeping with the disjunctive nature of mimeticism—its lack of practical integration—Butler explains this self-consciousness as parodic.

Of course, gays and lesbians are crucially different from a colonized society in that there was, it seems, no development of gay and lesbian traditions independent of and prior to compulsory heterosexuality. This necessarily has consequences for any discussion of "orthodoxy" and sexual preference. Butler's arguments indirectly remind us of this. On the other hand, it does not at all follow that distinctions regarding identity are irrelevant here. For example, unlike orthodoxy—and assimilation—mimeticism and reactionary traditionalism have a forced or strained quality resulting from stereotypical or purgative disconnection. They appear as a response to denigration and that context marks them. There is no reason similar patterns might not appear with respect to sexual preference. Butler's homogenous and ubiquitous mimeticism occludes such differences. Moreover, Butler's argument that there is no original for imitation relies on an ambiguity in her use of "original." She may have shown that there is no absolute origin, no Platonic Idea of gender behavior. It hardly follows that there is no original in the sense of some prior behavior that people are imitating. Her arguments do, however, suggest that there is at least an element of mimeticism—or reactionary traditionalism—in everyone's identity. For example, we often acquire practical identity in part by imitating stereotypes. Indeed, this is one aspect of cognitive monitoring by reference to the semantic component of identity categories, as discussed above.

Finally, we may consider Chinweizu, Jemie, and Madubuike in this context. The main program of *Toward the Decolonization of African Literature* may also be reformulated with greater clarity in terms of the distinctions outlined above. This program is roughly the following. Whatever the claims of African writers and critics, whatever their affirmations of categorial identity, the great majority do not have competence in African traditions of literature and orature. Their practical identity is disconnected from African traditions of verbal art. As Chinweizu et al. emphasize, "the fact that you are an African does not make you automatically a master at traditional oral story-telling" (53–54). In this context, concerted training in European literary principles and patterns will not produce an egalitarian integration of European and African traditions. It will largely reproduce European tradition. Thus a great deal of post-colonization African literature is syncretistic only in a trivial way—incorporating bits and pieces of African culture, without thorough understanding or internalization, into a fundamentally European structure. Chinweizu, Jemie, and Madubuike are not, I believe, aiming to foster a purified African literature, as it would have evolved had European colonialism never occurred. Nor are they trying to purge African literature of all European influences. Rather they are seeking the development of more literature that is genuinely syncretistic, literature that is not so fully European. At the same time, they are urging a form of criticism that emphasizes and encourages this development.

In their denunciations of critical Eurocentrism, Chinweizu, Jemie, and Madubuike are denouncing an exclusive categorial identification with metropolitan culture (e.g., mimeticism), for this prevents the serious cultivation of competence in African culture. Though the point may not be as clear, their argument goes equally against stereotypical reactionary traditionalism, which has much the same consequences. In place of these, they urge a consistent engagement with tradition that will result in genuine competence of the sort found in orthodoxy. Thus they write that African authors "need more than a haphazard and unconscious exposure to the African tradition in order to develop the proper sensibility and skill for working in it. They need *conscious, determined, meticulous* and *thorough study*. They need extended *immersion* in the traditional mode and *apprenticeship* in its methods" (234); "The need for reimmersion in the traditionalist sources, and for sustained apprenticeship in traditionalist attitudes and craft, cannot be underestimated, especially for those nurtured in a disorienting euromodernist sensibility" (285). There is no other way to produce work that is truly syncretistic; African authors "should apprentice themselves to African orature so that our narrative prose literature can become a thorough synthesis from African and non-African narrative traditions" (146).

Since they are never entirely clear about the relevant distinctions, Chinweizu, Jemie, and Madubuike often appear to contradict themselves. Indeed, they probably do contradict themselves. Sometimes they seem to advocate an orthodox or even reactionary traditionalist *categorial* identity, which would certainly contradict their references to syncretism. But there is no *necessary* contradiction here, for their arguments only require the cultivation of a particular practical identity. The difference is consequential, for metropolitan and indigenous practical identities need not be broadly contradictory. Though they are likely to be contradictory on particular beliefs and procedures, they do not in general exclude one another. Practical identity is like—in fact, includes—linguistic knowledge. Competence in French does not contradict competence in Yoruba. Categorial identity, in contrast, is not so permissive.

All this has some perhaps surprising results. First, despite their apparent fundamentalism, there is nothing in the main arguments of Chinweizu, Jemie, and Madubuike that requires the affirmation of categorial identity. Second, despite their opposition to identity politics, both Bhabha and Butler end up advocating forms of identity politics, for they articulate and valorize particular identity categories, if in unusual forms. All these writers discuss issues and ideas in ways that help sharpen our understanding of identity. But Chinweizu, Jemie, and Madubuike are the ones who give us the deepest sense of what is at stake in literary identity, especially when we rearticulate their arguments in terms of the distinction between practical and categorial identity, and in terms of the varieties of categorial identity.

This is not to say that I believe Chinweizu, Jemie, and Madubuike are correct in all their arguments. Personally, I agree with some of their contentions and disagree with others. I have enormous sympathy with their call for more writers and critics to gain competence in African orature. I greatly appreciate the generosity of spirit evidenced when an African nationalist—faced with the horrors of colonialism—still says that "you don't have to be an African to master an African oral story-telling art" and even names a White woman as one of two exemplars. At the same time, I have little patience with broad prescriptions telling a group of artists and critics that one set of practices is right and another is wrong. I am particularly unsympathetic when such prescriptions are aimed at an ethnically or racially defined group. (While Chinweizu, Jemie, and Madubuike welcome Whites into African tradition, they clearly see Black Africans as having a special moral obligation to precolonial African traditions.) Finally, I have no more investment in the genuine syncretism advocated by these writers than I have in a real continuation of African orature or in the development of more straightforwardly European trends by African, Indian, Afro-Caribbean, or other authors. All three options, and others, seem to me valuable.

In my view, the importance of *Toward the Decolonization of African Literature* does not lie primarily in its specific conclusions, but in the way it foregrounds what is at stake in literary identity and explores the complexity of that issue. Indeed, without the benefit of the conceptual analysis presented above, Chinweizu, Jemie, and Madubuike have made clear that literary identity is inseparable from practical identity. Moreover, despite their focused appeal to Black Africans, they have also shown in effect—and perhaps contrary to their intentions—that literary identity has no necessary relation to ethnicity or any other categorial identity. In this way, despite some superficial problems with exposition, *Toward the Decolonization of African Literature* is a model of the way postcolonial theory should be done.

APPROACHING LITERARY IDENTITY

Needless to say, this hardly means that there is nothing left to write about literary identity after Chinweizu, Jemie, and Madubuike. They have focused on particular problems in one region at a particular historical moment. In the following pages, I set out to present a broader account. Of course, this too will not be exhaustive. The possible relations between postcolonization authors, on the one hand, and metropolitan and indigenous traditions of literature and orature, on the other, are countless. They cannot be treated in a single book, nor even in many books. Instead of pursuing an impossible exhaustiveness, I have tried instead to present a series of illustrative cases that indicate some of the subtlety and complexity that is often overlooked by readers and critics.

Despite the positive example of Chinweizu, Jemie, and Madubuike, critical treatments of postcolonization literary identity and literary tradition have been relatively few in number and limited in scope. Moreover, even those few works that do take up these topics have tended to conceive of them very narrowly. Individual critics have certainly considered a range of relations between individual authors from colonized groups and precursor traditions. Nonetheless, the general tendency of criticism and theory has been to ignore such relations or, when examining them, to focus on one of two topics: hybidity and resistance. Treatments of hybridity most often address the way postcolonization works explore mixed or transitional cultural phenomena, touching only briefly on the syncretism of specifically literary traditions. The emphasis on resistance has commonly taken one of two forms. The first is "writing back." This is the postcolonization author's response to a metropolitan precursor (e.g., Achebe's response to *Heart of Darkness* in *Things Fall Apart*). The second common way of understanding resistance is by reference to an anticolonial tradition in the writing of the colony. This approach emphasizes the way authors from colonized groups read and influence one another.

Though undoubtedly important, these approaches do not adequately represent the multiple and complex relations of postcolonization authors to metropolitan and indigenous traditions. Moreover, even hybidity and resistance tend to be understood too narrowly. For example, discussions of writing back tend to assume that the indigenous author has a critical intention and that this intention actually produces resistance. In other words, such discussions tend to assume that authors from colonized groups not only tend to adopt a corrective attitude toward metropolitan tradition, but that this intent produces works of resistance. In fact, things do not operate in such a straightforward manner. The mere categorial identification of oneself as a resistant or anticolonial author is not sufficient to produce a corrective work in practice. More generally, critical and theoretical writing on colonialism and literary tradition tends to suffer from two limitations: first, an overly narrow understanding of the postcolonization author's relation to metropolitan tradition; second, the virtual absence of reference to the postcolonization author's relation to indigenous tradition. There are individual exceptions at the level of textual criticism, and occasionally at the level of theory (again, Chinweizu, Jemie, and Madubuike come to mind). But the general trend seems indisputable. There has also been a tendency to treat individual precursor works, and to pass over broader patterns from the traditions in question.

In responding to this situation, I have first of all sought greater balance of numbers. Of the following six chapters, three address metropolitan traditions, while three take up indigenous traditions.[3] I treat individual books in the first and second chapters. However, I turn to larger structures in the remaining chapters. The third and fourth chapters take up myth, the shared stories that are in some ways the reference points for literary traditions, both in explicit retellings and in implicit incorporations. The fifth and sixth chapters turn to the shared patterns of genre, for perhaps the most basic manner in which traditions are organized and internally differentiated is through genre.

I have also sought greater balance in representing the quality of postcolonization authors' responses to tradition. Thus, for each pair of works, I take up a different attitude toward tradition as well. The first and second chapters treat resistance, specifically writing back. Though this particular topic is fairly common, there are two ways in which these chapters are different from standard accounts. First, I give examples of writing back to both the metropolitan and indigenous tradition. Second, in the case of metropolitan tradition, I explore the discrepancy between the categorially defined aim and the practical result, arguing that, in specifiable circumstances, the work of the postcolonization writer may end up being more complicit with colonial ideology than the metropolitan work to which he/she is writing back. The third and fourth chapters take up positive attitudes toward tradition, but again with a difference. First, the positive relation may occur with respect to either tradition. Second, it may take widely different forms. In the case of metropolitan myth, I emphasize the selectiveness of the postcolonization writer, the ways in which he/she may choose or even in effect create a subtradition within metropolitan writing. In the case of indigenous myth, I discuss the ways in which a postcolonization author's relation to indigenous tradition may be defined by the ephemeral quality of that tradition and its impending loss—one of the problems that gave urgency to the appeals of Chinweizu, Jemie, and Madubuike. The final chapters take up relations that are more ambivalent, but also more general, more characteristic of literary relations outside of colonialism—for postcolonization authors are, after all, authors with literary interests, ambitions, and sensibilities much the same as those of authors anywhere. The fifth chapter considers what is involved in a competitive relation to precursors, an attempt to outdo the paradigms of one's chosen genre. The sixth and final chapter addresses the ways in which an author might neither compete with nor simply imitate his/her precursors, but rather continue the trajectory of a generic tradition, extending it along paths suggested, but not followed out, by precursors.

More exactly, in the opening chapter, I consider the relation between Anita Desai's novel *Baumgartner's Bombay* and Joseph Conrad's *Heart of Darkness*. This chapter argues in part that Desai's revision is complicit with colonial ideology, perhaps even more so than its precursor. Desai's novel involves an almost entirely uncritical use of Conrad's novella as a model for understanding India. This has significant ideological consequences—most obviously, in assimilating India to a "heart of darkness," even to the point of implying indigenous practices of cannibalism. This novel thus serves as an apt counterexample to standard views of indigenous literature as ideologically critical writing back. On the other hand, one may wish to argue that Desai's novel is not really an instance of writing back at all. Perhaps it is not. Its ideological affinity with Conrad's work indicates at the very least that not all such rewritings by postcolonization authors are aptly conceived of as ideologically critical. But one might still ask whether more "genuine" instances of writing back—works that have a self-consciously critical or corrective purpose—are liable to the same sort of ideological complicity. In the final pages of this chapter, I briefly discuss George Lamming's *Water with Berries*, which is widely cited as a paradigm case of writing back. I argue that much the same sort of ideological complicity is indeed to be found in this novel, and for much the same reasons.

The second chapter turns from the metropolitan to the indigenous tradition, considering Rabindranath Tagore's *The Home and the World* in relation to its major precursor, one of the foundational works of the Indian literary tradition and of Hindu cultural ideology—Vālmīki's *Rāmāyaṇa*. Tagore's revision of this poem, in contrast with Desai's reworking of Conrad, is highly critical. Indeed, it is similar to the paradigm cases of writing back against metropolitan works. In keeping with this self-conscious critical purpose, this revision is of more direct thematic significance than is the case with Desai's novel. Indeed, the relation between Tagore's story and this major text of Hindu ideology is thematically central to the novel—so much so, that it is very difficult to isolate and understand the aims of the novel without recognizing that Tagore has set out to write a critical corrective to this revered epic, an epic that has provided Hindus with one crucial set of gender ideals, in the figures of Rāma and Sītā, and one crucial model for the ideal society, in the "rule of Rāma."

As the case of the *Rāmāyaṇa* suggests, literary traditions—European and non-European—are deeply bound up with a culture's narratives about divinity. As Northrop Frye put it, "the structural principles of literature" are almost inseparable from "mythology and . . . religion" (134). Frye is probably the critic most famous for emphasizing the pervasive presence of Judeo-Christian stories in European literature from the Middle Ages to our own day (see, for example, 140). However, any reader of European literature should recognize this on his/her own. After all, two of the most prominent plot structures in European literature, two structures found explicitly or implicitly in countless works, are the stories of the Fall and the Redemption, the story of Adam and Eve and the story of Jesus. The general point holds no less for the literatures of, say, Hindu or Muslim regions. Moreover, this link between religious and literary stories is not at all confined to traditions with sacred texts. Indeed, in oral traditions, myth and literature—or, more properly, myth and orature—are hardly even separable.

It seems clear, then, that, in virtually any tradition, engagement with common religious myths is likely to be important to an author's establishment of literary identity. This is particularly true for writers in colonies and former colonies, for the colonizer almost invariably imposes metropolitan myths on colonized people through school and church. At the same time, colonial ideology commonly labels indigenous myths Satanic. For these reasons, myth almost invariably becomes central to crises of indigenous cultural identity in general and indigenous literary identity in particular.

In the following chapters, then, I take up two uses of myth. Chapter 3 concerns Walcott's isolation of a, so to speak, "subaltern" tradition within Christianity. Specifically, Walcott structures *Dream on Monkey Mountain* in part around a version of the story of Jesus. But Walcott's version is not the standard one, as taught in colonial missions or in middle-class suburbs. Rather, it is a version drawn from a tradition of revolutionary interpretation, which emphasizes Jesus' position as a non-European in a European colony.

Chapter 4 considers a very different relation to myth, in this case indigenous myth. One of the effects of colonization is the rapid transformation of traditional culture among the colonized people. In the case of oral traditions, including oral traditions of verbal art, this transformation is often mere loss. As men and women move to the cities, children come to be educated in European traditions, and large numbers of people are converted to new religions, the old myths may stop being told and thus simply disappear. In this context, one obvious and important task for an author, a task which forms a sort of necessary condition for any concern with or attention to indigenous tradition and literary identity, is preservative. In conditions where there is an impending loss of tradition, an indigenous author's relation to that tradition is, at least in part, a matter of keeping that tradition from fading entirely from human memory and practice. Of course, preservation alone is not a literary task. That is anthropological. The literary task is to shape the complex of oral myths into an aesthetic whole, not just preserving them individually, but at the same time transforming them into a coherent literary work that manifests the central beliefs and aspirations of the culture, exposes their interrelations and inner logic. That is one accomplishment of Amos Tutuola's *The Palm-Wine Drinkard*, taken up in this chapter.

Again, the concluding chapters consider one broad, structural element of literary tradition—genre. Clearly, literary structures, such as genre, are of central importance to any author establishing his/her literary identity. An author necessarily writes in a particularly close relation to the conventions and expectations of the literary category he/she has chosen—conventions of tragedy, love lyric, historical romance, and so on. Here as elsewhere indigenous authors face the general problem of literary identity, a problem faced by any writer. But they do so, once again, in the context of colonial relations. Indeed, colonialism is much more bound up with genre than one might at first expect. For one thing, many of the most influential colonial tales, such as those in popular novels or cinema, are pervaded by genre conventions—most obviously, the conventions of the adventure story. Perhaps more importantly, the cultural denigration aimed at colonized societies included attention to what literary genres they did or did not have (e.g., tragedy) and what characteristics defined their genres (e.g., whether or not they had requirements for unity). For example, in his highly influential lectures on aesthetics, Hegel confined non-European art to the first or most basic moment in the dialectic of art. This categorization was inseparable from considerations of genre (see my "Beauty," especially 5–6 and 16–24, and citations.)

In the fifth chapter, then, I examine Derek Walcott's *Omeros* as a sort of challenge to the Western epic tradition. Historically, the epic has been considered the culminating and preeminent genre, the pinnacle of literary achievement. Walcott, I argue, set himself the task of taking on that culminating genre, and thereby of placing himself in the company of the greatest poets in the European tradition. There are points when he could be seen as writing back to Virgil or Homer, and points at which he could be seen as drawing subaltern elements out of their works. But his major task in composing this poem seems to be different from either of these responses to metropolitan tradition. It appears to be, rather, a matter of outdoing his competitors—not Homer and Virgil, necessarily, but the contemporary poets who would, ordinarily, be his rivals. Put differently, his task is not one of denouncing the white epic, nor is it one of finding suppressed black epics, nor of highlighting a subversive strain in the European epic tradition. Rather, it is a matter of working through the major European epics in order to establish that his work is of their caliber and deserves a place among them, that he should be listed in the company of the "paradigm" epicists: Homer, Virgil, Dante, Milton. This is not, as it might at first appear, a purely egocentric task. It is not, in other words, a simple matter of individual poetic identity, isolated from broad cultural concerns of colonialism. Rather, it is an assertion of poetic voice that is inseparable from the author's sense of colonial history, and the continuing implications of that history. The poem takes as its subject the lives of common Afro-Caribbean people. In consequence, the establishment of this poem as a paradigm epic is at once an assertion that the ordinary people of Walcott's island should be understood as equal in excellence and literary splendor to the renowned heroes of the *Odyssey,* the *Iliad,* the *Aeneid.*

The final chapter takes up a very different relation to genre—Agha Shahid Ali's use of the ghazal tradition of Persian and Urdu lyric in his long poem "From Another Desert." The responses to literary tradition considered thus far appear to have been largely a matter of self-conscious reflection and self-conscious decision. Certainly, Ali thought about the issue of tradition, and about his own relation to tradition. Indeed, he wrote directly about the topic in his dissertation, subsequently a book, on T. S. Eliot, one of the most influential theorists of tradition in the modern era. But Ali's relation to the long history of the ghazal appears to have been almost entirely spontaneous. He did not consciously choose to draw on the images and motifs of that tradition. Rather, he directly imagined his poetic world in those images and motifs, as a speaker conceives his/her assertions directly through the concepts of his/her language. Ali internalized the practices and principles of this genre to such a degree that he, in effect, thought his poetry already in these terms. Moreover, his relation to the ghazal was consistent with his explicit views on tradition. For his self-conscious attitude toward tradition was much like that of Eliot: he saw tradition as having force and significance, not as a distant artifact, but as a a living part of the present. He also saw tradition, not as the antithesis of poetic individuality, but as the means by which a poet finds his/her voice. The ease and fluency in indigenous tradition displayed by Ali provide a fitting conclusion to the study. They are, in a sense, the antithesis of the troubled writing back that is so often seen as the paradigm for literary identity after colonization.

Again, these are not the only ways in which an indigenous author can work to establish poetic voice in the face of colonial ideology. However, I believe these chapters set out the major components of that work. Many of the most common alternatives may be generated simply by joining these components in different configurations. For example, chapter 3 treats "writing through" subaltern metropolitan myth as one common strategy. Here and below, I use "writing through" to refer to a positive or enabling relation between a new author and a precursor; I have drawn the phrase in part from Virginia Woolf's famous statement that "a woman writing thinks back through her mothers" (101). Clearly, one can also write through a single subaltern metropolitan precursor work—indeed, in *Omeros,* Walcott's relation to *Ulysses* is a case of this sort. Similarly, the following chapters consider both writing back and genre, but not writing back to a genre, as when Wilson Harris in effect writes back to the colonial adventure romance in *Palace of the Peacock.* A wide range of such combinations is possible.

In keeping with the broader purposes of this study—which undertakes the interpretation of particular works not only for its intrinsic value, but because these interpretations are illustrative of larger patterns—each of the following chapters begins with a theoretical treatment of its topic. The interpretations themselves are founded upon cultural and historical analyses, analyses that are "particularist" in the sense that they address the cultural and historical uniqueness of the works under consideration. In contrast, the theoretical sections are aimed, not at particularity, but at generality. In the theoretical discussions, I set out to isolate common patterns, shared structures and practices in the establishment of literary identity. For this reason, these sections do not draw on cultural studies. Rather, they are based largely on cognitive science. Cognitive science articulates ways of understanding the human mind generally—its organization, its operations, its aims and means for achieving those aims. The rigorous and lucid formulations of writers in cognitive studies, with their empirical underpinnings from linguistics, experimental psychology, and related fields, provide a way of formulating the principles of literary identity with clarity, precision, and explanatory force. In this way, the theoretical premises of the following chapters are very different from those of most writing in "postcolonial" studies. The theoretical grandparent of this book is not Jacques Derrida, but Noam Chomsky; its most important influences are not Spivak and Bhabha, but theorists and researchers such as Amos Tversky and Eleanor Rosch, along with such classical non-European thinkers as al-Fārābī and Abhinavagupta, whose analyses are much closer to cognitive science than to the post-Romantic principles of Deconstruction and Postmodernism (for the case of Abhinavagupta, see chapter 2 of my *The Mind and Its Stories*).

The opening chapter takes up the common cognitive distinction among schemas, prototypes, and exempla to analyze what is involved in drawing on and writing back to a precursor text. It considers particularly the ways in which a precursor text operates as an exemplum, a cognitively definitive instance, and thereby serves to shape the new author's perception of the colonial situation, even when that new author has set out to write against the precursor work. It is in the nature of the cognitive use of exempla that they render certain properties salient and obscure others, that they lead us to infer certain causal relations and not others. Thus, however much he criticizes Shakespeare, once Lamming takes up *The Tempest* and writes back to it, he simultaneously employs it as an exemplum for understanding colonialism. As a result, his characterization of colonizer and colonized and of their relations to one another is almost necessarily guided in some degree by that play—or, rather, by his interpretation of that play. (The use of exempla is not a matter of the precursor text per se, whatever that might mean, but rather of the precursor text as understood by the new author.)

The second chapter, which also focuses on the revision of single precursor texts, takes up the structure of the mental lexicon and the cognitive processes which operate that lexicon, in order to anatomize and clarify the fundamental techniques employed by authors in such revisions. This chapter considers such cognitive processes as the systematic transformation of a precursor text through a lexically specified alternative. For example, within Hindu ethical theory, there are two sharply opposed types of principle: *sādhāraṇadharma* or universal duty, which includes nonviolence, and *kṣatriyadharma* or ruler/warrior (kṣatriya) caste duty. This division enters individual lexicons as an exclusive disjunction—either universal duty or warrior caste duty, but not both—which, in turn, establishes them as transformational alternatives. One way in which Tagore alters Vālmīki's *Rāmāyaṇa* is through a systematic transformation of Rāma's actions from conformity with kṣatriya duty, in Vālmīki, to conformity with universal duty.

The third chapter considers a further aspect of lexical structure—the domain or semantic field, a set of related lexical entries, such as days of the week or grades of temperature. Through a sort of metaphorical mapping, domains often serve to structure more abstract ideas, as when we use temperature as a model for feeling, and say that a former friend was cold or gave a warm greeting. Domain mapping serves an important function in colonial and other sorts of racism, as well as sexism and related forms of bias. It allows the establishment and elaboration of a division within the category "human," so that some humans may be considered genuinely human, while others are considered subhuman and treated accordingly. Myth provides one of the most important domains for this sort of mapping. For example, the division between human and demonic may serve as a model for defining the differences between Europeans and Africans or Jews (see chapter 4 of my *The Culture of Conformism*). The subaltern reversal of this mapping—in this case, Walcott's identification of (divine) Jesus with an impoverished Afro-Caribbean charcoal burner—becomes politically consequential, for it is not merely the development of some character in an isolated story. Rather, this reversal undertakes to revise a set of cognitive relations that have been structurally established in the lexicons of many people, both colonizers and colonized, and which therefore have practical, and deleterious, consequences.

The fourth chapter considers what might be called "situational identification." We develop a sense of intimacy with someone directly as we sense a sharing of unstated feelings, ideas, inferences, expectations. Conversely, we grow estranged from someone as we are forced to unfold presuppositions which we always assumed tacitly to be shared by everyone, and thus to be unquestionable. This sharing is best understood as a matter of overlapping lexical structures. Here, too, myth is tremendously important. It provides one of the most crucial sets of presuppositions—lexically specified, as usual, in terms of exempla, prototypes, schemas, and domains. Indeed, our broad, experiential sense of cultural identity, as it develops in real conditions of human interaction, relies to a considerable degree on a tacit presumption of shared narratives about important and troubling aspects of life—its purpose, its end or continuation, the meaning of human misery, and so on. In other words, it relies on myth. This, in turn, makes the preservation and dissemination of myth all the more significant, both within a culture and, perhaps even more importantly, across the lines of colonial cultural estrangement. This is just what Tutuola has undertaken.

The fifth chapter takes up categorial identity, examining it in terms of an internalized or lexicalized self-schema. The very nature of a self-schema indicates that an individual's identity will be a function of his/her various group identities, and that his/her sense of self will be bound up with a structure of "reference sets," classes of paradigm individuals or groups that are evaluatively determinative for a particular category. In part, we judge ourselves and define our aspirations by reference to communally esteemed instances of the groups to which we belong—exemplary Catholics (hence the stories of the saints), exemplary Americans (hence national heroes), and so on. This provides an important psycho-social context for understanding the nature and significance of Walcott's relation to the genre of epic. Walcott is attempting to place himself in the same paradigm category, in the same reference set, as the great European epicists—Homer, Virgil, and the rest. Moreover, he is doing this in such a way as to incorporate the history and culture of Afro-Caribbean people into the same epical/heroic reference set as the Homeric Greeks and Virgil's Romans. Thus Walcott celebrates an Afro-Caribbean categorial identity that has been demeaned since the beginning of the slave trade—and that has been demeaned in part by reference to this literary tradition.

The final chapter adds a further type of structure to the mental lexicon in order to clarify what it means to write, unselfconsciously, within a tradition. Specifically, this chapter considers procedural schemas, introduced briefly above. Procedural schemas are not objects of thought or communication, but structures of action that are almost entirely closed to introspection. We have a "representational" schema for shoe laces, but a procedural schema for tying our shoe laces. This chapter also introduces a distinction, drawn from linguistic theory, between obligatory and optional procedures. A living tradition may be viewed as a series of internalized obligatory and optional procedural schemas, operating on representational schemas, prototypes, and exempla. Finally, this chapter considers how the ghazal tradition may be understood in these terms, thus establishing the cognitive context for an analysis of Ali's fluent, spontaneous use of that tradition in "From Another Desert."

Because these chapters introduce a great deal of theoretical material, I have listed and briefly redefined the most important theoretical concepts in an appendix.

Literary traditions are important. One need not be uncritical of such traditions to recognize that, in specifying or "filling in" the cognitive structures and
processes we all share, they provide us with otherwise unavailable means for
understanding and articulating the world around us. This crucial function of
traditions is undermined when they are denigrated, or simply ignored, and
equally when they are made singular and univocal—two tendencies of colonialism and of some indigenous reactions against colonialism.[4] One thing I
hope the following study shows—in addition to the diversity of indigenous
responses to metropolitan and indigenous literature, in addition to the cognitive and social complexity of literary identity after colonization—is the wealth
and variousness of both metropolitan and indigenous traditions. As the following chapters will make clear, I am far from advocating some sort of neo-
traditionalism, for all traditions are marred by a sort of blindered conformism,
by oppressive ideologies of class, gender, race, and other hierarchies. Yet, I am
farther from dismissing tradition. For, along with the oppressive ideologies, all
these traditions include resistance and humane sensibility as well; along with
the conformism, genuine utopian vision.

That humane sensibility and utopian vision are dulled, or even lost, not
only when traditions are suppressed, forgotten, or reified, but when they are
narrowly confined to an imaginary national or ethnic—or even hybrid—heritage. As Edward Said wrote in *Culture and Imperialism* (xxv):

> We are still the inheritors of that style by which one is defined by the nation,
> which in turn derives its authority from a supposedly unbroken tradition. In
> the United States this concern over cultural identity has of course yielded up
> the contest over what books and authorities constitute "our" tradition. In the
> main, trying to say that this or that book is (or is not) part of "our" tradition
> is one of the most debilitating exercises imaginable. . . . For the record then,
> I have no patience with the position that "we" should only or mainly be con-
> cerned with what is "ours," any more than I can condone reactions to such a
> view that require Arabs to read Arab books, use Arab methods, and the like.
> As C. L. R. James used to say, Beethoven belongs as much to West Indians
> as he does to Germans, since his music is now part of the human heritage.

The same holds for Homer or Jesus, Yoruba myth, Vālmīki, and the great
writers of Persian and Urdu ghazals.

I take up the ethnic confinement of tradition more systematically in an
afterword. Extending the discussion of "internalization" from the final chapter,
I argue that traditions, literary or otherwise, exist only in individuals (a point
implied, if not fully recognized, by Chinweizu, Jemie, and Madubuike). Traditions are entirely and solely a matter of "idiolect," personal systems of belief,
expectation, preference, and the like. These systems overlap from one person to
another, but they never entirely coincide. One consequence of this individual-

ity of tradition is that it makes no theoretical sense to refer to a tradition as belonging to one group more than another. Traditions belong equally to everyone, or to no one. Like a language, it only makes sense to say that some persons have greater or lesser communicative ease, fluency in shared idioms, that their idiolects are, as a contingent, changeable, empirical fact, more similar to one another than to the idiolects of some other persons. Moreover, that ease, fluency, and so on, in no way imply convergence in opinions or attitudes. In that sense, too, traditions are individual. Indeed, this diversity of both idiolect and attitude is largely what is at issue in the other chapters.

In sum, my hope is that the following studies suggest the worth, not only of the literary works discussed, not only of the cognitive and social theories developed in the course of these discussions, but of a simultaneously critical and universal traditionalism: a cross-cultural acceptance of the aesthetic, cognitive, and moral excellences to be found variously in African, Indian, European, and other traditions, though an acceptance tempered by caution, aware of the ugliness, falsity, and cruelty that are to be found in these traditions as well. My aim, then, is a sort of critical sharing across lines of cultural estrangement, as I put it earlier—lines that are, in the end, illusory anyway, resulting as they do from a false assertion of categorial identity; an assumed communal unity of ideas and attitudes that are always in fact idiosyncratic, contradictory, personal; an imagined ethnic heritage that is shared by individuals only in virtue of being acquired, sometimes laboriously, and that can be acquired, like a particular language, by anyone.

Chapter One

Ideological Ambiguities of "Writing Back"

Anita Desai and George Lamming in the Heart of Darkness

LITERATURE, MIND, AND THE STRUCTURE OF EXPERIENCE

It is a virtual commonplace of cognitive psychology that we do not perceive, recall, understand the world, other people, ourselves, by some direct and immediate experience of reality. The "manifold of intuition," as Kant called it, must be shaped and oriented, structured by concepts, schemas, categories of understanding. A world of pure sense data would not be a world of perfect knowledge, but a chaos. This is true in our everyday lives and, even more obviously, in literature. We cannot live our lives, perform ordinary tasks, without organizing in our minds the properties and relations of things and ideas. Still less can we tell a story about lives without selecting, from the welter of inconsequential detail, the relevant elements, without ordering and relating those elements, without stressing one and subordinating another.

There are different ways of extracting meaning from the muddle of experience. The most obvious is through schemas, broad and abstract structures under which we subsume particulars. I glimpse a small, hairy, moving thing on a leash; some mix of features, inconclusive in themselves, but with collective value, triggers a schema: dog. Or, rather, in an imperceptibly rapid sequence, one sensation (small and motile thing) triggers a range of schemas (dog, cat, rat, etc.). These guide my selection of further details, leading me to notice, say, the leash. This, in turn, selects the schema: dog.[1]

This is one way experience is structured. More often, our thought and inference are more concrete, guided by instances or types of instance, not broad structures. We do not, in the usual course of things, see a particular as a dog because we subsume it under a category. Rather, we compare it with a prototype—a typical dog, not the bare idea of dogness. Consider birds. We recognize a flitting thing as "bird" because we see its similarity to such proto-typical birds as robins, not because we fit it into the general category: "warm-blooded, egg-laying feathered vertebrate," as the *American Heritage Dictionary* has it. At times our identifications are more specific still, linking the object at hand to a particular case or "exemplum"—"I knew right away that he must be a Carter; he looks just like our former President."[2]

Thus schemas, prototypes, and exempla guide our perception and our thought, bring parts of the world into structure and emphasis, discarding or downplaying others. They also guide our literary construction of sensation and of cognition. Of course, the ordinary structures and instances that gather our daily lives into coherence figure in literature. But, perhaps more importantly, literary schemas provide broad principles for new literary compositions, and literary exempla guide the detailed choice of plot, character, and diction in new works. Indeed, such literary elements pervade ordinary life as well—for we understand our friends and foes in part through literary characters, our experiences and aspirations in part through literary plots. That is, among other things, what gives literature its moral and political force. As the great Arabic theorists, al-Fārābī, Ibn Sinā, and Ibn Rushd argued, literature fosters moral or immoral action through *takhyīl*, the simultaneously creative and mimetic imagination that guides the way we think about and react to the world, unconsciously tying our understanding of love to romantic fiction, as stressed famously by Flaubert, or our feeling about members of some ethnic group—Irish, Italians, African Americans— to particular characters from that group in movies or on television. As this suggests, *takhyīl* is perhaps best understood as the tacit use of literary or other exempla to body forth, to give substance and definition, to our other-wise ghostly and confused experience. This unwitting use of art in daily life is at least part of what makes literature consequential.

Writers, then, draw on schemas and prototypes—the broad structure of the novel or the drama, the repertoire of motifs and techniques (as Wolfgang Iser might put it) that are standard in a particular a genre, and so on. At the same time, they form their new works by comparison or contrast with works of precursors employed as exempla—seeking to avoid the failures of one work, seeking to emulate the successes of another. This use of exempla figures most obviously in self-conscious imitation, but it is crucial also in unconscious influence, negative or positive. (For a fuller development of these ideas in relation to influence, see chapter 1 of my *Joyce, Milton, and the Theory of Influence*.) Most important for our purposes, it is a central part of "writing back."

There are many canonical works which, though written by members of dominant groups, set out to portray the lives, feelings, and society of "subalterns." Writing back is the process by which an author from a dominated group takes up and revises one of these canonical works. (The now-classic discussion of writing back is to be found in Ashcroft, Griffiths, and Tiffin.) This process is commonly conceived of as highly antagonistic. But it is not necessarily so. A subaltern author may set out to deny entirely the validity of the precursor work. But he/she may equally seek to create a sort of complement of the precursor text, filling in absent perspectives, histories, and contexts; he/she might undertake to extend or to modify the canonical work or to re-apply its structure to another object. Writing back to *Kim* in *Gora*, Tagore certainly set out to undermine Kipling's racialism. But, simultaneously, he developed another aspect of the novel, the contradictory emphasis on upbringing, on the Indianness of the Irish child raised as Indian. Thus Tagore's writing back is partially antagonistic, but partially sympathetic also. Despite Achebe's harsh criticisms of Conrad (see "An Image"), *Things Fall Apart* does not so much critique *Heart of Darkness* as provide a missing perspective: the social life and human subjectivity of Conrad's obscure, anonymous natives. Bapsi Sidhwa takes up the relation between Europeans and Africans in *Heart of Darkness* as one model for the relation between urban and tribal Pakistanis—a use which does not so much criticize as, so to speak, extend and "apply" Conrad, among others. In short, the aims and attitudes which underlie writing back are far more diverse than is typically imagined (for further discussion of the varieties of writing back, see my "Gora").

More important for our purposes, even highly critical revisions, even uncontroversial instances of writing back in the full, antagonistic sense, almost necessarily involve the use of the precursor work as a model for selecting, structuring, and stressing elements of character, theme, and plot. As such, writing back is always at risk of being complicit with the ideology—or, rather, the perceived ideology—of the precursor work. There are at least four significant variables affecting this possible complicity: (1) the extent of modeling; (2) the pairing of elements in the precursor work and the new work; (3) the ideological complexity of the precursor work; and (4) the subaltern author's interpretation of the precursor work.

As to the first, a new work may write back to a precursor work in a very general way, or in detail. A revision of *Robinson Crusoe* may involve nothing more than a man stranded on an island, or it may incorporate precise correlations of plot and character. Clearly, the greater the degree to which one adheres to the structure of the precursor text, the more one is likely to choose details of one's own work on the basis of the ideological presuppositions of that precursor text. On the other hand, even in simpler cases, the precursor work typically defines the terms of debate, the issues discussed, the general parameters of the discussion. Patrick White's *A Fringe of Leaves* clearly and effectively criticizes the standard portrayal of cannibalism as savagery. Yet the very fact that, in rewriting Conrad (see Brydon), he feels compelled to treat cannibalism indicates the degree to which the discussion of non-European peoples has been bound within a narrow problematic.

As to the second variable, a new author may map the elements of the precursor text onto different elements of the new text. It is, for instance, possible to map Marlow onto an African traveling in Europe and Conrad's African's onto Europeans. This would tend to render salient the "civilized" behavior of the African and the "barbarity" of the Europeans. In that sense, it would invert the stereotypes. Margaret Atwood's use of Conrad in *Surfacing* does something along these lines, in its straightforward identification of savagery with the United States. (For a discussion of Atwood's novel as a reworking of Conrad, see Brydon.) However, most cases are more ideologically complex. For example, to the degree that Sidhwa identifies Conrad's Europeans with urban Pakistanis, she removes urban Pakistanis from colonialist stereotypes; however, to the extent that she identifies Conrad's Africans with tribal Pakistanis, she tends to repeat colonialist stereotyping with respect to those tribal peoples.

Thirdly, a precursor work may involve a complex range of ideological elements, or it may be ideologically simple. This point is perhaps most easily seen in the case of patriarchy. Women are, of course, a dominated group in the relevant sense and engage in writing back, though it is not usually referred to in this way. For example, many Victorian women in effect wrote back to John Milton, as Gilbert and Gubar have shown. A short poem may, more or less explicitly, reduce a woman's legitimate aspirations to those of physical beauty and selfless devotion in the home, but introduce little ideological complication beyond this. In this case, the ideological elements may be easily isolated, and thus easily criticized, by the later author. In contrast, a lengthy and complex novel might involve a wide range of highly specified elements of patriarchal ideology, embedding these elements in details of setting, character, and plot. In this case, much of consequence is likely to escape a new author's self-conscious notice, and thus may guide that author's work in ways of which she is entirely unaware. In other words, due to their extent and complexity, these elements are more likely to affect the unconscious or implicit aspects of modeling that are often a part of writing back.

As to the final variable, a new author may interpret a precursor work in many different ways. Our understanding of a literary work is no more unmediated than is our understanding of anything else. When reading, we select, structure, emphasize, and subordinate. Moreover, we fill in details, extend events and ideas, infer links and causes. In consequence, as we all know, readers interpret works differently, often very differently. Thus, for instance, some critics see Conrad as vilely racist, while others find him enlightenedly anticolonialist. Certainly one interpretation may be more plausible than another. But in writing back, what matters is not so much the text itself as the new writer's version of the text—his/her understanding or, in phenomenological terms, "constitution" of Conrad, Kipling, or Shakespeare, rather than Conrad, Kipling, or Shakespeare per se.

The point can be made more rigorously in cognitive terms, simply by introducing the important notion of the internal, idiolectal lexicon—a mental structure of words, meanings, morphological forms and principles, "encyclopedia" information, personal recollections, and so forth.[3] This lexicon exists in individual human minds, with no separate, autonomous existence (as, for example, Chomsky has argued influentially; see chapter 2 of *Knowledge*). It is composed of lexical entries, which are related to one another through various links, which allow and guide access from one entry to another. For example, the entry for "Wednesday" in my lexicon includes such information as "middle of work week" and "day for departmental meetings"; it also includes links to such entries as "week," "Thursday," and so on. *Ulysses* in my lexicon includes such widely shared "encyclopedia" information as "written by James Joyce," as well as links with other epics, such as *Omeros*, which are less widely shared, and entirely personal associations—for example, memories of particular times when I read a part of the novel—which are not shared by anyone else.

Given this concept of the mental lexicon, we can return to the issue of writing back and say that what matters for a new author is not the precursor text per se—a notion that becomes almost meaningless in this context—but the new author's lexical internalization of the work, his/her incorporation of the precursor work into a complex of mental lexical entries, linked in specific ways with other, related entries. One important consequence of this formulation is that it highlights the significance, not only of the properties a new author attributes to a precursor text, but also of the lexical context in which that author locates that text. For example, does he/she link Conrad's Africans with entries for Victorian racist pseudo-science which he/she rejects unequivocally, or current racist pseudo-science such as *The Bell Curve*, which he/she might take more seriously? Clearly, this will affect his/her response to Conrad, whatever his/her strict interpretation may be.

In any case, however one accounts for this in detail in a particular case, it is clearly one's understanding of a precursor work that guides one's writing back to that precursor work. This has at least one noteworthy and perhaps surprising consequence. Other things being equal, the ideology of a new work is likely to be more colonialist to the degree that the author tacitly construes the precursor work as colonialist. For example, if a new author is modeling some group of people on Conrad's Africans, he/she will be more likely to characterize that group as barbaric precisely to the degree that he/she understands Conrad's Africans as barbaric; he/she is likely to link that group with animals precisely to the degree that he/she links Conrad's Africans with animals, for this animalism will be part of the exemplum that tacitly serves to guide his/her construal of that group.

In sum, writing back is a highly cognitively complex activity and, quite often, an ideologically ambiguous activity as well. Though writing back is often seen as a fairly straightforward anticolonial gesture, there are many types of writing back, and there are many ways in which and many degrees to which writing back—even self-consciously critical or corrective writing back—may be complicit with colonial ideology, as a cognitive account of the process makes clear.

"EVERYTHING MENACING AND DEGRADED
IN INDIAN LIFE": DESAI AND CONRAD

Anita Desai's novel *Baumgartner's Bombay* provides a particularly good example of writing back in this context. Part of Desai's novel clearly revises *Heart of Darkness*. Moreover, it revises Conrad's novella in such a way as to criticize English colonialism. But, at the same time, Desai tacitly models aspects of her novel on *Heart of Darkness*. In part because of this, Desai ends up linking Indian culture and Indian people with mad violence, historyless primitivism, gross animality, and even imputing to Hinduism the celebration of cannibalistic rites. In short, Desai has, I believe, in effect transformed the general population of India, especially Hindu India, into the semihuman savages of Conrad's Africa, in the most colonialist interpretation of that work.[4]

There are many minor but significant ways in which Desai draws on and revises Conrad. For example, prior to the anticolonial focus of recent critics, the standard interpretation of Conrad's novella was psychological: Africa presents to the European, in undisguised and thus horrific form, the savage darkness that lay always within his/her own heart, however much he/she might seek to conceal it with layers of civility. At least at times, Desai presents India in similar terms, for, from Baumgartner's first arrival in Bombay, he realizes that "India flashed the mirror in your face. . . . You could be blinded by it" (85). In both works, immersion in the alien culture produces the same shock and disequilibrating recognition of what is hidden within oneself.

Beyond this broad and, admittedly, common theme, there are parallel narrative moments and images, also limited and localized, but significant.[5] When traveling upriver by steamboat, Marlow recurrently meditates on the impenetrable darkness of the African bush and on its oneiric, hallucinatory quality: "the dream-sensation that pervaded all my days at that time" (Conrad 42); "It seems to me I am trying to tell you a dream—making a vain attempt, because no relation of a dream can convey the dream-sensation, that commingling of absurdity, surprise, and bewilderment" (27; see also 58). The incongruity of steamship, Kurtz, Marlow, the long-staved pilgrims, inscrutable nature, makes it all "unreal," "absurd" (Conrad 25, 23), ghostly— "we glided past like phantoms" (Conrad 36). Likewise, "Baumgartner on the steamship traveling to Dacca," looks out at the densely wooded shores: "The forest that was like a shroud on the bank, ghostly and impenetrable" (92). Baumgartner wonders if it is not "a mirage, a dream." It is all too incongruous. "If it had been a real scene, in a real land, then Baumgartner with his hat and shoes would have been too unlikely a visitor to be possible. . . . If he were real, then surely the scene, the setting was not. How could the two exist together in one land? The match was improbable beyond belief" (93). Compare Marlow on the Russian encountered in the bush, "His very existence was improbable, inexplicable, and altogether bewildering. He was an insoluble problem. It was inconceivable how he had existed, how he had succeeded in getting so far, how he had managed to remain—why he did not instantly disappear" (Conrad 55).

Indeed, the incongruities of the situation redouble incomprehension, pile opacity on opacity in both texts. Marlow surveys the unfed cannibals on his steamer and wonders why they do not kill and eat him—"Why in the name of all the gnawing devils of hunger they didn't go for us," he wonders (42). He cannot fathom their restraint: "Was it superstition, disgust, patience, fear—or some kind of primitive honour?" (42). Baumgartner similarly baffles at the reserve of street people in their makeshift home on the curb outside his building: "They saw him bring bags of food, knew he had a wallet in his pocket, wore a watch on his wrist, good shoes on his feet . . . and he wondered what prevented them from grabbing him by his neck and stripping him in the dark" (145). Marlow worries that perhaps the cannibals find him "unappetising," and feels his vanity offended by their culinary disdain (42). This concern too recurs with Baumgartner. In an empty rural temple, Baumgartner, like Marlow, ruminates on his unfitness for "cannibalistic rites" and, not without self-pity, names himself: "Indigestible, inedible Baumgartner. . . . Not fit for consumption" (190).

Desai's criticisms of the British also recall Conrad. Like Conrad's Belgian Congo, Desai's British India is a chaos of malign incompetence, portrayed to itself and to the home population as civilizing order. This is most obvious in the tragically irrational confinement of German Jews along with other Germans. There are other instances also: the befuddlement of the camp commandant at the end of the war and, before that, the general confusion of camp life, the British surrender of control to fascist thugs. The few documents available do not indicate that this is an accurate portrait. It is, rather, a portrait formed by a Conradian view of colonialism.

Consider the internment of German Jews. At the outset, British policy was to arrest German nationals. The policy was a gross violation of civil rights, involving as it did a presumption of guilt rather than of innocence. However, once this presumption of guilt was in place, it appears to have been applied indifferently to all German nationals. Thus the refugee status of any given individual (e.g., a Jew) had to be demonstrated. Indeed, the British established the Darling Interrogation Committee to determine "friendly enemy aliens." As a result of work done by this committee (and by the Jewish Relief Association), "within a couple of months, practically all [German Jews], some 317, were released" (Roland 220).

Admittedly, more Jews were detained later, and some probably did remain in confinement for the entire war. However, this too did not result from Conradian chaos. It too was the outcome of self-conscious policy. Consider, for example, the disturbing decision by the British Indian government that "even German Jews who had been deprived of their German nationality by the German Ordinance of 25 November 1941 were still liable to internment" (Roland 220–21). This was far from an imperial muddle in the heart of darkness. It was, rather, calculated colonialism in its standard form. The British were apprehensive about Jewish "antecedents and connections in Europe" (Roland 223) and were particularly fearful of Nehru-allied "Jewish communists" (183) who might support and further radicalize the Indian nationalist movement.

Finally, it does not appear that the British camp commandants were in fact the abstracted bumblers depicted in *Baumgartner's Bombay,* nor that the camp was a Conradian slop of randomness and organizational confusion, a vacuum of structure which Nazis could enter and form to their own will. Katherine Smith argues convincingly that Desai's primary source for the internment scenes was Heinrich Harrer's *Seven Years in Tibet.* Smith notes that Desai follows Harrer in numerous details, but "downplays the presence in Harrer of a hostile English military force" with "inviolable power" (151). In short, Desai's imagination of detention is defined at least as much by Conrad as by history.

But the structure of Conrad's novella operates most importantly and most obviously in the narrative sequence that concludes Desai's novel. A young man travels from Europe deep into the heart of colonial darkness, first mingles with the natives, then penetrates into their cults, excels them in their own perverse practices, degrading both his mind and body in the process. Half mad and deathly ill, he is nursed by another European voyager, but turns ungratefully on his benefactor. This precis partially summarizes both *Heart of Darkness* and *Baumgartner's Bombay.* In the first case, the crazed adventurer has no given name. His patronym is "Kurtz." In the second case, he has no patronym. His given name is—"Kurt." Both are tall and mad and in physical decline (Desai 13, 144; Conrad 60). A German Jew takes up the role of Conrad's Russian, nursing the dazed, half-nativized adventurer back to a provisional health (see Conrad 56). Baumgartner's murder is simply the playing out of Kurtz's threats against the loyal Russian, with a slight shift: Kurt murders Baumgartner for his silver, while Kurtz threatens the Russian for his ivory—"He declared he would shoot me unless I gave him the ivory . . . and there was nothing on earth to prevent him killing whom he jolly well pleased" (Conrad 57).

Kurt's desire for the silver is, of course, desire for the heroin it can buy. This fits too, echoing with Kipling as well as Conrad. Kurt draws his debilitating habit from Kim's father, colour-sergeant O'Hara, who "fell to drink and loafing up and down the line . . . till he came across the woman who took opium and learned the taste from her" (Kipling 19). Desai interwove this brief, sad figure from *Kim,* who "died as poor whites die in India," with the differently deteriorated Kurtz, switching O'Hara's taste for opium with Kurtz's equally addictive taste for ivory, "the appetite for more ivory" that in the end "had got the better" of him (Conrad 58), linking Kurt's injections of heroin with the ivory which, along with the "wilderness," the darkness, the primitivism, "got into [Kurtz's] veins, consumed his flesh" (Conrad 49).

But Baumgartner is not only founded upon Conrad's Russian. He also plays a sort of unwilling Marlow to Farrokh's company manager. Most obviously, Farrokh takes on the manager's role in aiming to rid himself and his business of Kurt/Kurtz; Farrokh fears patronage will decline, just as the manager conjectures "trade will suffer" (Conrad 63). More interestingly, Farrokh, recalling the company manager's disdain for Kurtz's "unsound method" (63)—his intimacy with the indigenes—denounces Kurt for nativism, and, indeed, Africanism. Despite his height, Farrokh terms Kurt a "pygmy," and adds that he is a "jungly heathen" (13). The reference to pygmies reethnicizes—indeed, racializes—an irony from Conrad: "Kurtz—that means 'short' in German. . . . He looked at least seven feet long" (60).

Most importantly, Farrokh's slurs are not the only instances of racialism in the novel. In keeping with many interpretations of *Heart of Darkness,* such racialism is widespread. This is not to say there is race hatred in the novel. There is not. There is, however, a consistent strain of "racial thinking," the conceptualization of individual people and of human relationships in terms of race and putative race properties, invariably stereotypical.

Consider, for example, the paranoic view that Jews can always recognize one another—a central part of the delusion of Jewish conspiracy. Desai presents a broadened and thus relatively innocuous, but nonetheless racialist version of this. Early in the novel, Desai has Baumgartner think that Germans can always recognize one another, and especially that Jews and Aryans can recognize and distinguish one another. Indeed, like beasts, they sometimes do so by *smell* (21).

More significantly, Baumgartner, though greatly sympathetic, is characterized in fairly straightforwardly stereotypical terms—a "dirty Jew." He "rarely washed his clothes; they emanated a thick, cloudy odour that he himself found comforting in its familiarity but some considered offensive" (6). In his room there is "mess spread and heaped everywhere" (148) and "filth" (226) giving rise to a noxious odor which drove away guests, but which "was to him a kind of fertiliser" (148). In terms of physical appearance, he is a stereotype too: he has a "nose like a thumb" (38); in Lotte's words, he is a "turnip-nosed *Jude*" (96; *Jude* being the German word for "Jew"). Even his stance is a racialist type: "his hands dangling, his knees buckling" (108; on the stereotype of this posture, see chapter 2 of Gilman, especially 46).

Moreover, Baumgartner is not alone in this. Reb Benjamin too is greasy and "odorous" (37). And Lotte—a Yiddish speaker (67) and thus, one must assume, Jewish—is formed in part from related, if somewhat different, racialist images, Desai stressing in particular her vulgarly corpulent sexuality: "her fat legs . . . always contrived to show so much of themselves under her skirts" (65); her thighs formed "a generous meaty triangle" (68); the "loose flesh" of her legs was "bulging with maturity, with experience" (75); playing cards, she "pulled her skirts up over her thighs" (208) and, kneeling down, she had her "dress rucked up to the thighs" (228).

Admittedly, there is an element of critique in Desai's treatment of Lotte. Her gross sexualization counters an opposition common to exploration narratives—that between licentious or bestial native women and angelic White women. The motif runs from James Bruce's eighteenth-century writings through many intermediaries to *Heart of Darkness* and beyond. Thus, in Bruce, we find his European beloved referred to as "Virgin Mary" (Hibbert 44) and placed in contrast with group after group of native women anxious to bestow their sexual favors (30–31) in loud, orgiastic romps (36). We find the same structure in Conrad's famous opposition between Kurtz's demure Intended, with her "halo" of "unextinguishable light" (76), and his native mistress, "wild" (61), "savage" (62), "barbarous" (69).[6] In portraying Lotte as the "whore" and the Indian woman—the wife of Lotte's lover—as chaste, Desai is in part responding to this common stereotype. Indeed, a similar point might be made about the native worship of White men, another recurrent motif in exploration narratives, obviously repeated in Conrad. In rendering Baumgartner physically repugnant and in depicting Indians as disdainful of him, Desai is to a degree responding to the rather bizarre idea that indigenous people see Europeans as akin to gods ("the tribe . . . adored" Kurtz [Conrad 56–57]). But this is a merely partial critique. For the colonialist idea was never that Jewish women were pure or that Jewish men were godlike. Rather, it was, of course, precisely the opposite. In that sense, even at the moment when Desai is offering a critique of Conrad, she is simply shifting from one discriminatory and stereotypical opposition to another.

Moreover, none of this prevents Desai from characterizing India and Indians in demeaning ways that have clear affinities with the vision of the natives in *Heart of Darkness*. Throughout Desai's novel, the Indian masses are unindividuated and inscrutable. In the very first sentence, they appear to us as a "collected crowd of identical individuals—one-legged, nose-picking, vigilant-eyed" (1). Elsewhere, they become "one restless, heaving mass" (83), formed into slithering fish, wild animals, swarming insects. Baumgartner thinks of the milling Indians on Colaba streets: "So much naked skin, oiled and slithering with perspiration, the piscine bulge and stare of so many eyes" (18). Elsewhere, the Indian people form and scatter "Like knots of ants" (229)—the image, taken in part from Conrad, is largely a matter of color: "A lot of people, mostly black and naked, moved about like ants" (Conrad 15). Worse still, at home, the urban masses form "families that lived in the cracks and crevices of the building like so many rats, or lice" (174).

Individual Indians, when they appear as such, do not necessarily escape this dehumanization—one, for instance, is merely a "small brown monkey of a man" (102). More importantly, even Indians who receive a fuller treatment remain inscrutable for other reasons. Baumgartner decides "that he would never fathom Chimanlal's motives, that under all that bland guilelessness there was an unfathomable guile" (191): stereotype of the endlessly duplicitous Asian. (Compare Mr. Bennett's claim in *Kim:* "My experience is that one can never fathom the Oriental mind" [99]—though, unlike Baumgartner, Bennett is far from sympathetic and his view is discredited directly by Father Victor and the lama.)

Desai not only refers to the Indian masses through metaphors of animals and vermin, she characterizes their lives as, in many ways, the lives of animals and vermin. In keeping more with broad colonialist views than with the details of Conrad's novella, she is particularly unremitting in her stress on virulantly unhygienic conditions. A malnourished child sucks "something brown and slippery," then drops it on the filthy pavement; the mother retrieves the now foul "brown lump" and "pop[s] it back in the child's mouth" (144–45). Perhaps a realistic scene, but at the very least one rendered salient by schemas linking the Indian masses with bestial dirt, disease, and ignorance. Only a few pages into the novel, we are informed that the homeless family outside Baumgartner's flat washed their "cooking pots . . . in the gutter," "the same gutter" which held their "heaps of faeces" (6). Subsequently, Desai repeats the information, telling us again that they wash "pots and pans in the thickly moving water of the gutter" (144). Later, she reiterates the point another time: "pots and pans being washed in the gutter" (207). This third time, she accompanies the information with an account of Kurtzian reactions: "the tenants stopped on their way in or out to express their *horror* . . . for the ragged creatures who *hardly seemed human*" (207, emphasis added). Recall Marlow standing "horror-struck" before a "picture of . . . pestilence" in which "woolly" headed "creatures . . . went off on all fours" and "lapped" water from a stream (Conrad 18); or, later, his complaint that "the men were—No, they were not inhuman. Well, you know, that was the worst of it—this suspicion of their not being inhuman . . . the thought of their humanity—like yours—the thought of your remote kinship," though what they did was "horrid" and "ugly. Yes, it was ugly" (36–37). Then there is Kurtz's repeated, culminating judgment on his experience of the heart of darkness: "he cried out twice, a cry that was no more than a breath: 'The horror! The horror!'" (71); "his stare . . . could not see the flame of the candle, but was . . . piercing enough to penetrate all the hearts that beat in the darkness. He had summed up—he had judged. 'The horror!'" (72). Elsewhere, Baumgartner too experiences the "horror" of Darkness, a horror linked closely with what Desai seems to present as a special Indian affinity for fecal matter: "horror at the sight of women carrying excreta on their heads, and digging their hands into it as they might into wet dough or laundry" (111).

Feces and other filth seem so pervasive in Desai's India that it is sometimes difficult to discern any vigorous human life on the part of poor, ordinary Indians—except, of course, the ugly, remote, primeval version of life that assailed and discomfited Marlow. The smell and sludge are there from Baumgartner's first arrival, when he hires a carriage that "stank of horsedung" (84). They recur in such passing, repeated images as the walls stained by urine (100, 213). They are central to the characterization of Baumgartner's homeless neighbors—and also of many others who use the gutter as toilet, bath, and washing basin: "Open gutters ran outside . . . along which children squatted, women washed and dogs lapped" (187). Indeed, the water tap shared by a community is little better than the gutter; the mire seems coextensive with the people: "nowhere could one see any sign of cleanliness—the tap only created a morass of mud and slime; children squatted anywhere to urinate or defecate" (175).

Wallowing in verminous offal, and equally immersed in violence ("He knew the absolute degradation of their lives; he knew the violence it bred—the brawling in the night, the beating, the weeping" [7]) the Indian masses are also locked in an eternally primitive condition outside of history. Baumgartner, observing Indian peasants, wonders at "lives so primitive, so basic and unchanging" in "the absence of choice and history" (111). Compare Marlow: "I don't think a single one of them had any clear idea of time, as we at the end of countless ages have. They still belonged to the beginnings of time—had no inherited experience to teach them" (Conrad 41; elsewhere in *Heart of Darkness* they are "simple people" [54], "rudimentary souls" [51] living in "the night of first ages" [37]).

Moreover, in *Baumgartner's Bombay*, this putative atavism is linked repeatedly with Hinduism—here appearing in its full colonial guise as grimly savage idolatry. In a wasteland of dust and stone, Baumgartner finds a crude temple "ancient and primitive" (189), but still in use. Inside there is "total blackness," a Conradian "darkness" which is "a presence" (189). It is here that Baumgartner calls up to his mind's eye the fantastical practice of "cannibalistic rites" (190). In addition, these rites are strangely associated with phallus worship—they include an "engorged penis" (189)—thus tacitly taking up the image of the native as an oversexualized and bestial savage. Indeed, this scene suggests further complexities of literary and ideological relations as well. Specifically, in the course of her novel, Desai spends relatively little time on the hierarchical and largely Aryan aspects of Hinduism, or the Christianlike devotional strains of Hinduism. However, the mystical strain of Hinduism, especially in its Śaivite and thus indigenous South Asian form (see Wolpert 18–19, 35–36) is taken up directly into Desai's Conradian structure. It defines, in fact, the very heart of Indian darkness in *Baumgartner's Bombay*. The most striking, and the most fully Conradian, instance of this is Kurt's recollection, or fantasy, of cannibalism.

Alone with Baumgartner, Kurt narrates his trip into the obscure depths of Indian culture. He had lived for a time in the burning ghat, the cremation place at the river's edge. Baumgartner asks, "And—the bodies? Did you—also eat?" Kurt replies, "I was a tantric then—I was with the tantrics. With them, yes, I ate. I ate. Why? Why do you look like that? Is only flesh, only meat. For eating. For becoming strong. Strong" (157). One recalls Kurtz "presid[ing] at certain midnight dances ending with unspeakable rites" (51) and living in a compound marked out by severed heads, "black, dried, sunken, with closed eyelids" (Conrad 58). Certainly, much that Kurt says in this monologue is untrustworthy, but this boast of uninhibited Indo-primitivism is in effect corroborated by Baumgartner's question—after all, he introduces the topic of cannibalism, and Kurt replies without hesitation—and by Baumgartner's earlier meditation on Hindu "cannibalistic rites" (190).

It is worth considering this temple scene again. It is, perhaps, a scene from Rushdie read through Conrad, for Rushdie's presence pervades *Baumgartner's Bombay* as much as Conrad's. Saleem, "in a murky corner of the abandoned shrine . . . saw the remnants of what might have been four small fires— ancient ashes, scorch-marks on stone—or perhaps four funeral pyres; and in the center of each of the four, a small, blackened, fire-eaten heap of uncrushed bones" (Rushdie 440). In Rushdie, this is the end of a consuming dream in "the forest of illusions" (440). It says nothing of Hindu practices, and still less of cannibalism. It is only when the passage is read through Conrad, when Saleem's trip into the forest is a trip into the heart of darkness, when the Hindu shrine is the place of those savage rites first witnessed, then celebrated by Kurtz—it is only when the passage is structured and filled in by this exemplum, that Rushdie's scene might seem to speak of cannibalistic rites, and be transferred as such into another novel.

After recounting his eating of burned corpses with the tantrics, Kurt goes on to explain that he "learnt yoga" and "meditated till one night the devil came to him, dressed only in white ashes. . . . They had danced together on the rock" (157). Here Kurt portrays Hindu spiritual discipline as Satanic, and identifies Satan with the ash-covered God of yoga and of dance—which is to say, Śiva. He goes on, "Yoga, yes. I learnt. . . . To be like the devil" (157): a standard colonialist view, that the religious practices of the colonized peoples are demonic, that their gods are Satan and his cohorts. Moreover, it is crucial that the deity in question is Śiva. Of the two major Hindu deities, Viṣṇu is clearly more in line with Christian conceptions of divinity and devotional practices. Moreover, as we have already noted, Śiva was indigenous to South Asia. In other words, Śiva and Śaivism are the remnant of the pre-Aryan darkness—what those first Aryan invaders found in their ancient civilizing mission. Put differently, they are the part of Indian society that any Indian might wish to repudiate, insofar as he/she identifies him/herself as the descendant of those Aryans and not of the "barbarians" they brutalized. Here, modern colonialism repeats the structures and motifs of an earlier colonialism, both aligned with and structured by Conrad's novel.

Here, too, Kurt repeats Kurtz, who engaged in "the inconceivable ceremonies of some devilish initiation" (49) and "had taken a high seat amongst the devils of the land—I mean literally" (Conrad 50). But, despite the final adverb—"literally"—it seems that Desai's portrayal of Śiva as Satan goes beyond even a staunchly colonialist interpretation of *Heart of Darkness*. It degrades the subtle and powerful system of Hindu yoga, and—literally—demonizes Hinduism's great ascetic, metaphysical, and indigenous deity. This is, of course, all in the voice of Kurt. But there is nothing to contradict Kurt's view, nothing to rebut the characterization of Hindu yogic discipline and Śiva as demonic.

Indeed, Farrokh extends the vilification of mystical Hinduism, characterizing Hindu hermitages as drug dens; people like Kurt, he insists, "get drugs in . . . ashrams" (14); Kurt later corroborates this linking of Hinduism with narcotics: "At Holi, he and the pilgrims had . . . drunk opium in milk, eaten opium in sweets, smoked opium in pipes" (159). Holi is a Hindu festival, given different interpretations. In one common view, it commemorates Śiva (see Knappert 119). It is a popular festival involving "a reversal of relationships in which the lowly can abuse the high-born" (Knappert 120). It is a good example of a Bakhtinian carnival in which social hierarchies are disrupted and a "contradictory . . . fullness of life" (Bakhtin 61) is affirmed. In Farrokh's speech, however, it is presented as a day of addiction, vice, debauchery.

The West's worst nightmare of barbaric Hindu paganism seems confirmed in this novel by an Indian author, writing in, about, and from India—and thus, one might assume, rich with authenticity. Rosemary Dinnage, reviewing *Baumgartner's Bombay* for the *New York Review of Books*, provides an excellent and disheartening illustration. She explains Kurt thus: "Everything menacing and degraded in Indian life has moved into the empty drugged spaces of his brain" (36).

My point here is not to single out Desai, to impugn her motives, or even to criticize her political views, of which I am largely unaware. Desai has written a novel which develops great human sympathy for a person with whom she has no ethnic or other connection—and that is always difficult and admirable. Nonetheless, she has, at the same time, created a work which, while responding to and revising *Heart of Darkness*, seems not only to repeat but to further what is, under one interpretation, its dehumanizing characterization of non-White people and its denigration of their culture. In doing this, she has shown with disturbing clarity that, contrary to common presumptions, writing back is not necessarily a full and politically progressive repudiation of the precursor work.

BUT IS IT WRITING BACK? IDEOLOGICAL AMBIGUITY
IN GEORGE LAMMING'S *WATER WITH BERRIES*

There are, however, two obvious objections to this argument. One is that there are successful cases of writing back. For example, Tagore's *Gora* does not appear to succumb to the sorts of blatant stereotyping that mar Desai's novel. This is true. I do not mean to say that any postcolonization writer who sets out to revise a metropolitan precursor is thereby condemned to repeat the colonialist ideology of that precursor work. However, success or lack of success in avoiding the ideological pitfalls of writing back is a function of those variables discussed above—the degree to which the writer follows the precursor work in detail, the degree to which he/she interprets the precursor work as expressing colonialist ideology, and so on. Tagore's *Gora* does not repeat colonialist ideology, at least not in any obvious or extended way, primarily because Tagore writes back to Kipling's *Kim* only in the most general terms: an Irish boy orphaned and raised as an Indian—and, in keeping with this, there is in fact a certain amount of Irish stereotyping in Tagore's novel. Moreover, the preceding analysis does not set out laws of nature, intended to cover every individual case with ironclad necessity. It isolates broad tendencies that individual authors may overcome, due to circumstances, effort, or features of their particular intellects or compositional processes.

The second obvious objection to the preceding analysis is more specific and concerns *Baumgartner's Bombay* in particular. Perhaps Desai never set out to "write back" to Conrad. Rather, she simply set out to use *Heart of Darkness* as a model for her own novel. Thus, her evident ideological complicity with Conrad is not an "ambiguity" of writing back—it is not a matter of writing back at all. This too is a reasonable point. Desai does not appear to have begun with a critical or corrective attitude toward Conrad, and an attitude of this sort might be considered a necessary condition for writing back. Still, if Desai is not "writing back" to her metropolitan precursor in this narrow sense of the phrase, then a common working assumption of much postcolonization literary analysis appears to be mistaken. If asked, critics and theorists would, no doubt, acknowledge that postcolonization writers sometimes adopt a positive attitude toward metropolitan texts, even texts which those writers find to be pervaded by colonialist ideology. (It seems clear that Desai understands *Heart of Darkness* in this way, whether she would put it like that or not.) However, the most common working assumption of critics and theorists is that writers from colonized groups do write back to colonialist metropolitan texts in a corrective manner, that they do not "write through" such precursors. In other words, the most common working assumption is that the postcolonization writer begins with a critical or corrective attitude. At the very least, Desai's case indicates that this working assumption is overly simple.

More importantly, the ideological ambiguity we have been discussing is not confined to works such as *Baumgartner's Bombay*. It arises in paradigm cases of critical/corrective writing back as well. It does not seem to be a matter of the postcolonization author's self-conscious aims, but rather of the other variables set out above: the interpretation of the precursor (e.g., how colonialist Conrad is taken to be), the degree of detail in the parallelism, and so on. It is worth considering an unequivocal case of this sort before concluding.

George Lamming has been one of the most articulate and forceful critics of Shakespeare's *The Tempest*. His essay "A Monster, a Child, a Slave" is a standard instance of the anticolonial reading of metropolitan texts. As Ashcroft, Griffiths, and Tiffin point out, "Shakespeare's *The Tempest* has been subject to many such readings. . . . Perhaps the most influential rereading of the play has been George Lamming's" (189). For example, Lamming directly links Prospero's treatment of Caliban with the torture of slaves in Haiti after emancipation. There, and in "Caliban Orders History," he takes up Caliban as an image of anticolonial resistance. Fortunately for our purposes, Lamming's concern with Shakespeare is not confined to critical essays. In his novel, *Water with Berries,* Lamming has set himself the task of writing back to this play (from which he takes his title) along with Shakespeare's *Othello* and, perhaps, Jean Rhys's *Wide Sargasso Sea,* published five years before Lamming's novel.

Water with Berries is, in many ways, a finely crafted exploration of the psychological harm done by colonialism. Moreover, Lamming's self-conscious motives in writing this novel were straightforwardly anticolonial—opposed to colonial political economy, deeply critical of colonial ideology, and so on. Indeed, the entire plot leads toward Teeton's return from England to the Caribbean on 12 October. It is no coincidence that 12 October is the anniversary of the day Columbus landed in the new world. The novel is, in effect, an exploration of the deleterious consequences of that landing.

Yet the overall effect of the novel can hardly be said to undermine the racist beliefs that are so central to colonialist ideology. There are three main non-White characters in this work—Teeton, Roger, and Derek. By the end of the novel, all three have engaged in reprehensible actions. Teeton has killed an old White woman—the "Old Dowager"—who had been kind to him for many years. Roger has driven his White wife to suicide and has committed multiple arson. Derek has tried to rape a girl. Admittedly, none of these men is entirely in his right mind when committing his particular crime. Moreover, there are indications throughout the novel that this mental disequilibrium is the result of the colonial conditions in which they live. There is also an allegorical element to this, as several critics have noted (see, for example, Nair 66–67). Nonetheless, every one of these men engages in violent criminal behavior—and violent behavior that is entirely in keeping with racist ideology. As Supriya Nair points out, "the black man as rapist is hardly a radical breakthrough against . . . stereotyping" (67). More generally, Helen Tiffin notes that all three major non-White characters "might be expected in their individuality and creativity to escape their respective pasts," but, instead, all fall into "false stereotype" (qtd. in Joseph 71).

In contrast, the White characters seem relatively decent. Though far from perfect, their crimes are less than those of the non-White characters. The one apparent exception to this is the Old Dowager's estranged husband, who is reported to have treated his servants very badly on his estate in the Caribbean. However, while we more or less directly witness the crimes of the non-White characters, we are only told indirectly about this man's actions, which are, for that reason, less salient, less consequential for our reaction. Moreover, the evil of this character's behavior is more than counterbalanced by that of the servants themselves, who gang rape his apparently innocent young daughter. In short, the novel involves White men who are often bad, but evidently not as bad as the non-White characters with whom they are linked; White women who are more or less unequivocally good; and non-White men who brutalize the good White women in horrible ways. One would hardly expect this summary to apply to a work written by such a politically self-conscious novelist as Lamming. But it does.

At least part of the explanation for this lies in Lamming's project of writing back. He tacitly interprets his precursors as highly colonialist and follows their texts in detail—with the predictable results. The perfidious acts of his three non-White protagonists are exactly the crimes of the Blacks in those precursor works. *Water with Berries* became an ideologically ambiguous work at least in part because Lamming's composition of the novel was necessarily to some degree guided by the very texts he was setting out to criticize and correct.

More exactly, we may isolate three interrelated stories in the novel, surrounding three related characters—Derek, Roger, and Teeton. Derek is an actor who once played Othello at Stratford, but is now unable to get any role other than that of a corpse. The thematic point is both literal and metaphorical. Literally, there are too few good roles for non-White actors—more generally, too few good jobs for non-White people. Metaphorically, life as a colonized person has made Derek a sort of living corpse. For our purposes, Derek introduces the link with Othello, calling the reader's attention to Shakespeare's tragedy, making the reader sensitive to links between the novel and the play. But Derek does not enact the Othello story. Rather, he enacts the story of Caliban; he tries to rape an innocent girl, a young actress—"It's the girl's debut. She's just fresh from drama school" (237). This occurs shortly after he has been given shelter by the theater, his apartment building having been burned to the ground (241–42):

> There was a wildness of butterflies in the girl's eyes, and her voice went ripping through the footlights like a wail of angels in agony. The silence grew like the horror of the body which was now pricking its way violently through the girl's thighs. Some hurricane had torn her pants away, as the body struggled to split open her sex.

Lamming makes it clear that Derek's life is emotionally debilitating, that he has, as just noted, become a living corpse. But to have him rise up from his role as a corpse to attempt rape—a "uniquely brutal . . . assault" (242)—makes no sense. Or, rather, it makes sense only on the model of a certain interpretation of Caliban—for Caliban's crime, according to Prospero, was an attempted rape of innocent Miranda, after he, like Derek, had been taken in and housed (*The Tempest* I.ii.421–27):

> Prospero: Thou most lying slave,
> Whom stripes may move, not kindness! I have used thee
> (Filth as thou art) with humane care, and lodged thee
> In mine own cell till thou didst seek to violate
> The honor of my child.

This speech immediately follows the one that provided Lamming with the title for his novel. There, Caliban speaks of Prospero's change from early kindness to cruelty and exploitation and notes that, when he first came, Prospero "made much of me" and would "give me / Water with berries in't" (I.ii. 408, 409). Moreover, the rape passage in Lamming's novel calls attention to this link by comparing the rape to a hurricane (242), thereby alluding to the storm from which *The Tempest* takes its name.

Roger is a musician, also formerly successful, also down on his luck. He is married to an angelic White woman named Nicole. She gets pregnant and he accuses her of infidelity. She evidently commits suicide. In any event, she ends up dead in Teeton's room—precipitating Teeton's flight, with the Old Dowager. Though Derek introduces the theme of Othello, it is clearly Roger who lives out the story of Othello—the non-White man with a pure White wife, against whom he makes wild, jealous accusations. Indeed, the connection is explicit in the novel: Derek is thinking of "the man whom Roger had imagined to be Nicole's lover" when "suddenly Derek was back to the days of *Othello*" (133). It is even possible that Roger killed Nicole.

Of course, by the end of the novel, it is clear that Roger is somewhat deranged. His mental imbalance is suggested by his final criminal acts of arson. But, ultimately, this only makes matters worse, for his arson is not really explained at all. It too seems to make sense only by reference to a precursor text. Roger's fire starting evidently results from Lamming tacitly assigning him the role of the (dehumanized) Blacks who burn down Coulibri in *Wide Sargasso Sea*. Unlike *Othello* and *The Tempest*, there are no clear, direct references to Rhys's novel. However, the position of that novel as a precursor text may be suggested in the repeated references to "Saragasso." It was the place on San Cristobal where the dead were supposed to return in order to face their accusers (107)—an image of central importance in Lamming's story. Moreover, Derek was raised "by the pastors of the Saragasso chapel" (238). Finally, when the revolutionaries of San Cristobal plan to return to their island and reconvene, their meeting place is "Saragasso cemetery" (244).

Teeton is the main character in the novel. He is a successful painter, but also a member of an underground organization determined to liberate San Cristobal—largely the island of Hispaniola, comprising Haiti and the Dominican Republic. He is living in the home of the Old Dowager, a kindly lady who obviously cares for him. His story in effect combines those of all three precursor texts, though with a particular emphasis on *The Tempest*. One night, in the dark, Teeton meets a woman who introduces the theme of *The Tempest*—or, rather, reintroduces the theme, for the title itself has already linked the novel to that play. Her name is Myra, a version of "Miranda." One night, she tells Teeton about a horrible storm that killed her father. She then explains that she had lived alone with her father and their servants "on that island. . . . Five thousand miles from home" (145). Her father had suffered some sort of robbery—later, we learn that her mother is the Old Dowager and that the "robbery" was the sexual liaison between the Old Dowager and Fernando, her father's brother. We also learn eventually that the father had treated his servants very badly and that Fernando killed him—all variations on Shakespeare's story. But, whereas in Shakespeare, there is only an uncertain accusation of attempted rape, here Myra tells a brutal story of vicious gang rape by all of her father's servants (150). Evidently, this derives from a tacit interpretation of Shakespeare's play in which Caliban is truly guilty of the accusations against him, and an interpretation in which this guilt is more salient than any actions of Prospero.

Interestingly, Teeton immediately identifies with the servants and is "tortured by regret and guilt," feeling "as though he had been the agent of these barbarities" (151). Evidently, he was not a part of these actions, but assumes their guilt because he sees himself as racially identified with the perpetrators—in clear contrast with the White characters, who show no tendency to assume that the crimes of one or another White person are somehow shared by the entire race. Of course, White people do share Teeton's sense that all Blacks are linked in this way. Thus Fernando too identifies Teeton with the rapists and characterizes him as a "monster" due to the actions of other Blacks; for example, speaking to Teeton, he refers to "your monstrous kind" (224). In one way this operates only to expose Fernando's racism. But the actions of Derek, Roger, and Teeton appear to bear out his assertion. In any event, as we have already noted, Teeton eventually kills the Old Dowager. In this respect, he ends up acting like the "tribe of monstrous butchers" with which Fernando linked him (226) and with which he linked himself. He does this by taking on the role of Othello, murdering the good White woman who had loved him selflessly. Moreover, the full act draws on *Wide Sargasso Sea* as well, for "He had made arson on the Old Dowager's body" (247).

Lamming clearly conceives of himself as writing a critique of or corrective to these precursor works—two metropolitan plays, one settler novel. And he does clearly indicate the debilitating effects of colonialism on the hearts and souls of the non-White men he portrays. But, at the same time, he closely models his own novel on these precursor texts, following them in the most politically consequential details, which he interprets as highly colonialist and highly racist. The result, in this paradigmatic case of writing back, is a novel that, perhaps, does more to reenforce negative stereotypes of non-White men than any of the works it sets out to critique.

In sum, whether or not we conceive of *Baumgartner's Bombay* as writing back, it seems clear that writing back is far from an ideologically unambiguous undertaking—which is just what one would expect from an understanding of its cognitive structure. Fortunately, there are many variables which affect the ideological development of a new work. Moreover, the revision of a single metropolitan precursor—whether a case of writing back or not—is by no means the only way, nor even the most important way, postcolonization writers respond to literary tradition.

Chapter Two

Revising Indigenous Precursors, Reimagining Social Ideals

Tagore's *The Home and the World* and Vālmīki's *Rāmāyaṇa*

Many Hindus refer to the ideal state, the perfect society, as "Rāmarājya," the rule of Rāma. In saying this, they identify this ideal with the legendary kingdom of Rāma, depicted in one of the two great Sanskrit epics, Vālmīki's *Rāmāyaṇa*. Within the Hindu tradition, to reimagine the ideal state almost necessarily involves reimagining the story of Rāma. This is particularly significant, because, despite his status as ideal, many of Rāma's actions have caused readers a great deal of discomfort. Two of his acts are particularly notorious. One is the abandonment of his pregnant wife, Sītā. The other is his murder of a low-caste boy for practicing religious asceticism—the boy was forbidden from engaging in such practices due to his caste status. More generally, the *Rāmāyaṇa*, like most early epics, is a tale of battle and military conquest, which many readers—including many Hindu readers—find anything but ideal. In short, any Hindu who is opposed to the oppression of women, casteism, or war, is likely to find Rāmarājya an imperfect and even highly objectionable ideal. In *The Home and the World*, Tagore undertook to revise this social ideal, and he did so by revising Vālmīki's epic, adopting a revisionary attitude toward that foundational work of indigenous tradition.[1]

Specifically, Tagore took up two topics of great historical importance in early-twentieth-century Bengal. The first is the swadeshi movement, the boycott of foreign goods which spread throughout Bengal after the 1905 decision of the British Indian government to divide Bengal into two separate states—one, Hindu majority; the other, Muslim majority. Secretary of Government Risley explained that "one of our main objects is to split up and thereby weaken a solid body of opponents to our rule" (qtd. in Sarkar, *Swadeshi*, 18). This strategic pitting of Hindu against Muslim was not so much a matter of the administrative division itself, but of how the administrative division was used to convince Hindus and Muslims—especially Muslims—that their interests were mutually opposed. From 1904, the viceroy toured Muslim majority East Bengal to convince Muslims that the partition was advantageous to Muslims. This insistence on the contradictory interests of Hindus and Muslims in part inspired the formation of the Muslim League in 1906 (see Gordon 92 and Sarkar, *Swadeshi*, 80). In connection with this, the antipartition agitation and the associated swadeshi movement tended to take on a sectarian Hindu character—all of which led to the Hindu/Muslim riots of 1907, depicted in the novel.

The other topic taken up by Tagore was purdah, the confinement of women to the inner apartments of the home and their veiling in public. In fact, this practice was already greatly declined by the time of the novel. At least in retrospect, it seems that Tagore presented the breaking of purdah as far more daring and radical than it really was in 1907. (For a discussion of the dissolution of purdah, see Borthwick.) Nonetheless, it allowed Tagore to broach questions of gender relations simultaneously with the issue of nationalism. Moreover, this fit well with the *Rāmāyaṇa* and with the problems of Rāmarājya—for purdah itself is a topic of discussion, albeit briefly, within that epic, as Rāma explains in what limited circumstances a woman may appear in public (III, 334). (It is worth stressing this point, due to the common belief that concealment of women came to India with the Muslim conquests.)

In order to address these two topics, with all their implications regarding political, economic, and cultural ideals, Tagore fashioned a story based largely on the *Rāmāyaṇa*. In doing this, he systematically revised those elements in the epic that are militaristic, patriarchal, and casteist. However, as we shall see, he did not import European ideas and principles to undertake this revision. Rather, he reworked the *Rāmāyaṇa* on the basis of Hindu principles—the very principles that the epic itself putatively celebrates.

Reimagining the story of Rāma is not an easy task, especially given the fact that this legendary figure is widely worshiped as God—not merely as one partial incarnation of one God, Viṣṇu, but as the preeminent manifestation of divinity. As the great sixteenth-century Hindi poet Tulasidasa put it, "there is no other means of grace, neither abstract meditation, sacrifice, prayer, penance, vows, nor ritual worship. Meditate only on Rama; sing only of Rama;

and give ear only to the sum of Rama's infinite perfections" (663). A revision of Rāma's story, especially one that, explicitly or implicitly, criticizes his abandonment of Sītā, his militarism, his murder of the low-caste boy, immediately risks being identified as sacrilege.

Yet, at the same time, there is a long tradition of reworking Rāma's story, a tradition extending back two millennia. First of all, there are numerous explicit revisions. For example, there are regional versions of the story throughout India, the most famous being Tulasidasa's Hindi retelling (just quoted), followed, perhaps, by Kamban's Tamil revision. There are also dramatic versions of parts of the epic, most notably Bhavabhūti's *Uttararāmacarita*, which alters the original epic in significant ways, softening the two crucial scenes of Rāma's apparent cruelty. Moreover, many rewritings of the epic are highly critical. Paula Richman refers to these as "oppositional tellings" ("Introduction" 11). These include women's versions in which Śūrpaṇakhā, a "demoness" mutilated by Rāma, takes revenge on Rāma (see Rao), Tamil revisions and versions by untouchables that celebrate Rāma's demon enemy, Rāvaṇa (Richman "Introduction" 14–15; see also Ramanujan 33–34 on Jaina characterizations of Rāvaṇa, and Seely on an important Bengali version of this sort, prior to Tagore), and so on. Finally, there are indirect revisions of the story as well—and these are particularly important for Tagore's project. For example, the most famous play of all Sanskrit literature, Kālidāsa's *Śakuntalā*, is in many ways a rewriting of the *Rāmāyaṇa* (see Hogan, "Beauty," 30). Kālidāsa does not name his characters "Rāma," "Sītā," and so on. However, he clearly structures his story on the basis of the *Rāmāyaṇa*, and does so in such a way as to alter and reexplain the abandonment of Sītā, and even to limit or criticize the militarism and casteism of the original.

In this way, Tagore's project is doubly traditional, for it revises a work of unsurpassed importance in the Hindu literary tradition, and, in doing this, it follows one common practice within that tradition as well. This contrasts nicely with Desai's novel. For while Desai draws on a Metropolitan work as a model for understanding indigenous society, Tagore "writes back"—in the narrow, critical sense—to a great precursor in his own tradition. In other words, Tagore is undertaking a project of corrective revision here, but he is doing so with respect to indigenous traditions, not with respect to traditions of the colonizer. In this way, Desai and Tagore almost exactly reverse the attitude toward literary precursors that appears to be widely assumed in studies of postcolonization literature.

ON ALTERING A PRECURSOR WORK, AND ON WRITING BACK

In the preceding chapter, we discussed how a precursor work often serves as a cognitive model for the new writer. It provides what we might call "selection principles" for describing or narrating real events and it guides the addition of properties and relations to imagined events. Suppose I am writing a novel based on some recent historical occurrence. As part of this, I wish to describe daily life in India. Again, daily life anywhere is too diverse, too multiple to be described in all its detail. I necessarily select. A precursor work can serve to guide my selection, rendering certain properties salient and occluding others. This process of selection is, of course, largely unselfconscious. It involves "encoding" experience—making it available as information for cognitive processing—synthesizing that information, linking it to further lexical structures, and so on (on encoding, see John Holland et al. 55–56). Typically, I do not even choose what models I am using to guide encoding, inference, and so on. Rather, these are triggered automatically.[2]

More exactly, suppose I wish to include in this novel a particular sort of fictional character—a European adventurist, say. I need some way of deciding what properties to give this character, where to place him in India, how to define his connections with other people, what events to have him experience or initiate, and so on. In one cognitivist idiom, I need a way of generating "situation-specific" cognitive entities (e.g., characters), their attributes, and their functional relations (for a general treatment of the creation and synthesis of such entities, see Radvansky and Zacks; see also Garnham). I may self-consciously choose to draw on some particular exemplum. Or I may spontaneously begin to draw on such a model without any such choice. In either case, I will begin to articulate this character—his feelings, ideas, actions, relations—in part through a sort of "feature transferral" from a precursor character to the new character. (On the general operation of feature transferral, see Tversky and Ortony.) Thus, I may take parts of Kurtz in order to shape this character's relation to a native colonial population. Or, what is more likely, I will attribute features to the new character on the basis of feeling that they "fit," that they are "right." This feeling results from the fact that I have unconsciously linked this new character with the character of Kurtz—that is, the lexical entry "Kurtz"—and have drawn the features from that entry without being aware that I have done so. Technically, just as the leash and the hair serve to "probe" my lexicon and trigger the prototype for "dog," so, in this case, some condition of my new character—say, his alien presence in a European colony—serves to probe my lexicon and trigger relevant exempla, of which the most prominent is Kurtz. (On the operation of lexical or memory probes, see Radvansky and Zacks 180 and Estes 27.) The exemplum of Kurtz will, in turn, serve to provide properties and relations for this new character.

But, clearly, this process cannot be one of mere repetition, the simple re-creation of Kurtz. In the most extreme case, such repetition might constitute plagiarism. In less extreme cases, it would mark the writer as "derivative," as unworthy of serious attention, because he/she is too similar, and too obviously similar, to a precursor. In consequence, the new writer's relation to a precursor text must involve some sort of cognitive processing which changes the properties and relations of that precursor text, or rather of the relevant, lexicalized part of that text—in this case, the lexicalized complex of features defining the character Kurtz.

To understand this, we need to consider the lexicon and lexical operations in more detail. We may define the "internalized" or "lexical" precursor work as a set of linked lexical entries—"Conrad," "Kurtz," "Marlow," etc.—with each of these entries, in turn, comprising a complex of lexical "features" and further links. I use "features" to refer to any element of a lexical entry. These features would include abstract properties and relations, such as a character's moral propensities; more concrete properties, such as physical attributes; specific perceptual memories (e.g., visual images perhaps from a film version of the work), and so on. These features are, obviously, derived in part from the precursor work itself. But they are also the product of the new writer's "concretization" of that work, as Roman Ingarden would call it—his/her inferences about it, the conclusions he/she draws from it, the ways in which he/she tacitly visualizes it, imagines its unspecified details, and so on, the way he/she fills in its "gaps," as Iser would say. It is worth noting that this lexical structure includes elements of style and phrasing from the precursor work, and a whole complex of aesthetic, political, and other reactions—one's own, and those of others. Indeed, it includes a sort of personal version of a Jaussian history of reception.

There are many ways in which these items are linked and thus many ways in which they may be activated. For example, characters—here understood as lexicalized hierarchies of features—are accessible not only by character name ("Kurtz"), but by author ("Conrad"), literary work ("Heart of Darkness"), genre or subgenre ("colonial adventure," or whatever one might call it), etc. Again, suppose I am writing an historical novel. "Romantic" (i.e., relating to love) or "heroic" entries may be triggered by my need to include a love scene or battle scene at a certain point—this need itself probably deriving from some further, lexicalized structure, for example, that of genre. These entries would include instances of works I find particularly effective and ineffective in the romantic and heroic modes—thus works to emulate or to avoid emulating—as well as instances I know to be widely considered effective and ineffective. For example, in the "romantic" category, I might have positive or admired instances—scenes, characters, metaphors, lines—from Kālidāsa and Neruda, while in the "heroic" category, I might have positive instances from Homer and Chikamatsu. In composition and revision, I tacitly compare my own writing to these exempla, judging the effect of my own work relative to these (successful) precursor works, ending the process of revision when I feel that the final result is "right," which is to say, produces the effect that I have experienced in reading the relevant precursor works, perhaps an effect of beauty or sublimity.

But, again, the new writer cannot simply repeat the features of the precursor text. There are two necessary parts to the transformation of a precursor work: abstraction and reparticularization. Reparticularization may occur through the selection and shaping of personal experience, simple transferral of features from distinct lexical items, or systematic transformation of feature complexes in relation to an alternative within a domain, often within a reference set. A domain is, roughly, a set of systematically related lexical items, usually linked with a further lexical item—such "hot," "cold," etc., for the domain "temperature." These methods of reparticularization are not mutually exclusive, but may be combined in various ways.

Abstraction is just what it sounds like—repeating the features of a precursor work at a more general level, not at the level of full particularity. Clearly, abstraction of some sort is necessary for almost any sort of writing. More exactly, our lexical entry for any given literary work will involve hierarchies of general structures in which the particularity of the work is embedded. (On the structure of lexical entries, see, for example, John Holland et al., 12–21). Consider, for example, the *Rāmāyaṇa*. At the most particular level, it is a text consisting of certain words, characters with precise properties, given in those words, actions with very specific courses and consequences, and so on. But one may abstract from any of these particulars. Thus the plot may be understood as a form of love triangle, or as a story dealing with duty. Rāvaṇa may be seen as a rival in a love triangle, or as a demon, or as a purveyor of illusion.

Clearly, there are many possible levels of abstraction for any work—infinitely many, in fact. They form a sort of continuum from the most general categories to the particular concreteness of the text, as lexicalized by the later author. Some abstractions are so large that they have little bearing on the unique text in question. For example, the structure "love triangle" applies to the *Rāmāyaṇa* equally with innumerable other plots. Insofar as an author is drawing on the general conventions and motifs of the love triangle plot, we would say that he/she is writing in a genre, but not necessarily that he/she is transforming a particular precursor. In order to say that the new author is revising the work of a precursor, the level of abstraction from the precursor work must drop below a particular threshold. We could call this the "threshold of distinctiveness," the "highest" point where an abstraction remains distinctive of the work in question.

For example, an author might develop the love triangle in such a way as to characterize the rival as a politically powerful manipulator of illusions, the husband as a devotee of moral duty, the wife as suffering a metaphorical fire ordeal, with the metaphor stated explicitly or implied through imagery.

Within the Indian literary tradition, this would be distinctive of the *Rāmāyaṇa*. On the other hand, this is not to say that either the author or a reader will be self-consciously aware of the relation of the new work to the *Rāmāyaṇa*. An author may perfectly well draw on the structure of the *Rāmāyaṇa* without realizing that he/she is doing this. He/she might think of various possibilities for characterizing the rival in a love triangle, then choose a politically powerful manipulator of illusions merely because it "feels right"—without realizing that this "feeling right" is, at least in part, a matter of its conformity with a distinctive structure of the *Rāmāyaṇa*. The same point applies to the reader and his/her reaction to a work. We could refer to the point at which an author or reader becomes aware of the link with a precursor work as the "threshold of salience."

But, of course, abstraction will not do on its own. Abstraction alone leaves us not with a plot, but with a plot summary. It necessarily requires "reparticularization," the respecification of the abstract structure in a manner different from its initial specification in the precursor work. One way in which this reparticularization may occur is through the application of the precursor structure to some personal experience, condition, observation, belief, or the like—as when Desai applies the structures of *Heart of Darkness* to her experiences of and ideas about India. We stressed above the degree to which the precursor work serves to guide a new author's observation and remembrance, the way that *Heart of Darkness*, as understood by Desai, serves to select details and to organize scenes out of her beliefs about and personal memories of India. In fact, the process is more complex than that. Daniel Schacter explains that we do not simply remember past events as they happened. We do not store complete, detailed records of past events. Rather, we store fragments (40). When we recall some episodic memory, we do not simply activate a complex set of data. Rather, we re-create the memory out of the fragments—and out of present experiences, interests, goals, and so on (8, 104–13). Thus Desai does not merely use Conrad (unconsciously) to highlight factually accurate memories. Her understanding of and interest in Conrad serve to refashion her memories of India and to develop her current experiences (just as my current interests, etc., do the same for my reading of Desai and any reader's interests, etc., do for this book).

Of course, personal experience is not the only way an author reparticularlizes an abstraction from a precursor work. This brings us to the second type of alteration, the transferral of features from another lexical item. One primary way in which a new author alters a precursor text is through the combination of lexical features. For example, Desai seems to have taken Conrad's Russian and added to him features from her lexical entry for "Jew" (a transferral probably facilitated by the common lexical association of Jews with Russia) deleting the features in her entry for Conrad's Russian that contradict these additions. In revising Rāvaṇa, the demon king of the *Rāmāyaṇa*, into the character of Sandip, Tagore adds features drawn from his lexical entries for particular politicians and activists (contemporary and historical), along with more general political entries (e.g., "revolutionary") and entries for other literary figures, such as Milton's Satan. It is worth noting that feature additions need not be confined to character traits, but may include actions, personal relations, scenery, rhetoric, and so on. For instance, in the case of Milton's Satan, Tagore drew most obviously on metaphor and imagery. An interesting case of this may be found in Sandip's account of his relation to Bimala: he must "steal into the garden of paradise in the guise of a snake, and whisper secrets into the ears of man's chosen consort and make her rebellious." In the immediately following sentence, he explains Bimala's condition: "My poor little Queen Bee is living in a dream." Beyond the obvious links with the story of the Fall, the specific images of the whispering and the dream are drawn from *Paradise Lost* IV.799ff., where Satan, having stolen into the garden, whispers in the ear of sleeping Eve, giving her a "troublesome dream" ("Argument" to V) which prepares her for the final seduction and loss of Paradise. Indeed, according to Milton, that seduction and loss "Brought Death into the World, and all our woe" (I.3). The same consequence is described directly by Sandip: "then farewell to all ease; and after that comes death!" (55).

It is unsurprising that Tagore conjoined just these two literary figures, Rāvaṇa and Satan. Indeed, this is just the sort of feature-synthesis one would expect, given the general structure and processes of human cognition. Simply put, our experiences and recollections of different literary works are bound up with one another through lexical connections. More exactly, our lexical entries are cross-indexed for a wide range of features. If two entries are strongly linked, they are likely to be activated simultaneously, if nonconsciously, in our minds, and thus both are likely to enter into our generation and evaluation of new characters, scenes, plot developments, and so on. Satan and Rāvaṇa are likely to be linked in a number of ways. They are both demons and the greatest enemy of humankind; both try to seduce a woman; both are involved in battle against God, which they lose. Thus an activation of one—especially when that involves a probe that draws on these links, such as "demon seducing a woman"—is likely to activate the other, rendering *both* functional in interpretive, productive, or other relevant cognition.

We could think of literary creation in the following way. We have some sort of aim—to write a story dealing with a love triangle, for example. This itself may have its source in some personal experience or in some allegorical concern or in something else. In any case, this aim combines with experiential particulars to activate a range of relevant entries in our lexicon. These entries are not directly accessed; we do not become explicitly conscious of them. But they are brought to the fore; they are "primed" for access, as cognitive scientists put it, brought near to consciousness and made directly accessible, but not directly accessed (on priming, see Garman 494 and John Holland et al., 57). This range of entries serves to provide a series of possible character traits and the like, by guiding experiential observation and reconstruction or through direct feature transferral.

In this way, general tasks already call up sets of related entries, making feature transferral very likely. For example, in writing *The Home and the World*, Tagore clearly had as one goal the composition of a national allegory. This goal activated several lexical entries right at the outset, presumably including "epic," the standard genre of nation founding. This did not lead Tagore to write in verse, but it is one reason why he did put the novel in the lexical context of such precursor epics as *Paradise Lost* and the *Rāmāyaṇa*. In combination with other lexical links between these two epics in particular, it fostered the sort of feature combination we have been discussing.

This placing of the new, or prospective work in the context of a goal-defined set of precursor works, brings us to our final mode of alteration—the systematic transformation of feature complexes via some alternative within a domain. As the preceding discussion indicates, we do not merely choose to combine features randomly. Most often, we do so based on some prior lexical connection, related to the goal of the work at hand. Thus, Tagore fuses Vālmīki and Milton, epics dealing with demonic evil and seduction, works already likely to be linked in Tagore's lexicon. Indeed, the relation is more systematic than lexical linkage alone suggests. We could say that these works are part of the same reference set. Again, a reference set is a subset of elements in a particular category that one uses as an evaluative standard for other elements in that category. For example, in judging my salary, I might compare it with the salaries of other professors or other people in my family. In this case, the other professors or the other people in my family would constitute a reference set and they would provide a basis for my evaluation of my salary (see Ortony, Clore, and Collins 102). The simple transferal of features, just discussed, appears to take place most often within a literary reference set. In addition to facilitating feature combination, reference sets afford the new writer structures for guiding the systematic transformation of complexes of features, for such transformation most often takes place through parallel items in a reference set.

Consider a simple instance from the reference set for European epic. In writing *Omeros*, one of Walcott's primary precursor texts is Joyce's *Ulysses*. He alters this text in many ways. For example, he clearly abstracts and reparticularizes. But he also transforms structures based on reference sets. Thus, while Joyce models his story of Ireland primarily on the *Odyssey*, the most important classical precursor for Walcott—or at least the one he chooses to stress, as Joyce stressed the *Odyssey*—is the *Iliad*. In this way, Walcott chose not only another work from the reference set for "European epic," he chose the only other work from the narrower set, "Homeric epic" (equivalently, he chose the member of the reference set for "epic" that is nearest to the *Odyssey*). Moreover, he did not merely transfer some features from the *Iliad* onto a prototype provided by the *Odyssey* or *Ulysses,* he systematically substituted the character and plot structures of the former for those of the latter. In other words, he did not simply add features from one precursor work to those from a second precursor work, as Tagore did in joining Satan to Rāvaṇa . Rather, he systematically transformed his use of *Ulysses* by substituting one member of a reference set, the *Iliad,* for another, the *Odyssey*. Instead of abstracting from and adding features to Joyce's use of the *Odyssey,* he substituted the *Iliad*.

Unsurprisingly, Tagore too used systematic transformations of this sort in composing *The Home and the World*. Consider Hindu ethical theory, which provides one central structuring principle for Tagore's novel. Within Hindu thought, there are several distinct types of duty, as we shall discuss below. The two most sharply opposed types of duty are "universal" duty and "caste" duty. Clearly, these form parts of one lexical set or domain. Throughout the *Rāmāyaṇa*, Rāma is faced with situations in which he has to choose between caste duty and universal duty—and he always acts on caste duty. In revising this epic, Tagore does not abstract from these acts and combine features from other characters or actions. Rather, he consistently and systematically transforms the Rāma character from a character who follows caste duty into a character who follows universal duty.

Before going on, it is worth dwelling for a moment on the notion of reference sets, for they are crucial to understanding literary identity—influence, poetic voice, and so on—in a variety of ways. Reference sets are, after all, what define relevant precursor texts to begin with. Suppose a writer sets out to develop a love triangle. By that decision, he/she already begins to locate his/her work in relation to a tacit reference set of possible precursors. Moreover, the different degrees of influence exerted by various precursor works are in part a function of the different ways in which the works fit into literary and nonliterary reference sets. Joyce's *Ulysses* became a primary precursor text for Walcott largely because his project in *Omeros* included *Ulysses* in a wide range of reference sets. Walcott set out to write an epic about a former British colony, an island and so forth. The intersection of these various reference sets made Joyce's work particularly forceful or salient. One could think of the different reference sets as providing their constituent works with a degree of activation or prominence. As the number of project-relevant reference sets increases—"epics," plus "works treating a former British colony," and so on—so too does the activation or prominence of any given work that is included in these sets. A work included in many of these sets will have a higher degree of activation than a work included in few of these sets. Such a work is therefore likely to become a dominant precursor. (The idea that lexical entries may have different levels of activation is common in cognitive science; for a discussion of this sort, in relation to a different set of problems, see Chandler.)

Finally, the concepts we have been discussing allow us to add further to our conception of writing back, in the narrow sense of an alteration in which the new author is self-consciously setting out to revise the precursor text with the aim of correcting some politically objectionable aspect of that text. First, since it is a self-conscious and corrective undertaking, the new author typically tries to raise the links with the precursor work above the threshold of salience for a reader—to make the reader aware of the connection. This is clearly the case in such classic cases of writing back as Jean Rhys's *Wide Sargasso Sea* or Aimé Césaire's *Une Tempête,* as well as Lamming's *Water with Berries.* It is also the case with Tagore's use of the *Rāmāyaṇa* in *The Home and the World.*

Second, writing back is often based on some systematic transformation calculated to serve the political purposes of the new author. For example, *Wide Sargasso Sea* is to a considerable degree based on one very important and common type of transformation—the shift to a complementary point of view. Specifically, Rhys transfers the point of view from Jane Eyre to Bertha/Antoinette. This serves as a generative principle guiding a whole series of other transformations—not only in physical location and narrative detail, but in the development of empathy, in tacit ethical evaluation, and so forth. This systematic transformation was clearly designed to serve Rhys's political purpose of correcting the misrepresentation of creole women.

As already noted, Tagore's writing back to the *Rāmāyaṇa* involves a similarly consequential transformation, in this case based not on point of view, but on the fundamental ethical principles guiding the action of the main character. This is the result of Tagore's political purposes as well, specifically, his desire to advocate a particular sort of politics for India—a politics that is not Hindu nationalist and violent, but universalist and nonviolent. In this way, Tagore's relation to this foundational text of the indigenous, Indian literary tradition may be seen as a paradigm case of writing back.

HINDUISM AND NATIONALISM

Differences in object and method between Tagore's novel and the novels by Desai and Lamming may seem to suggest that Tagore's work is relatively free of colonial ideology. This is not really the case. Tagore presents a picture of Indian goods that is, at best, prejudicial. He repeatedly characterizes Indian products as expensive and inferior. This is part of his opposition to the swadeshi campaign, the boycott of foreign goods, which he portrays as violent and, to a great extent, economically harmful. But, in fact, this boycott was tremendously valuable for the Indian economy. As Wolpert points out, during the swadeshi campaign, "Mills in Bombay, Ahmedabad, and Nagpur enjoyed a half decade of industrial boom" (275). Perhaps more importantly, it "helped revive the dying cottage industry of hand spinning and weaving" and "served . . . to stimulate indigenous production of most other things that had hitherto been imported from England, including sugar, matches, glass objects, shoes, and metal goods" (276). The representation of the violence of the movement is misleading too. While there were no doubt objectionable incidents, it is strange for Tagore to represent the violence of Indians while ignoring the far greater violence of the government during this period (see, for example, Ray 23; Sarkar, *Swadeshi,* 24). As Wolpert puts it, "Ruthless repression spread like plague throughout Bengal" at this time (275).

It is particularly important to stress this, for some of the most influential critical analyses of *The Home and the World* have ignored this point, treating the novel as if it were a precisely accurate and representative historical portrayal of the period in general and the swadeshi movement in particular. For example, Martha Nussbaum's sensitive discussion of Tagorean universalism is marred by an assumption of this sort. Indeed, this is part of the reason Nussbaum's argument is open to Immanuel Wallerstein's objection: "Had there not been *swadeshi,* India would still be a British colony. Would this have served Kantian morality more?" (122). There is a similar, but in some ways deeper, problem with Ranajit Guha's attack on swadeshi in his important collection *Domination without Hegemony.* In this attack, Guha relies for his historical claims almost entirely on a "dossier compiled in 1909 by the Director of Criminal Intelligence" (110), *Memorandum showing how far the boycott agitation has gone beyond the advocacy of mere boycott of British goods in the interest of native industries. Prima facie* this would hardly seem to be a trustworthy source. Moreover, like Tagore, Guha fully ignores the benefits of the movement and the great violence against which the movement was struggling.

However, the ideological ambiguity or complicity in Tagore's novel does not appear to have resulted from Tagore's relation to any particular precursor text. Rather, this novel—published in serial form, in Bengali, in 1915, then in book form in 1916—was simply written in Tagore's most pro-British period. In 1911, King George had rescinded the partition of Bengal, which had sparked the swadeshi movement. In 1913, Tagore had been awarded the Nobel Prize in literature, which he understandably took not only as a personal honor but also as a sign that Europeans were beginning to recognize the value and importance of Indian civilization and culture. He was knighted in 1915— an apparent indication that English racism was declining. Of course, one could just as easily give this a cynical interpretation, to the effect that Tagore saw his personal interest in siding with the British—much as his ancestors had collaborated with the invaders to begin with (see chapter 1 of Dutta and Robinson). In any case, however one understands Tagore's response to these honors, he does seem to have become sincerely disillusioned with Indian politics, especially its apparently increasing violence and sectarianism—tendencies evidenced in the Hindu/Muslim riots of 1907, which conclude the novel.

The violence and sectarianism were at least in part a result of the Hinduization of Indian nationalism. Tagore had several objections to this. Most importantly, it excluded Muslims, as well as smaller minorities such as Parsis, Christians, and Jews. From early on, Tagore emphasized what we would now call the "multiculturalism" and "multiracialism" of India and advocated an acceptance of that diversity. In his lectures on nationalism (published in 1917), he argued that "The history of India does not belong to one particular race but is of a process of creation to which various races of the world contributed—the Dravidians and the Aryans, the ancient Greeks and Persians, the Mohamedans of the West and those of central Asia" (27).

In addition, this Hinduization of nationalism simultaneously distorted Hinduism. It reenforced the worst aspects of Hindu thought by valorizing all those practices criticized by the British—child marriage, caste, and so on—while simultaneously degrading much that is spiritually excellent in Hinduism. Consider, for example, the important nationalist leader, B. G. Tilak, part of the "revolutionary" wing of the Congress Party and a supporter of the Swadeshi movement (Wolpert 277). In 1891, the age of statutory rape in India was only 10. The British sought to raise the age to 12. Tilak spearheaded a campaign against the measure, decrying it as a danger to Hindu tradition. In his home state, he instituted a festival commemorating the birth of the Hindu god, Gaṇeśa. Wolpert reports that "The annual Ganesh . . . festivals were usually accompanied by violent conflicts between Hindus and Muslims, especially when paramilitary bands of young 'Ganesh guards' . . . marched noisily past mosques" (260). Moreover, Tilak took up the Bhagavad Gītā, a Hindu spiritual text, to argue that killing is fully in accord with, and perhaps even required by, Hindu principle (see Wolpert 261)—this in a religion that exalts nonviolence as a central ethical principle (we will return to this point below).

And this is only one case. In Bengal, the Mother Goddess became a focus of political attention—as is evident in the novel through Sandip's insistence that the nation is the Mother Goddess and his identification of Bimala with that goddess. First, this focus on the Mother Goddess tended to consider one aspect only. The goddess has many faces. She is maternal love, tenderness, generation, eros, understanding, beauty, delight, intellect, devotion. She is also destruction—first of all, time that devours all living things. It was this aspect of destruction that the Hindu nationalists stressed above all others. That was already a serious distortion, occluding all aspects of the goddess except one. In addition, nationalists twisted and further narrowed this remaining bit, redefining the destructive goddess as a force of active violence. Sarkar refers, for example, to a 1905 work that "offered a startling reinterpretation of the goddess as incarnated in the sword" (*Swadeshi* 485). Another version of the same principle was the stress on the goddess as "Śakti," meaning "Power"—here understood not as spiritual power but as a sort of brute force, used for national ends. Of course, historically, the goddess did have a martial aspect, and there are important texts (e.g., the *Devī-Māhātmya;* see Coburn) that present her as assuming bodily form in order to defeat evil in battle. However, these mythological conflicts bear little relation to the revolutionary violence advocated by some nationalists—whether one sympathizes with that violence or not. And, once again, this is only one narrow function of the goddess, over-balanced by so many others, that were left out of the nationalist account. These are distortions that should disturb any devoted Hindu.

Of course, Tagore was far from being an orthodox Hindu. Indeed, he was a member of the Brahmo Samaj, a sort of religious fellowship that combined elements of Hinduism with aspects of Christianity, Islam, and other religions. Individual members of the Samaj stressed one or the other component according to their own preferences. The leaders of the Samaj most admired by Tagore, leaders such as Keshub Sen, were universalists who believed that each religion could learn from all the others and that the fullest spiritual development could be achieved by combining the best elements from different religions (on Sen's project of creating a "universal" religion, see Kopf 267–86). At the same time, in Tagore's own understanding of this universalist synthesis, Hinduism loomed particularly large. Indeed, his own universalism could be seen as a version of Hinduism—in part because Hinduism itself is already so diverse and inclusive in its ideas and practices. But he clearly felt that Hindu nationalists were doing just the opposite of what such a universalist project required. They were dividing religions, opposing them to one another, rather than bringing them together. Moreover, they were stressing the most retrograde and harmful aspects of their own religion.

Indeed, Tagore was far more interested in human spirituality than in national independence. He actually went so far as to argue that India should not seek national independence but should strive to lead all humankind to greater spiritual elevation, drawing on its strength as a land of many spiritualities, many profound and beautiful traditions—including many traditions within Hinduism itself. In a poem written on the last day of the nineteenth century, Tagore expressed his view of nationalism as a spiritually—and physically—destructive force: "The last sun of the century sets amidst the blood-red clouds of the West and the whirlwind of hatred. / The naked passion of self-love of Nations, in its drunken delirium of greed, is dancing to the clash of steel and the howling verses of vengeance" (in de Bary 234). In contrast to nationalism, Tagore urged "disinterested faith in ideals, in the moral greatness of man" (239). He maintained that "We, in India have to show the world . . .

truth," specifically "The truth that moral force is a higher power than brute force." Because of this, Tagore argued, national independence "is not our objective." Rather, "Our fight is a spiritual fight—it is for Man. We are to emancipate Man from the meshes that he himself has woven round him—these organizations of national egoism." In this way, India will "win freedom for all humanity" (in de Bary 239).

Though this universalism is obviously linked with Brahmoism, Tagore's analysis of nationalism and his advocacy of human liberation are situated firmly within Hindu thought. It is worth stepping back for a moment to consider some of the relevant underlying principles of Hindu philosophical tradition. According to this tradition, human life is animated by four goals: love (kāma), prosperity (artha), dharma, and mokṣa. Love and prosperity govern the majority of lives. But the two greater goals are dharma and mokṣa. Dharma is ethical obligation or duty. Mokṣa is spiritual enlightenment or "liberation." Both are of central importance to Tagore's thought in general, and to *The Home and the World* in particular.

More exactly, Hindu ethical theory distinguishes a variety of types of dharma. Some forms of duty are particular to one's position in the family—being a parent or child, for example. Others are related to one's stage of life—whether one is a student, say, or a householder. The two forms that are most crucial for our concerns are one's caste dharma and the "universal" dharma that applies to everyone. Caste dharma is a function of one's caste. Hinduism distinguishes four broad categories of caste: the priestly and learned or Brahmin caste, the ruler/warrior or kṣatriya caste, the cultivator and merchant caste, and the servant caste. The first three castes are considered to be significantly superior to the fourth. In consequence, orthodox Hinduism forbids members of the fourth caste from studying the sacred books, practicing spiritual discipline, and the like. We have already alluded to this prohibition in connection with Rāma's murder of the low-caste boy. The dharma of the ruler/warrior caste involves war, murder, treachery, and deceit in the service of the state—and it pervades the *Rāmāyaṇa*. This is one aspect of Hinduism that Tagore sought to oppose in his novel. In effect, Sandip is advocating a sort of kṣatriyadharma, as were many Hindu nationalists in real life.[3]

One would expect Tagore, the spiritual universalist, to be more partial to universal dharma than to caste dharma—especially ruler/warrior dharma. In fact, he was. But his opposition to kṣatriyadharma was more particular, and more Hindu, than one might at first realize, for it was based on the specification of universal dharma within Hindu belief. There are many lists of universal dharma in ancient Hindu texts. They differ from one another, sometimes considerably, but almost all seem to agree on two properties of universal duty: truth and ahiṃsā—usually translated as "nonviolence," but often understood as a broader refusal to take part in or go along with harming others. In this

way, universal dharma and kṣatriyadharma are, obviously, antithetical. There
was disagreement among Hindu thinkers as to which should take precedence.
The standard view was that, in cases of conflict, caste dharma should
supercede universal dharma (see O'Flaherty 97). Tagore's view was the precise
opposite of this. Thus he made Nikhil an example of universal dharma. As
such, Nikhil is a character continually concerned to avoid himsā, harm to or
violence against others—even in subtle forms of indirect coercion.

In this universal scheme, especially as it is taken up and developed by
Tagore, the largest goal of any person's action should be to bring the entire
world into truth and ahiṃsā, into a practice of universal dharma. For the most
part, other goals, to be genuinely justified, should conduce toward the achievement of this universal ethical society. Thus the establishment of independence
for India is an important goal only insofar as it conduces toward universal
dharma. This, in and of itself, would be likely to make Tagore uncertain that
national independence is a goal worth great effort. But if those who seek
national independence do so by means of deceit and violence, then that makes
the whole pursuit positively reprehensible. Indeed, from this point of view, one
might argue that it hardly matters what the colonizer is doing. If the colonial
government is propagating far more deceit and violence than Indians, that
does not really matter, because the concern of Indians should be with their
own moral duties, their own dharma. The adharma (violation of dharma)
enacted by the British has no bearing on the obligations of Indians. Duty, in
this view, is not a contract between people, broken when one party fails to fulfill his/her commitments. It is absolute, and binding in all circumstances.
Indeed, it is particularly binding on Indians, in Tagore's view, for they have the
task of leading all other erring peoples back onto the path of duty. Like parents or teachers, faced with delinquent youths, Indians must be particularly
careful to persevere in truth and ahiṃsā, for their example is crucial to the
future of the entire world.

This pursuit of absolute, universal duty is, obviously, difficult. It is continually undermined by other pursuits—largely the pursuits of desire or wealth. In
Vedantism and related schools of Hindu metaphysical thought, this continual
disruption of duty is the result of the fact that our minds are suffused with egoistic attachments. We can truly pursue dharma only when we have freed ourselves from these attachments, when we are no longer driven by lust for that
person or greed for this thing, but can pursue duty for its own sake. Put differently, we can follow dharma only if we renounce all interest in the fruits of our
actions—the concrete gains or losses that might result for ourselves. This
renunciation of gain is not simply an evaluative matter regarding the purity of
our motives. It is a practical condition for the fulfillment of duty. If we fail to
renounce the fruits of our actions, we will always be distracted by those fruits,
and we will not be able to follow universal duty consistently.

This all leads us to the final and most encompassing goal of life—mokṣa or liberation. The problem with attachment is not, in the first place, ethical. It is prudential. Attachment is error, untruth, delusion. It is based on an idea of material things, which, in turn, is based on a continual flux of sensations. But these sensations are mere appearance. The solid things they seem to reveal are seeming only. They are not genuine substance, but illusion, "māyā." Only that absolute spirit, brahman, that pervades and includes every individual soul—only that is real. All other things (physical substance, memories and ideas, differences between person and person) are mere fancy, a web of deceit made up from strands of desire. Mokṣa, liberation, is the recognition of this—not merely its intellectual acceptance, but the full realization of the oneness of spirit, the unreality of ephemeral things, a realization that suffuses one's thought, feeling, and action. When Tagore looks for liberation, he cannot confine it to the political independence of a nation state. For him, it must be a broader, more encompassing pursuit—the liberation of the human soul, of all human souls, for they are one and only appear different in the dim light cast by desire. That is why he says that political independence "is maya" and why he insists that India's "spiritual fight . . . for Man" is "to emancipate Man from the meshes that he himself has woven round him—these organizations of national egoism" (239).

Thus, Tagore's view of the ideal India is deeply antinationalist. Indeed, it is an ethical and metaphysical view, more than a political one. But the ethics here cannot be a matter of isolated individuals. Indeed, the metaphysical ideas ultimately contradict such isolation. That is why the liberation Tagore advocated had to pervade the entire populace.[4] That is also why, in revising the *Rāmāyaṇa* in order to reimagine the perfect society, Tagore has not set out to write a story that simply concerns two contending individuals—one, who misuses kṣatriyadharma to egocentric ends; the other who seeks to follow universal dharma. Rather, he has worked the revision into a national allegory.[5]

Bimala is not merely an individual wife, but the people of Bengal, or even the people of India as a whole. At one point, she thinks, "I who before had been of no account now felt in myself all the splendour of Bengal itself" (50). Later, Sandip links her with all of India, saying, "in you, I visualize the *Shakti* of our country" (73). Moreover, as Bimala herself notes, Sandip is "not a mere individual" (50), and neither is Nikhil. Rather, they represent broad tendencies of action and of thought—alternatives for the future of Bengal. Here, Tagore has taken up what is perhaps the most common structure for national allegory in postcolonization literature—the conflict of two men over the love of a woman, representing the conflict of two political tendencies over the heart of the people. Just as Bimala must choose Sandip or Nikhil, the people of Bengal too—and, beyond them, the people of India; and, beyond them, the people of the world—must choose the way of destructive nationalism or the way of universal dharma and renunciation, the way toward liberation of the human soul.

RĀMĀYAṆA

Before discussing Tagore's use of the *Rāmāyaṇa*, it is necessary to give a brief overview of the main elements of the story, particularly those elements important to Tagore's revision. The *Rāmāyaṇa* is the story of one incarnation of the god Viṣṇu. Viṣṇu, widely characterized as the "preserver" god in the Hindu trinity, is believed to be born in mortal form whenever the world is particularly at risk due to some evil force. He defeats the evil and saves the world. In this case, evil is incarnate in the demon king Rāvaṇa. Even here one begins to get a sense of Tagore's reappropriation of this story—for "national egoism" is such a force of evil, and Tagore, as we have noted, hoped that India would serve as savior to all of humankind in defeating this demon. Rāma is born the eldest son of King Daśaratha. When Rāma is still a youth, the sage Viśvāmitra comes to Daśaratha to take Rāma and his brother Lakṣmaṇa into the forest in order to teach them their kṣatriyadharma and to train them in killing demons. It is worth noting that many readers of the *Rāmāyaṇa* view the "demons" as indigenous South Asian peoples despised and conquered by the invading Aryans. In this view, the war against these people and their characterization as demons is in part based on racial antagonism and dehumanization. (For discussion of a particularly politically consequential reading of this sort, see Richman "E. V. Ramasami's.") In any case, in the course of Rāma's education, Viśvāmitra impresses on Rāma that he should not have any qualms about killing the enemy, and that he should not let universal dharma interfere with his performance of kṣatriyadharma. For example, Rāma "must not be squeamish about killing a woman" if she is a demon. More generally, "a prince must do whatever is necessary to protect his subjects, whether it be cruel or otherwise" (I, 58). In short, kṣatriyadharma overrules any imperative toward ahiṃsā. This is not some aberration on Viśvāmitra's part. The Hindu tradition includes elaborate treatises on the importance of deceit in politics, the use of weaponry, and so on.

In the course of these travels, Rāma meets and marries Sītā, an incarnation of Viṣṇu's consort Lakṣmī, goddess of wealth. Then the entire group proceeds to Ayodhya, the capital of Daśaratha's kingdom. Daśaratha decides that he will enthrone Rāma as king. However, Daśaratha has three wives—Kausalyā, Kaikeyī, and Sumitrā. Kausalyā is the mother of Rāma. Kaikeyī is the mother of Bharata. Sumitrā is the mother of Lakṣmaṇa and Śatrughna. Because Kaikeyī once saved Daśaratha's life, Daśaratha promised to grant her any two things she wanted. She had never chosen her two boons, but now decides that she will have her son, Bharata, enthroned, and Rāma exiled. Daśaratha has little choice and agrees, but the pain of separation from Rāma quickly brings about his death.

Sītā and Lakṣmaṇa go with Rāma into exile. When Kausalyā asks to go along as well, Rāma replies that this would be a violation of her dharma as a wife, for, "To a woman her husband is verily god himself" and "Even a pious woman who is otherwise righteous, if she does not serve her husband, is deemed to be a sinner. On the other hand, she who serves her husband attains blessedness even if she does not worship the gods, perform the rituals or honour the holy men" (Venkatesananda 62; see also Vālmīki I, 222–23). This is a recurrent theme in the poem—though it is implicitly undermined at points by Sītā's independence of thought and strength of character, especially in her final act of defiance.

While wandering in the forest, Rāma and Lakṣmaṇa cut off the nose and ears of Rāvaṇa's sister, who had rushed at Sītā threatening to eat her (Vālmīki II, 39). In response, Rāvaṇa decides to kidnap Sītā. He sends one of his followers in the form of a beautiful wild deer to distract Rāma. Sītā sees the deer and asks Rāma to catch it. Rāma leaves Sītā in the care of Lakṣmaṇa. But, when he is gone, the demon imitates Rāma's voice, and calls out for help. Sītā insists that Lakṣmaṇa go to Rāma's aid. In some versions, Lakṣmaṇa tells Sītā not to step outside "a magic circle drawn around her cottage" (Dutta and Robinson 47). Meanwhile, Rāvaṇa has taken on the appearance of a holy ascetic wandering in the woods. He approaches and Sītā, leaving the circle, welcomes him. Rāvaṇa then abducts Sītā, and takes her to his island kingdom of Laṅkā. There, she lives in his grove and he tries to seduce her, but she resists him.

When Rāma discovers that she is missing, he sets out in search of her. He meets with the monkey people and forms an alliance with them. One of them, Hanumān, the son of the Wind God, finally discovers Sītā in Laṅkā. He speaks with her in private, learns of her despair, and receives from her a jewel to give to Rāma as a sign of her identity. Afterward, he causes great havoc in the place, burning most of it, and killing many guards. He is finally arrested and bound. Rāvaṇa's men try to burn him, but Sītā prays to the god of fire not to affect Hanumān, who is thereby saved. He quickly frees himself, burns more of Laṅkā, then rejoins Rāma.

Rāma, Hanumān, and their armies return to Laṅkā for war, which culminates in a great battle between Rāma and Rāvaṇa. Rāvaṇa uses such weapons as śakti, or spiritual "power" (Venkatesananda 311). Moreover, as the incident with the deer indicates, he is a master of illusion, and in some versions, the final battle itself culminates in a battle between "weapons" of truth and māyā (see, for example, Tulasidasa 552–53 and Narayan 156—Narayan's retelling is based on Kamban). Ultimately, Truth/Rāma triumphs over Illusion/Rāvaṇa. In Kamban's version, as retold by Narayan, the death of Rāvaṇa allows the release of an "inner" Rāvaṇa who was good and who had all the qualities lacking in the "outer" Rāvaṇa (159); similarly, Dimock et al., point out that, in Tulasidasa's version, "Ravana was a devotee [of Rāma], fallen into a demon's body and struggling for . . . release" (76).

After the battle, Rāma and Sītā are reunited. But Rāma will not accept Sītā until she proves her chastity by passing through a fire and remaining unhurt. Sītā dutifully passes through the fire, proving that she had not given in to Rāvaṇa's advances. After the ordeal, Sītā rewards Hanumān by giving him a set of her pearls (3.369). They return to Ayodhya and are warmly welcomed by everyone. Rāma honors Kaikeyī, who eventually dies and ascends to heaven. Unfortunately, rumors begin to circulate among the people that Sītā did not resist Rāvaṇa. Heavy at heart, Rāma realizes that he must repudiate his wife. So he has Lakṣmaṇa deceive her, telling her that they are going to take a trip to a hermitage in the forest, recalling their peaceful days together. When they are far into the wilderness, however, Lakṣmaṇa abandons Sītā— who is now pregnant with Rāma's twin sons.

During their separation, Rāma rules a perfect society, where everything is good. And he does many good deeds. Noteworthy among these is the killing of the lower-caste boy. One day the young child of a Brahmin died. Sages informed Rāma that this death occurred because a lower-caste boy— Śambūka—had been trying to achieve spiritual excellence by reading religious texts and practicing meditation. Rāma found the boy and faced him with the accusation. Śambūka admitted that he had been doing this. Rāma beheaded him immediately.

Many years later, Rāma and Sītā meet again. Rāma announces that he will accept Sītā back if she will only pass through a second fire ordeal. Sītā, who is the daughter of the Earth, instead calls on her mother to take her. The ground opens and a chariot rises from the depths of the land. Sītā enters the chariot, in a shower of lotus petals, and descends into the earth. Rāma falls into despair, and eventually decides to jump in a river and die.

Throughout the poem, Rāma is explicitly characterized as the incarnation of dharma itself. His repeated violations of truth and nonviolence are all explained as necessary and he is repeatedly presented as committing those violations with much regret. On the other hand, there are moments in the poem when Vālmīki comes close to acknowledging weaknesses in Rāma's character. Two such weaknesses are particularly prominent. The first is jealousy. This is most obviously manifest in his tendency to treat his wife cruelly when he has even the slightest suspicion of her infidelity—however unsupported that suspicion might be. Again, this treatment is usually explained as a mere show, necessary for reasons of state. However, there are points where Vālmīki suggests that there is more to it. For example, there is a hint of this when Rāma says to Lakṣmaṇa, "There is no grief greater for me than that another should touch Vaidehi [i.e., Sītā], a grief greater far than that issuing from the loss of my father" (II, 4). The context makes clear that "touch" here means, merely, "touch"; it is not a euphemism for sexual relations. Thus Rāma literally says that he would rather see his father dead than his wife *touched* by another man. His treatment of her after the defeat of Rāvaṇa , after the rumors in Ayodhya, and at their final reunion suggest that this jealousy had a prominent place in his actions as well.

The second main flaw in Rāma's character is a propensity toward hiṃsā— violence or cruelty. There are many incidents of this in the poem, including the killing of Śambūka. But, again, these are explained as necessary. Occasionally, however, another view of Rāma appears, primarily in statements from Sītā. She recognizes this tendency in Rāma and explains it, not as some innate property of Rāma's soul, but rather as the result of daily activity. For Sītā, it is the very practice of violence that makes one violent, the practice of cruelty that makes one cruel. One may think: "This violence is necessary; I will commit it in order to protect non-violence. Then I will return to non-violence myself." But, according to Sītā, this is impossible. Violence is self-perpetuating. Once one begins behaving according to hiṃsā, one will not stop. Sītā warns Rāma against "the infliction of cruelty without provocation—to which men yield from delusion" (II, 16). She explains that the "bow inflames" the warrior "as fuel does fire." She tells the story of a holy man, living alone in the woods. One day, a soldier came to the holy man and asked him to take care of a sword until he returned. The holy man "carried [the sword] with him." But the results were terrible. "Carrying that weapon constantly with him, he who has been noted for his austerities lost his faith in them and inured his mind to cruelty. The sage fell in love with cruelty from the failure to watch himself, and lapsing from virtue by constant association with the weapon, went to hell." She concludes that "The mind . . . is perverted" by the mere handling of weapons (II, 17). How much more perverted will it become by the regular practice of violence.

This statement by Sītā, delivered to Rāma with much self-abasement— "You know verily all that there is to be known in the three worlds regarding these things. I have spoken out of a woman's foolishness" (II, 18)—could be understood as a central theme of Tagore's novel, and a central part of Tagore's view of liberation. Violent methods will lead only to an habituation to violence. They may lead to political freedom, but they will inhibit spiritual freedom. Of course, Tagore leaves out a number of things here—most obviously the fact that people who are hungry and oppressed are likely to be very inhibited in spiritual liberation, and thus that political freedom may be a necessary condition for mokṣa, as B. N. Pandit and others argued (Pandit 100–101).

Nonetheless, he is, I believe, right to follow Sītā in protesting that violence hardens the heart and deters the soul from dharma, whatever else it might do.

Again, we may understand Tagore's revision of the *Rāmāyaṇa* as a revision that makes the Rāma character conform to the ideals of universal dharma, not those of kṣatriyadharma. Moreover, in doing this, Tagore makes his new Rāma, Nikhil, struggle against the same flaws to which Vālmīki's Rāma succumbed: jealousy and violence, the latter generalized to include any urge to bend another person's actions to one's own will. But, in this case, Rāma/Nikhil is successful in the struggle—precisely because he abjures cruelty entirely. In refusing to take up weapons at all, his heart remains uncorrupted by himsā. Put differently, this revision systematically recasts the story in order to follow Sītā's argument to Rāma, as well as those statements by Rāma himself that elevate universal dharma, despite his own behavior. For Rāma, who more than once uses trickery to achieve his ends, even deceiving Sītā when he decides to abandon her, says "That Dharma which exalts truth is regarded as the highest in the world . . . there is no Goal higher than Truth" (I, 413). In the same passage, he says, "Those great sages who are devoted to Dharma, with whom the wise associate, who are endowed with the power of austerities and are noted for their generosity; who are wedded to non-violence and are free from sin—it is these that all men honour" (I, 415). He even goes so far as to announce, "I repudiate that Kshattriya Code which is predominantly unrighteous in its tenets" (I, 414). Tagore seeks to rewrite the character of Rāma in accordance with these statements—and thereby to revise the notion of the ideal society, Rāmarājya, in a similar way. Of course, in order to do this, he must revise the other main characters as well—most importantly, Sītā and Rāvaṇa.

CHARACTER IN VĀLMĪKI AND TAGORE

Clearly, the three main characters in the novel—Bimala, Sandip, and Nikhil—are the most important in the revision of the *Rāmāyaṇa*. However, before going on to these, we should briefly consider some lesser characters—Bimala's sister-in-law, Amulya, Nikhil's teacher, and Panchu.

Tagore introduces the "Bara Rani" or senior wife of the household—the widow of Nikhil's deceased elder brother—as a jealous, competitive, Kaikeyī-like figure.[6] She is less than kind to Bimala and, like Kaikeyī with Daśaratha, she "never failed to get from [Nikhil] whatever she wanted" (22). Tagore introduces this figure, however, not to criticize her, but to criticize the situation—specifically, the severe inhibitions placed on widows in Bengal at that time. For Tagore, it is this situation that creates jealousy and competitiveness, not some innate propensity. Bimala explains that Nikhil "felt more the sorrow of her lot than the defects of her character." Indeed, Tagore intends the point to be generalizable. At one point, Bimala complains that women are often "petty" and "crooked." This alludes to Kaikeyī's maid, Manthara, who convinced Kaikeyī to demand Bharata's enthronement and Rāma's exile, for she, a "hump-back" was "deformed, crooked" (I, 175), both metaphorically and literally. Nikhil responds to Bimala, saying, "Like the feet of Chinese women.... Has not the pressure of society cramped [these women] into pettiness and crookedness?" (22). In other words, Tagore takes up these figures from Vālmīki's epic in order to make a point about the deleterious effects of patriarchal oppression. Women are taxed with many faults in a patriarchal society. Tagore uses Kaikeyī and Manthara to indicate that these faults are not a justification for patriarchal society, but a result of patriarchal society.

Of course, one could rightly object that Tagore is mistaken in assuming that women are more faulty in these ways than are men. Indeed, it seems clear that Tagore's assumption here is part of the same patriarchal ideology that he sets out to criticize. On the other hand, Tagore sometimes portrays the cruelty of a patriarchal system more impartially, and with moving empathy. The most striking case of this is when Nikhil comes upon his sister-in-law as she is packing to leave the family home with Nikhil and Bimala—a moment that recalls Kausalyā's insistence that she will travel with Rāma and Sītā into exile and thus transfers features from Kausalyā to this otherwise Kaikeyī-based character. Nikhil remembers how she was married into that house at the age of nine, when he himself was six. He reminisces on how they played together, in particular recalling "the marriage celebration of her doll" (188–89), how they developed a bond that she was never able to find with her own husband. Now a widow, with no prospects for future fulfillment, development, or self-expression, she has nothing of human value beyond her ties with Nikhil: "She had only this one relationship left in all the world, and the poor, unfortunate, widowed and childless woman had cherished it with all the tenderness hoarded in her heart" (189). Feeling particularly close to her at this moment, Nikhil expresses nostalgia for their youth, saying, "How I should love, Sister Rani, to go back to the days when we first met in this old house of ours." But she replies in a sentence that summarizes the entire point of her character in this novel, and the pain Tagore knew from real women who shared her plight: "No, brother dear . . . I would not live my life again—not as a woman! Let what I have had to bear end with this one birth. I could not bear it over again" (190).

As to Amulya, there are several parallels that link him with Hanumān.[7] His private audiences with Bimala, in which she alternates between hope and despair, parallel the meeting between Hanumān and Sītā in Laṅkā, where Sītā's mood fluctuates similarly. His receipt of the jewels recalls both the single jewel Sītā gives to Hanumān as a token and the reward of pearls she gives him after the battle. Moreover, the entire incident in the treasury recalls Hanumān's destructive romp through Laṅkā, with Amulya's wounding of Kasim being a much softened transformation of Hanumān's killing of many guards. Bimala's prayers for his safety are also reminiscent of Sītā's prayer to Agni that Hanumān escape injury by fire. Finally, his arrest and release recall the arrest and escape of Hanumān in Laṅkā.

There are, of course, changes, some very significant. The one apparently major difficulty with drawing the parallel in this way is that Hanumān is an ally of Rāma, whereas Amulya is an ally of Sandip—the Rāvaṇa figure. However, this actually works well with Tagore's purposes. As we have already noted, Tagore has transformed the Rāma figure from an incarnation of kṣatriyadharma into an incarnation of universal dharma. In keeping with this, all the deceitful and military aspects of Rāma's personality and action are transferred onto the Rāvaṇa character. He becomes the incarnation of kṣatriyadharma—as, in many ways, he already is in Vālmīki, for the behavior of Rāma, judged intrinsically and without reference to his divine origin, is little if at all better than that of Rāvaṇa. Indeed, it is arguably worse—compare, for example, Rāvaṇa's abduction of Sītā into an opulent pleasure grove and Rāma's abandonment of Sītā in the wilderness. In any case, given this general transformation, Tagore is faced with the problem of how to deal with Rāma's military allies. If they remain oriented toward kṣatriyadharma, then it would seem that he has to shift them to the Rāvaṇa figure, which is to say, Sandip. On the other hand, he could make them nonviolent allies. In effect, he does both with Amulya. Amulya begins as a militant follower of Sandip. Moreover, he bases his militarism on Hindu religious texts, such as the Bhagavad Gītā (see 139)—the teachings of Kṛṣṇa, another incarnation of Viṣṇu. But, through his interaction with Bimala, he realizes that Sandip is a hypocrite and turns away from that sort of kṣatriyadharma at the end of the novel.

Allegorically, Amulya represents the segment of the population that has been sincerely convinced by Hindu nationalist leaders that violence in the service of the nation is true dharma. Through his development of this character, Tagore indicates that genuine service of India, allegorically represented by Bimala, will reveal to these sincere militants that their leaders are at best mistaken and at worst corrupt. Thus, it will lead them to see that true dharma lies not in militancy, but in ahiṃsā. Tagore takes up Hanumān as a parallel figure from the *Rāmāyaṇa*. Hanumān initially agrees to join Rāma for strategic and, so to speak, nationalist reasons. He is the minister of Sugrīva, king of the Vānaras, who has been deposed by the usurper, Vāli. Hanumān's relation to Sītā is initially a function of his desire to restore political authority, to reclaim it from an illegitimate usurper, just as Amulya's relation to Bimala and to the nation is initially a function of his desire to end the British usurpation and division of Bengal. On the other hand, Hanumān is also driven by a genuine devotion to Sītā. For example, when he sees her imprisoned by Rāvaṇa , he is "overcome by sorrow" and "his eyes filling with tears, he laments Sita's fate" (III, 379). Similarly, Amulya was driven by a genuine devotion to India, and to Bimala personally. Indeed, Hanumān does a far better job regarding Sītā than Rāma does himself, for he is the one who finds and meets with Sītā in Laṅkā. This too provides an obvious parallel to student militants, such as Amulya, who have been convinced by Hindu nationalist leaders to devote themselves to Mother India, and who undertake this task with far more devotion—and at far greater personal risk—than do those leaders.

Another relevant minor character is Nikhil's teacher, Chandranath. He is implicitly established as a parallel to Viśvāmitra and other sages who taught Rāma. But here Tagore uses the opposite strategy from that he used with Hanumān. Instead of having the teacher instruct Sandip in military practices, he has the teacher instruct Rāma/Nikhil in nonviolence. In other words, he transforms Viśvāmitra from a teacher promulgating caste dharma to a teacher promulgating universal dharma. As we have seen, Viśvāmitra instructs Rāma on the importance of violating universal dharma in favor of caste dharma, on the necessity of acting violently against the enemy. He tells Rāma that, as a kṣatriya, he "must" commit even "a sin," even an act that is "cruel," if his kṣatriyadharma demands (I, 58). In contrast, Chandranath instructs Nikhil in the importance of universal dharma. In keeping with the focus on nationalism in the novel, Chandranath makes a special point of arguing—precisely in the manner of Tagore—that India should not aspire to national independence but to spiritual release, for national independence is itself merely a form of destructive egoism. "I tell you, Nikhil, man's history has to be built by the united effort of all the races in the world" (recall Tagore's statements on how India was built in the past) "and therefore this selling of conscience for political reasons—this making of a fetish of one's country, won't do." Instead of dying for the nation one should wish to "die for the truth," the truth that will free all humankind from māyā, desirous illusion, of which nationalism is one particular form. In keeping with Tagore's own views, and in sharp opposition to Viśvāmitra's lessons concerning murder of the alien Rākṣasas, Chandranath expresses the hope that it will be the mission of India to lead all other nations of the world toward this true independence: "Here, in this land of India . . . may the feeling for this truth become real!" (166).

Another sage who teaches Rāma is Nārada. He instructs Rāma that the low-caste boy, Śambūka, must be killed. Tagore implicitly takes up this aspect of caste dharma as well in the story of Panchu. Panchu is a poor and presumably lower-caste man. His wife has died recently and the Hindu priests are demanding huge sums of money from him to perform the proper ceremonies. This already suggests the theme of caste-based oppression. But what follows more directly recalls the story of Śambūka, for Panchu begins to practice the sort of asceticism practiced by Śambūka. "In a desperate attempt to gain consolation of some sort he took to sitting at the feet of a wandering ascetic, and succeeded in acquiring philosophy enough to forget that his children went hungry" (99). Eventually, he leaves home to become a wandering ascetic himself. In doing this, Panchu may have violated caste dharma. At the very least, he has violated "stage of life" dharma, the duties based on his current station in life—specifically, duties central to his current "householder" stage. In any case, unlike Nārada, Chandranath does not propose a punitive response to this violation. Rather than increasing cruelty, Chandranath seeks a solution to the problem that reduces cruelty, for he "take[s] Panchu's deserted children under his own roof and . . . car[es] for them" (99–100).

Moreover, in this response, Chandranath is opposed directly to Sandip, who acts coercively toward Panchu, when Panchu violates the boycott. Here, too, it is Sandip who takes up the violent actions of Rāma, the actions taught by Viśvāmitra and adjured by Nārada—for, again, in Tagore's view, actions of that sort are adharmic, and thus should be associated with Rāvana . Of course, here as elsewhere, nationalist leaders—and even ordinary anticolonialists— would be right to object to Tagore's implicit colonialist bias in having Nikhil send Panchu to the police, as if they were not prime agents of himsā in colonial India, and as if the British legal system were not, at least in part, a system of colonial violence (on some racist discrepancies in British legal practice in India, see Ray 23 and Sarkar, *Swadeshi,* 24). If Panchu and Nikhil have no qualms about cooperating with agents of imperial cruelty, it seems nothing short of hypocrisy and collaborationism that they object so strongly to the far more limited cruelty of the anti-imperialists.

But, again, these are only minor characters. Indeed, our identification of their prototypes in the *Rāmāyana* is contingent on our isolation of the main parallels between Bimala and Sītā, Sandip and Rāvana, Nikhil and Rāma. The parallels we have been discussing are only suggested indirectly in the novel. They have force insofar as the main parallels have fuller textual support.

In the case of Bimala, the link is clear. On the very first page, Bimala explains that she prayed to "my God" that "I might grow up to be a model of what woman should be, as one reads it in some epic poem." In the very next sentence, we learn that an astrologer has predicted "she will become an ideal wife" (17). Even the most basic knowledge of Hindu culture allows a reader to identify these as clear references to Sītā. Throughout Hindu society, there is only one "model of what woman should be," and certainly only one "in some epic poem"; there is only one "ideal wife"—Sītā, as portrayed in the *Rāmāyana*. She is, indeed, the archetype of wifely dharma in the Hindu tradition, up to this day. Thus, right from the first page of the novel, it is clear that we are to think about Bimala in relation to Sītā, and we are to think about her situation in relation to "some epic poem," which is to say, the *Rāmāyana*.

Of course, this does not mean that they are simply identified. Again, this is a critical revision of Vālmīki's poem. But they are systematically linked.

This is not the only point at which Tagore alerts us to this connection. Sandip repeatedly identifies Bimala with the goddess. When she is first introduced to Sandip, he immediately refers to her as "the Goddess of Plenty" (33; "Annapurna" in the Bengali, not Lakṣmī, but the general identification of Bimala as an incarnate goddess is maintained). Shortly thereafter, he identifies Bimala as the "goddess" "of the country" (34–35), a motif that recurs throughout the novel. This is particularly important because the Hindu nationalist song "Bande Mataram," sung by Sandip and his followers, identifies Bengal, or India, not only with the goddess of destruction, Kālī, but also the goddess of wealth, Lakṣmī (see de Bary 159)—thus stressing two aspects of the goddess that are not particularly conducive to universal dharma. The link is clearly important for Hindu nationalism generally, and for Tagore's criticism of nationalism, for, in practice, nationalism values desire for prosperity or wealth, not striving after mokṣa, and it pursues its goals through destruction, rather than ahiṃsā. The first point, concerning wealth, recurs most significantly in Sandip's requests for funds from Bimala. It is, of course, this concern for wealth that leads Bimala—and Amulya as well—to recognize Sandip's hypocrisy. Amulya recounts to Bimala how Sandip has not used her money for the cause, but has hoarded it, "gloating" over it, "pouring it out in a heap on the floor." It is no accident that Amulya quotes Sandip as referring to the money as "Lakshmi's smile" (171), thus again linking Bimala with the goddess of wealth. Indeed, this suggests another systematic transformation to which Tagore has subjected Vālmīki's epic. While Vālmīki's Rāvaṇa seeks to seduce Sītā for sexual enjoyment, Tagore's Sandip has as his primary goal seducing Bimala for material gain—in some ways a more rational goal, given that Sītā incarnates Lakṣmī, the Goddess of Wealth, not a Goddess of Love.

On the other hand, Bimala is not Lakṣmī only. "I was *Shakti*" (97), she explains. She was the goddess understood as power, physical force, coercion—the sort of coercion she demands that Nikhil employ to enforce swadeshi on his estates. She complains, "our district was backward, for my husband was unwilling to put any compulsion on the villagers" (94) and argues that it is mere weakness not to ban foreign goods from his markets. Beyond being the goddess understood as power, this śakti is also the weapon of Rāvaṇa, which he thought would finally defeat Rāma. In Tagore's novel too, this weapon of Śakti—which is, in this case, Bimala—is used by Sandip against Nikhil. First of all, the idea of Śakti is what he uses to seduce Bimala away from Nikhil. Second, he tries to employ Bimala, now understanding herself as Śakti, to seduce Nikhil into joining the cause. In keeping with this, the relationship of these men, especially in connection with Bimala, is repeatedly linked with battle. For example, in recounting their very first meeting, Bimala notes that

Sandip initiated "a passage at arms" with Nikhil; as she later noticed, he did this repeatedly, "whenever I happened to be present" (36). Just like his epic prototype, however, Sandip fails to defeat Nikhil, even with the weapon, śakti/Śakti.

Of course, in reality, Bimala is neither the weapon nor the goddess. Referring to Sandip's seductions, Bimala says, "Listening to his allegories, I had forgotten that I was plain and simple Bimala." (97). This is important to Tagore's allegorical use of the *Rāmāyaṇa* as well. For it is not only true that Bimala is not a goddess. It is equally true that Bengal is not a goddess, and neither is India. For Bimala to conceive of herself as a goddess is to succumb to a form of egocentric illusion, to fall prey to māyā. As Tagore argued repeatedly, to believe that the nation is a goddess, to devote oneself to a nation, rather than to humanity, is to succumb to a different instance of the same general type. It too is "māyā," not as personal egoism, but as "national egoism" (Tagore in de Bary 239).

There are other, more specific links as well. In their own first meeting, Sandip alludes to the first meeting of Sītā and Rāvaṇa by referring to "the impulse of the wild deer to run away" (36). The statement is general, but in context it suggests the deer that lured Rāma away from the camp, so that Rāvaṇa could abduct Sītā. Indeed, just as Rāvaṇa approached Sītā in the guise of a mendicant, a spiritual liberator, Sandip approaches Bimala in the guise of a national liberator, drawing her out of the inner chambers of her home, just as Rāvaṇa drew Sītā from the protective circle around her cottage. Of course, while Lakṣmaṇa insisted that Sītā remain within, Nikhil/Rāma encourages her departure from this false and stifling protection. The point of this change is that such "danger" is necessary for her own development, and for the development of her relationship with Nikhil—allegorically, the risks inherent in free democratic choice are necessary for the development of the nation. In keeping with this parallel, once she has realized Sandip's true nature, Bimala implicitly compares Sandip to the demon Rāvaṇa , and tacitly relates his influence over her to Rāvaṇa 's abduction of Sītā. "Some demon has gained possession of me," she reflects. Then, referring to their first meeting, she thinks, "This demon," like Rāvaṇa in his first approach to Sītā, came in a false form of holiness, "the guise of a god . . . saying, 'I am your Country'" (141). The violence and illusion that characterize the demonic Rāvaṇa are here transferred entirely onto "radical" and Hinduizing nationalists. The abduction of Sītā becomes a subtler seduction of the people of Bengal.

In keeping with this, Bimala alludes early on to the story of Ahalyā. This story is taken from early in the *Rāmāyaṇa,* where it serves to prefigure Sītā's deception by Rāvaṇa. Indra had wished to have sexual relatons with Ahalyā. When her husband was away, Indra appeared before Ahalyā, disguised as that husband. The difference with the story of Sītā and Rāvaṇa is that Ahalyā succumbs to Indra, even though she recognizes who he really is. There are several reasons why it is important that Bimala alludes to this story. First, it re-enforces the link between Tagore's novel and the earlier epic. Second, it lays particular stress on the relation between Sandip and Bimala as one of illusion or māyā. Indeed, it to some degree universalizes this relation. By giving another case of the same general sort, it indicates that the relation between Sītā and Rāvaṇa or Bimala and Sandip is not so unique, but part of a broad pattern—the very pattern, in fact, that defines egocentric illusion, personal or national. Finally, it is clear that Tagore is combining the two stories from the *Rāmāyaṇa* in his representation of Bimala and Sandip. This is true most obviously in the sense that, more in keeping with Ahalyā than with Sītā, Bimala is at least partially seduced (i.e., she is seduced into giving money illicitly, if not into adultery—again, in keeping with a general transformation from kāma to artha, sexual enjoyment to material prosperity). It is true also in the sense that Bimala initially confuses Sandip, not precisely with her husband, but with a noble, dharmic Rāma figure. She mistakenly attributes to Sandip all the characteristics that in fact belong to Nikhil.

One of the most striking transformations of the *Rāmāyaṇa* comes in Tagore's revision of Sītā's fire ordeal. In Vālmīki's poem, Sītā has done nothing wrong, but Rāma insists that she pass through a fire in order to prove her innocence. Clearly, Nikhil would never subject Bimala to any sort of ordeal or proof of this sort. It is directly contrary to his noncoercive principles. But, at the end of the novel, Bimala refers back to all the suffering she has experienced because of her attachment to illusion—illusion about herself, about Sandip, about the nation—and says, "I have passed through fire." First of all, the fire ordeal of Bimala is not a trial forced on her by someone else. Rather, it is the direct result of false attachment. Second, it is not a test, designed to prove or disprove her purity. Rather, it is a purifying experience. Because she has gone through the suffering of attachment, she can recognize its falsity, and turn away from it: "I have passed through fire. What was inflammable"—the mere material and ephemeral part, not the soul—"has been burnt to ashes; what is left is deathless" (199). This thoroughly transforms the significance of the fire ordeal. It highlights the cruelty of Rāma's actions, in contrast with Nikhil's noncoercion, and it simultaneously stresses the self-imposed suffering—the hiṃsā against oneself—that results from illusory attachments, including those to the nation.[8]

Much of what might be said about Sandip is already clear from our treatment of Bimala and the other characters. The most benevolent interpretation of Sandip would say that he advocates caste dharma over universal dharma. To some extent, his anti-Muslim attitude fits with this view. When he says that "the Mussulmans . . . must be suppressed altogether and made to understand that we are the masters" (120), he expresses an attitude not unlike that of

Rāma to the "demons," or of any dominant group to any minority group. His caste prejudice fits here as well. Consider his response when he is blocked by a guard in Nikhil's house. Whether born into the servant caste or not, the man has clearly taken the role of a servant. Sandip is infuriated at being "touched by a flunkey" and gives "the man a sounding blow" (53)—in some ways recalling Rāma's treatment of Śambūka, and certainly contrasting with Chandranath's treatment of Panchu. (Recall that, in Tagore's revision, the caste-based characteristics of Rāma are transferred to the Rāvaṇa character.)

Of course, someone might argue that this is not true kṣatriyadharma, for it often involves cowardice and hypocrisy. For example, Sandip has a tendency to attack only those who are defenseless—as his abuse of the servant illustrates. He also acts in concealment, as when he has his followers sink Mirjan's boat, rather than facing his opponents directly. But Rāma himself adopted this tactic, notoriously in his assassination of Vāli. In order to gain military support from Sugrīva, Rāma killed Vāli from hiding, not in open combat (see cantos xiv–xvii of the "Kiṣkindhā Kāṇḍa"). On the other hand, perhaps the dharmic authenticity or inauthenticity of Sandip's violence does not really matter. Tagore's portrayal of Sandip seems to suggest that any advocacy of violence—whether "genuine" kṣatriyadharma or not—will necessarily degenerate into bullying and deceit. In any case, Tagore clearly had little sympathy with violence of any sort, and he makes it perfectly clear that Sandip's advocacy of himsā is an advocacy of adharma. Indeed, Sandip himself states this: "the Great is cruel. To be just is for ordinary men—it is reserved for the great to be unjust" (78). Sandip goes on to assert that "Successful injustice and genuine cruelty have been the only forces by which individual or nation has become millionaire or monarch" (79). Tagore might well agree. But, of course, for Tagore, these goals of material prosperity and political power—the two primary forms of artha—are precisely the opposite of genuine independence. They are webs of māyā, trapping one in illusory attachments.

These links to himsā and adharma are the thematically crucial points about Sandip's relation to the *Rāmāyaṇa*. But it is important to note that there are more specific connections with Rāvaṇa as well. Demonic "rākṣasas," such as Rāvaṇa, live by consuming human flesh. In consequence, Sandip and those like him—the political rākṣasas of Hindu nationalism—"are the flesh-eaters of the world" (47), by Sandip's own admission. In keeping with this, Nikhil later links him with "cannibalism" (160; metaphorical cannibalism, of course—this is not *Baumgartner's Bombay*, after all). Just as Rāvaṇa is a master vīṇā player, Sandip is a "master-player" of the "flesh-and-blood lute" of people's "feeling and fancy" (68; "lute" here is "vīṇā" in the original Bengali). In these instances, Tagore takes up literal features of Rāvaṇa as apt metaphors for the attitudes and behavior of the Hindu nationalists. In addition, Sandip's flattery of Bimala at their first meeting and his ongoing work to seduce her have obvious parallels in Rāvaṇa's treatment of Sītā. Indeed, just as Sandip first greets Bimala as "the Goddess of Plenty" (33), Rāvaṇa first greets Sītā as "the Goddess of Prosperity" (II, 97). Sandip's later praise of Bimala's beauty, when his eyes fill with "fire" (73) and shower "scorching sparks" (74)—"passion" deceitfully presented as "worship" (73)—is also similar to Rāvaṇa's more elaborate and sexually explicit statements when he poses as a mendicant (II, 97–98).

If this all seems too indirect, however, Sandip makes the connection explicit less than half-way through the book. Sandip is now thinking of seducing Bimala sexually—though this is not, of course, unrelated to his seduction of her for material gain. He regrets that he has let moments "slip by" when he could have grabbed hold of her. He regrets that there were moments when he could have acted with absolute self-assertion and definitive force. The problem, he says, is that "hidden elements in my nature have openly ranged themselves as obstacles in my path" (82–83). This takes up a motif from a few pages before, where Sandip contrasts his exterior harshness with "the inner me, which by a curious freak of fate has been created tender and merciful" (79)—a point reminiscent of Rāvaṇa's character in Kamban and Tulasidasa. As noted above, both authors contrast the good inner Rāvaṇa with an evil outer Rāvaṇa. In any event, immediately after regretting his failure to force himself upon Bimala, Sandip compares himself directly to Rāvaṇa, thinking, "That is exactly how Ravana, whom I look upon as the real hero of the *Ramayana,* met with his doom. He kept Sita in his Asoka garden, awaiting her pleasure, instead of taking her straight into his harem" (83). Note that this passage not only makes explicit the relation of Sandip to Rāvaṇa, it repeats and thus reenforces the characterization of Bimala as Sītā also.

Finally, Nikhil. As I have stressed throughout, Nikhil is both Rāma, and not Rāma. He is Rāma as Rāma would have been had he systematically followed universal dharma, not kṣatriyadharma. This status as Rāma and not Rāma is suggested right at the outset of the poem. Just after Bimala thinks of herself in terms of "a model of what woman should be, as one reads it in some epic poem" (17)—that is, just after she thinks of herself in relation to Sītā—she discusses her marriage. She explains that, as a child, she "was quite familiar with the description of the Prince of the fairy story." Unfortunately, "my husband's face was not of a kind that one's imagination would place in fairyland" (17–18). His personality only makes him less of the enchanting warrior hero represented by Rāma. She suspects him of "cowardice" (28)—because he refuses to "worship" his country, and will only worship "Right" (29). Indeed, in the very first chapter, she explains, "I used to feel that goodness has a limit, which, if passed, somehow seems to make men cowardly. Shall I tell the whole truth? I have often wished that my husband had the manliness to be a little less good" (22)—that would have made him more akin to Rāma, more like the prince of the fairy story.

While Sītā worries over Rāma's tendency toward cruelty, Bimala explains that Nikhil's "gentleness knew no bounds" (22). In the following chapter, she expresses much the same feeling about Nikhil's devotion to the other main principle of universal dharma, "his fanaticism for truth" (32). In these respects, then, Nikhil is the precise opposite of Rāma.

On the other hand, insofar as Rāma is the true incarnation of dharma, as Vālmīki repeatedly asserts, Nikhil is Rāma—or, rather, he takes up Rāma's role as representative of dharma. This identification is strongly implied when Sandip contrasts men of his own type with "those *avatars* who come down from their paradise to talk to us in some holy jargon" (46), clearly including Nikhil in this group. In Hinduism, an "avatar" is an incarnation of Viṣṇu, such as Rāma. The link is made even more forcefully when Bimala, in the depths of despair, calls out to God, "Lord . . . I will lie here, waiting and waiting, touching neither food nor drink, so long as your blessing does not reach me." Alluding to the worship of Rāma's "lotus feet," she continues, "Come, oh come, come and let your feet touch my head. Come, Lord, and set your foot upon my throbbing heart, and at that moment let me die." Just then someone comes: "He came and sat near my head," she thinks, implicitly linking this person with the Lord on whom she called. "Who?" she asks. "My husband!" The conjunction of Bimala's invocation with Nikhil's appearance clearly links him with the Lord Rāma, and she receives from him "his blessing" (186).

Again, the most obvious way in which Nikhil is a revised Rāma is in his devotion to ahiṃsā. Tagore develops this in two areas. The first concerns Nikhil's relation to women. Part of the point of Nikhil's character is that forcing one's spouse to behave in a certain way or to think in a certain way is an act of hiṃsā—just the sort of act committed by Rāma in abandoning Sītā and in demanding the fire ordeal. From the very start, Bimala remarks on how "my husband" "did not . . . compel me. . . . He did not use his power" (26). Indeed, Nikhil insists that marriage is sahadharma, the sharing of dharma between husband and wife, and thus marriage, in its deepest ethical sense, is violated by any coercion of one party by the other: "My husband used to say, that man and wife are equal in love because of their equal claim on each other" (20).

Indeed, Tagore takes up Rāma's other character flaw, jealousy, in this context as well. When Bimala has in effect betrayed him—not with her body, but with her deceit, her monetary dealings, her attachment to Sandip—Nikhil does not blame her, but questions and criticizes himself. It strikes him that Bimala's deceit about the money could only have been motivated by a feeling that she could not be open with him about her intentions: "I have begun to suspect that there has all along been a vein of tyranny in me. . . . She has had to steal this six thousand rupees because she could not be open with me, because she felt that, in certain things, I despotically differed from her" (198). Nothing could be more strikingly distinct from Rāma, or more consistent with ahiṃsā. Completing the point, while Rāma abandoned his entirely faithful wife, Nikhil blames himself for Bimala's actions (is not marriage, after all, the sharing of dharma?) and plans to leave *with* her.

Nikhil's devotion to ahiṃsā is perhaps even more obvious in relation to social and national activism. "Those who make sacrifices for their country's sake are indeed her servants . . . but those who compel others to make them in her name are her enemies" (94), he explains to Bimala. Hence, he consistently opposes the tactics of Sandip and his followers. He also denounces the anti-Muslim attitudes and actions of the swadeshi activists. Acknowledging that the British have fomented anti-Hindu feeling among Muslims, he asks "Why is it possible . . . to use the Mussulmans thus, as tools against us? Is it not because we have fashioned them into such with our own intolerance?" (162). The question is parallel to his self-blame over Bimala's deceit.

This nonviolence is of a piece with his commitment to renunciation. The reason one tries to coerce another person is that one has not renounced the fruits of one's actions, and pursues pleasure or prosperity, not dharma or mokṣa. Sandip argues that "Every man has a natural right to possess, and therefore greed is natural." He advocates taking what one wants "by force" (45). Nikhil, only two pages later, expresses the directly contrary view: "The strength I believe in is the strength of renouncing" (47). Elsewhere, Bimala explains that, according to Sandip, "'I want!' . . . was the primal word at the root of all creation" (77). Nikhil, and Tagore, would agree—but only insofar as that creation is understood as māyā.

Of course, Sandip and his followers—like Tilak and other Hindu nationalist leaders, and like Viśvāmitra and Rāma—certainly advocate renunciation (see, for example, 59). But they do so only to justify adharmic acts. In their view—or, at least, in their self-justifying rhetoric—if an adharmic act is done "with renunciation," then it is not adharmic, because the agent did not seek gain. This sophistical version of renunciation is explicitly articulated by Amulya. He is ready to kill the cashier, due to "stock phrases from the *Gita—Who kills the body kills naught!*" (139), as Bimala expresses it. She asks him, "Don't you know that the dear old man has got a wife and children." But Amulya will not let her continue, arguing that "pity is, at bottom, only pity for ourselves" (139) and thus the most renunciatory act is the most pitiless. This is not only sophistry, it is also hypocritical, at least on Sandip's part. For, as Nikhil stresses, and as Sandip's own statements reveal, "Sandip's love of country is but a different phase of his covetous self-love" (43).

In sum, due to attachment, one does not strive to do what is right or dharmic—that is, practice ahiṃsā. Rather, one labors to achieve some illusory success of pleasure or gain, often through hiṃsā, itself justified by a false appeal to renunciation. Nikhil explicitly contrasts "success" of this sort with genuine spiritual achievement. He says to Sandip, "Winning your kind of success . . . is success gained at the cost of the soul." This is a matter of attachment, thus a matter of personal or national egoism. Referring to the national variety, Nikhil argues that "where our country makes itself the final object, it gains success at the cost of the soul. Where it recognizes the Greatest as greater than all, there it may miss success, but gains its soul" (80).

This leads us to the other aspect of universal dharma, truth, as well as the other great goal of human life, mokṣa. Clearly, the sort of attachment Nikhil is condemning is, in Tagore's view, an attachment to māyā. Just as clearly, truth will bring genuine release, genuine freedom—not the deceptive freedom of national independence. In keeping with this, truth is bound up with renunciation. Nikhil explains that, in trying to shape Bimala into an ideal, he made her into an idol—like the ideological image of Sītā as the perfect Hindu wife—and thus concealed her truth. To act noncoercively toward her is at once to "divest" her "of all the ideal decorations with which I decked her," when "I indulged in . . . idolatry," and was "greedy" (65). Later, when he feels sorrow over Bimala's neglect, he realizes that this is the result of attachment, and it keeps both Bimala and himself trapped in illusion: "So long as I continue to suffer, Bimala will never have true freedom. I *must* free her completely, otherwise I shall never gain *my* freedom from untruth" (86).

The point is clear enough at the level of personal relations. Nikhil will be trapped in māyā and egoism, as long as he remains attached to his idea of what Bimala should be. Moreover, as long as he does not renounce this image, as long as he is still attached to shaping her into an idol, she too will never be free. But the point is equally clear when understood allegorically. For it is only when all the people of the country have renounced their own personal idolization of the nation, only when they have renounced the egocentric illusion of nationalism, that anyone in that nation can be truly free. As Nikhil puts it, referring this time to nationalism: "To try to give our infatuation a higher place than Truth is a sign of inherent slavishness. . . . Our moribund vitality must have for its rider either some fantasy, or someone in authority, or a sanction from the pundits, in order to make it move. So long as we are impervious to truth and have to be moved by some hypnotic stimulus"—which is to say, an illusory attachment—"we must know that we lack the capacity for self-government" (42).

Though the caution regarding nationalism is valid, it should be clear that the conclusion about self-government is not only a non sequitur, but a horribly colonialist non sequitur. It would follow logically only if the British were themselves committed to truth and ahiṃsā—which was patently not the case. Tagore seems to assume here that Indian self-government requires some sort of justification. But, in fact, it is the deprivation of self-government that would require justification—and a very strong justification at that.

In any event, the theme of truth relates to our concerns more narrowly as well. For just as the battle between Rāma and Rāvaṇa is in part a battle between truth and illusion, so too is the conflict between Nikhil and Sandip. As we have already noted, Bimala, early on, expresses concern over Nikhil's "fanaticism for truth" (32). The occasion for this concern is his potential opposition to Sandip. In Nikhil's first debate with Sandip, Bimala's apprehensions prove justified. Nikhil begins by asserting "I would know my country in its frank reality" and thus refuses what he calls "hypnotic texts" (36). He maintains that Sandip and the Hindu nationalists are trying "to pass off injustice as a duty and unrighteousness as a moral ideal" (37). Subsequent discussions center around the same theme. For example, Sandip insists that his movement "require[s] a great deal of untruth." He insists that, faced with the British, we "must see whether we cannot erect a defensive fortification of untruth." Chandranath replies in Nikhil's place, "How can they who do not feel the truth within them, realize that to bring it out from its obscurity into the light is man's highest aim—not to keep on heaping material outside?" (105)—material which conceals the truth, because it is opaque, but also material which draws attachment, and thus lures the soul away from dharma and mokṣa.

But what, precisely, is this truth advocated by Nikhil? In part, it is plain, empirical fact, literal honesty, of the sort rarely exhibited by Sandip. At the same time, it is the spiritual reality that, in Tagore's view, underlies empirical fact, the spiritual reality achieved by renunciation, the spiritual reality that defines genuine liberation and release from māyā. At one point, Nikhil reflects on the problem of māyā, as the problem of attachment to either the idealization and fetishization of a wife—most obviously in a Sītālike image— or the idealization and fetishization of a nation. Drawing on one standard image of māyā, he says, "We must tear away the disguise of her who weaves our net of enchantment . . . and know her for what she is. We must beware of clothing her in the witchery of our own longings and imaginings" (110). Elsewhere, the debate between Sandip and Nikhil takes on these same metaphysical implications, much like the final battle between Rāma and Rāvaṇa . For example, Sandip insists that "Illusions are necessary for lesser minds." Illusion, in this view, is an appropriate weapon in fighting colonialism. But Nikhil replies, "No" it "is necessary to clear away our illusions" (121). Sandip, like Bimala, criticizes Nikhil for his "prejudice in favour of truth," even going so far as to deny truth entirely: "truth—as though there exists such an objective reality!" (121).

Elsewhere, Sandip's māyā is more fully related to Rāvaṇa through the image of weapons and conquest. For example, in discussing his techniques, at one point Sandip says he conquers Bimala—and thus, allegorically, that Hindu nationalism conquers India—using "no weapons—but just . . . delusion" (124). Later, Bimala takes up the image of Rāvaṇa and his weapons of māyā more straightforwardly when she says that "the shafts" in his quiver "are of the demons" (149). Most significantly, almost at the end of the novel,

Sandip describes his battle in terms that fit well the final battle between Rāma and Rāvaṇa (especially in such versions as those by Tulasidasa and Narayan, cited above): "All the fights in the world . . . are really fights between hypnotic forces. Spell cast against spell—noiseless weapons which reach even invisible targets . . . magic weapons" (174–75). Weapons, in short, of māyā—and of truth.

THE FUTURE OF THE NATION

Tagore has clearly delineated two options for the future of India—Sandip's hypocritical and egoistic Hindu nationalism, pervaded by māyā, or Nikhil's universal dharma and renunciation, pregnant with truth. Of course, these never were the only options. Unsurprisingly, Tagore sees his own view as opposed only to the most extreme and most objectionable alternative. In any event, that is the way Tagore has framed the possibilities. What, then, is the conclusion of the novel? Vālmīki's *Rāmāyaṇa* in effect has two endings. One is the killing of Rāvaṇa and the reunion of Rāma and Sītā. The other is their second and final separation, leading ultimately to what appears to be their suicides—Sītā descending into the earth; Rāma entering "the holy stream Sarayu . . . with its swirling whirlpools" (III, 625). The second ending does not seem possible here. It is clear that Nikhil would never abandon his Sītā. Thus the whole train of events leading to his suicide could never occur. But, since Sandip incorporates many of the characteristics of Rāma, it is also not clear that Nikhil will win the battle fought with weapons of truth and illusion. After all, Sandip predicts the opposite: "Who says 'Truth shall Triumph'? Delusion shall win in the end" (125). Of course, there is an answer to Sandip's question, and it is an important answer: the statement that truth shall triumph derives, within the Hindu tradition, from the Upaniṣads (as the translator notes, 125n.1), which are among the most important Hindu spiritual texts. It seems likely that Tagore put his faith in the Upaniṣads more than in the deceptions of a Hindu nationalist.

But, again, what is the conclusion of the novel? Most of my students—guided by Anita Desai's introduction to the recent Penguin edition (Desai herself guided I imagine by Satyajit Ray's movie)—believe that the novel ends with the probably fatal wounding of Nikhil. Personally, I always took the dying character to be Sandip. There has been a riot. A doctor accompanies a group bearing a wounded man. Someone asks, "What do you think, doctor?" He answers, "Can't say yet. . . . The wound in the head is a serious one" (203). Who has been wounded here, Nikhil or Sandip? The point is not explicit. And there is probably good reason for the ambiguity. The ending of the novel is, in effect, a prediction about the future of India. If Nikhil dies, then the future of India is with Sandip. Indeed, the future of India may be a sort of national suicide. For as Bimala is waiting to hear what happens, she thinks, "if only I could die," and she "remember[s] the pistol in [her] box" (202–203).

But, despite Desai's and my students' virtual unanimity in this interpretation, it does not seem to me likely. Right at the beginning of the novel, we are told by Sandip that no one in his family has "survived their thirtieth year," that he is twenty-seven, and that "My horoscope tells me I am to die early" (34). In contrast, Bimala's horoscope predicted that she would become the ideal wife—perhaps what she will now become, having "passed through fire" (199). More importantly, the Muslim anger is directed against Sandip and his followers. Nikhil informs Sandip that "Mahomedan preachers have been about stirring up the local Mussulmans. They are all wild with you, and may attack you any moment" (157–58). Sandip himself leaves the house only moments before Nikhil, explaining, "The Mussulmans, I am told, have taken me for an invaluable gem, and are conspiring to loot me and hide me away in their graveyard" (200–201). In contrast, Nikhil is the one Hindu in the area that they have no reason to harm, for he has been supportive of them since the beginning. It seems very unlikely, for example, that they would be unaware that he refused to enforce swadeshi in his markets. Finally, when the group returns to the house, there is one other person who has been shot—and he is dead. That is Amulya. Though Amulya had become disillusioned with Sandip, this would hardly have been widely known. Rather, he would have been recognized as Sandip's close associate. It would seem odd that the Muslim rioters would set out to kill Sandip's associate and Nikhil. It seems far more likely that they would pursue the two leaders of the anti-Muslim activists—Amulya and Sandip. Finally, the doctor's tone seems oddly indifferent, if he is speaking about Nikhil. If the injured man were Nikhil, one would imagine that the doctor would say something more than "Can't say yet. . . . The wound in the head is a serious one" (203). This neutral tone seems more appropriate if the victim is Sandip.

The implication, then, is that Tagore saw his own nonviolent view—represented by Nikhil—as ultimately succeeding, truth emerging triumphant, as the Upaniṣads have it, and India emerging, perhaps, as the epitome of universal dharma, to lead the world, not to national liberation, but to a fuller, spiritual liberation. Still, this is not fully explicit. The letter of the text is ambiguous between the death of Sandip and the death of Nikhil. Indeed, even the death is uncertain ("Can't say yet"). And this ambiguity is no doubt intentional. Tagore seems to have expected—or at least hoped for—the eventual triumph of Nikhil and all he represents. But he could not be sure. The conclusion of the novel is necessarily uncertain, for the choice of the nation was uncertain as Tagore wrote. He could not look into the future and see which set of principles and practices would "live" and which would "die." He could only urge one option over the other, portray the alternatives in terms of hope and tragedy.

Tagore's vision here, his new version of Rāmarājya, may be too upper class, too founded on unquestioned assumptions of food, clothing, personal security to be directly applicable to real life. It is all well and good to speak of spiritual development when one never has to worry about how to feed one's family or oneself. First, one needs material security. That is a basis for any other development. Tagore had that. Millions do not. Second, this lack is not unrelated to the relations of colonial exploitation that Tagore systematically occludes in this novel.

Yet, to say that this vision of an ideal society leaves out crucial matters is not to say that it has no worth. In fact, it serves as a valuable corrective to the pure emphasis on material gain. Tagore, following Hindu tradition, is no doubt right about many things. Romantic love and prosperity are not the highest goals. Not because they are evil, not because they are sinful. But because their pursuit ultimately brings pain, longing, dissatisfaction. They do not bring peace, and peace is the most perfect feeling of the soul. Drawing on Hindu tradition, and revising the *Rāmāyana*, Tagore presents us with a vision of an ideal society in which all people avoid cruelty, and pursue truth, and strive to free themselves from the illusions that spur desire and disrupt peace. It is a beautiful vision. And a necessary one. For, while any just vision of the future should include universal material security, any such vision should also include a recognition that peace cannot come from accumulating things. Peace can come only if we live in a world where we can act every day according to what is true, and according to the universal principle of ahiṃsā, which adjures us not only to avoid behaving cruelly ourselves, but to refrain from any cooperation with the cruelty of others—a point argued powerfully in Tagore's novel, but a point that emerges with full clarity only when one recognizes the novel as a corrective revision of Vālmīki's foundational epic.

Chapter Three

Subaltern Myths
Drawn from the Colonizer

Dream on Monkey Mountain and the Revolutionary Jesus

And I remember his telling me the story—I do not think it could
ever have been so told before or since—of the carpenter whom the
rich men killed, and many and many a time saying, "After all we
can forgive Christianity much."

> —Eleanor Marx, from reminiscences
> of her father, Karl Marx (150)

SUBALTERN TRADITIONS IN THE METROPOLIS

Though postcolonization writers no doubt rarely conceived of the issue
explicitly in these terms, one solution to the problem illustrated in the two
novels by Desai and Lamming is to explore subaltern strains in the metropolitan tradition. As I argued in the first chapter, Desai's representation of India
and Lamming's representation of Afro-Caribbeans appear to have been distorted, at least to some degree, by the use of ideologically oppressive metropolitan models. Insofar as this is the case, one obvious way of responding to

this dilemma is by seeking out those elements in the metropolitan tradition that work against oppression. When one looks at the metropolitan tradition from a colony, it may initially appear that the metropolis is a unitary oppressor. But clearly this is not the case. There are rifts within the metropolitan society—by class, sex, ethnicity, and the like. Moreover, these rifts manifest themselves in the literature. Some metropolitan literary works take a self-consciously proletarian, feminist, or minority stance, exploring the mechanisms through which people have been oppressed in terms of these divisions, and responding to that oppression.

Of course, to say that a work is feminist is not to say that it adopts a progressive stance on any other issue. A feminist work may be racist, classist, and colonialist. A proletarian work may be sexist and imperialist. However, each work that opposes oppression in some form provides a potentially suitable model for opposition to oppression in other forms. Each type of subaltern metropolitan literature provides potentially valuable models for postcolonization writers. Thus we find Tagore, in *Gora*, drawing on the protofeminist writing of Jane Austen, specifically *Pride and Prejudice* (see my "Gora"), and the, at least to some degree, class-conscious work of Turgenev, specifically, *Fathers and Sons*. (Turgenev's writings helped to expose the condition of the Russian serfs and, in connection with this, explored the conflicts between "Westernizers" and those Russians who wished to affirm a distinctive Slavic culture.) We find Ousmane Sembene drawing on the proletarian *La Condition Humaine* in *Les Bouts de Bois de Dieu* (see, for example, S. Ojo 118). We find Wole Soyinka rewriting works by Euripides *(The Bacchae)*, the dissident voice of classical Greek drama, and by Jean Genet (see *Play* v), a thief and homosexual prostitute.

This use of metropolitan tradition seems particularly common in the Caribbean, which is unsurprising. Indian and African authors have readier access to indigenous traditions, and these traditions can provide them materials and forms for anticolonial writing. But Caribbean authors are much less directly linked to the traditions of their ancestors. Certainly, Afro-Caribbean cultures have retained many elements of their various African sources. But these are necessarily attenuated, relative to the original traditions from which their ancestors were torn and sold into slavery. This is particularly clear when one recalls that slaves were intentionally mixed together from different linguistic and cultural groups in order to prevent them from forming a unified block against the slave holders. Moreover, they were virtually all converted to Christianity generations ago. Again, elements of African traditions certainly survive. But for the most part in a diminished, concealed, and in many ways Europeanized form. For this reason, the literary traditions in which Caribbean writers developed have been largely European. They do not have direct access to some counterpart for Sanskrit drama and epic, or Arabic poetry and tales.

Yet, when they look at the mainstream of the metropolitan tradition, they see a set of works that appear to ignore or demean them, or at least to give tacit support to the system that brutalized their ancestors and continues to weigh down upon themselves. It is, then, particularly important for Caribbean writers to find subaltern elements in the metropolitan tradition, to discover a part of that tradition which provides a model for opposing oppression.

Many postcolonization writers have found a particularly fruitful source of subaltern literature in Ireland. Ireland was a late addition to the metropolitan tradition. For most of the nineteenth century, mainstream Anglo-Saxonists considered the Irish to be racially inferior—indeed, closely akin to Africans and high in the "index of nigrescence" (see Curtis 72, 136–37). Moreover, Irish literature came to colonial peoples as a part of the metropolitan tradition—but a part that opposed English colonialism and racialism, and that participated actively in the development of Irish independence. Boehmer notes that "both Tagore and Mulk Raj Anand found helpful correspondences for their own work in Irish literature" (114). Yeats's drama is no doubt one source for Soyinka's poetic theater, and the general inspiration provided to Nigerian writers by the Irish Renaissance is suggested by the fact that Achebe took the title for his first novel from one of Yeats's poems. Joyce had a significant impact on a range of postcolonization, Anglophone writers as well, including, for example, Raja Rao, R. K. Narayan, and Salman Rushdie. The list could be extended.

Caribbean writers seem to have drawn on Irish precursors with unusual frequency. This is due in part to their greater general reliance on the metropolitan tradition. In addition, however, Ireland and the English Caribbean share a number of similarities that distinguish them from other British colonies. Unlike Africa or India, the mother tongue of virtually everyone in Ireland and in the English Caribbean is English. Moreover, it is a particular form of English, strongly influenced by other, ancestral languages, now retained in pitch and inflection, idiom, vocabulary, even aspects of morphology and syntax. They are, or were until recently, small, beautiful, sparsely populated islands, tied to the sea, and little marred or advanced by industry. This parallelism of language and of circumstance seems to have resulted in a special sense of literary affinity. Thus we find a range of poets working to use and beautify Caribbean English, in part inspired by the work of Synge, Lady Gregory, and others in Ireland. We also find a surprising number of novelists drawing on Joyce's *Portrait of the Artist as a Young Man,* the story of a child growing into a poet in the backwaters of empire, then preparing, at the end of the book, to leave home, with the hope of forging a conscience for his race. This novel served as a crucial model for George Lamming's *In the Castle of My Skin,* Jamaica Kincaid's *Annie John,* and V. S. Naipaul's *A House for Mr. Biswas,* which also draws on *Ulysses. Finnegans Wake* was an important precursor for

Kamau Brathwaite's *Mother Poem,* an appreciation of his native Barbados as a physical place, much as *Finnegans Wake* is, in part, an appreciation of Ireland as a physical place.

Walcott is a particularly good instance of this, so to speak, strategic influence. In *Omeros,* as we shall see, Walcott turned to Joyce as a primary model for outdoing the European epic tradition. In some of his early plays, most obviously *The Sea at Dauphin,* Walcott clearly drew on John Millington Synge. Indeed, *Dream on Monkey Mountain* itself is not entirely dissimilar to some of Yeats's plays, and it certainly fulfills Yeats's program for a poetic theater, though there are a number of other possible sources for this aspect of the work.

But, of course, Ireland is not the only source of subaltern elements in the metropolitan tradition, nor is it necessarily the most important source even in those instances where it has exerted a strong influence. In the case of *Dream on Monkey Mountain,* the most systematic, thematically significant, and rhetorically consequential use of metropolitan tradition concerns the story of Jesus. This brings us to a particularly valuable type of subaltern modeling, and revision, of metropolitan tradition—the retelling of myth.

MYTH AND COGNITION

Religious narratives are, so to speak, the common coin of a culture. They are central to a wide range of traditions, or subtraditions, within a culture. Perhaps most obviously, these include the literary tradition, which is imbued with such tales in every society of which I am aware. Stories of the sacred are no less crucial to the formation and development of ethical traditions, or to the structure and history of political debate and theorization. Indeed, myth is central to almost every system of thought that contributes to the understanding, articulation, and intellectual defense of colonialism. This is not to say that religious belief is in any way at the foundation of colonialism, politics, or anything else. In my view, economy is the most important basis of these. However, religion plays a very large and consequential role in the *discussion* of these issues, in the way they are conceived, in the way alternatives are formulated. It plays a particularly important role in *justifying* social and political structures—especially those that, at first, appear unjustifiable, such as slavery. In short, religion and myth have deep and pervasive ideological functions.

The close historical link between religion and colonialism does not imply, however, that religion and myth are intrinsically oppressive forces. Rather, it seems that all religions have what might be called "hierarchy-preserving" and "hierarchy-disrupting" aspects. Marx and Engels saw religion as necessarily of the former sort, and they were right, in a sense. The hierarchy-preserving aspects of a religion are invariably the aspects stressed by the ruling elite. And the aspects of religion stressed by the ruling elite are almost always the aspects that achieve social dominance. Put simply, if George Bush quotes the Bible in talking about the Gulf War, he will not be choosing a passage that promotes pacifism or generosity to those who are ethnically different. But this is not to say that there are no such passages in the Bible. There are many. Those passages may be quoted by antiwar activists. But, clearly, it is George Bush's quote that will be widely reported, read, cited, requoted, and so on, not those of the antiwar activists. In part because of this discrepancy, and because of the great psychological importance of religion and myth for most people, it is particularly valuable for postcolonization writers to draw out and make prominent the hierarchy-disrupting aspects, so often occluded in the mainstream or dominant uses of religion. Indeed, this is particularly clear in the case of Christianity, because Christianity has played a central ideological role in the establishment and preservation of European colonial hierarchies right from the beginning of European colonialism—despite the fact that its origins are, in fact, anticolonial and antiracist.

Before going on to discuss the subaltern strain in Christianity, however, it is worth considering the cognitive operation of myth more carefully in relation to colonialism. Up to this point, we have considered the lexicon primarily in terms of schemas, prototypes, and exempla. These are all subsumed under lexical entries. But lexical entries themselves are organized into further patterns, sometimes referred to as "semantic fields" (on the structure of semantic fields, see chapter 6 of Kittay; for a broader discussion, see Cruse on lexical relations and lexical configurations, chapters 4 and following.) I refer to them as "domains." As noted briefly in chapter 2, domains are sets of lexical entries linked into a structure by some general principle and, most often, named by a further lexical item. Obvious examples of domains include "months" ("January," "February," "March," etc.) and "weekdays." Domains are also marked out by terms that have less rigidly defined extensions, including, for example, scalar terms, such as "temperature," comprising "hot, "warm," "cool," and so on. Often scalar terms involve a small number of "basic domain terms," such as "hot" and "cold" in the case of temperature. These may then be augmented by a series of more finely discriminating terms—"freezing," "frigid," "stifling," and so on.

George Lakoff, Mark Johnson, Mark Turner, and others have shown that a great deal of our thought is guided by the mapping of one domain onto another—typically, the mapping of an abstract domain onto a more concrete domain in a sort of complex or systematic metaphor. Thus we understand passion by reference to temperature ("Their once-fiery feelings had begun to cool") or emotional well-being by the vertical axis of our bodily experience ("Jones was feeling down today, but Doe was in high spirits"). This sort of mapping operates virtually whenever we encounter a new domain and, indeed, whenever we are forced to alter an old domain in unexpected ways. Clearly, any mapping of this sort will guide our understanding of the new or unfamiliar domain. It will select certain details, not others; render some patterns salient, while occluding others; lead us to draw certain causal inferences unreflectively; guide us in the phenomenological "concretization" of objects within the domain, and so on. Moreover, it should be clear that, in certain cases, it will orient our emotional reaction to those domains. For example, one of the most commonly used concrete or "source" domains for understanding new, abstract, "target" domains is that of health and sickness. We commonly conceive of certain sorts of behavior, certain systems of thought, certain emotional attitudes as healthy or sick. Often, these behaviors, and so forth, are extensionally equivalent to common and uncommon or standard and eccentric behaviors, respectively. If we come genuinely to consider a certain behavior as "healthy" or "sick," if we genuinely map the domain of health and sickness onto that behavior and its correlates, we are likely to have a rather different emotional reaction to it than if we merely understand it as common or uncommon. Consider homosexuality. Some people think of it as sick; others think of it as uncommon. (There are obviously other possibilities. I am simplifying for the sake of exposition.) A person's emotional response—and behavior—are likely to be different in one case than in the other. Of course, part of this feeling and behavior preceded the mapping. One person may have mapped homosexuality onto "sick" because he/she began with an aversive response to homosexuality. But part is also likely to be the result of the mapping itself.

For our purposes, the most important type of mapping is that which operates to distinguish and hierarchize groups, specifically the colonizer and the colonized. The gross exploitation of an entire race of people cannot proceed without some sort of sharp conceptual distinction between the exploiting and the exploited groups. This is most obviously the case with slavery. If Africans are slaves or potential slaves (i.e., their race makes them liable to sale as property), whereas Europeans are slave owners or potential slave owners (i.e., their race does not make them liable to sale), then there must be some cognitive division—and, correlatively, some emotional division—between Africans and Europeans. This distinction cannot be made by invoking the concept of humanity. Rather, these two groups must be understood, their hierarchization must be justified, by reference to some further domain—typically a domain that includes the lexical entry "human" and thus, through a mapping of domains, allows a sort of paradoxical distinction between the human and the nonhuman within humanity.

One obvious set of such categories is biological. The division between European and African—or man and woman, English and Irish, Aryan and

Jew, my high school football team and the rival high school football team—is mapped onto the division between human and animal, very often the most humanoid animal, a monkey or ape. Put differently, "human" and "monkey," or some variant, become basic domain terms for this mapping, the nearest non-human item in the domain operating as the primary alternative to "human." Clearly, Walcott seeks to examine this sort of mapping in his play about an Afro-Caribbean man who has forgotten his name and calls himself "Makak," which is to say, "macaque."

However, we will not be concentrating on this aspect of Walcott's play. A domain of equal importance in colonial ideology—and in other ideologies based on hierarchical group divisions—is drawn from myth. Specifically, part of the cognitive structure that underlies colonialist attitudes and actions involves a systematic mapping of the domain of mythic beings onto the domain of colonial relations, with colonized peoples most often taking up the place of demons within this mapping. This tends to foster, or at least justify, not only broad colonial policies—primarily policies of murder, including "ethnic cleansing" (for demons must be sought out and killed)—but also individual feelings of fear and hatred, individual behaviors (often paranoid) of cruelty. This sort of mapping serves to highlight and "explain" certain sorts of behavior on the part of colonized people. It leads colonizers to "encode"—to perceive, understand, and remember—only certain behaviors on the part of colonized people, and to interpret those behaviors in particular, demonic ways. Indeed, the encoding itself already involves tacit interpretations of this sort. In short, it leads colonizers to see colonized people as demonic and thus it tends to be self-confirming. Moreover, such mapping tends to stifle empathy, to replace curiosity or wonder at unfamiliar customs with fear or Conradian horror. (For a fuller discussion of these topics, see chapter 4 of my *Culture*.)

It is in this context, at once social and cognitive, that the project undertaken by Walcott assumes political importance. By placing an Afro-Caribbean man in the position of Jesus, Walcott is reorienting a type of cognitive mapping that is standard, and ideologically consequential, within European colonialism. He is redirecting the oppressive use of a cognitive domain so as to alter the way it operates in construing the character and culture of Afro-Caribbean people—and thus the way it functions to guide the actions and color the feelings of colonizer and colonized alike. On the other hand, Walcott does not simply reverse the standard structure. First, he draws on a subaltern strain of colonial myth, exploring anticolonial views within metropolitan tradition itself. Second, he complicates that strain, ultimately mixing together the divine and the demonic, for he does not wish to repeat the simplifications of a colonial ideology that identifies one race with angels, gods, or humans, and another with devils.

CHRISTIANITY IN THE COLONIES

Readers of postcolonization literature and theory are familiar with the ways in which Christianity was used by colonizers to secure and extend imperial control, especially among Africans, both within Africa itself and in the New World. This operation was both practical or administrative and ideological. As to the former, the close practical relation between Christianity and colonialism in the Caribbean—specifically, in Walcott's home, St. Lucia—is nicely ilustrated in Charles Gachet's *A History of the Roman Catholic Church in St. Lucia*. Gachet notes, for example, that "The Caribs who inhabited the island at the time of its discovery"—that is, its discovery by Europeans, for clearly the Caribs themselves already knew about the place—"continued to live in it . . . up to 1660, when, by a treaty of Peace with the French and the English, they renounced all claims to ownership of most of the Lesser Antilles." This treaty—little more than formally legalized theft—"had been signed through the mediation of Missionaries working among the Caribs." Gachet notes with some surprise that, despite the missionaries' work on this treaty, "very few Caribs became Christians in St. Lucia" (2). Gachet goes on to trace the continual presence and operation of the Catholic Church and its relation to French colonial forces. He also suggests the parallel function of Protestantism in English colonialism on the island.

As to ideology, Christians invoked the putative superiority of their religion and its associated ethics as justification for imperialism. They were fighting against heathens and against demonic practices—what could be more in keeping with God's will? Moreover, the colonists saw their triumph over these heathens as evidence of divine support for the colonial enterprise. Indeed, this heinous sentiment—according to which, Might, however exercised, really is Right—extends back to some of the earliest colonial conquests. Consider, for example, John Milton's characterization of the "Papists of *Ireland*" (*Works* VI, 243) as "our most savage and inhuman enemies" (VII, 525), "a nation cursed and set apart for destruction" (V, 39), who are "justly made our vassals" (VI, 244). He approves the policies that brought the "godless" Irish (V, 39) "every where either to Famin, or a low condition" (V, 199), explains that the "Irish Campaign" is "so acceptable to Almighty God" (V, 197), and maintains that the English victories over the Irish were concrete evidence of God's favor (III, 340).

Needless to say, Christianity was not used solely for self-justification among the colonizers. It was taught to the indigenous people as well. This had at least two functions. The first was to undermine indigenous culture and the solidarity that this culture might underwrite. In *The Joys of Motherhood*, Buchi Emecheta illustrates the ways in which some groups of Igbos (e.g., many domestic servants) were coerced into attending Christian churches, following

Christian marriage and other practices, and so on. Over time, and especially across generations, this operated to sever these people's ties with ancestral traditions. This inhibited their distinctive, practical identification with other Igbos and perhaps their categorial identification as well. In short, it weakened the ties binding the Igbo community together, and thus inhibited collective anticolonial action. Moreover, initially , Christianization contributed to the creation of a stratum of Europeanized Africans who served as a sort of buffer between the colonizers and the African masses.

The second function of Christian proslytization had to do with the precise version of Christianity that was preached throughout the colonies—a Christianity of nonresistance and passivity. When faced with oppressed indigenous people, the same Christians who saw colonial conquest as an act of God now determined that Christianity was the religion of unqualified nonviolence, and emphasized just those passages in the Gospels where Jesus adjures stoic acceptance of injustice, cruelty, and exploitation—as, for example, in the following passage from Matthew (5:39–42):

> I say this to you: offer the wicked man no resistance. On the contrary, if anyone hits you on the right cheek, offer him the other as well; if a man takes you to law and would have your tunic, let him have your cloak as well. And if anyone orders you to go one mile, go two miles.

As Walter Rodney put it, "The church's role was primarily to preserve the social relations of colonialism. . . . Therefore, the Christian church stressed humility, docility, and acceptance. . . . [C]hurches could be relied upon to preach turning the other cheek in the face of exploitation" (252–53).

Of course, Africans who were converted to Christianity did not merely accept the new religion as it was given to them. Well, some did—especially those who aspired to be accepted into European circles and who repudiated their fellow Africans. But many paid only lip service to the new religion. Others combined elements of the new religion with their own traditional practices, synthesizing the two in ways that they found emotionally satisfying—or, as emotionally satisfying as one could reasonably expect, given the circumstances. For example, it is well known that Afro-Caribbeans often fused Christian saints with West African deities. They used the Christian names, but gave these saints the attributes of ancestral gods and goddesses, following many traditional rituals in their regard.

On the other hand, this grudging and superficial acceptance of a colonial imposition is not all there is to African and Afro-Caribbean Christianity. Many Africans and Afro-Caribbeans fully accepted a version of Christianity. And they did this in part because they saw Christianity as *anti*-colonial in its deepest impulses. Exposed to Jesus' teachings for the first time, untainted by years of habituation in middle-class churches, many

Africans heard a revolutionary message, a message that the Kingdom of God was not the kingdom of man, that it belonged not to the wealthy, but to the poor. They heard religious teaching that did not elevate the elite, but rather the ordinary people—and they saw that, from ordinary people, Jesus chose the most downcast to celebrate and raise up. In short, they saw a religion that addressed them as colonized people, as slaves, and told them that they—not the colonizers, not the slave owners—were God's chosen people. Right alongside the colonialist use of Christianity, there was always a revolutionary countertradition emphasizing just this point. Indeed, this tradition did not begin with African Christianity. It extended all the way back to the time of Jesus himself.

JESUS AND ANTICOLONIAL STRUGGLE:
IMPERIAL ENGLAND AND IMPERIAL ROME

Those of us who were raised as Christians and learned about the teachings of Jesus in suburban schools and churches tend to forget that Jesus was born into and lived his entire life in a colonized country. This one fact pervades the gospels—though it is virtually absent from common teaching about the gospels in the mainstream denominations. (It is not absent from the scholarship, of course.) Jesus is born when his parents are on the road because of an imperial census, ordered for purposes of colonial taxation. Jesus dies on a cross marked with the legend, "King of the Jews." As Cullman explains, this was precisely the *charge* leveled against Jesus: "Translated into the legal parlance of the Roman State, this means: Jesus was condemned to death . . . as a rebel against the Roman State in one of its subject provinces" (*State* 6; see also 42–43, and Pagels 6–7). The entire story of Jesus is the story of an ordinary man—a man who was not wealthy or from a powerful family, a man without position—in a land in which daily life is pervaded by colonialism. Roman soldiers, images of the emperor, concerns about Roman law, poverty resulting from Roman taxation, and rebellion against all these things, were ubiquitous.

Indeed, all the concerns of cultural and political identity were there, just as they appeared later in Ireland, Africa, India, the Caribbean. Thus we find collaborators and militant revolutionaries, mimeticists and reactionary traditionalists. Josephus, in his historical memoirs of the period, portrays a place in constant anticolonial turmoil, a land in which Jews were continually forming new alliances, developing new strategies, to throw off the yoke of colonial domination—and a land in which Jews were continually divided by their cultural responses to that domination.

Traditional interpretations of the gospels emphasize the role of the Sadducees, chief priests, and Pharisees, rather than the Romans, in Jesus' life and death. This emphasis in and of itself is not unreasonable. However, there is a tendency for those who emphasize these groups to see them as representing Judaism or, worse still, Jews as a race—a horrible bit of racist nonsense, combined with a serious misreading of the historical situation. Clearly, this is not an issue we can discuss at length in this context. But the crucial point here is that the Sadducees, chief priests, and Pharisees were not separate from the colonial structure. They were a central part of it. They were, to a great extent, the elite, collaborationist stratum. Cullmann notes that the Sadducees "assented without reservation to the Roman domination" and were "indeed the collaborationists of that time" (*State* 9). Cassidy stresses that "It was a general feature of Roman policy in their provinces to utilize local leaders and existing institutions whenever possible." One such institution was the Jewish Sanhedrin or supreme council in Jerusalem (92). The chief priests "were among the wealthiest groups of society" (110) and were notorious for their "collaborationist stance" (118). Moreover, the high priest—"president and convenor" of the Sanhedrin (93)—was a Roman appointee (see Aelred Cody in Metzger and Coogan 611). Clearly, the Jewish religious hierarchy of the time was in effect part of the colonial machinery. To criticize that hierarchy is, at once, to criticize the colonial structure of which it was a part.

John Brown nicely summarizes the situation: "To a greater degree than source critics and form critics of the Gospels have allowed, it is possible to visualize the Jesus movement among the rural poor of Galilee and in confrontation with priestly-Roman rule in Jerusalem. The Gospels are saturated with glimpses of how Rome ruled Palestine through the native Jewish elite, with the result that the imperial effects were felt everywhere, although more visibly in the capital than in the countryside" (357).

Admittedly, the role of the Pharisees is somewhat more complex than that of the Sadducees and chief priests. For example, Cullmann sees the Pharisees as opposing the Roman occupation. However, their opposition to Roman rule was based entirely on the hope of establishing a theocracy in which they would be the rulers (*State* 10). Moreover, Cassidy presents a picture of the Pharisees as far from resistant to colonial domination. In short, their opposition to Roman rule was narrowly self-interested and, in actual practice, inconsequential. For all practical purposes, they were collaborationist. Moreover, at a cultural level, they were reactionary traditionalists whose behavior was self-righteous and demeaning to ethnic minorities, such as Samaritans, and to women. This is typical of reactionary traditionalism in colonial situations. Thus we find reactionary Catholics in Ireland attacking Protestant Irish more vehemently than they attack the British; reactionary Hindus in India attacking Muslims; reactionary Yorubas attacking Igbos, and so on. This reactionary ethnocentrism, even racism, is usually combined with a sort of rigid patriarchalism.

Though not directly part of colonialism, these attitudes are clearly part of the colonial situation; they are produced by the conditions of colonialism.

There were two other politically prominent Jewish groups during this period. One was the Essenes. They were, in effect, socialist utopians, who formed their own communities outside the mainstream of Jewish and Roman life—sometimes in cities, but also in isolated communities in the desert (Riches 198). They held land and property in common, sought to treat each other with love, and so on (see Josephus 605). There are some fairly clear connections between their teachings and those of Jesus. Moreover, this sort of "independence within the colony" is another common response of colonized peoples. There are some elements of it in the cooperative movement in Ireland (see Lyons 209–20) and in certain strains of the swadeshi movement in colonial Bengal (on the different currents of that movement, see Sarkar, *Swadeshi,* 32ff.). While the broader politics of these movements vary, there is often an element of reactionary traditionalism in them. This appears to have been true of the Essenes, who showed dogmatic, ethnocentric, and patriarchal/misogynistic tendencies. Riches points out that they believed themselves to be in sole possession of "the true understanding of the Law," and referred to all non-Essenes as "sons of darkness" (198). Josephus notes their concern with purity, alluding to the washing they must undergo if they have "intermixed themselves with the company of a foreigner" (607) and he reports that "they guard against the lascivious behavior of women, and are persuaded that none of them preserve their fidelity to one man" (605).

The final group were the "Zealots," open revolutionaries against Roman rule. Both Josephus and Cullmann associate the Zealots' views with those of the Pharisees (see Josephus 477, Cullmann *State* 10). However, the Zealots had an interest in reducing economic inequality (see Cassidy 123–24), which connects them with the Essenes as well. In the years 60–70 C.E., the Zealots fought an open war against the Roman Empire (see Cullmann *State* 10) and for a time held Jerusalem. But the Romans recaptured the city and, in retaliation, leveled the great temple. The Zealots remained active, however, and rose again, later in the first century (Cullmann *State* 10–11). Indeed, these famous uprisings were not the beginning of the Zealot movement. As Cassidy discusses, a Zealot uprising, led by a man named Judas, occurred in 6 C.E. (124); it is referred to in *Acts* (5:36–37).

Some writers—most famously, or notoriously, Robert Eisler—have argued for a close connection between Jesus and the Zealots. In any case, messianism was deeply bound up with zealotry. As Cullmann points out, there were two concepts of the Messiah at Jesus' time, "According to the one, which was more or less official and shared by the majority of people, the Messiah was a victorious warrior, who as king on earth will establish a powerful kingdom of Israel through which God would then rule over the world"

(*Jesus* 38). Moreover, Jesus was widely believed to be such a military messiah, even, it seems, by some of his own apostles. At least one of these apostles was drawn from the revolutionaries, "Simon the Zealot." Moreover, Cullmann argues that the "Iscariot" in the name "Judas Iscariot" derives from the Latin word for a Zealot, "Sicarius," and that Peter, Jesus' appointed successor, was a Zealot as well (*State* 15–17). In keeping with this, as we have already noted, Jesus was crucified under a charge of treason—which is to say, the charge of being a Zealot.

Whether one chooses to believe that Jesus was or was not a Zealot, the important point here is that there is a tradition of interpreting the Jesus story that links him closely with this militant anticolonial movement. Moreover, independent of this, it is clear that Jesus' teachings take place in the context of a colonial situation with direct parallels to the situation of Africans, Indians, Irish, and other people colonized during the modern period. Indeed, it seems clear that the entire Jesus story, leading to Jesus' execution by colonial authorities, is strongly anticolonial, and anticollaborationist.

Before going on, it is worth noting two points in connection with this. First, the "liberatory" tradition of Christian thought, which extends from Jesus' own time through such movements as the Diggers in revolutionary England to Liberation Theology in our own day, often places particular emphasis on Luke's gospel. Luke is far more consistent in his emphasis on uplifting the poor, and more ambiguous about violence against the oppressor, than the other evangelists. For example, while Matthew's version of the Beatitudes elevates "the poor in spirit" (5:3), Luke's Jesus celebrates "the poor" (6:20). While Matthew praises "those who hunger and thirst for what is right" (5:6), Luke's Jesus refers instead to those "who are hungry now" (6:21). Repeatedly, Luke stresses the actual material conditions of the poor and the rich, the ruled and the rulers; over and over again, he indicates that God favors the downtrodden and reviles the oppressor. Moreover, Luke's gospel exposes the anticolonial nature of Jesus' teachings, if somewhat less vehemently. As Cassidy observes, "In Luke's gospel Jesus shows virtually no deference to any of the political authorities to whom he theoretically owes allegiance" (74).

The second point that it is important to stress in this context is that the gospels are not the only books of the New Testament that concern colonialism. Acts of the Apostles (probably written by Luke [see Bruce 6]) certainly touches on issues of colonialism—though it has relatively little relevance to Walcott's play, perhaps because it concerns events following Jesus' death. Even more strikingly, Apocalypse or Revelation is almost entirely concerned with Roman colonial rule. The Beast of Revelation has been widely recognized as an allegorical representation of imperial Rome (see *Jerusalem* 441n.k), and the story of the liberation of those subjected to the beast—characterized as "saints" (13:7)—has clear implications for any colonized people. Thus, in Revelation, the colonizer is directly represented as a demonic force. Moreover, the opposition to that colonizer is led ultimately by Jesus himself and it is a straightforwardly military opposition (see 19:19–21). Of course, one might argue that this militarism is not intended literally. But, again, the issue here is not which interpretation of the text is most accurate. Rather, the point is that there is a strain of Christian tradition that is explicitly and militantly anticolonial, and that links Jesus with revolution against colonial power.

In *Dream on Monkey Mountain*, Walcott draws on just this tradition in order to remake the story of Jesus into the story of an impoverished charcoal burner in St. Lucia—or, rather, in order to remake the story of an ordinary, poor Black Caribbean man into a story of Jesus.[1] More generally, he sets out to elevate those who are most oppressed, in a manner entirely consistent with the teachings of Jesus as manifest in this subaltern tradition. Also in keeping with this tradition, he draws particularly, though not exclusively, on Luke's gospel and on Revelation.

SAINT MAKAK

As just noted, Walcott draws primarily on the story of Jesus, as understood in the radical and anticolonial tradition, in order to shape the life of Makak, and that is what I should like to consider in most detail. However, Walcott draws, in a limited but significant way, on the legends of St. Christopher as well. As this is part of the same general project of revising the myths of the colonizer, I should like to treat this aspect of the play briefly before going on to examine the Jesus motifs.

Early in the play, Lestrade informs the audience of the date: 25 July. It is no accident that this is the Feast of St. Christopher. According to the standard account, drawn "from the *Golden Legend* as put into English by William Caxton" (Thurston and Attwater 185), St. Christopher was baptized "Christopher, which is as much as to say as bearing Christ" (184). This strange name is explained by the following story. Christopher went looking for Christ. He met a hermit and asked what service he should perform for Jesus. The hermit told him to go to a river, to live by the river, and to "bear over all them that shall pass there, which shall be a thing right pleasing to our Lord Jesu Christ" (185). Christopher bore many people across the water. One night, as he slept, he heard a child calling, "Christopher, come out and bear me over." Christopher took up the child and entered the river. But the child, despite his small size, grew heavier and heavier, and the river grew stronger, until Christopher feared he would not succeed in crossing. When, after much pain and fear, he reached the other shore, he said to the boy, "Child, thou has put me in great peril; thou weighest almost as I had all the world put upon me."

And the boy answered, "Christopher, marvel thee nothing; for thou has not only borne all the world upon thee, but thou hast borne Him that created and made all the world, upon thy shoulders" (185), for the boy was Jesus.

Though Walcott only alludes to this legend by making his story take place on St. Christopher's Day, the implication is clear. Makak's great message to his people is the message of many Afro-Caribbean religious leaders, from Marcus Garvey to the Rastafarians: Return home to Africa. Makak too wishes to lead his people across the water. The more "sophisticated" Christians tend to look down on this as crazy, as a wild fancy, a "dream," confused with reality by some macaque living on Monkey Mountain. But by this simple allusion to St. Christopher, Walcott has implied that Makak's aspiration—to bear his people across the water to their home—is the most noble act a Christian can perform. For to bear men and women against the currents, to carry the weight of their pain and history—that itself is to bear Christ. The very tradition of the colonizer tells us that it is Makak, and not his colonial masters, who truly bears the burden of the world, and thus who truly carries, and thus serves, Jesus—that his dream, the dream on Monkey Mountain, is the dream of being a genuine Christian.

MAKAK, THE MESSIAH

But, again, *Dream on Monkey Mountain* is most directly aligned with the story of Jesus. Specifically, the characters in the play break down along roughly the following lines. Makak is Jesus.[2] Moustique appears to represent a Messianic Zealot—perhaps Judas, leader of the Zealot uprising, or Judas "Iscariot," the apostle who betrayed Jesus, or perhaps both, as well as Peter, a Zealot (according to Cullmann [*State* 15–17]) and Jesus' successor. In the last role, he represents the history of Christianity after Jesus, when it becomes a temporal power—in keeping with the general aspirations of the Zealots.

Lestrade is ambiguously Herod and Pilate in the first half of the play. Herod, though not Jewish, was not Roman either. His father was half Jewish, while his mother was Samaritan (Hoehner 281–82). (Samaritans were closely related to Jews, but Jews denied this link—see 2 Kings 17.) He was, in effect, an ethnically intermediate character—a sort of "straddler" like Lestrade, himself a mulatto (209), thus neither African nor European. Herod was, of course, a collaborationist with Roman occupation, his power dependent upon their good will (see Hoehner 283), again, just like Lestrade. In the second half, Lestrade shifts his allegiance and becomes a corrupt reactionary traditionalist, more akin to the Pharisees (as discussed above). In connection with this, he is closely associated with St. Paul, his conversion in some ways recapitulating that of Paul.

Market Inspector Caiphas Joseph Pamphilion (224) is, of course, the high priest Joseph Caiaphas, who "played a leading part in the plot against Jesus" (*Jerusalem* note f at 3:2). Clearly Caiphas has all the collaborationist characteristics of the high priest. As regards his official position of market inspector, it is worth recalling that the chief priests objected to Jesus in part because he evicted the dealers from the Temple (Luke 19:45–46). As Ringe notes, "the sale of animals for the temple sacrifices and the exchange of imperial money into the currency used for temple offerings . . . would have been types of commerce on which the temple itself enjoyed a monopoly" (Ringe 242). In other words, the accusation that the Temple had become "a robbers' den" (Luke 19:46) was an accusation against the chief priests. More importantly, the eviction of the dealers was a blow to the finances of those priests and their use of the temple as, precisely, a market. In making Caiphas a market inspector, Walcott highlights the economic interests that underlay Jesus' conflict with the chief priests—a point of obvious relevance to a political and anticolonial interpretation of Jesus' life.

Tigre and Souris are the two men crucified with Jesus. Eisler argues that these men were Zealots, and that certainly fits their characterization in Walcott's play. Of these, Tigre is the thief/zealot who is not saved; Souris is the "good thief" or good zealot. This division is found only in Luke.

Basil's place is less obvious. He is a carpenter, like Jesus' earthly father, Joseph. However, his position as "figure of death" (209) makes him more like the Old Testament God of law and punishment—in other words, Jesus' heavenly father.

The apparition alternates between the Virgin Mary and the Whore of Babylon from Revelation. (There is a degree of feminism in Jesus' teachings, especially as represented by Luke. This strain of progressive Christianity does not appear to have found a prominent place in Walcott's play.)

The play begins with a note on psychosis and colonialism. This is first of all a general statement about colonial oppression as a cause of mental illness. It is important to point out that this link between madness and colonialism was not historically new or unique to Africa and the Caribbean. John Brown notes that, in Roman Palestine, "Serious economic dislocation and deprivation, as well as social stigmatization of the poor, stand out starkly . . . in the psychosomatic 'demonic' diseases by which oppression was internalized" (357). Moreover, Makak himself is presented as ambiguously insane or inspired. In part, this repeats a standard cliché about inspiration. But it also repeats one view of Jesus held by his contemporaries. Mark reports that Jesus' own "relatives" were "convinced" (or perhaps "were told") that Jesus "was out of his mind" (3:21).

Makak is soon introduced by Lestrade with the mocking title "King of Africa" (214). This clearly links Makak with Jesus, officially charged as "King of the Jews," as already noted. The mockery continues—from Lestrade, as well as Tigre and Souris—supplemented by an interrogation of Makak that itself recalls the interrogation of Jesus. In fact, throughout this scene, Lestrade's words and actions recall Jesus' treatment by Pilate, and even more his treatment by Herod—for Luke records that "Herod, together with his guards, treated [Jesus] with contempt and made fun of him" (23:11).

Two pages after the introduction of Makak, Tigre identifies himself and Souris as "two thieves"—literally true, perhaps, but also clearly suggestive of the men crucified with Jesus. Tigre then goes on to say that they have "fallen by the wayside" (216). This appears to allude to the story of the Good Samaritan. The point of the Good Samaritan story is usually taken to be something about judging people by their works. And that is certainly true. But what this interpretation misses is that Samaritans were a demeaned group. They were an ethnic minority among Jews and were considered inferior and impure (see Massey 14 and Ringe 149). Indeed, that is the reason Jesus stresses judging people by their actions—for most people in Jesus' audience would have been prejudiced against Samaritans and would have been inclined to condemn them because of their ethnicity, whatever their acts might be. In short, the story of the Good Samaritan is not aimed merely at repeating an obvious platitude. It is aimed at opposing ethnic bias. It is no accident that, immediately after this allusion to the Good Samaritan, Lestrade refers to the three prisoners as "animals, beasts, savages, cannibals, niggers" and enters into a perverse, pseudo-Darwinian condemnation of Africans (216–17). Lestrade demonstrates precisely the sort of prejudice against which Jesus is arguing through that parable.

This speech also serves to further the identification of Makak with Jesus. Specifically, Lestrade parodies the opening of John's gospel—"In the begining was the Word" (1:1). Makak, named for a type of monkey, is implicitly—if parodically—identified with that Word, hence Jesus, in Lestrade's statement "In the beginning was the ape" (216). Lestrade continues his speech, mocking Makak as "the Lion of Judah" (217). In part, this is a reference to Rastafarianism. However, it also has more direct Judeo-Christian significance. The Biblical source is Genesis 49:9ff. The passage in question predicts, through rather violent imagery, the coming of a messiah who will triumph over other nations so that "the peoples shall render obedience" (49:10). It is clearly a passage very much in keeping with the militant messianism of the zealots.

This parallel is made more fully explicit a few pages later, when Lestrade says that he will have pity on the prisoners as "Roman law" had "pity on our Blessed Saviour" (220). Those who recall that Roman law crucified Jesus are likely to ask just what Lestrade has in mind. Unsurprisingly, then, Lestrade's instance of this pity is strange—for he refers to the point just before Jesus' death when he is given vinegar for his thirst. Lestrade uses the French word here, but not the standard, "vinaigre"; rather, he says *"vinegre."* Evidently this is a pun on *vie nègre,* negro life. Lestrade links this act of giving vinegar with the life *(vie)* of Blacks *(nègres)*—implying, perhaps, that their life is marked by receiving vinegar instead of wine or water, that they live a life of continual crucifixion. At the very least, the alteration suggests an identification of Afro-Caribbeans today with the crucified Jesus and perhaps with Jews more generally at the time of Roman imperial rule.

The biblical incident itself fits well with the implications of this pun. John reports that Jesus took the vinegar to fulfill the prophecies (see 19:28–30). Specifically, Jesus refers to Psalm 69, a lament over the condition of Zion. The speaker of this psalm, like Christopher bearing Jesus, is near to drowning in a swelling water. Calling out to God for help, the speaker explains this condition in terms that could be spoken by any victim of racism: "people hate me for no reason" (1.4). The speaker goes on to express the despair that always threatens the oppressed, the despair discussed by Walcott in his essay "What the Twilight Says" (printed as an introduction to *Dream on Monkey Mountain and Other Plays*); these words too could be spoken by Makak or any of those who follow him: "You know all the insults I endure, / every one of my oppressors is known to you; / the insults have broken my heart" (ll.19–20). The prophecy concerning vinegar, referred to by Lestrade, directly follows (1.21).

Indeed, the relevance of this passage to *Dream on Monkey Mountain* is even more extensive than might at first appear. It relates to the Afro-Caribbean situation not only in portraying the condition of an oppressed and demeaned people. It is also part of militant messianism, as indicated in the following verses, that call for the destruction of "oppressors" (1.19) and assert that "Yahweh will always hear those who are in need, / will never scorn his captive people" (1.33). The bearing of this last verse on the condition of Afro-Caribbeans is too obvious to require elaboration.

A few pages later, Lestrade explains the nature of Makak's crime. He damaged a bar, calling the proprietor "an agent of the devil" (224). This appears to be roughly parallel to Jesus' expulsion of the dealers from the Temple. As Mark recounts the incident (11:15–17), Jesus

> went into the Temple and began driving out those who were selling and buying there; he upset the tables of the money changers and the chairs of those who were selling pigeons. Nor would he allow anyone to carry anything through the Temple. And he taught them and said, "Does not scripture say: *My house will be called a house of prayer for all the peoples?* But you have turned it into *a robbers' den.*"

There are two points worth stressing about this passage. First, in denouncing these practices, Jesus quotes a passage from Isaiah, "My house will be called a house of prayer for all the peoples" (56:7). Through its reference to "all the peoples," this passage stresses the nonracialism of Jesus' teaching, and the implicit racialism of the high priests—a point with obvious relevance to Walcott's play and to his use of this tradition of Christianity. The second important point about this passage is that Jesus not only accuses the chief priests of racialism; he accuses them of robbery, and of violating the very scriptures they pretend to obey. As Mark explains, "This came to the ears of the chief priests and the scribes, and they tried to find some way of doing away with him" (11:18). In short, this incident is the beginning of Jesus' trouble with Caiaphas, just as it is the beginning of Makak's trouble with Caiaphas.

In addition, Lestrade explains that, just before damaging the bar, Makak engaged in a "blasphemous, obscene debate" with Market Inspector Caiphas Joseph Pamphilion—much as Jesus' conflict with the chief priests and other religious leaders often involved debate in which each side viewed the other as, in effect, blasphemous and obscene. One might recall, for example, the discussion on purity, where Jesus was criticized for not following religious prescriptions and in turn criticized the Pharisees, saying, "You clean the outside of cup and plate, while inside yourselves you are filled with extortion and wickedness" (Luke 11:38–39). Perhaps even more significant are the debates with the chief priests immediately following the expulsion of the money changers. Specifically, Makak was "urging destruction on Church and State, claiming that he was the direct descendant of African kings, a healer of leprosy and the Saviour of his race" (225). In a similar way, the first "debate" Jesus has with the high priests after he clears the Temple concerns his own status and authority. The chief priests ask him, "what authority have you for acting like this? Or who is it that gave you this authority?" (Luke 20:2)—Jesus manages to avoid answering, but the implication of the gospel is clear: He is the descendant of kings, the healer of leprosy, the Savior who will lead His people to the Kingdom of God, and thus the overcoming, the final destruction of Church and State, Caiaphas and Herod.

In short, Makak was playing the role of Jesus to Caiaphas's role of Caiaphas. Just as Jesus opposed the practices of the chief priests, who were collaborating with the Roman imperial state, so too does Makak oppose the church and the British imperial state. Just as Jesus claimed descent from King David (see, for example, the end of *Revelation:* "I, Jesus . . . am of David's line, the root of David" [22:16]), Makak claims descent from African kings. Just as Jesus healed leprosy, Makak heals the disease that makes his fellow Blacks turn white—if not through the decay of leprosy, then through the decay of mimeticism. (Makak performs miraculous cures of physical ailments as well, of course.) Just as Jesus offers himself as divine Savior, Messiah—and was seen as a worldly savior as well—Makak offers himself as the one who will save his people from their oppression, first their worldly oppression, but also their spiritual desolation, the oppression of the heart. All this is met with "pious horror" (225)—perhaps not the response one would expect from a market inspector, but certainly the response one would expect from a high priest.

Shortly after this, Makak begins to recount his dream, the dream in which "I feel I was God self" (227). This discussion of his dream is immediately preceded by Tigre telling Makak: "you so damn ugly. You should walk on all fours" (226). His blackness is, of course, equally emphasized—and related to his ugliness. For example, Moustique tells him, "You is nothing. You black, ugly, poor, so you worse than nothing" (237). Indeed, the theme of Makak's ugliness, and blackness, recurs throughout the play. Accustomed as we are to pictures of a beautiful, white Jesus, this may seem to be a point that does not fit the Jesus story. But according to Eisler's arguments, Makak is much more similar to the historical Jesus than are the common icons. Eisler notes that "a number of passages in the Church Fathers" concern "the plain, nay, ugly appearance of 'Jesus when in the Flesh'" (393). One writer characterized him as having "a face from which spectators might shrink" (413). Eisler finds evidence that Jesus was hunchbacked (416). He finds no evidence that he was beautiful—a point that fits with other aspects of Jesus' background and status, for he was repeatedly associated with the downcast and the reviled. After all, he was not born wealthy or in a dominant ethic group, but to a relatively poor family in a colonized land. If he did not have privileges of class or ethnicity, why should we expect him to be part of an elite in physical appearance? Perhaps even more importantly, Eisler argues that Jesus was "dark-skinned" (420)—not necessarily what we would call "black," but certainly much darker than the average European icon, certainly closer to Makak than to Charlton Heston. This view of Jesus is not confined to libraries and musty scholars. Michelle Cliff presents the same view in popular Afro-Caribbean Christian iconography when she describes one family's "picture of Our Saviour" as "a small dark man with a hump on his back—a gift from the pastor of the Church of the Lickle Jesus" (35).

The center of Makak's vision is "this woman . . . like the moon walking" (227), a "Lady in heaven" (228). Here, the woman is Mary—specifically, Mary as she appears in Revelation: "a woman . . . standing on the moon" (12:1). In Revelation, this woman is pregnant, and threatened by the dragon that is in part a representation of Rome—or, perhaps, a deeper evil that gives rise to the Roman empire in the form of the beast. The woman gives birth to a boy, "The Messiah considered simultaneously as an individual person and as head or leader of the new Israel" (*Jerusalem* n.e at 12:5). The Biblical image is clearly of direct relevance to the function of Makak's vision—for this vision is what inspires Makak to take up his messianic mission of opposing church and state. On the other hand, though he is drawing on the "subaltern" elements of Christianity, Walcott evidences ambivalence about this image right from the beginning.[3] Lestrade immediately characterizes

Makak's relation to the woman as a "rage for whiteness" (228). The point will become particularly important at the end of the play.

The introduction of the vision ends the prologue. Scene one begins with Moustique, "a little man with a limp" (231), a "breakfoot nigger" (234), recalling the gospels' continual emphasis on Jesus' ministry to the poor and crippled. The opening pages develop the ambivalence of the apparition, linking her with a white spider. At the end of this scene, Makak has decided to descend the mountain and begin his ministry of bearing people across the water. He calls to Moustique, "Saddle my horse" (240)—his "horse" being a "half-starve jackass" (241). The jackass recalls Jesus' entry into Jerusalem on the "colt of a donkey" (John 12:14). This too was done to fulfill the prophecies, in this case, the prophecy of Zechariah 9:9, "your king comes to you . . . riding on a donkey." Here as elsewhere, Walcott's choice is particularly apt, for the entire Old Testament passage makes clear that this messiah king is a leader who will deliver his people from their sufferings, a military commander who will conquer vast lands on their behalf. In a statement particularly relevant to Afro-Caribbeans seeking return to Africa, Yahweh announces, in connection with this messiah, that "In compensation for your days of banishment / I will give you back double" (9:12).

Having set out, Makak and Moustique immediately encounter a group praying for a man who is dying from snakebite "and no medicine can cure him" (245). The choice of a snakebite is, obviously, not accidental. It serves to recall the origin of all death, in Eve's temptation by the serpent in the Garden of Eden. A snake, in other words, is the cause of all death, because it is the cause of the Original Sin that was our Fall. Jesus' primary task in the incarnation was to redeem humankind from this fall. The purpose of his entire life was, in effect, to cure humankind of the poison of the serpent-induced bite from the forbidden apple. Thus it is deeply appropriate that Makak's first miracle should be the restoration of a man bitten by a snake. It does not merely parallel Jesus' miracles in general, but in effect allegorizes the purpose of his entire incarnation.

Indeed, that first fall is referred to as a "happy/fortunate fault" or *felix culpa,* because it led to the birth of our savior. At the end of the play, we learn that Makak's real name is "Felix Hobain." This links him with the *felix culpa.* But, at the same time, he is not the *felix culpa,* the happy/fortunate fault. Rather, as a messiah, he is a happy/fortunate response to or result of that fault; perhaps he is an *"aubain"*—pronounced the same as "Hobain," thus indistinguishable in performance—a windfall, a piece of good fortune, just what is produced by the "felix culpa."

In treating the sick man, however, Makak indicates that the Original Sin which he sets out to cure did not take place in the Garden of Eden—just as his own project is not to return all humankind to that Garden of Paradise.

Rather, the implication of Makak's teaching is that the Original Sin which bears on his mission is the sin that occurred in slavery. The fallen condition for which he serves as savior is not exile from Eden, but exile from Africa. In keeping with this, Makak cures the man by calling on those present to have faith—not in a transcendental deity, but in their own people: "Faith, faith!/Believe in yourselves" (249). He diagnoses them all as ill because they are "like trees without . . . roots" (248), for they are people removed forcibly from their own home and traditions, their "roots." As a result, they have fallen, not into spiritual despair, but into "racial despair" (see Walcott "What" 21).

This explicitly anticolonial purpose is developed in relation to other Biblical images as well, most obviously that of "Moses" and the "blazing bush" invoked by Makak in his cure (248). Like Makak, Moses had no knowledge that he was to be called to ministry. But the "sons of Israel, groaning in their slavery, cried out for help" (Exodus 2:23), and so God appeared to Moses in the form of a burning bush and announced that he would "deliver" his people "out of the hands of the Egyptians and bring them out of that land to a land rich and broad, a land where milk and honey flow" (3:8). This is precisely the mission that Makak envisions himself undertaking, leading his fellow African people out of the land of the "slave drivers" (3:7) and to the promised land of Africa. Here Walcott is drawing on a long tradition of Afro-Christian religious belief, which repeatedly assimilated repatriation to the exodus from Egypt.

After the cure, Moustique takes up the standard role of the priestly caste and collects money. He labels himself both "Secretary-Treasurer" and "Saint Peter." This passage seems to turn from myth or religious/revelatory narrative to history. In referring to the "Secretary-Treasurer," Walcott is presumably referring to the general tendency of the priestly hierarchy to exploit ordinary people for their own monetary advantage—a point made repeatedly by Jesus. By referring to "Saint Peter," Walcott is probably referring in part to the historical development of the Catholic Church, which, as we have already noted, played an important role in the French colonial domination of St. Lucia. On the other hand, the most important aspect of this identification is probably more directly Biblical, referring to the social conformism purveyed by "Peter," the author of two canonical epistles. (Though attributed to Simon Peter, the apostle, the letters were almost certainly written by someone else; see Best 584–85 and Bauckham 586.) Peter's first epistle is one of the New Testament writings that veer most strikingly away from the subaltern interpretation of Jesus' message, and one of the writings most serviceable to colonialism. For example, Peter admonishes Christians in the following terms: "For the sake of the Lord, accept the authority of every social institution: the emperor, as the supreme authority, and the governors as commissioned by him. . . . God wants you to be good citizens" (2:13–15). Indeed, Peter's first letter seems to have been written by a New World slave holder: "Slaves must be respectful and obedient to their masters, not only when they are kind and gentle but also when they are unfair. . . . This, in fact, is what you were called to do, because Christ suffered for you and left an example for you to follow" (2:18, 21). In all these ways, Moustique's characterization as Secretary-Treasurer and Saint Peter serves to suggest the historical perversion of Jesus' teachings, a perversion that eventually allowed their use in defense of colonialism.

At the beginning of scene three, Lestrade enters. Having already been linked with Roman law, he is now linked with "Mosaic" law, and thereby with the Sadducees and chief priests. Appropriately, he is at the market with "Market and Sanitation Inspector Caiphas J. Pamphilion" (256). As noted above, Caiphas's role as market inspector alludes to the involvement of the chief priests with the changing of money and the selling of goods in the Temple. The addition of "sanitation inspector" is fitting as well, for one great obsession of strict Jews at the time was ritual purity, and one of the most common objections to Jesus was that he refused to follow the restrictions governing purity, but instead ate with those who were impure, such as prostitutes and tax collectors (see, for example, Matthew 9:10–11 and *Jerusalem* 29n.9e; on the impurity of tax collectors, see Salo 77). It was in response to this concern—in this case, among the Pharisees—that Jesus complained that they "clean the outside," while "inside" they "are filled with extortion and wickedness" (Luke 11:39). The high priest is, in this context, appropriately conceived of as a "sanitation inspector."

As these two men walk through the market, people are recounting Makak's miracle. One woman says that the dying man "could see hell" before he was saved—implying once again that Makak saved not only his body, but his spirit. But the political, revolutionary nature of this messiah is made clear quickly. Lestrade notes that they are "in a state of emergency" and Caiphas remarks on "the strikes and cane-burning taking place in the district" (260)—methods of resistance extending back to the period of slavery. Lestrade summarizes the situation: Makak "give them hope, miracle, vision, paradise on earth, and is then blood start to bleed and stone start to fly" (261). Perhaps the crucial part of Lestrade's summary is the statement that Makak gives the people "paradise *on earth.*" The colonizers and their intermediaries have no objections to promises of paradise *after death.* Indeed, the promise of eternal reward for earthly subservience can serve the rulers' ends quite well. The danger of this messiah is that he is speaking of justice, not in heaven, but here; not in eternity, but today.

The first part of the play ends with Moustique pretending to be Makak and trying to take on the role of messiah, even to the point of wondering if he should say, "I am the resurrection, I am the life" (271); the reference is to Jesus' statement to Martha and prefaces his miracle of raising Lazarus from the dead (see John 11:25). However, Moustique's concern is not resurrection, but gain. He is not a liberator, like Makak, but an opportunist. As he puts it at one point, "Daughter of heaven, Makak will remember you. But I prefer cash" (267). Later, he tells Makak, "I take the dream you have and I come and try to sell it" (273). Ultimately, he dies on the crossroads, and thus in a sense he dies upon a cross. Moreover, the crowd turns against him, much as it turned against Jesus (see Luke 23:13–23). However, several points make clear that he should not be identified with Jesus. Most importantly, perhaps, the crowd attacks him with sticks crying "Break his legs!" (271). This alludes to the practice of breaking the legs of the crucified in order to speed their death. The most famous case of this concerns Jesus and those with whom he was crucified. The Roman "soldiers came and broke the legs" of the men who were crucified with Jesus, but "when they came to Jesus, they found he was already dead" and did not break his legs (John 19:32, 33). The point is stressed as a fulfillment of "the words of scripture: *Not one bone of his will be broken*" (19:36). In this way, Moustique is opposed directly to the messiah and implicitly characterized as an ordinary zealot—in this case, a hypocritical and self-serving zealot, though one closely related to Makak/Jesus (perhaps like Peter).

The second part of the play begins with Lestrade bringing figs. Tigre and Souris demand their figs in the course of the scene, as Lestrade declares that "the law is a whore" (280). This declaration implicitly links Roman/Mosaic/English law, the law of the oppressor, with the prostitute of Revelation—a predictable link as she is in league with the beast (Revelation 17). The point of the metaphor is, of course, that the law is purchased by whoever has money, desire, and no scruples—thus the beast, which is to say, in this case, the colonial powers. The repeated references to figs seem to be based on the Biblical significance of figs, which emerges most strikingly in Jeremiah 24. There, Jeremiah has a vision of two baskets of figs—one good, the other inedible. Yahweh tells him, "As these figs are good, so I mean to concern myself with the welfare of the exiles of Judah. . . . My eyes will watch over them for their good, to bring them back to this land" (24:5–6). In the context of these biblical resonances, the prisoners' demands for their figs come to suggest demands for a broader justice and even for the realization of Makak's dream—a return to Africa, the end of exile, as symbolized by figs in the dream of Jeremiah.

In this scene, Makak takes on his role as Lion of Judah, but here in a more literally destructive way, for he kills Lestrade, calling out that he is a lion (285). This is in part drawn from Revelation—which is increasingly important in this part of the play—where the lion of Judah has now triumphed (5:5). But it is even more significantly a revision of the Last Supper. Here Walcott departs even from the revolutionary tradition of Christianity. It is central to the story of Jesus—even in the subaltern tradition—that Jesus offers himself as a blood sacrifice. Makak, however, offers someone else as the sacrifice: Lestrade. When Lestrade asks what Makak wants to drink, Makak answers "Blood!" (285). This recalls the institution of the Eucharist, where Jesus offers his own blood to be drunk by his apostles. However, at this point Makak proclaims himself, not the sacrificial lamb but the lion, and kills Lestrade. He then orders the others—"Drink it! Drink it! . . . I will drink blood. You will drink it with me" (286). In keeping with this transformation of the Last Supper, the crucifixion is altered also. Rather than Makak being crucified, he kills Lestrade with a knife, the blade of which is attached to "the crucifix of the handle" (284).

Though this represents a significant departure form the gospels, it is not entirely without precedent. The appearance of the knife at the "Last Supper" recalls Jesus' statement to his apostles, shortly after the supper, "if you have no sword, sell your cloak and buy one"—to which the apostles reply that they have two swords ready (Luke 22:36, 38). It also recalls Peter's attack upon the men sent by the high priest (John 18:10). However, if the parallel were exact, it would be Moustique, not Makak who drew his sword. This skewing of the parallel begins to suggest Makak's transformation in this part of the play, a transformation that will bring him closer to the zealots and the hypocrites despite his own more genuine impulses. This scene also recalls the prophetic precedent for the Last Supper found in Zechariah. We have already noted the relevance of Zechariah 9 to Walcott's play. In that chapter, Yahweh promises his people that due to the messiah, a victorious king "riding on a donkey" (9:9), "the hopeful captives will return" and will be compensated doubly for their "days of banishment" (9:12). It continues with a passage prophesying a Eucharist different from those in the Gospels. Specifically, Yahweh will lead his people to military triumph so great that "they will drink blood like wine, / they will be soaked in it" (9:15). This is precisely the sort of Eucharist instituted by Makak. But that does not mean it is positive. Quite the contrary, it is a Eucharist that, a reader might already fear, will be repeated continually in Makak's name, as Jesus adjured his apostles, "do this as a memorial of me" (Luke 22:19).

Following this section, the story returns to the biblical narrative, with Tigre and Souris straightforwardly linked to the thieves in Luke's gospel. Referring to Tigre and Souris, Makak says, "The Lord on the day he dead . . . had two thief by him." Souris completes the account, saying, "Only one went in heaven." Tigre indicates that he is the one who is condemned to hell: "I see myself burning there, forever and forever" (293). Subsequently, Tigre betrays Makak, but Souris refuses to go along with the betrayal, directly recalling the "good" zealot or thief crucified with Jesus. Souris proclaims, "I believe this old man," much as the good thief/zealot expresses his faith in Jesus (see Luke 23:43). Souris then explains his faith. As with the miraculous cure of Josephus, this is not a matter of supernatural belief, but of a directly political faith, faith in oneself: "I believe I am better than I am. He teach me that" (302); recall Makak's words to those around Josephus, "Faith, faith! Believe in yourselves" (249). As a spiritual messiah to Afro-Caribbeans, Makak ends his people's racial despair, and gives them a sense of their own worth and possibilities.

Just after the reference to the thieves, Makak calls for his crown. Souris *"twist[s] a vine and crown[s] him."* This is another alteration of the gospel, alluding first of all to the mockery to which Jesus was subjected by the Roman soldiers, particularly the fact that they "twisted some thorns into a crown" (John 19:2). However, for Souris, this is not mockery, even if it is not yet entirely an act of devotion. In keeping with this, Makak's crown is not a crown of thorns, but, again, a vine. In part, by making it a vine, Walcott steps outside Christian mythology and connects Makak with Dionysus. The point of this connection is presumably related to the Rastafarianism of the play. The Rastafarians' emphasis on the religious/cultural importance of marijuana associates them with the sort of intoxication represented by Dionysus, and thus makes the connection between Makak and Dionysus not only plausible, but resonant, in an Afro-Caribbean context. Indeed, Makak himself advises his followers to smoke marijuana, saying, "Here, look, you see this plant? Dry it, fire it, and your mind will cloud with a sweet, sweet-smelling smoke. Then the smoke will clear. You will not need to eat" (288). In response, Tigre calls him, "You crazy ganga-eating bastard" (289). On the other hand, Jesus himself is directly associated with vines in very positive ways as well. The institution of the Eucharist makes wine, the drink of Dionysus, a central part of Christian ritual commemorating Jesus. Moreover, the imagery of vineyards is common in Jesus' teachings. Indeed, in some instances, God's people themselves are represented by a vineyard (see, for example, *Jerusalem* note g at Matthew 21:33), making the vine a particularly apt crown for a messiah whose task is to lead the chosen people out of bondage and return them to the land of their roots. In short, Walcott's image here too has many relevant biblical associations.

Shortly after this, Lestrade begins to link the moon, and thereby the apparition, not with the Blessed Virgin, but with the Prostitute of Revelation: "the pock-marked moon . . . the siphylitic crone" (296). The link is not unprepared for. He had earlier identified her with "rage for whiteness" (228), and thus with the very racial despair against which Makak preaches. But the later statement marks the beginning of a more systematic degradation of this figure. It also shortly precedes Lestrade's own conversion and acceptance of Makak. As already noted, this conversion is reminiscent of Paul. Paul, then named Saul, had been persecuting Christians (see Acts 9:14). But, on the road to arrest Christians in Damascus, he was struck to the ground by a blinding light and addressed by Jesus (Acts 9). Lestrade is physically overwhelmed, in a similar way, when in pursuit of Makak and his followers in order to arrest them. There is the apparent difference that Lestrade finds himself in "darkness" (300). But, first, Saul was blinded by the light—thus he too experienced darkness. Second, and more importantly, the conversion of Lestrade is a conversion to the acceptance of blackness, a conversion that repudiates the identification of that which is good with that which is white—which is to say, European—and this leads to a reversal of the imagery. Finally, this is hardly a benevolent conversion, hardly genuine enlightenment, anyway.

Paul's conversion may be said to mark the beginning of the vast expansion of Christianity that was eventually to have such deleterious effects on African culture. As Gerald Hawthorne notes, Paul was a Pharisee, and he carried his Pharisaism over into his Christianity (Hawthorne in Metzger and Coogan 576). Perhaps in keeping with this, Lestrade becomes a reactionary traditionalist and opportunist in Makak's postrevolutionary government—pharisaical characteristics, as we have already noted. On the other hand, Paul was one of the strongest advocates of converting the gentiles, and one of the most active missionaries to the gentiles, as well as a tireless worker for Jewish/gentile cooperation (see Hawthorne in Metzger and Coogan 577). Thus the xenophobia exhibited by Lestrade, which may be seen as Pharisaical, seems very un-Pauline.

This leads us to the ending of the play, which is somewhat difficult to interpret. One thing at least does seem clear: Makak's career diverges increasingly from that of Jesus. It is as if Jesus' life were rewritten as the story of a triumphant zealot. But the purpose of this revision is not to praise zealotry. Rather, it seems, the purpose is precisely the opposite—to expose the dangers of zealotry, primarily using imagery drawn from Revelation. Clearly, Walcott sympathizes with Makak's dream of ending racial despair, and clearly he does not share the elite disdain for Makak's dream of repatriation, of bearing his African brothers and sisters back across the water to their home. But he does seem to see this dream as almost invariably leading to violence and cruelty, to actions that are far from the teachings of Jesus, but all too similar to the actions of colonialist Christians—their mirror image, in fact.

In any event, there is a change in Makak right after Lestrade's conversion, perhaps as there was a change in the early church after Paul's conversion. Makak begins to sound more like the vengeful God of the Old Testament, and he cries out "I have brought a dream to my people, and they rejected me. Now they must be taught, even tortured, killed. Their skulls will hang from my palaces. I will break up their tribes" (301). In connection with this, Makak himself comes to refer to the historical development of Christianity, and its use by Europeans in justifying and stabilizing colonialism: "I an old man . . . beaten down by a Bible, and tired of looking up to heaven" (304). It is as if, having manifested Jesus, having acted as the messiah to this point, Makak now repudiates Jesus. This can be understood in two ways. It may mean that Makak repudiates Jesus because of the use to which Jesus was put by colonialism. Or it may mean that Makak's repudiation of Jesus is itself a sort of unconscious or allegorical recapitulation of Christianity's own effective repudiation of Jesus in its early days, after Paul's conversion.

Either way, the result of this, a sort of shift from Jesus to full-fledged zealotry and ideological Pharisaism, is far from beneficial. After Makak talks of divine vengeance, echoing any number of passages in the Old Testament, he then prophesies mutual destruction of the tribes—not the tribes of Israel, but those of Africa: "The tribes! The tribes will wrangle among themselves, spitting, writhing, hissing, like snakes in a pit . . . devouring their own entrails like the hyena, eaten with self-hatred" (305). The passage recalls the universal violence spoken of in Revelation on the breaking of the second seal: "out came another horse, bright red, and its rider was given this duty: to take away peace from the earth and set people killing each other" (6:4). Moreover, the image of snakes recalls the snakebite from which Josephus suffered. As we have seen, in that case, the snake represented a primal Fall that was not other-worldly, but was, instead, very historical—the loss of Africa. Again, the cure, the salvation brought by the messiah, Makak, was belief in oneself, the ending of racial despair. But here Walcott, through Makak, envisions a very different result of broad revolutionary triumph and return to Africa—not the curing of racial despair, not the curing of the snake bite, but the intensification of "self-hatred" and the consequent transformation of the entire society into a society of snakes, continually biting one another, continually repeating and extending the Fall. For the loss that characterizes the Afro-Caribbean condition is ultimately not one of land, not a mere displacement from Edenic Africa, but one of hope and vision and a sense of self-worth and possibility.

I should perhaps note that I do not entirely agree with Walcott on this point. In my view, what is called "self-hatred" is most often a matter of hating members of your own group, not yourself, or of assuming that other people hate you because of your membership in that group, and seeing no way of escaping that hatred. The difference is significant.

In any case, it is right after this that Lestrade proclaims himself "Bastard, hatchet-man, opportunist, executioner" (307) and sets about establishing Makak as demagogue and Roman emperor. He says that this is demanded by "the people, Vox Populi" (307), the use of Latin functioning to indicate that "Jesus"/Makak has been transformed from an anticolonial figure into another version of colonial authority—much as occurred in the history of Christianity itself, and much as occurred with other revolutionary figures and ideas in the history of Africa and other colonies.

This ends the second scene. The third scene is marked "Apotheosis" (308)—ironically, for here Makak does not rise into heaven, following out the story of Jesus. Rather, he rises to imperial rule, to a genuinely blasphemous pretense of divinity—not the "blasphemy" with which he was charged earlier in calling for the "destruction" of "Church and State" (224, 225), but a true blasphemy that strengthens those oppressive institutions. From here, the parallel between Makak and Jesus is extended, but now in every case it is simultaneously inverted. Most obviously, Jesus was condemned to death by imperial power, and when interrogated about his kingship said, "Mine is not a kingdom of this world" (John 18:36). In contrast, Makak becomes the imperial power, with a very worldly kingdom. While Jesus preached, "Do unto others as you would have them do unto you" (Luke 6:31), Makak becomes the one "Who shall do unto others as to him it was done" (310). Whereas Jesus became truly God through death and resurrection, Makak finds himself now "only a shadow. . . . A hollow God" (311). While Jesus achieved life through death, Makak finds only death in life. This is, again, parallel to the Christian church after Jesus. In Walcott's representation, the Christian church in effect obliterated Jesus' teachings, making him a "hollow God," and the revolutionary zealots of our own day perform the same violence against any genuine message of Afro-Caribbean salvation—which, again, works not against spiritual despair, as in Christianity, but against the closely related racial despair.

Indeed, Lestrade explains the implication of this new regime directly. One could say that, through the resurrection, the biblical account presents Jesus—champion of the miserable, the colonized, the unorthodox—as apotheosized. In contrast, in this scenario, the scenario of both the institutional Christian church after Jesus and of the postrevolutionary society, we see, not Jesus, but the corrupt high priest elevated: "Behold [Caiphas] Pamphilion, apotheosised" (310). Of course, this is apotheosis with a twist. The new rulers are no longer overt collaborationists. Rather, they have entirely reversed their position, repudiating their former mimeticism, substituting a reactionary form of traditionalism—a transformation most thoroughly developed in the case of Lestrade. The violence and racialism that standardly characterize reactionary traditionalism are worked out through the condemnations of all White people, and all people of partially European ancestry (312)—though evidently Lestrade has managed to exempt himself, hypocritically, from this judgment.

Here the imagery of the Last Supper recurs, but again altered, turned upside-down. First, there is the trial of Moustique, who has "betrayed our dream." He is clearly linked with Judas here. But, unlike Judas, he does not turn the messiah over to Caiaphas. Rather, he is condemned by the Messiah and turned over to Caiaphas/Caiphas and Pilate/Herod/Lestrade. Indeed, he is led in to Makak *bleeding and broken* (314), recalling Jesus when he is brought before Pilate, the chief priests, and the guards, and condemned to death, after being scourged and crowned with thorns (John 19:1–6). In keeping with this inversion, while Judas may have been a zealot disillusioned with

Jesus' refusal to lead an armed rebellion, Moustique/Judas here is the one who calls for "love" rather than "Power" (314), speaks out against "All this blood, all this killing" (315), explaining that, though Makak believes himself to be free of colonial domination, he is "more of an ape now, a puppet" (315)—an accurate statement about the neocolonialism of many postrevolutionary governments.

This may seem to contradict Moustique's earlier characterization as self-serving and his association with the Catholic Church. But in fact it fits the latter perfectly. For in recent decades, ordinary clergy in the Catholic Church have been active in opposing the oppression of common people. As the example of Latin America shows, the Catholic Church—as represented by parish priests and by nuns—may be a significant force against brutality. Moreover, many of these ordinary priests and nuns have shown great bravery, even accepting martyrdom in order to speak against dictatorship. In this way, Moustique's alterations in behavior are fully in keeping with those of the church itself.

This shift in Moustique's character may also relate to his representation as Peter, author of the epistles. If his earlier appearance as secretary treasurer corresponded to Peter's first epistle, with its development of Christianity into a tool for colonialism, this appearance may be linked with Peter's second epistle. It should be clear that, in relation to the subaltern interpretation of Jesus, Peter's first letter and the more general colonialist use of Christianity constitute a betrayal of Jesus fully comparable to that of Judas. Thus having a figure who is ambiguously Judas and Peter makes sense in that context. And, again, according to Cullmann, both Judas and Peter the Apostle were zealots. In any case, Peter's second letter is addressed to the issue of the Second Coming and thus is in keeping with the apocalyptic concerns of this section of the play. Moreover, it is written shortly before Peter's death, and thus fits with the impending doom of Moustique. Peter announces his vision of the Second Coming, experienced when he was "with [Jesus] on the holy mountain" (1:18)—a link to Moustique's time on Monkey Mountain with Makak, and to their ascent up Monkey Mountain at the end of the play. In this letter, Peter denounces the "false prophets . . . who will insinuate their own disruptive views . . . with insidious speeches" (2:1, 3)—just what Moustique suggests regarding Makak's advisors, especially Lestrade: "Look around you, old man, and see who betray what" (314). Speaking of these advisors, he asks, "can you trust them for true?" (315). Moreover, in keeping with Moustique's accusation that Makak is "more of an ape now, a puppet" (315), Peter says that these false prophets "may promise freedom but they themselves are slaves"—slaves who are "in a worse state than [when they] began" (2:19–20). Peter particularly denounces the false prophets for their offenses against angels (2:10–11). This point is recalled by Moustique's statement, "Once you loved the moon, now a night will come when, because it white, from your deep hatred you will want it destroyed" (315) and by the subsequent execution of the apparition, who has been characterized in angelic imagery from the beginning of the play. This execution is demanded precisely by Lestrade (318–19).

In any case, in keeping with the inverse parallel to Judas, rather than fleeing from the last supper, turning Jesus in, and hanging himself, Moustique is ordered away to his execution by Makak/Jesus. As in the gospels, this departure of Judas/Moustique leads to Jesus' agony. Makak prays, "Why have you caused me all this pain? Why are you silent? Why did you choose me?" In doing this, he echoes Jesus' prayers in Gethsemane. But, here too, there is an important change. While Jesus suffers agony over the prospect of his own death, Makak is considering the murder of the apparition, the White woman. Indeed, in this scene, Makak is more similar to Pilate than to Jesus. Just as Jesus is silent in the face of Pilate's questions, it is the apparition who is silent in the face of Makak's questions. When Lestrade calls out to Makak, "Kill her! Kill her!" it recalls the response of the chief priests to Pilate's offer that he would release Jesus: "Crucify him! Crucify him!" (23:21).

At this point, Makak takes the sword, much as Peter takes the sword in the Garden of Gethsemane, and kills the woman—the precise opposite of Jesus, who forbids his followers to use their swords against those who have come to arrest him and who, in Matthew, chastises Peter, saying "all who draw the sword will die by the sword" (26:52).

But the result of this is strange, and evidently beneficial.[4] After the murder, Makak calls out "Now, O God, now I am free" (320). This ends the scene, and in the immediately following epilogue, Makak announces his name, Felix Hobain, alluding to the felix culpa, as we have already discussed. At first, this might seem to indicate that the violence was in fact necessary or valuable in ending racial despair, that the way of Jesus—even the way of Jesus as represented in subaltern traditions of interpretation—is not the way to overcome racial despair. Rather, such despair is overcome by the apotheosis of Caiaphas.

But this seems highly implausible on the surface. Moreover, when Makak repeats his name, he announces "I believe in my God. I have never killed a fly" (322). In other words, far from the apocalyptic slaughter that ended the dream, Makak's new self-understanding is based on a form of nonviolence that goes beyond that advocated by Jesus. Indeed, it is precisely this nonviolence that is accompanied by Makak's final refusal of the "white mask" that had come to represent his racial despair and self-hate (see 324), and by his discovery of rootedness, his feeling that he is no longer homeless, a man without a proper place in the world, without identity, but has "found ground." Indeed, Makak's refusal of the mask, thus of mimeticism and racial despair, and his finding of ground or a sense of positive identity, are a sort of resurrection. It is clearly not by chance that this takes place on "Sunday morning" (324), the day on which Jesus rose from the dead. Makak has now passed through death and entered the New Jerusalem of Revelation.

The play concludes with Makak announcing that he is "going back home, back to the beginning, to the green beginning of this world" (326). But now, it seems that this return to Eden is no longer a return to Africa. Rather, this return to his "father's kingdom" is spiritual, not physical (as Breslin has noted [155]). In other words, Makak seems to have shifted away from zealotry to a spirituality based on Jesus' message. He is now going to ascend his mountain and seek spiritual salvation, rather than revolution. Perhaps he is following Jesus' advice at the Last Supper, advice addressed to the apostles' own colonial situation: "When you see Jerusalem surrounded by armies, you must realise that she will soon be laid desolate. Then those in Judaea must escape to the mountains" (Luke 21:20–21). Lestrade says, "Our life is a prison" (325). Perhaps Makak's way of escaping that prison is no longer a matter of killing the jailer, but of spiritual retreat. Moreover, this talk of ascension following the imagery of the resurrection on Sunday morning fits well with the story of Jesus, who, after his resurrection, announced "I am ascending to my Father" (John 20:17).

It may be, then, that the violence of the dream serves as a lesson to Makak, and to the reader, that one should indeed imitate Jesus, that one should follow the teachings of Jesus. These teachings should be understood in their radical and anticolonial sense, but, at the same time, one must be careful not to confuse Jesus with the zealots, for their practices will lead only to a worse bondage, an apotheosis of Caiaphas. Perhaps the dream, and the messianic zealotry on which it is based, are like the "lying prophecies" denounced by Jeremiah, who explains that false prophets proclaim "I have had a dream" and "announce their private delusions as prophetic" (23:25–26). Perhaps what Makak has learned is that his dream is not prophetic, but a delusion—which itself then becomes a sort of prophecy, by turning us away from the wrong path.

Yet, if this is so, the alternative offered by Walcott at the end of the play seems only slightly less bleak than the vision presented in the dream. What can Makak hope to achieve by returning to his mountain? Perhaps he can live his miserable life with a sense of hope in divine salvation. Perhaps that will make his crushing poverty more bearable. But isn't that just the *colonial* function of Christianity? It seems by the end of the play that there are only two options for poor Afro-Caribbean people, at least with respect to Christianity. One option is to invoke Jesus as a messianic leader in the struggle for political change—which, if successful, will lead from one high priesthood to another, both oppressive. The second option is to withdraw from the struggle, ascend the mountain, and live whatever life one can eke out, remembering Jesus' love of the poor. Liberation theology and similar movements suggest that these are not the only possibilities. If they are, the prospects for a specifically Christian politics among the oppressed seem grim.

In any case, whatever one thinks of Walcott's reflections on Afro-Caribbean politics, and however one interprets the conclusion of this very dense and difficult play, it is clear that Walcott has drawn on the story of Jesus—and particularly on subaltern traditions of interpreting and developing that story—in order to think through those politics, and to give them literary shape. Moreover, he has done this in such a way as to suggest a different mapping of cognitive domains from that which dominates colonial ideology. He has shifted the order of the mapping, so that the divine and salvational figure is projected onto the African, making him Jesus, not Satan. At the same time, he has done this in such a way as to avoid an idealizing simplification. He has undertaken this mapping of domains, but he has not given us a mere counter-ideology, a simplified and implausible image of pure and angelic Blacks to serve as a mirror image of the colonialists' simplified and implausible picture of demonic Blacks. That is one reason why the complexity of the ending is necessary—it is part of the play's rejection of the "white mask," the structure of ideas and alternatives established by European colonialism and White racism, a structure that necessarily operates on the basis of simplistic identification across domains. Put differently, Walcott initially reverses the cognitive mapping of race onto metropolitan myth, and he does so by drawing on subaltern traditions of that myth. But, by the end of the play, he has not only reversed this mapping, he has passed beyond this reversal to suggest the limitations of any projection from the mythic onto the human. He has, in this way, repudiated—or at least vastly complicated—the entire colonialist project of understanding the domain of race via the domain of religion.

Chapter Four

Preserving the Voice of Ancestors

Yoruba Myth and Ritual in *The Palm-Wine Drinkard*

As we saw in the case of Tagore, indigenous religion and myth can operate in much the same way as metropolitan religion and myth. For while Tagore was writing back to a single indigenous work, he was simultaneously writing back to a work of singular religious and mythic importance. Clearly, he saw this work as perniciously hierarchy preserving and he set about writing back to it for that reason.

On the other hand, there are some very important differences between metropolitan and indigenous religion and myth. While both have oppressive and subaltern strains, one religion is itself in a position of cultural domination over the other. Hindu, Igbo, Yoruba, and other systems of belief indigenous to the colonized world are continually endangered by Christianity. As discussed in the preceding chapter, Christians have widely maintained that their views are morally and ontologically superior, and have proselytized in those terms. Moreover, they have the economic and political power to undermine indigenous religions, directly or indirectly—as when European employers effectively required their domestic servants to attend Christian services, be married in a Christian church, and so forth (see Emecheta 50). Thus there is a strong tendency for indigenous religions to be eroded by the influx of Christian teaching and conversion. In contrast, there is no risk in the opposite direction. While there might be an occasional European who "goes native" and is accepted into Yoruba, Igbo, or Hindu society, the number of these "reverse converts" is minuscule—and clearly no threat to the colonial religion.

The risk to indigenous bodies of faith is particularly great when the beliefs, stories, practices, and so on, are not codified in sacred texts, and when they are highly localized. For a number of reasons, a religion such as Islam or Hinduism is far more stable than, say, Igbo or Yoruba custom. First of all, Islam and Hinduism cover broad geographical areas, which makes their practices transportable. More importantly, their central tenets are recorded in sacred texts, which makes them enduring. In contrast, Igbo or Yoruba practices are very difficult to preserve when one is living away from Igboland or Yorubaland. Whereas a Hindu could go anywhere in India and find temples, festivals, and the like, and thus preserve his/her faith, an Igbo could not travel even to Lagos and expect to find his/her traditions preserved. More significantly, without a set of sacred texts, every loss to such a religion threatens to be both permanent and absolute. If a ritual is practiced only in one set of villages in Igboland, and is not preserved in any texts, then if that ritual is not practiced for a single generation, it will die.

In this way, a postcolonization author from an oral tradition is likely to be faced with a dilemma very different from that facing an author from a written tradition. Far from having to assert his/her individual voice in response to powerful precursors, he/she may be confronted with the possible loss of the entire indigenous tradition in which his/her own work would be located. In this way, one prime task of a postcolonization author may be the preservation of indigenous tradition.

Of course, the author cannot merely present that tradition as it is. Indeed, that does not even make any sense. A tradition is a wide range of practices, stories, ideas, organized and articulated in different ways, at different times, with different relations depending upon context and immediate purpose. The author who sets him/herself the task of preserving this tradition has to refashion some part of it, shape elements of tradition into a literary work—just as the living tradition is itself always refashioned, for particular purposes and for a particular audience at a particular time. In this case, the author must structure tradition into a work that can be read on its own, and read by a general and unfamiliar readership—not a present audience, with shared experience and memory. In this way, the author is not merely preserving tradition, as if he/she were an anthropologist. Rather he/she is sculpting it into a coherent work of art, oriented to a new readership. The new author cannot simply set up a microphone and record an oral performance, delivered by a poet to a familiar audience, all of whom are living within that tradition of culture and orature. The nature of the postcolonization writer's task is such that he/she cannot presuppose a privileged reader, a reader who is living in the tradition. Consider Tutuola. Even his own children or grandchildren are unlikely to know Yoruba beliefs, stories, and customs in the way he knows them. Indeed, this is part of what motivates his project to begin with.

On the other hand, this is not to say that an author cannot seek to preserve something of the experience one has when one is part of a living, familiar tradition. To reshape the tradition into an autonomous work is not to museumize it. That too is the anthropological tendency—taking up something within the culture, removing it to a strange building in a foreign land, and placing it in a glass case. Reshaping tradition with a sense of readership and medium does not mean forgetting or repressing the contextual specificity and human animation of that tradition as it was practiced. It means orienting these qualities in a way that fits the medium and is comprehensible to the reader.

This is precisely what Tutuola has done in *The Palm-Wine Drinkard*. As Quayson has noted: "For Tutuola, all the vague stories about spirit-figures encountered by hunters in the bush acquired a strange intensity precisely because they were at threat of being lost to the conceptual force of Christianity. To what extent he saw this as a danger for the whole culture it is futile to speculate, but he has been quoted as saying that 'it seemed necessary to write down the tales of my country since they will soon all be forgotten'" (61). I should perhaps note that I see nothing vague about Yoruba tales, and believe that the triumph of Christianity has more to do with its economic and political force than with anything conceptual. But the sense of threat and preservation is the same in either case—or, rather, the sense of threat and preservative recreation. For, again, what Tutuola does is more than record, "write down the tales." He refashions them into new, literary wholes.

SHAPING THE BREATH OF TRADITION

In the following pages, I will focus on the content of Tutuola's novel, the way in which the story manifests and synthesizes central motifs from traditional Yoruba religion and myth; the way it preserves not only a few tales, but, more importantly, main characters and themes, central religious ideas and practices from a disappearing culture; the way it forms these traditional elements into a whole that gives them fullness and coherence. But before going on to this, it is worth remarking briefly on Tutuola's manner of presenting this material. As is well known, Tutuola wrote his works in a form of Nigerian English—indeed, in a form of English that is filled with "errors" and neologisms derived directly from the Yoruba language (see Zabus 113–18). This serves the same literary function as the similar use of Hiberno-English by James Stephens, Lady Gregory, and others, the use of Caribbean English by Louise Bennett, and so on. It gives the reader a fuller sense of the oral elements of the work, probably through the indirect sensory experience produced by subvocalization (the reader's internal pronunciation of the text). Zabus points out that Tutuola's language is not simply an indigenous form of English, but involves many apparently inadvertent fusions of Yoruba and English. In this way, it is less "indigenous" English than "indigenized" English, English refashioned through Yoruba spontaneously, by the individual speaker, at the time of speaking. It is not, in other words, a stable form of English regularized by a community, as in the case of Hiberno-English or the various Caribbean Englishes. However, the same general point still holds; there is still an oral preservative function here, a continuity of the new work with the oral tradition—for, in this case, the oral tradition would be in Yoruba, not in an indigenous form of English, and thus "indigenized" English is the most appropriate medium, once the author has chosen not to write in Yoruba. (In fact, the same point applies to some of the Irish material.)

The other feature of Tutuola's writing that readers often remark upon is his use of repetition and capitalization. This appears to serve much the same function as his indigenization of English. Indeed, it is in some ways part of that indigenization. Zabus notes that the "repetition of words, phrases or even whole sentences is an incantatory device used in traditional Yoruba narrative" (119). Tutuola's use of this and related techniques is, in effect, a further shaping of an oral context into a written text—or a further shaping of that text in such a way as to preserve and communicate the oral mode and situation of telling. These techniques extend the imagination of the scene from one in which the narrator is speaking aloud—in an indigenous language, represented through indigenized English—to one in which the narrator is speaking aloud *to an audience.* For example, the written repetitions and capitalizations can be understood as spoken emphases used by a teller interacting with the audience: "we did not know other money, except COWRIES" (7); "When I reached his (Death's) house, he was not at home. . . . But when he (Death) heard the sound of the drum . . ." (12). As Walter Ong explains, oral tellings are never simply verbal, but "always modifications of a total, existential situation, which always engages the body" (*Orality* 67). More specifically, Mack et al. note that "movement and gesture, with which the narrator dramatizes action or provides a visual delineation of character" are "crucial factors" in the "direct relationship" of the oral poet with his or her audience (2337; see also Chinweizu, Jemie, and Madubuike 80). Such physical activity cannot be represented directly in writing. However, it may be suggested, and that is what Tutuola does with repetition and capitalization. In the case just cited, it is easy to envision a teller turning from one audience member to another, saying first "his," then "Death's," with some comic or ominous change of tone, or shaking a pouch of shells as he shouts "COWRIES."

To an unusual degree, then, Tutuola's work in effect preserves elements from the form of Yoruba oral storytelling, as well as the content. This is appropriate to Tutuola's larger task for reasons beyond the simple mimetic one of representing or recalling an oral context. One main purpose of preserving an oral mythology is to memorialize the intimacy of a group, the feeling of common experience that gives people a sense of shared, communal identity. The cultural function of orature is not solely a matter of its religious or other teachings. It is a more formal matter as well. It is a matter of "achieving close, empathetic, communal identification," as Walter Ong puts it (*Orality* 45). Indeed, this is true not only for the group present at a particular telling. The communal nature of traditional myth extends identification across tellings. It intimates that other people of own's own generation have heard or will be hearing the same stories, that these same stories were shared also by one's parents, and by earlier generations still, and will continue through generations that follow. As Richard Delgado puts it, writing about the relation between law and narrative, "stories build consensus, a common culture of shared understandings, and deeper, more vital ethics" (2414). Whatever those stories might be, part of their significance is merely that they have been heard by all the members of the community. Like the reminiscences of an old couple, such stories bind people together with threads of memory. To recount them in a way that mimics a communal gathering is, thus, relevant beyond any mere issue of their actual oral form, for it foregrounds this communality.

MYTH AND IDENTITY

As we noted briefly in the introduction (and will discuss more fully in the next chapter), the sense of cultural identity is largely a matter of categorial attribution. Directly or indirectly, I am told that I am European or Irish or American. This is not something that I learn about myself through introspection, through looking in a mirror, or through any other means of self-investigation. Indeed, the social malleability of identity is almost absolute. For example, as one famous study demonstrated, people will tend to form themselves into in- and out-groups—complete with ideological and behavioral preferences for other in-group members—simply on the basis of such trivialities as whether their social security number is odd or even (see Hirschfeld 1, 23; for a fuller discussion, see Tajfel.)

But such categorial identities cannot be sustained in the face of all circumstances. We might distinguish categorial identities from *situational identifications*, identifications among people in concrete situations of action or communication, contexts of work, play, or conversation. Part of this second sort of identification is a matter of agreement, whether on issues of deep communal conviction or on highly idiosyncratic matters. We find ourselves drawn to people who share our deepest beliefs and commitments about, say, politics or religion; but we also find ourselves drawn to people who share our private and trivial preferences, for an unusual food, odd card game, or obscure type of music. These obvious points of contact are, however, mere surface manifestations of a broader determinant. Our sense of situational identity is, fundamentally, a sense of shared presuppositions, both conceptual and practical, both in speech and in action. Our sense of intimacy results, most importantly, from what does not need to be spoken, especially from an unexpected breadth or depth of unspoken understanding. Conversely, estrangement results from the need to unpack presuppositions, to explain oneself, to render expectations explicit. We feel alienated when we expect someone to behave in a certain way, and he/she does not. We feel that a barrier is thrown up between ourselves and someone else when we need to explain what we meant or how our reasoning led to particular conclusions, when we need to fill in information or inferential assumptions which we had, unreflectively, assumed to be shared.

Ted Cohen put the point nicely in talking about jokes and metaphors. Esoteric jokes produce a feeling of intimacy with those who get the joke. Estrangement intrudes when we need to spell out the humor. What Cohen says about jokes and metaphors is generalizable to all of speech: a "sense of close community" results from "the awareness that not everyone" could make a certain joke and not everyone could understand it, that a certain statement or action may be "inaccessible to all but those who share" specific "information," and tacitly know that they share it (9). In his influential essay "The Writer's Audience Is Always a Fiction," Walter Ong makes a similar point about certain literary styles. They forego introducing the unknown, but act as if the characters, scenes, events, are already shared, familiar to writer and reader. He cites the opening of Ernest Hemingway's *A Farewell to Arms:* "In the late summer of that year." "What year?" Ong asks; "The reader gathers that there is no need to say." Because the author presupposes "shared" experience, he counts on "sympathy" (63). Of course, in this case it is a sort of deceit, a sleight of hand in which shared experience is supposed even though it is not there. But this can only work in such literary illusions because it is so common in reality, because situational identification is founded, in actual experience, on genuinely shared presuppositions—semantic or experiential.

In "The Myth of Myth: Dialogue with the Unspoken," Ong notes that all "expression has about it an obliquity, an indirection," and every explicit statement "carries with it something it is not, an implicit" (135). Ong refers to this implicit as "myth," the "nonexplicit complement accompanying any body of expression. . . . Myth in this sense is that which fills in the voids" between utterances and acts (133). Here, Ong is using "myth" in an expanded sense, the sense in which we speak of "the myth of democracy" or "the myth of America." But the point applies perhaps with particular force to myth in the narrow sense of divine and demonic narratives, especially those narratives that people accept as connecting them with something sacred. Myth, in this narrow sense, fills many of the empty spaces in a person's words and actions within his/her culture. Consider the degree to which such Christian ideas as the Fall, incarnation, salvation, and resurrection—even such specific doctrines as the Immaculate Conception—shape the discourse of people in a predominantly Christian society. They operate as literal beliefs, explicit metaphors, implicit analogies, and so on. As this suggests, myth often has a significant, shaping influence on the way we think and speak—even (perhaps especially) when not explicitly invoked. Moreover, it is often critical to our sense of fellowship—especially cultural fellowship, what is most obviously at stake in a colonial context.

These points can be put with greater precision in terms of lexical structure. Any utterance or action draws on entries in the speaker's lexicon. These entries include elements of various degrees of commonality and idiosyncracy. On the one hand, entries necessarily overlap to some degree from one speaker to another—otherwise communication would not be possible. On the other hand, entries are composed of schemas, prototypes, and exempla that form complexes almost necessarily unique to each particular speaker. Moreover, the commonality is a matter not only of all speakers of the language, but of subgroups defined by class, profession, region, and so on. Take the word "blue." My entry will share the basic color and mood meanings with virtually all English speakers. However, it also includes rarer connections, common only within smaller groups—for example, connections with Monet, Picasso, William Gass's *On Being Blue*, and passages in Collette. It also includes personal memories that are shared only by members of my family, or perhaps by no one. Or consider "idealism." My lexicon includes a distinction between a common meaning—"committed to ideals"—as well as various philosophical uses, such as "viewing ideas as having an autonomous history, independent of material conditions," "viewing ideas as more real or causally determinative than material conditions," and so on. These different elements in my entry for "idealism" are marked for situational use in speech or interpretation. In one situation, I hear "Jones is an idealist" and assume he/she is committed to ideals; in another situation, I hear the same sentence, but assume that he/she holds certain philosophical views.

In any given conversation, I automatically set my lexical access at a certain level. I tacitly presuppose certain commonalities with my interlocutor. Put differently, I presuppose a certain level of lexical overlap. This results in my unselfconscious reliance on particular sorts of implicitness in that conversation. I use certain lexical items, relying on a particular level of lexical content. Most often, this is a very general level, with "blue" standing simply for the color or mood. In other cases, it is a more idiosyncratic level, perhaps one involving specific personal memories of blue. Thus, when I refer to something as "cobalt blue," I may simply be reporting a color, or I may be alluding to a shared memory. Situational identification, and the correlated feeling of intimacy, are fostered by a recognition of lexical overlap beyond what one anticipated. Conversely, estrangement is fostered by a recognition of nonoverlap beyond the initial set point.

Levels of expected overlap are fixed by reference to specific information about addressees (e.g., memories regarding friends) and by group categories (e.g., professions). Thus we assume that people in, say, medicine will know certain things (e.g., medical terms), but not other things (e.g., terms from narratology). Our lexical entry for each individual and each group presumably marks some default or standard level of lexical overlap that guides our expectations in their regard.

This has obvious bearing on ethnic groups and myth. One of the most important things shared by an ethnic group is, precisely, myth—sacred stories that give structure and purpose to matters that are obscure but deeply important in human life: death, evil, pain. Thus myth is one of the most important elements of lexical structure for a sense of ethnic identification in that it may serve to define a distinctive level of expected lexical overlap. This is an obvious reason for preserving a body of myth told by one's ancestors. It can help to maintain (or perhaps even restore) the sense of exclusive intimacy that ties together members of an ethnic group, a sense of intimacy often lost under colonial rule (and often replaced by a defensive assertion of shared identity in reactionary traditionalism).

Yet that is not Tutuola's project. After all, for he is retelling the tales in English, and he submitted them initially to the Lutheran World Press (Thelwell xiv). Tutuola seems to explain his project in ethnic terms (qtd. in Thelwell xiv):

> What was in my mind? Oh . . . the time I wrote it, what was in my mind was that I noticed that our young men, our young sons and daughters did not pay much attention to our traditional things or culture or customs. They adopted, they concentrated their minds only on European things. They left our customs, so if I do this they may change their mind. . . . To remember our custom, not to leave it to die. . . . That was my intention.

But what he does is not, in fact, ethnically centered at all. He certainly wishes to preserve Yoruba culture and customs, not let them die. But he does not seem to have confined his concern to Yoruba people. He seems to have sought, entirely self-consciously, to have Europeans concentrate their minds on Yoruba things, just as Yorubas were concentrating their minds on European things.

The idea seems odd due to our deep habit of identifying culture with ethnicity and ethnicity with some sort of biological ancestry. As Walter Benn Michaels has argued, Americans at least have developed a form of "racial pluralism" according to which cultures are, in effect, racially grounded. Certain people do "Jewish things," express and act on loyalty to "Jewish culture," because they "are" racially Jewish. The same holds for Navajos or Irish or anyone else (see 137–42). But, Michaels stresses, this racial pluralism makes sense only if we accept some sort of racial identity that is distinguishable from cultural choice and serves as its justification. In any case, it is only because of our tendency to think in this way, to adopt racial pluralism, that Tutuola's actions appear odd. For Tutuola's project, however he might describe it, is not racialist in the sense discussed and criticized by Michaels.

More exactly, Tutuola is as concerned to alter the lexical structures of Europeans as he is to alter those of Yorubas. He is not setting out to give Yoruba people a sense of ethnic identity, but rather to extend the intimacy consequent upon shared myth to Yoruba and non-Yoruba alike. He is setting out to integrate Yoruba stories into the unspoken presumptions of literary Europeans as well as literary Yorubas and other Africans. In this sense, his project is precisely the opposite of securing ethnic identity. Ethnic identity fosters intimacy among "us" by opposition to "them." "We" share something noteworthy precisely insofar as "they" don't share it. Conversely, the shared myth of one culture is typically an element of indirection, of presupposition, alien to another culture; what produces the particular intimacy within one group impedes communication and cooperation between two groups, and thus fosters mutual estrangement. Tutuola sets out to preserve a set of myths for their ethnic community of origin, certainly. But, simultaneously, he seeks to carry those myths—along with their underlying conceptual, ethical, and metaphysical systems of belief and imagination—over the border into the opposed community as well, making Yoruba myths common currency, just as Christian myths are. This is very much in keeping with the perhaps overly optimistic narrative response to racism and law advocated by such theorists as Delgado: "Stories at times can overcome . . . otherness"; they are "the oldest, most primordial meeting ground in human experience. Their allure will often provide the most effective means of . . . forming a new collectivity based on the shared story" (2438). Tutuola's project, his resolution of the problem of poetic voice in the face of colonialism, manifests, in this way, a sort of universalism, a balancing of the imbalance produced when Yoruba people took up Christian stories, but Christians failed to take up Yoruba stories—and, indeed, Yorubas themselves began to forget those stories.

Needless to say, this is not a homogenizing universalism, to borrow Ashis Nandy's term (*Illegitimacy* x). Tutuola is not transforming Yoruba myths to make them more European. In that case, his project would be only superficially different from the practices of the young mimeticists he describes. It would entirely fail in its task of preservation—serving, instead, to speed the process of disintegration. He is, rather, maintaining and reshaping these myths *as* Yoruba, manifesting traditional Yoruba beliefs and practices, though he is doing this, not only for Yorubas, but for everyone.

In short, Tutuola sets out genuinely to preserve Yoruba myth, to teach it, to bring it into cognitive presuppositions of idea and act, in all its cultural particularity, imbued with Yoruba ethics, cosmology, ritual, and social structure. But at the same time, he dissociates that myth and that culture from their putative racial identities.

TUTUOLA'S CRITICS

Strangely, however, this deep cultural particularity has been largely ignored by critics of Tutuola's novel. (Here and below, I refer to this work as a "novel" for lack of a better category. As should become clear, what is most culturally valuable—and what is most aesthetically exciting—about Tutuola's book does not appear to have much to do with metropolitan genres, novelistic or otherwise.) In this way, its preservative function has been obscured—for its cultural detail and resonance are precisely what give it value in preserving and communicating tradition. Indeed, its artistry and thematic unity, even its most basic implications regarding the structure of human life and human society have hardly been touched on.

More exactly, since its publication in 1953, Tutuola's first novel has received considerable critical attention. However, relatively little of this attention has been focused on interpreting the text in its details and thus understanding its deep and systematic relation to Yoruba traditions. When not debating the value of the work, critics have tended to devote themselves to linguistic analyses of Tutuola's English and to largely noninterpretive and very narrowly focused source studies (see, for example, Collins 96–116 and Zabus on the former; Lindfors *Folklore* and "Amos Tutuola," Roscoe, and Beilis on the latter). Most remaining critics (e.g. Moore, Edwards, or Coates) stress the mythological or folkloric commonality of motifs found in Tutuola's book (a point noted by Irele [188]; Quayson has stressed these tendencies as well [44]).

Much of this criticism is quite valuable. But it leaves virtually all the semantic and narrative details of the novel unexamined. It provides a literary source for the fight with Death, but does not treat the significance of fighting Death with the ropes of yams or suggest the specific cultural implications of such a fight; it tells us that annual sacrifice is a common folklore motif, but does not indicate why Tutuola links this to the color red, nor does it explain the place of sacrifice in Yoruba society. Still less does it integrate these incidents into a more encompassing and deeper understanding of Yoruba mythic thought. The common assumption of this critical work seems to be that the meanings of Tutuola's tales are self-evident; the language of the tales, some of their specific sources or their relation to broader folkloric patterns may need to be treated, but not their significance. In keeping with this, the vast majority of Yoruba cultural references in the work have not even been identified, not to mind explained. Moreover, all this is closely related to the view that the book is unstructured, "little more than a cleverly woven string of loosely connected episodes," in Bernth Lindfors's words (59; Snead stresses that critics of the novel "rarely . . . give the artist credit for willed craftsmanship" [240]).

But, in fact, the stories which constitute *The Palm-Wine Drinkard* are not mere semantically obvious fancies with little symbolic or social depth. Nor are they a random collection of disparate if fascinating elements. Rather, each episode repeats and elaborates the central themes of the novel, which are equally the central themes of Yoruba culture. Indeed, that is what makes *The Palm-Wine Drinkard* a successful literary work—and a successful manifestation and preservation of Yoruba traditions of verbal art. In this novel, Tutuola preserves religious myth, not merely as a sequence of engaging events, but as systematic manifestations of a coherent, underlying cosmology.

Specifically, both the novel and Yoruba traditional culture largely center around fertility, the continuation of human life through the growing of food and the birth of children. As G. Ojo explains, "The Yoruba have always been preoccupied with the problems of fertility of human beings as well as crops. Every worship, no matter what the deity, is incomplete without solicitations for children or for their long life; otherwise, it is for land fertility or better crop yields" (185; see also Hallgren 13, 91, and throughout). Tutuola has taken these themes, along with relevant motifs and tales from Yoruba myth and legend, and, through a series of variations, fashioned them into a complex and highly interpretable work.

THE MECHANICS AND ETHICS OF FERTILITY IN YORUBA CULTURE

More exactly, we may understand the relevant aspects of Yoruba culture as structured by two parallel sets of beliefs. The first set centers around fertility as the *mechanism* of life. Life is *sustained* through the fertility of the soil—or, more generally, through nourishment recurrently provided by nature. Life is *reproduced* through the birth of children—or, rather, through the birth of children who will themselves continue the cycle of reproduction. Note that each aspect of fertility—that which sustains and that which reproduces—is cyclical. Note also that in each case the cycle may be broken. Nature may not provide food. A couple may have no children, or their children may die and thus fail to continue the cycle of reproduction. In other words, the mechanism of life may fail.

This possibility of failure leads us to the second set of beliefs. These are not mechanical, but ethical. If the mechanism of life fails, we need to explain why it does so. Every society accepts that there is a purely material aspect to such a failure, a physical cause. But, colonialist clichés about the scientific attitude of Europe notwithstanding, every society also has a set of ethical principles that at least certain members of the society see as underlying the life-sustaining mechanisms. A failure in those mechanisms may then be explained by an ethical failure on the part of the society or of some group within society (cf. the way some Americans explain the AIDS epidemic as divine retribution for sexual promiscuity).

In Yoruba society, perhaps the most crucial ethical principle is *reciprocity*. The mechanisms of life fail when there is a failure of ethical reciprocity. This typically occurs when a society or some members of a society have become greedy, not so much about necessities as about excess. Life, for the Yoruba—or, really, for anyone else—is not merely a matter of having or lacking. We may conceive of normal circumstances as varying between the poles of *adequacy* and *scarcity*. In times of adequacy, needs are fulfilled with little surplus. In times of scarcity, mechanisms of life fail in part but without precipitating a crisis, for needs are still fulfilled by the slim surpluses of other times. But outside of adequacy and scarcity there are other circumstances. On the far side of adequacy, we find *abundance*. This is the ideal life. On the far side of scarcity, we find *devastation*. This is life at its worst. Where abundance is characterized by massive harvests, devastation is marked by drought and famine. Where abundance yields many offspring, devastation leaves one with no children, or, what is usually the same thing, with children who are *àbíkú* or *tohosu*, children who are abnormal and will not continue the cycle of regeneration.

Before going on, it is worth saying a few words about these two types of children as they figure in *The Palm-Wine Drinkard*. An àbíkú child is a child "born to die" (Parrinder 98) or "possessing death" (Ellis 111). Like the *ogbanje* child of Igbo culture, it is a spirit who haunts its mother by being born, dying at a young age, then reentering the mother's womb to be born again, only to die again, and so on. Ellis explains that, in Yoruba folk belief, the bush is inhabited by a great number of spirits who have not achieved the status of ancestors, and thus do not live peacefully in the land of the ancestors. They wander aimlessly and suffer from "hunger, thirst, and cold since nobody offers sacrifice to them" (112). When one of these wandering ghosts manages to enter a woman's womb and be born, he/she is obligated to share with all the companion spirits whatever food he/she acquires. Because of this sharing out of the food, the child does not retain adequate sustenance for him/herself and thus "begins to pine away and become emaciated" (112). The child's mother does everything to keep the child alive, but to no avail.

The tohosu is, first of all, a physically abnormal child. As Herskovits and Herskovits explain: "Among the things that distinguish a *tohosu* from a normal child are hermaphroditism and gross physical anomalies. Abnormal traits include macrocephaly," and so on (30). More significantly, the tohosu is prodigious and dangerous: "The *tohosu* are able to speak at birth, and . . . to pit their strength against giants, sorcerers and kings" (31; see also Ellis 120). In other ways, tohosu children are, in effect, the inverse of àbíkú children. They consume massive quantities of food (see Ellis 120)—roughly in the amount that would be required to maintain an àbíkú spirit and all his/her parasites—but they do not waste away. Moreover, while the parents of an àbíkú child would seek ways of keeping the child alive, tohosu children were often "exposed at the water's edge shortly after birth" (31).

I should note here that "tohosu" is in fact a Fon term, not a Yoruba term. The two groups are closely related—sharing, for example, not only the concept, but the term "àbíkú" (Parrinder 98). More importantly, belief in and concern with tohosu children is part of "an important cult made by the Fon and some Yoruba to abnormal children" (Parrinder 100). Among the Yoruba, the two types of child are not always clearly distinguished and the term "àbíkú" may be used for abnormal, prodigious children, and not merely for normal, sickly ones. Indeed, sometimes the two are, in effect, combined. For example, in Tutuola's *My Life in the Bush of Ghosts,* the burglar ghosts (53–55) are prodigious children who pretend to pine away, and thus to be àbíkú, in order to extort sacrifices from the parents. On the other hand, Ellis finds the two distinguished among the Yoruba. He refers to the prodigious child as a "changeling," on the model of Northern European folk beliefs. According to Ellis, this child "is possessed by an evil spirit, just as an Abiku possesses a child, though with different results" (122). For the sake of clarity, I will distinguish the two and use the Fon term "tohosu" for the abnormal, prodigious child.

Again, the birth of a tohosu or àbíkú child, as well as any form of devastating human or agricultural infertility, requires an explanation that is not merely mechanical, an explanation that accounts not merely for the physical facts, but for the great human suffering that these facts entail. This is where the ethical account enters, positing a violation of reciprocity as the ultimate cause of devastation. More exactly, in Yoruba myth and folklore, devastation is most often viewed as resulting from excessive appropriation of abundance, greed regarding something which is in excess of need. To produce homeostasis, and thus to return the mechanisms of life to their normal cyclical path, such excessive appropriation requires a sacrifice—specifically, a propitiatory sacrifice aimed at a deity angered by this excess (see Awolalu 152–56). In the most extreme circumstances, the society must sacrifice one of its own members. In those cases, when balance and reciprocity have been radically disrupted, society must sacrifice what is nearest and most important: human life, precisely what is to be preserved by the mechanisms of fertility once reciprocity has been restored.

In the following pages, I examine the stories of *The Palm-Wine Drinkard* in this context, arguing that each tale manifests these structures of belief, and that the entire novel operates to work through these central Yoruba concerns of ethical reciprocity and material fertility. Tutuola occasionally departs from strict Yoruba ideas. But for the great bulk of the novel, he fashions his story by integrating and developing motifs and imagery, real practices and imaginary plots, from Yoruba myth, folklore, and ritual, forming them into a coherent and deeply resonant narrative. Far from a mere stitching together of tall tales from a more or less random selection of sources, *The Palm-Wine Drinkard* is a developed work of art pervaded by Yoruba symbolism, structured by Yoruba ethics and cosmology, asserting and playing variations on the fundamental Yoruba principles of fertility and reciprocity. Indeed, in connection with this, it is doubly appropriate that Tutuola drew on the central Yoruba themes of devastation, reciprocity, and reproduction. In writing his stories, Tutuola in effect labors like the drinkard with the food-producing egg, given by the ancestors—only Tutuola is working to reproduce a heritage, rather than a generation of people; he is working to prevent cultural, rather than biological death or devastation. Moreover, he is doing this in opposition to a great violation of reciprocity that he finds in Africans who reject African culture for mimeticism—and, of course, in Europeans who have hardly considered African traditions at all.

THE TALES

1. The Myth of Land and Heaven

Perhaps the most obvious instance of the pattern outlined above (excess leading to greed, then to violation of reciprocity, devastation, and so forth) is to be found in the story of Land and Heaven recounted at the end of the novel under the title "THE CAUSES OF THE FAMINE" (118ff.). Land and Heaven go hunting together, but capture only a mouse. Clearly, a mouse does not satisfy any need. In good Lacanian fashion, therefore, it becomes an object of desire. Both Land and Heaven become "greedy" (119) and refuse to divide the mouse in two. Heaven returns to heaven; the mouse remains on earth. Due to this failure of reciprocity, Heaven withholds rain from the earth. This causes drought and famine which can be stopped only by a sacrifice. When the sacrifice is accomplished and successfully transported to Heaven, reciprocity and balance are restored and rain begins to fall immediately. In this case, the sacrifice does not involve the literal killing of a human being, but it does involve symbolic killing. Specifically, a slave is chosen to act as "carrier" for the sacrifice, bringing it to heaven. In taking the sacrifice, he is, so to speak located in the area of death. For this reason, immediately following the ceremony, he is excluded from human social life, separated as if he were dead, even though he is alive. This is why "nobody would allow him to enter his or her house at all" (125—cf. Taiwo 96).

The overall structure is clearly in accord with the centrally important Yoruba cultural themes outlined above. Some of the details, with their particular cultural resonances, extend these connections further still. Consider the precise object of dispute between Land and Heaven. Tutuola draws this story from a common Yoruba myth in which the rodent in question is an *"emon"* (see Idowu 50), which is to say, *"praomys Tullbergi"* (see Abraham under *"emon"*), which can be equally referred to as a mouse or a rat (see Grzimek 375 and 351; Idowu prefers "rat"). This is relevant for, as G. Ojo points out (222), the rat is an important symbol of reproductive fertility among the Yoruba.[1] Thus, while the dispute focuses on sustenance, there may also be a suggestion of reproduction. Indeed, Heaven's withholding of water could be understood as a symbolic destruction of reproductive fertility as well as sustenance. As Margaret Drewal points out, in Yoruba cosmology water is "the source of all life," not only in agriculture, but in the womb (74). Of course, these associations would not have any interpretive implications were it not for the fact that the theme of reproduction enters the tale more literally also. During the famine, reproduction is not merely stopped, but reversed; parents not only fail to bear children, but "many parents were killing their children for food" (118). The cosmic failure of reciprocity—a failure not only of an individual or of a society, but of the earth itself—has completely devastated fertility, both sustenative and reproductive.

2. The Frame Narrative (Second Story)

The preceding myth is integrated into a larger frame narrative which is open to the same sort of analysis. The frame narrative has two parts which may be treated separately. The first narrative concerns the acquisition of the magic egg; we will turn to that in a moment. The second concerns the use and destruction of that egg. It is this second story that is integrated with the myth of the famine. Specifically, the narrator returns to his home with a magic egg given to him when he left the Deads' Town. The egg is clearly associated with life, with the avoidance of/departure from death. Moreover, it is both a food and a symbol of reproduction—we eat it, and it contains an embryo. Given what we have just noted about water, it should come as no surprise that the egg functions to provide sustenance once it is placed in life-giving water. People from all villages come to be fed by the egg. As the egg not only satisfies their needs, but produces a surplus, they become greedy. They refuse to go home, and do not let the narrator rest even for a moment; he must constantly supply them with food and drink. Ultimately, their raucous behavior breaks the egg. When the egg no longer works, they depart, and begin to suffer again from the famine. Moreover, they spurn the man who had fed them so untiringly. Subsequently, he repairs the egg, but now it will produce no food, only whips. He calls back the greedy villagers and commands the egg to punish them. They are beaten by "millions of whips" (123) so that "many of them died" (124). Then the egg disappears.

For the most part, this tale too fits clearly into the pattern we have elaborated: abundance of fertility leading to greed leading to devastation. But subsequent to the devastation come the whips. To understand this resolution, we must look at the parallel scene in the myth of Heaven and Earth. There, the slave is completing the sacrificial ceremony when he is "beaten" by rain. Like the villagers at the narrator's home, he runs about trying to "escape from the rain," but "nobody would allow him to enter his or her house" because he was now, symbolically, dead or "of the dead," as we have already noted. (Typically, this abuse and exclusion precedes the "carrying" of the sacrifice, as illustrated in Soyinka's *The Strong Breed.* But the function is the same.) The beating of the villagers and the resulting deaths have the structural position, and thus function, of a sacrifice. They restore normalcy. This link gains greater resonance and cultural depth when we recall the use of whips by Egúngún (members of the community who take on the identities of important ancestors for ceremonial purposes; on their use of whips, see Johnson 29), the importance of beating in the Egúngún ceremonies (Simpson 49, 51), the juridical and punitive function of the Egúngún (Ellis 107), and the association of the Egúngún with rebirth and with agricultural fertility (Johnson 30–31). In some degree, the beating of the greedy villagers recalls the Egúngún ceremonies and parallels what happens to villagers when they displease the ancestors prior to or during these ceremonies and are, in consequence, chased and whipped by them.

After the beating, the egg disappears and we are back to the status quo. Of course, due to the insertion of this tale in the myth of Heaven and Earth, the status quo at that moment is itself devastation and another resolution is needed.

Unsurprisingly, this sequence fits Yoruba beliefs and practices surrounding drought quite well. In a time of drought, the Yoruba would first call upon a rainmaker, who, in a scenario directly parallel to that of the narrator and the egg, "boiled the rain-inducing ingredients in a big pot set on a fire in a public place" (215; cf. the even more directly parallel Igbo practice, described in Elechi Amadi's *The Concubine,* where a "mysterious white smooth stone . . . when immersed in water, caused rain to fall even in the dry season" [8]). If this failed, the Egúngún maskers would be called out (215)—presumably with their whips and beatings. Finally, if this too failed, a human sacrifice would be undertaken (216). Tutuola's frame narratives clearly present a version of these practices.

It is worth noting that, in another story, the narrator steals a cola and is chased by a man with a whip. Here, again, greed for surplus is punished by whipping. Moreover, in this case, the whipping is also associated with death, and in a way that links the man directly with the ancestors, thus reenforcing the connection between the Egúngún and the whips/beating of the frame narrative. Specifically the man with the whip walks backwards and thus represents the inverted existence of the dead, as Tutuola portrays it in the Deads' Town.

3. The Frame Narrative (First Story)

The first story of the frame narrative is in many ways directly parallel to the second story, and the events of the two constitute a sort of reciprocity or balancing for the narrator. It begins with the narrator doing no work, but drinking palm wine the entire day. He is surrounded by friends who share his greed for palm wine and who keep his tapster constantly busy. One Sunday, he sends his tapster out to tap more wine. The specification of the day as the Christian day of rest underscores the excess of the narrator's demands. The tapster falls from the tree and dies. This deprives the narrator of his palm wine. Like the villagers in the second frame story, the community which has been consuming his wine disperses. This sorry state of affairs inspires him to set out on a quest to the Deads' Town, from which he returns with the magic egg.

This story is a sort of comic version of the structure we have been discussing. The narrator's sustenance has not been genuinely devastated, though he takes his loss of palm wine as seriously as others might take a drought. More importantly, the narrator himself operates as a sort of carrier or sacrifice. Just as the slave rises up to Heaven in order to restore the rain, which is to say, water, the narrator goes to the town of the dead in order to restore his palm wine—itself a sort of excess or superlative of water: "I could not drink ordinary water at all except palm-wine" (7). The result of both sacrificial journeys is the restoration of sustenance, though the narrator, unlike the slave, is not excluded from society for achieving this. Indeed, rather than being excluded from society, he assumes the burdens of sustenance. Of course, scapegoats always take on the burdens of society, but they do so symbolically. In this case, the narrator becomes responsible for producing the food for the community. At the beginning he "had no other work more than to drink palm-wine" (7). And at the end he "did no other work than to command the egg to produce food and drinks" for the community (122). In effect, he takes the position of his tapster, working ceaselessly to produce excess to satisfy the greed of others.

4. The Other Deads' Town (Alternative Frame Story)

Though, for the most part, I wish to consider episodes from the novel in their order of appearance, I would like to single out one further story for discussion out of sequence. The story of the journey to the Deads' Town in effect repeats an earlier story from the novel, but renders it comic, so that it can ultimately lead to the comic resolution of the novel as a whole. In this way, the earlier story can be loosely considered part of the frame narrative, a further frame story. This is the story of the "UNRETURNABLE-HEAVEN'S TOWN," clearly another town of the dead—though the two are very different. The Deads' Town is, in effect, a benevolent version of death; the Unreturnable-Heaven's Town, its malevolent counterpart. More exactly, the Yoruba distinguish two places of death. The Deads' Town is, more or less, the *òrun afẹ́fẹ́* or "heaven of breezes." This good heaven is often believed to be on this earth and to have a social and material structure directly parallel to our own. Moreover, it is the heaven or afterworld from which the dead are reborn into our world (see Bascom 68). In contrast, the Unreturnable-Heaven's Town is the *òrun apaadì* or "heaven of potsherds," a brutal place where cruel people are sent and everyone is "beaten and made to walk in the midday sun" (Bascom 68). Tutuola derives his name for the place from the fact that, unlike the heaven of breezes, no one can be reborn from the heaven of potsherds (see Bascom 68). It is truly unreturnable.

Within the novel, both places are marked by an inversion of the practices of life. In the Deads' Town, everyone walks backward (96). In the Unreturnable-Heaven's Town, people "were doing everything incorrectly" (58). More importantly, the two towns invert one another. The backwardness of the Deads' Town is benign, while the incorrectness of the Unreturnable-Heaven's Town is malign. The narrator has to sneak into the Deads' Town, whereas he is forced to enter the Unreturnable-Heaven's Town. In the Deads' Town, everyone has a fear of blood; therefore the deads drive the narrator and his wife from the town when he is accidentally cut. In the Unreturnable-Heaven's Town, in contrast, the inhabitants cut visitors to pieces (59). In the Deads' Town, the narrator and his wife are forbidden to stay, but are well treated. In the Unreturnable-Heaven's Town, they are beaten (58). Most interestingly, in the Deads' Town, the narrator falls into a pit—here, as elsewhere in the book, reminiscent of a grave—but he gets out of the pit and leaves the town, in effect enacting a scenario of rebirth. When he leaves the town, his tapster provides shelter, food, and drink—in other words, all the necessities for sustaining life. In contrast, the inhabitants of the Unreturnable-Heaven's Town bury him and his wife up to the jaw—reminiscent of interment, but also planting; place food nearby, so that they can see it, but not eat it; and flog them. However, they are able to escape when rain falls, softening the earth. They burn the town, eat a sheep, and leave.

In a sense, this trip to the Unreturnable-Heaven's Town provides, by way of the burial and beating, the sacrifice required of the narrator, the sacrifice which compensates for his greed. We have already seen the link between beating and human sacrifice in the myth of Land and Heaven and the second story of the frame narrative. More importantly, as Parrinder points out, in one method of human sacrifice among the Yoruba, the victim was "buried . . . with the head just showing" (72), precisely as represented in this episode. The ordeal of this journey, then, in effect restores the balance lost at the outset of the novel and allows the narrator's subsequent journey to the Deads' Town to be comic rather than tragic. In this way, Tutuola alters the heaven of potsherds, making it returnable—contrary both to the cosmology and to his name for the place—in order to make it fit the dynamics of the story, much as he makes the final sacrifice of the slave a symbolic death only, not a literal one. Moreover, within the story, this change is allowed by rain filling the earth— where they are, so to speak, "planted"—in a manner clearly connected with agriculture. Note that this too is linked with the return of the slave to earth in the frame narrative (second story), for the slave is in part driven back down to earth, and thus back to human life, by the "heavy rain" (125). Once again, it is the cyclical produce of the earth—fertilized by rain—that frees one, temporarily, from the grave or death. Indeed, in this case, the grave in explicitly linked with hunger through the inaccessible food. This theme of sustenance is further stressed when the narrator and his wife mark their destruction of the Unreturnable-Heaven's Town by eating a sheep.

5. The First Story of Death

These are the main sequences that structure the novel as a whole. However, there are, obviously, many further episodes incorporated into this structure along the way. All of these serve to develop and respecify the main organizing themes. It is unsurprising that the first of these episodes, occurring just after the narrator sets out on his sacrificial journey to the Deads' Town, is an encounter with Death.

At the start of his quest, the narrator meets an old man and asks for directions. The old man says that he will give directions only if the narrator performs a task. The narrator retrieves a bell for the old man. But the old man is not satisfied, so he asks the narrator to go and capture Death. Before going on, it is important to note that the parallel between these stories implies a parallel between death and bells. It links death with a type of sound. Specifically, this sound is not natural, but artificial; yet, at the same time, it is not articulate—it is not speech.

Whatever the link, however, capturing Death is, unsurprisingly, a much more complicated task than getting a bell. The old man gives the narrator "a wide and strong net which was the same color as the ground of that town" (11)—in effect, the net is the soil and thus he will use the soil to combat and capture death. The narrator encounters Death and Death immediately tries to subdue him with "the strings of the drum"—another artificial instrument of sound. But the narrator fights back and simultaneously subdues Death with "the ropes of the yams in his garden . . . the yams . . . and the yam stakes" (12). Thus, in a rather obvious way, Death is subdued by crops, by farming. From here, the narrator and Death struggle in various ways until the narrator causes Death to fall into a pit—here, presumably, more related to planting or to digging yams than to interment, but of course including the image of the death of Death. He then captures Death with the earth-colored net, in what is in effect an allegorization of the life-sustaining function of agriculture.

6. *The Abducted Daughter*

The next story is one of the longer, more complicated, and more fascinating episodes. Briefly, there was a young woman who refused to marry (18)—thus, implicitly, refused to fulfill her role in reproducing life. She sees a "complete gentleman" in the market and follows him into the forest. As the man travels in the forest he begins to remove parts of his body and return them to their owners, from whom he had them on loan. Ultimately, he is reduced to a skull. Allegorically, then, the woman has refused marriage, perhaps because she is seeking an ideal—the "complete gentleman." In refusing marriage, she has implicitly refused children. Thus, she has unwittingly "followed death," rather than following reproductive life. Indeed, this is almost explicit: "When the lady saw that she remained with only Skull, she began to say that her father had been telling her to marry a man, but she did not listen to or believe him" (21). And the Skull, implicitly identifying himself with death, tells her that "if she would die she would die" (21). He then begins "humming with a terrible voice," again linking death with inarticulate, contrived sound. The lady now tries to run away, but the Skull forces her to enter his house which "was a hole which was under the ground"—clearly a grave. Now she finds herself underground with many skulls, just as the narrator had found himself with many human skeletons in the house of Death. In order to prevent her escape, the skulls tie a cowrie around her neck. This cowrie prevents her from speaking, but itself makes "a terrible noise" when she tries to escape.

Here, the connection between death and inarticulate artificial sound is becoming clearer. Death means being unable to speak. It is marked by two different sorts of artificial sound: music and noise. Music seems to be connected with death by way of funerary practices. As Drewal points out, on the main funeral day, the "first public ceremony is a spectacle of playing and dancing. . . . Relatives of the deceased hire music groups and accompany them around the town dancing and singing praises of the family" (41–42). Dennett stresses the importance of drumming during a wake (29–30). More generally, Bascom points out that drumming, singing, and dancing are virtually continuous for days after a death. The bell may allude to the ringing of bells in a Christian church. Though they are fairly rare, Christian elements do enter into Tutuola's book at some points.

Noise is perhaps more akin to the keening, especially that for an inappropriate or premature death, a death that disrupts the cycle of fertility, as when the deceased person is childless. As Clarke reports, "As soon as death occurs, the friends of the deceased begin their woes and lamentations which they keep up at night for several days successive" (250). Indeed, "Humming with a terrible voice" may fit here as well, for the phrase could recall either singing or keening. In any case, while any death occasions some grief, a premature death gives rise to mourning with little or no celebration through music and dance (251; see also Idowu 187). Moreover, there are many sorts of inappropriately dead, such as suicides or àbíkú, for whom the Yoruba do not perform funerary rituals at all. Instead, they throw the corpse in the bush (see, for example, Talbot 470 and Bascom 65)—recall that the Skull's home is deep in the bush.

Fortunately, however, this simultaneously noisy and mute burial in the bush is not the end for this unmarrying young woman. The narrator follows the complete gentleman to his home and rescues her, helped by the sacrifice of a goat (23). But she still cannot speak; she is, in effect, still dead, though she has been retrieved from the bush. The narrator prepares a medicine for her from an "opposite" plant and a "compound" plant. In conjunction, the images of opposition and compounding imply balance and, therefore, a restoration of reciprocity. More importantly, when the opposite and compound plants allow the woman to speak once again, she immediately marries the narrator. Her "death," having been precipitated by a refusal of marriage, is necessarily overcome with marriage.

7. The First Tohosu

Having dealt with the problems of marriage, childlessness, and inappropriate death, Tutuola turns in the next episode to the problem of inappropriate reproduction with the introduction of a tohosu child. This child has the major characteristics of the tohosu. Though not initially deformed, he is born abnormally. More importantly, he is prodigious: he speaks immediately (31), is familiar with all the people at home "as if he had known them" (32), and has superhuman strength (33). He also has an enormous, indeed instatiable appetite (32), making him a particular threat to the survival of the parents. In addition, his name underscores the tohosu's abilities at self-transformation, stressed by Ellis (120–22): "'ZURRJIR' which means a son who would change himself into another thing very soon" (32).

While the tohosu child was often exposed at the water's edge, the narrator tries to kill this child by burning him. This is a fairly straightforward shift to an opposite, fire substituting for water. He believes he has succeeded and leaves to find his tapster. But his wife wants to return for a "gold trinket" (35). Her greed for this unnecessary item makes them return home, only to find the tohosu again, now returned as a "half-bodied baby" (35), a common version of the abnormal or aborted child (cf. the "half-child" in Soyinka's *A Dance of the Forests*). This child is linked with death in several ways. First, when the tapster and his wife refuse to obey him, he stops their breathing (35). This clearly mimics a real property of death, but it also alludes to the narrator's first encounter with Death, when Death prevented him from breathing (12). Second, the child begins whistling, which is to say, he produces inarticulate, artificial sound. Finally, when carrying the child, the narrator and his wife are chased away from homes and villages, precisely as if they were sacrificial carriers, associated with death.

Ultimately, they are able to escape from this tohosu only through "Drum, Song and Dance." Specifically, drum, song, and dance perform for five days, then lead the tohosu into their "premises" of "mud" (38). This is a fairly clear instance of music being identified as part of a funerary ritual, the five days evidently alluding to the duration of a funeral ceremony, prior to burial. (Yoruba preinterment festivities vary considerably in duration— Dennett reports seven days [30] and Bascom "as many as eight" [67], though Parrinder limits them to three [110] and Awolalu only says "two or more days" [55]; five falls neatly between these extreme estimates.) Thus, they are able to escape from this unnatural child, this spirit who blocks fertility and reverses the order of things, only by burying him. In general terms, the significance of this is clear: when the child is dead, he will no longer torture the parents. But one wonders if there is not a critical point here as well. Perhaps Tutuola is objecting to the mistreatment of these children and urging that they be given respectful interment rites. Insofar as the tohosu spirit is a wandering spirit, a spirit who has never been properly buried and thus allowed to travel to the Heaven of Breezes, a burial should put him/her to rest, remove him/her from the cycle of hungry wandering and torturous birth. In this way, the burial scene may represent Tutuola's criticism or revision of Yoruba practices.

8. The White Worms

The next episode is brief and somewhat obscure. After the narrator has earned some money by changing himself into a canoe, he and his wife resume their journey. They encounter a huge white creature with hands, but no head or feet. The narrator turns himself into fire and burns this enormous worm, only to find that a mass of identical creatures follow, crying "cold! cold! cold!" (42). These are a version of the tohosu child—malformed and prodigious. Just as the narrator failed to destroy the tohosu with fire, he fails to rid himself of these creatures with fire. Indeed, they crave warmth just as the tohosu craved food. The relation between warmth and food is perhaps clear enough through the suggestion of cooking, but it is reenforced when this episode is connected with a subsequent episode in which a tohosu figure cries "hungry—hungry—hungry," just as these creatures cry "cold! cold! cold!" (108; see number 17 below). This fits perfectly with Ellis's description of the wandering ghosts of the bush, "who suffer from hunger, thirst, and cold, since nobody offers sacrifice to them" (112; Ellis here is referring to àbíkú spirits, but, again, the two are often not sharply distinguished by the Yoruba). Finally, the narrator and his wife are able to escape these creatures only by leaving the bush—for the bush is the place of the inappropriately dead, the cold and hungry wandering spirits.

9. A Nonhuman Deads' Town: The Termites' House

The following episode involves a relatively simple encounter with death. The narrator and his wife enter the termites' house. They are surrounded by creatures of the kingdom and brought to their king—much as occurs in the Unreturnable-Heaven's Town, only without the violence. The king is, in effect, a compost heap: his "palace was almost covered with refuse . . . he himself was refuse" (45). He is, in short, the sort of natural death that gives rise to agricultural life. The inhabitants assume that the narrator cannot speak, as if he were dead. They subsequently take him to their god, with whom he speaks before leaving. This last development—which allows the narrator and his wife to leave this place of death—is a very attenuated version of the sacrificial mediation between earth and heaven by way of a carrier, as is indicated by the fact that the inhabitants "did not go near the 'god' because nobody would and return alive" (46).

10. A Tohosu Spirit on the Wraith-Island

From here the narrator travels to an edenic island, temperate and fertile, surrounded by life-giving water. The narrator plants, but he cannot harvest because a creature with a huge head eats all the crops. (Recall that macrocephaly is a typical feature of the tohosu.) As it turns out, this creature is owner of the land. He is eating the crops because the narrator failed to sacrifice to him, to give him his due. This failure of reciprocity is rectified, and the narrator's crops grow to abundance.

11. A Tohosu Child on the Wraith-Island

The following episode in effect repeats the one we have just discussed. The people of the island join together to clear a cornfield. However, they fail to include "a baby of one day of age" (50) who is clearly a tohosu. This child can speak and, more importantly, command the weeds to grow in the field, which is to say, undermine the mechanism of agricultural sustenance. When this is discovered, the king makes "excuses" to the child (50)—a mild form of reparation—and the child, appeased, goes away, allowing a good harvest.

12. The Greedy-Bush, the Birds, and the Spirit of Prey

The narrator and his wife enter a bush which shows no sign of death and which smells of food. The very smell satisfies their hunger. But the bush is "greedy" (51) and becomes too hot for them, so they leave. They come upon water which does not slake their thirst, and which dries up as they approach it. The earth becomes hotter. They meet huge trees with human heads, who are smoking pipes. They leave the "Greedy-Bush" and are threatened by carnivorous birds. But they make a fire and drive the birds away with the smell of burning powder. After this, they encounter the "Spirit of Prey," a large creature that kills its victims with its stare. They escape by climbing a tree.

Most of the sequence seems to form a single story which allegorizes the shift from abundance to famine and, correlatively, from rain to drought. Specifically, the narrator and his wife begin in a bush so filled with watery life that there is not even any dry material for a fire. Everything is so plentiful that their hunger is immediately satisfied. But then the temperature begins to increase, water becomes scarce, and the leaves disappear (52). The treetops smoke or burn in the heat and the land is ravaged by carnivorous birds reminiscent of vultures.

In keeping with the general themes of the novel and of Yoruba society, this shift from abundance to devastation is triggered by greed. Interestingly, however, in this case, it is not the greed of humanity, but of nature, evidently indicating that nature too sometimes fails in reciprocity on its own, and not in response to human failure. In any case, the greedy bush is a sort of agricultural equivalent of the tohosu child, an image of the way something that is supposed to sustain or reproduce life—nature, a child—may function malevolently to drain life away.

The next incident is that of the stolen cola, to which we have already referred. Following this is the tale of Unreturnable-Heaven's Town.

13. The Faithful-Mother

After escaping from the Unreturnable-Heaven's Town, the narrator and his wife are taken into a white tree by Faithful-Mother. In entering the tree, they "sell" their deaths and "loan" their fear (67), indicating that this is a utopia of immortality and perfect security, the precise opposite of the Unreturnable-Heaven's Town. The whiteness and shape of the tree recall the huge, tubular tohosu-worm. But they are not identified; rather, they are contrasted. This is already suggested by the mere fact that it is a protective tree, for this recalls the narrator's escape from the Spirit of Prey in the episode of tohosulike nature. Indeed, Faithful-Mother's white tree is the precise opposite of all that is associated with the tohosu. It is a place of endless giving, opposed to the tohosu principle of endless taking. Unsurprisingly, this principle of nurturant abundance is personified in a "faithful mother," just as the tohosu principle is personified in a greedy child. In keeping with this, Faithful-Mother's white tree is a place of abundance, with inexhaustible supplies of food and drink. There is also much music and dancing, but this is the music of entertainment (see 68), thus different from—again, opposed to—the implicitly funerary drum, song, dance, bell, and various hummings of the figures of death. It is the music and dance of abundance and festivity, not the music and dance of devastation and interment rituals. On the other hand, the loss of this utopia is marked by singing and is immediately followed by an encounter with dance (72), indicating a return to the world of mortality, with its ceremonial music.

14. Another Deads' Town: The Red-People in the Red-Town

After leaving the Faithful-Mother, the narrator and his wife meet a red woman, whom they later discover to be Dance, of Drum, Song, and Dance. She takes them to a town of red people, which is implicitly another town of the dead. As the king explains, the inhabitants of the town are people from "the olden days . . . when we were walking backwards and not forwards" (75), a mark of the dead, as we have noted. Moreover, their redness links them with death, for the Yoruba bury their dead in "red laterite soil" (see Beier 122), a point which turns up in Yoruba poetry and elsewhere (cf. the verse from a poem on àbíkú children: "the red soil in the grave belongs to Heaven" [Beier 49]).

The king explains how they turned red. Nature was topsy-turvy. He caught a red bird in the river and a red fish on the land. These unnatural animals are abnormalities of sustenance directly comparable to the tohosu as an abnormality of reproduction. Indeed, like the tohosu, they speak as if they were adult humans. The king tries to burn them, just as the narrator tried to burn the tohosu, but, again like the tohosu, they burn into halves. And just as the tohosu prevented the narrator from breathing, the smoke from the fire suffocates the king and his subjects. In addition, it makes them turn red. Finally, "the whole of us died" (77).

In keeping with the recurrent imagery of the novel, these two creatures of death—that is, death-causing abnormalities of sustenance—live in a hole in the ground. Continuing the motif of inversion, instead of providing food for people, as one might expect of a bird and a fish, they eat one human being each year; they demand a sacrifice. As the king puts it, "we are sacrificing one of us to them yearly to save the rest of us" (77). This is somewhat odd, considering that they are already dead. Perhaps the implication is that this "second" death would completely annihilate them, or transfer them from the Red-Town to some less hospitable place, such as the Unreturnable-Heaven's Town. In any case, it is clear that reciprocity is again out of balance. Nature, like the tohosu, is taking life rather than sustaining it. The narrator agrees to fight the creatures, and he eventually kills them. However, what is most interesting is his preparation for killing them. He has his head shaved and painted red and white; then he dances around the town. In other words, he imitates a brief version of the Yoruba initiation ceremony, where the initiates heads are shaved and painted white or white and red (see Drewal 66 and Drewal and Pemberton 32). This ceremony is, as Drewal emphasizes, a ceremony of rebirth, and thus of overcoming death, in part because it marks the initiate's entry into manhood, the social delimitation of his human reproductive capacity. In preparing as he does, then, the narrator contextualizes the battle as an initiatory combat with death. Note that, in the Unreturnable-Heaven's Town, the narrator and his wife had been scalped in a deathly perversion of this shaving. That shaving, like dance, occurs in both contexts is only to be expected, for shaving the head is part of the preparation of a male corpse as well as part of the initiation ceremony (see Awolalu 55, Dennett 30, and Parrinder 110).

When he returns, however, he finds that, fearing him, the Red-people have "changed into a great fire which burnt their houses and all their properties"—an inversion of the narrator's burning of Unreturnable-Heaven's Town, the tohosu child, and the white worms. After some intermediate events, they reappear and are "no longer red, because I had killed the two red creatures" (83). These people's earlier death, linked with the red soil of burial, has been undone by the narrator's defeat of the monstrous creatures.

At this point, Drum, Song, and Dance appear—appropriately, in this context of returning from death and avoiding death. As they play, all the dead rise up from their graves. But Drum beats itself into heaven, Song sings itself into a river, and Dance dances itself into a mountain, so that they can never be seen again in person. Then these dead people, who had just risen to life, die once more, and can never be resurrected: "since that day they could not rise up again" (85).

The ending of this tale is evidently an explanation of the relation between death and ritual. The Red-people were dead, but were brought back to life through ritual. Thus ritual could at one time move in both directions between life and death. One form of ritual could finalize death, as with the life-devouring tohosu in episode seven. But another form could return life to those who were dead. This is no longer possible. The Red-people were the last to be genuinely resurrected. From now on, life is a matter of sustenance and reproduction, not resurrection. Indeed, reciprocity requires this. After all, the mechanism of life is also the mechanism of death. Death obviously requires life. But life also requires death. Death makes way for new life. As if in confirmation of this, following this final return of death, the narrator acquires abundant sustenance; he plants seeds and "grains grew up and yielded fruits the same day" (85).

But there is still something unresolved. The Red-people had fled the narrator after he saved them, and they had stolen his wife, thus rather grandly failing in reciprocity. Therefore the story continues. The narrator has an invisible helper named "Give and Take" who is "head of all the Bush-creatures" (86) and who helps the narrator with communal work. Most importantly, he steals food. He also shaves the villagers' heads and paints them white. He is a sort of trickster figure that functions to address problems of reciprocity— hence his name. More exactly, he is based on the Yoruba trickster and messenger deity Èṣù. Èṣù serves as intermediary between humans and the gods, and has the particular function of transmitting sacrifices (see, for example, Awolalu 29). In addition, as Awolalu points out, "He is . . . the divine enforcer, punishing those who do not offer prescribed sacrifices and making sure that those who do are amply rewarded" (29). In his trickster function "Esu can and does instigate men to offend the gods—thereby providing sacrifices" (29). Due to Give and Take's Èṣùlike provocations, the villagers forget their obligations and threaten the narrator and his wife. In response to this redoubled violation of reciprocity, Give and Take kills them, in effect taking back the life restored to them by the narrator. Indeed, this death not only compensates for their treatment of the narrator, it also balances their own previous resurrection—for they were returned from death, by the narrator's initiatory victory, just before Drum, Song, and Dance ended forever the possibility of resurrection. Having been resurrected earlier, their continuing existence was a sort of anomaly after this event.

15. A Tale of Justice and Sacrifice

Continuing on his journey, the narrator meets a man who asks him to carry a bag. The narrator agrees, and unknowingly begins to carry the corpse of a murdered prince. They enter the prince's town and the man accuses the narrator of murdering the prince, thus undermining the reproduction of the society—both literally, due to the social disintegration caused by loss of succession, and metaphorically, due to the common identification of the monarch with the society as a whole. The king parades the narrator about the town in apparent honor. The man sees this and confesses to the murder, hoping for a reward. He too is paraded through the town in apparent honor. But, afterward, he is killed.

This tale fits into the general structure in two ways. First, it involves concerns of reciprocity in a fairly straightforward way and these relate to reproduction in a fairly straightforward way. More importantly, it implicitly presents the story of a human sacrifice operating to rectify an imbalance in reciprocity and a disruption in the cycle of reproduction, for in this episode the narrator and the murderer are treated as carriers or scapegoats. Though carriers are often reviled and excluded from society (as in the frame narrative or Soyinka's *The Strong Breed*), their treatment was in some cases precisely the opposite. As Talbot explains, "a person about to act as a scapegoat . . . was usually treated with the greatest respect and indulgence by all and given the best of everything. When the time came for his death . . . [he] was paraded through the streets, when many people took the opportunity of laying their hands on him" (858). The fact that both men are given the same ceremonial reverence indicates that the initial parading of the narrator was not merely a ploy to trap the true killer. Rather, it was part of a ritual sacrifice. This is made even clearer when the man is taken to the sacrificial place—"their bush reserved for such occasion" (95). Most strikingly, after the killing, "they presented his dead body to their gods in that reserve-bush" (95). This execution is not merely a secular punishment, but a ritual compensation, both for the murder of the prince, and for whatever prior crime the king or his people might have committed, thus allowing the prince's premature death.

Appropriately, this tale of sacrifice and retribution immediately precedes the episode of the Deads' Town.

16. Encountering the Dead

After leaving the Deads' Town, the narrator first encounters "over a thousand deads" who are "making bad noise" (101) and "not talking plain words except murmuring" (102)—in keeping with the motif of death and inarticulate, artificial sound. After this, and along the same lines, he meets "400 dead babies . . . singing the song of mourning" (102)—ambiguously tohosu and àbíkú children, their death a tacit violation of the principles of reproduction. Fleeing the babies, he meets a huge man—in effect, another Death figure—who captures him and puts him inside a bag. There are other creatures in the bag who make clear the connection with death. Most importantly for our purposes, "their bodies were as cold as ice" and when they spoke, their voices make a sound like "a church bell" (104). The huge creature takes his captives to his gravelike home, a hole in a hill. After a fight with these creatures, the narrator is knocked unconscious. His wife—who has been following along at a distance—uses plants to revive him, and thus to escape this form of Death. She thereby reciprocates his earlier act of saving her from the skull. Indeed, the entire episode repeats that earlier episode, balancing its onesidedness and thus providing balance in their marriage. This reciprocal (balanced) life-giving is particularly important here because marriage typically defines the most basic social unit for both reproduction and sustenance.

17. The Hungry-Creature and the Mountain Dance

Just as a tohosu episode followed the initial marriage of the narrator and his wife, a tohosu episode follows this reequilibration of that marriage. Moreover, just as this reequilibration inverts the initial sequence of events leading to the marriage—the husband is taken to a hole by death and rescued by the wife—so too does this episode involve significant inversions of the initial tohosu episode. Specifically, the narrator and his wife encounter an insatiably hungry creature, reminiscent of their own tohosu child. The creature wishes to eat the egg which they have been given in the Deads' Town and which, again, represents fertility in both sustenance and reproduction. In order to avoid this, the narrator transforms his wife into a small wooden doll (108). This is reminiscent of the wooden dolls that Yoruba women often have made after one of their twin children has died. Twins are revered by the Yoruba. But they are also seen as abnormal and, due to their unusually high mortality rate, are implicitly associated with both the àbíkú and the tohosu (see G. Ojo 178 and Parrinder 99). The purpose of the doll is to help protect the life of the remaining twin, by appeal to the good offices of the dead twin. In short, it operates to secure the continuation of the cycle of human fertility—a function further suggested by the fact that these dolls are often "shaped like phalli" (Parrinder 99). Indeed, they are even linked with "agricultural . . . fertility" through their common presence in temples dedicated to Oko, "the Farm God or Goddess" (Parrinder 40).

But, again, in this case, the doll is the wife, not the child. This makes sense in a general way, since the transformation serves to protect life and reproduction. However, at the same time, it places the wife in the position of the abnormal child, rather than placing the hungry-creature in that position. Continuing this inversion, the hungry-creature swallows the narrator and his wife, and they must cut themselves out of his belly in a perverse and violent twin birth that kills the creature.

This startling inversion may in part derive from the idea that one's own life is continued quite literally through one's offspring, and that a tohosu or an àbíkú child, or any child who dies without offspring, prevents this continuation. Specifically, it is a common view among the Yoruba that the spirits of one's parents or grandparents return in one's children (see, for example, Awolalu 60). Thus the failure to have children is not only a failure to reproduce society, but also a failure to reproduce one's forebears and thus, ultimately, oneself. In this way, the greatest threat of the tohosu or àbíkú child is to one's own life. The threat of the tohosu or àbíkú to the parents is that they themselves may not be reborn, that they may be deprived of a lineage which they can rejoin, through rebirth, in the future. In this context, it makes perfect sense that the "parents" should themselves be "born" in overcoming the tohosu or àbíkú.

There is a suggestion of these connections in one of the two remaining episodes also. Here the narrator and his wife have encountered some mountain creatures who—in another linking of dance with death—force the wife to dance until she is exhausted and perhaps may die. The narrator then changes his wife into a wooden doll and escapes. Here, again, the talisman that usually wards off a child's death—the wooden doll—becomes the talisman that wards off the mother's death.

18. Two Cases of Justice

The only episode we have not yet discussed is that in which the narrator becomes a judge and is faced with two cases. Both concern reciprocity. The narrator can resolve neither, and asks the reader to use his or her judgement, and to let him know of any solution. The first story concerns a borrower, a debt collector, and a passerby. The borrower decides to kill himself rather than pay his debt. The collector decides to kill himself in order to collect the money in the land of the dead. The passerby decides to kill himself in order to witness the result. Most obviously, the entire problem of debt is a problem of reciprocity. But in addition to this concern with reciprocity, this episode also manifests the recurring theme of greed leading to death. Moreover, it does so in a comic way that partially parallels the narrator's search for his tapster in the land of the dead.

The second case is similar. It concerns a man and his three wives. When the man dies, the first wife kills herself. The second wife goes to find a wizard who will bring him back to life. The third wife guards the husband's and senior wife's bodies in the bush. The wizard resurrects the man and his first wife. As payment, he requests a gift of one of the wives. Each of the wives refuses to marry the wizard. The court is to decide on proper reciprocation or sacrifice. It is significant that a wife is in question, for the gift of the wife would, in effect, be a gift of reproduction, an overcoming of death to parallel the overcoming of death performed by the wizard. Perhaps one reason that this is an irresolvable dilemma is that the wizard has created an anomaly by performing a resurrection, an event that should no longer occur. In a way, the only solution is for the man to die, much as the Red-people had to die after resurrection had ended.

TUTUOLA'S CRAFT

On the back cover of the Grove *Palm-Wine Drinkard* (copyright 1984), there is a quote from *The New York Times Book Review:* "Only a dullard who has buried his childhood under several mountains of best-selling prose could fail to respond to Tutuola's naive poetry." I am afraid that even the most sophisticated discussions of Tutuola's novel have frequently tended to assume its naiveté; they have tended to assume that it is all surface—a dazzling surface perhaps, but surface nonetheless. What I hope to have shown through the preceding interpretations is that *The Palm-Wine Drinkard* is not all surface. It develops and varies a small number of closely related themes that are central to Yoruba culture and it does so through images, character types, and narrative motifs that are incomprehensible outside a Yoruba context. In short, it is located firmly within a complex tradition of Yoruba myth and verbal art, which it serves to preserve, synthesize, and refashion as a unified and autonomous work.

Indeed, the point extends even to the sequence of the episodes. While not ordered by strict necessity of plot, the tales are not merely strung together at random. Dathorne points out, quite rightly, that they produce and illustrate the narrator's spiritual growth (67). But there is a further structural/thematic patterning as well, recognizable only by reference to Yoruba beliefs and practices. After the frame, which broadly introduces the main themes, Tutuola turns to an agricultural struggle with death, then to a tale of marriage, then to a tohosu tale about abnormal reproduction, followed by a variation on the tohosu theme (involving dancing and death). This traces a clear conceptual development from problems of sustenance to problems of reproduction. It is followed by the first town of death—precisely what one faces after the dilemmas of sustenance and reproduction are concluded. Thus the opening is quite rigorously organized. Unsurprisingly, the middle is looser. But there is a general pattern in this part as well. The major episodes stay in the spirit world, moving among various "heavens" and the bush of wandering spirits. The concluding sequence begins with the recapitulation of the marriage episode, which itself leads to another tohosu story and a story involving a relation between death and dancing (which also implicitly treats reproduction). This repeats a pattern from the opening of the novel. It is followed by the struggle with the famine. Thus the entire concluding series of tales inverts the opening movement from problems of sustenance to problems of reproduction. The one striking difference is that the conclusion is interrupted by a didactic if also comic episode that in effect recapitulates the main themes of the book as topics of ethical reflection (rather than motifs for narrative embodiment).

Having just mentioned that the didactic episode is not only didactic but also comic, I should probably note that the same comment could be made about virtually every episode in the book, which is sometimes laugh-out-loud funny. Tutuola's serious use of Yoruba custom and culture does not require him to adopt some sort of humorless puritanical attitude toward human frailty. He expresses the moral views of Yoruba tradition, and the significant material consequences that follow from greed according to that tradition. However, he does so in a way that emphasizes the comic absurdity inherent in human desire, a way that allows us to laugh at the ridiculous spectacle of a man who is willing to travel through Hell on account of a little palm wine. This attitude is not at all out of keeping with some strands of Yoruba culture—it would be particularly appreciated by Èṣù. It is also, I think, not out of keeping with our own experience of human life, which is both serious and silly, laughable, yet filled with horror. I have not emphasized the comic aspect of the novel as it appears to have been recognized, at some level, by virtually all critics. What they have missed is the seriousness of purpose underlying the humor—and thus the significance of the humor itself.

Needless to say, these interpretations are only a beginning. Tutuola's text is as subtle and as open to multiple interpretations as any other. And it is subtle and open to multiple interpretations at least in part because it is founded in an extensive tradition. Again, far from being naive poetry, it is a complex shaping of tradition into a literary whole, a shaping that preserves not only stories but the themes and cultural allusiveness that give those stories a place within society, within religious belief and ritual, within the shared practices and principles of a vanishing verbal art—and, indeed, within the fading intimacies of a communally shared culture. At the same time, Tutuola's project goes beyond an attempt to recapture that communal intimacy. Tutuola takes up these structures—these schemas, prototypes, and exempla, once central to Yoruba thought and practice—not only to preserve them for Yoruba people, but also to communicate them to people whose ancestors condemned that thought and practice as barbarism. He seeks to insinuate these stories and beliefs into the cognitive and affective processes of many people, and thereby to extend cultural intimacy across historical lines of racial and ethnic opposition.

Chapter Five

Outdoing the Colonizer

Homer, Virgil, Dante, Milton, Walcott

I saw myself legitimately prolonging the mighty line of Marlowe, of Milton, but my sense of inheritance was stronger because it came from estrangement. I would learn that every tribe hoards its culture as fiercely as its prejudices, that English literature . . . was hallowed ground and trespass, that colonial literatures could grow to resemble it closely, but could never be considered its legitimate heir. There was folk poetry, colonial poetry, Commonwealth verse, etc., and their function, as far as their mother country was concerned, was filial and tributary.

—Derek Walcott, "What the
Twilight Says: An Overture" (31)

REFERENCE SETS, CULTURAL IDENTITY, AND LITERARY EVALUATION

In the second chapter, I introduced the notion of reference sets and considered their place in the transformation of precursor works. Reference sets bear on the tasks of the postcolonization writer in a range of other ways as well. Perhaps most significantly for our purposes, they are of central importance to cultural and literary self-evaluation and thus to cultural and literary identity. Moreover, their consequences in this regard are not merely general. Reference sets enter into the creation of individual works by establishing models, standards of comparison (which guide an author at each stage of composition), and so on. Indeed, this is part of what Walcott is addressing in the preceding quotation. First, he is considering the reference set in which he aimed to locate his own work. At the same time, he is addressing the inhibitions colonialism places on the formation of reference sets and on one's self-location with respect to such sets. In this way, an author's self-placement regarding a reference set defines a more complex relation to literary tradition than any we have considered thus far. It is of particular, formative importance for Walcott's masterpiece, *Omeros*.

Clearly, self-evaluation is an important issue in postcolonization culture. The entire political, economic, and ideological structure of colonialism demeans colonized people, hammering away at the theme that they and their cultures are inferior. It is not so much that colonized people fully believe their detractors. But people who are living in relative poverty cannot help but feel some sense of failure. When they see a world of success—in films and on television, if not in their own towns and villages—they cannot help but look upon their own lives as less, not only less in monetary value, but less is social achievement. Indeed, no one—not even the most successful—can be free from insecurity and self-doubt. Colonial and racist ideology operate continually to probe those patches of tenderness in a colonized person's sense of self-worth. Sometimes, it works them from bruises into wounds.

As this already indicates, our sense of self-esteem is relative. We judge our own value comparatively. But we do not compare ourselves with others indiscriminately. Rather, we evaluate ourselves through reference sets, and through relative saliency within or across such sets (cf. Baron and Graziano 202). More exactly, we may distinguish two sorts of relative evaluation with direct bearing on self-esteem. The first is within a category; the second is across categories (on the general relation between these sorts of comparison and self-esteem, see Baron and Graziano 534–35, 543). In the first case, I evaluate myself relative to other individuals of my type. In the second case, I evaluate my type relative to other types of the same domain. I have phrased this abstractly, because the precise categories which operate in this way vary with circumstances. Sometimes a person might think of him/herself primarily in terms of a racial category, at other times the salient category is sex, sexual orientation, or nationality.

Intracategorial comparisons are the more obvious of the two. Often, these are perfectly rational, deriving from specific tasks or professions. Thus someone who runs the marathon will compare him/herself with other marathon runners, not with sprinters, or basketball players, or physicists. But sometimes one comes to compare oneself with other members of a group in irrelevant contexts. This typically happens in contexts where this irrelevant category has particular salience. Suppose I am at a dinner party. Some people are volunteering to help clean up. I am faced with a decision as to whether or not I should volunteer. My decision here is likely to be affected by the degree to which the volunteers fall into one or the other sex category. If only women are volunteering, I may be less inclined to volunteer.

Of course, one could argue that this sex-based categorization is not entirely irrelevant. And that is true. It is irrelevant in the sense that there is no rational basis for this categorization in terms of, say, knowledge. After all, who could be incompetent to carry plates to the kitchen? But it is, probably, in part a matter of social expectation. Women are expected to volunteer for these sorts of things. If it had been a question of repairing some piece of motorized equipment, perhaps the men would be more likely to volunteer. This suggests a general point. A large part of any decision regarding category relevance derives from social expectation. Although it is not intrinsically rational to compare myself to other men and not to women, a large part of the reason I do so is that my host and most of the people present are likely to draw comparison sets in this way. In contrast, I may notice that all and only volunteers are wearing a piece of blue clothing, but this fact, equally irrelevant to the task, will not lead me to form a reference set; it will not lead me to base my decision on the color of my clothes, because color of clothing involves no relevant social expectations.

But this is not the only thing this anecdote suggests. A second, and for our purposes more significant, implication is that intercategorial comparison may actually precede and allow intracategorial comparison. The point may be clarified by a further example. Suppose I am in India, eating with a large group of Indians, and two or three other Americans. The men are already seated together, and it becomes obvious that there is a sort of macho competition about who is able to stand the hottest food. I am likely to begin by comparing myself with other Americans, and only shift to comparison with Indians if I am successful in comparison with Americans. Clearly, this too is, in part, related to social expectations—my host and most of the guests are likely to compare us in this way. But it also indicates again that, in choosing to compare myself with Americans prior to comparing myself with Indians, I have already implicitly compared Indians and Americans and found the former superior in the relevant category. The fact that this is probably a rational conclusion—Indians are, on the whole, more accustomed to hot food than are Americans—does not affect the point. I still might have begun with individual comparison and shifted to group comparison only subsequently—or not engaged in group comparison at all, which is usually redundant after individual comparison anyway. In short, it appears that the parameters of individual comparison are set by a prior hierarchization of groups—a hierarchization that is also bound up with common social beliefs and expectations.

This last point is related to the way in which individual identity operates. As we noted in the introduction, identity is, first of all, a matter of "self-concept," one's own lexical categorization of oneself. (For an accessible overview of standard ideas about the self-concept, with its lexical self-schemas, etc., see Baron and Graziano 70–85.) That lexical categorization is largely a matter of what one is told about oneself. I am told that I am male, white, Irish, Catholic, and so on. I do not discover these categories by introspection or by looking in a mirror. Rather, I am classed in these terms from infancy. These categories are attributed to me. Moreover, this attributed identity goes beyond the mere statement of these categories, for the most socially crucial categories that go to constitute one's self-concept carry broad implications for everything from one's daily activities to one's future goals and possibilities. Gender categories provide an obvious case of attributions that function to structure our social activities in concrete practical detail. Even such seemingly objective characteristics as "male" are picked out by society in such a way as to guide a wide range of practical activities—professions, domestic obligations, etc. In being male, I am expected (and expect myself) to go into certain professions (e.g., doctor), not others (e.g., nurse), to do certain things at home (e.g., repair the windows), not others (e.g., match the curtains with the carpet). Moreover, these categories are linked with a wide range of putatively associated properties regarding intelligence, emotion, and other things, that go well beyond any supposedly defining feature—genitalia, chromosomes, whatever—and which thus have profound implications for self-concept (e.g., as a man, I am or should be better at math, but less sensitive and nurturant).

We may say that such categories as "male" and "female," certain racial and ethnic categories, categories of sexual preference—categories that have systematic consequences for one's life in a given society—are "socially functionalized." These categories operate, sometimes explicitly, sometimes implicitly, as organizational principles in a given society, and thus as guides for personal behavior, social aspiration, and so on. The categories that are functionalized in any given society tend to become the categories that are most central to one's self-concept; they tend to be the highest, most directly accessible, most easily activated, least alterable features in a person's lexical entry for him/herself.

To speak of an attributional self-concept or a lexical entry for oneself is not to deny that part of one's sense of identity is a sense of immediate experience, a history of particular memories, a set of unique aspirations. But even these features of one's singular individuality are largely structured by imputed categories. Our experiences result from the positions we can adopt in society; our memories too. The uniqueness of our aspirations is usually little more than an overlapping of pre-set categorial possibilities, oriented by accidents of circumstance.

Perhaps more importantly, our understanding of our unique, individual features is almost entirely guided by imputed categories. Consider introspection. A good deal of research shows that people have very little success in introspecting their own motives or the causes of their emotions (see, for example, Nisbett and Ross 226–27). Rather, they infer these from general evidence, much as they infer the motives and causes of emotion in other people. And this inference seems to be guided to a surprising degree by socially function-alized categories. In other words, when asked to describe our own behavior, we are, at least in some respects, much more likely to make statements that fit gender or other stereotypes than to make statements that actually fit our behavior. For example, when asked about their speech practices, men tend to characterize themselves as speaking in ways we would consider "masculine," while women tend to characterize themselves as speaking in ways we would consider "feminine"—even though these characterizations do not represent their actual speech (see Cameron 34). As to aspirations, John Stuart Mill's observation seems no less apt now than it did a century ago (309):

> Not only in what concerns others, but in what concerns only themselves, the individual, or the family, do not ask themselves—what do I prefer? Or, what would suit my character and disposition? Or, what would allow the best and the highest in me to have fair play, and enable it to grow and thrive? They ask themselves, what is suitable to my position? What is usually done by persons of my station and pecuniary circumstances? Or (worse still) what is usually done by persons of a station and circumstances superior to mine?

To a great extent, then, my own personal identity is simply a complex of imputed categories (e.g., "male") that have been rendered functional by the society within which I live. (Unless otherwise noted, here and below, I use "identity" to refer to categorial identity.) These imputed categories are, so to speak, "filled in" with personal experience, particular differences of personal situation. But the categories themselves, their organization, and their most important consequences are impersonal. I am not saying that we are trapped in these categories. In principle, I believe that there is considerable leeway for revision of one's sense of self. But I also believe that practical conditions make it very unlikely that such revision will occur with any frequency.

In any event, given this structure of identity, it is unsurprising that one's intercategory comparisons should precede and guide intracategory compar-isons, for it is the relations between the categories that are, in the first place, definitive of one's notion of oneself. This analysis leads us to expect several other things as well—all of which appear to be true. First, this indicates that intercategory comparison should have significant consequences for self-esteem. If I am in part defined by a particular category, such as "male," then comparison with another category of the same general domain—"female," for the domain "sex"—should have consequences for my sense of self as well. It is obvious from experience that this is the case. Whether I am judging men to be more mathematically adept than women or my high school to have a better football team than its rival, my self-esteem rises with the relative evaluation of my group—even if I myself am incompetent at math and hopeless at football. More importantly, research in social psychology strongly supports this intuitive view. Empirically, it seems clear that there is indeed a close relation between in-group/out-group hierarchization and self-esteem (see for example Duckitt 68–69 and 85).

It is worth noting that this does not imply that cross-category individual comparison never takes place. It does. But it is, so to speak, weighted relative to the categorial comparison—a point that is sometimes highly consequential in relation to such socially important domains as race and sex. To take a simple example, suppose a little boy gets in a fight and loses. He is much more likely to feel humiliated if his opponent is a girl than if his opponent is another boy. This is largely due to a prior, categorial evaluation—based largely on social expectations—that labels boys superior to girls in pugilism. The point is hardly confined to children. For example, though White professors of English certainly would never admit it, they often have a reaction to success by non-White professors of English comparable to the little boy's attitude, "No girl is going to beat me up!" Thus it becomes particularly important for White people to undermine potentially threatening achievements by non-White people, achievements that appear greater than their own individual achievements.

We could think of the issue in this way. Some categories—most obviously, race and sex—are so widely functionalized that they operate as "essential," which is to say, as relevant in any context. For this reason, race and sex hierarchies are salient in any evaluation. Consider hiring, or tenure evaluations. In both cases, candidates are not evaluated within separate racial or gender categories. They are all evaluated together. However, race and sex hierarchies remain salient in these evaluations, because broad functionalization means that race and sex operate as essential categories. Thus, the principles of weighted cross-category evaluation enter—perhaps not invariably, but certainly frequently—with all their bias and emotional force.

Clearly, this applies to literary evaluation as well, most obviously in standard colonial judgements regarding the relative merits of metropolitan and indigenous literatures. As Macaulay notoriously put it, "a single shelf of a good European library [is] worth the whole native literature of India and Arabia" (45). Evaluation of this sort affects a postcolonization author from a colonized group in two ways. First, it affects him/her categorially, as an Indian, African, or Afro-Caribbean writer—and it does so independent of any strategy of literary identity considered thus far. No degree of success in the approaches we have been discussing—for example, highlighting subaltern elements in metropolitan tradition—is likely to have even the slightest impact on the standard evaluation of European and non-European literature. No amount of writing back or preserving indigenous tradition is likely to alter the common social view, which is part of colonial ideology, that European literary art is superior to non-European literary art. At a more narrowly personal level, this affects an individual writer insofar as he/she aspires to be one of the very greatest writers in world literary history—not only a great writer "for an African" or Indian or whatever, but a great writer *tout court*. For example, until roughly the last decade, recipients of the Nobel Prize in literature were overwhelmingly White and male; women and non-Whites combined to only about one tenth of the prizes, though they comprise the overwhelming majority of the world population, and, I would imagine, a great majority of modern and contemporary authors—certainly far more than 10 percent.

Devotion to poetic craft, commitment to producing highly polished prose or verse, does not respond to these problems. Even a good deal of contemporary success leaves in tact what might be called the "high canon" of metropolitan literature—the elite stratum of the very greatest works that operates to define European culture, and to establish that culture as superior, along with the European peoples who produced it. A highly accomplished work of indigenous poetry might bear comparison with Philip Larkin. If tremendously successful, it might even go so far as to be linked with, say, W. H. Auden. But it leaves the core of the tradition, the foundation of putative European superiority, untouched.

WALCOTT'S CANON

Throughout his career, Derek Walcott has set out, almost systematically, work by work, to take on the metropolitan tradition and establish himself as achieving feats comparable, not to those of writers who are good in the tradition—not to Larkin, or Auden, not even to such modern Nobel laureates as Yeats—but to those figures who define the entire tradition. His "first published poem, at the age of 14" consisted of "forty-four lines, imitating the blank verse at the opening of *Paradise Lost*" (King 37). An early one-act play was "based on the Paolo and Francesca episode in Dante's *Inferno*" (King 75). Though these pieces respond to particular works, much of Walcott's early writing addresses genres and periods. In his best known early play, *Henri Christophe*, he took on English Renaissance drama. In *The Joker of Seville*, he addressed the Spanish Golden Age. In *Oh Babylon!* he turned to American popular culture—in this case, the Broadway musical—which is even more pervasively dominant in world culture than is English elite culture. In each case, he sought to confront a dominant genre of Euro-American literary hegemony and place himself in the company of the greatest writers in that genre. Walcott has, in effect, characterized this strategy as "mimicry." And it is a sort of imitation. (For an influential treatment of Walcott's work based on this self-description, see Terada.) However, the term is, I believe, misleading in several ways. Walcott has not really worked to imitate individual precursors. His actual practice has, unsurprisingly, been more complex than his public statements about that practice. As just noted, much research in cognitive psychology shows that our verbal accounts of our own motives and behaviors are only marginally more accurate than our accounts of other people's motives and behaviors. Poets are no different from anyone else in this respect. In Walcott's case, this is further complicated by the fact that he does not appear to be entirely forthright about his background, intentions, the characteristics of his work, and so on. In any event, Walcott's purpose seems best characterized, not as mimicry, but as what might be called "outdoing the tradition." (Obviously, this is not the sort of project about which Walcott could be forthright—unless he wished to appear almost insanely pompous.) Admittedly, this strategy was not terribly successful in the works just mentioned. Though undoubtedly accomplished, none of them has placed Walcott in the same category as the relevant precursors (e.g., Shakespeare). However, this strategy culminated in *Omeros,* and there it has been far more successful.

Put differently, we could divide the literary tradition into the "ordinary" tradition and the handful of "greatest" or "paradigm" authors in a tradition, the authors who define the reference set for general literary excellence. In English literature, Chaucer, Shakespeare, and Milton are the figures usually cited in this regard. In the broader European tradition, one would include the Greek dramatists, the great epicists mentioned in the title of this chapter, and a handful of other writers. Insofar as Walcott is able to put himself in their company, he in a sense lifts himself out of the mainstream. Other writers have undertaken this task before. Dante, for example, explicitly put himself into this sort of paradigmatic reference set in the fourth canto of the *Inferno.* Accompanied by Virgil, he meets Horace, Ovid, Lucan, and Homer. He then explains: "yet more honour unto me they paid, / For me into their band did they invite, / So that I a sixth amid such wisdom made" (4.100–103). But there is a difference with Walcott here. When Walcott elevates himself to a reference set of paradigm authors, now slightly different than at Dante's time, he not only elevates himself personally, but shows the possibility of paradigmatic literary achievement for other Afro-Caribbeans. His work thus stands as an implicit challenge to standard colonialist intergroup hierarchies in literary culture.

More exactly, in *Omeros,* Walcott has set out to place himself in the company of Homer, Virgil, Dante, and Milton. He has not set out to be another ordinary, successful poet—a William Stafford or Philip Larkin—nor even one of the top modernist poets, such as Auden. He has not tried to put himself in the company of Black Mountain poets, Beat poets, New York poets, or any similar group. He has sought to put himself in the company of a handful of paradigmatic writers—not merely those who are in the "Western Canon," but those who define it.

Moreover, he has chosen the paradigmatic genre in order to do this. In the history of European literature, the epic is the great, culminating genre. To write a successful epic is to achieve the apex of literary success. It is the definitive achievement of a writer's life. Novels, lyrics, even dramas are cheap and plentiful by comparison. In addition, it is a genre that has almost completely disappeared from contemporary literature—unlike tragedy, the nearest competitor for paradigm status. Thus to attempt an epic in this context is particularly daring, a particular challenge for a poet's virtuosity, and a particular challenge to the canon that elevates the epic.

Of course, Walcott has repeatedly denied this, insisting that *Omeros* is not an epic (see Bruckner 396). Many critics have taken him at his word. But this seems just obtuse on their part. Walcott also insists that the poem is not filled with "classical reverberations" (qtd. in Bruckner 399), though this is as patently false as any statement about a literary work can be. Indeed, it seems clear that Walcott is actually drawing attention to the "outdoing" aspect of his poem by these statements. And he is doing so through a classical technique—a *recusatio* or refusal, as Davis has pointed out (323; see also 327). It is not, so to speak, *merely* an epic, a rewriting of Homer—but it is to be put in the same category, evaluated in the same, paradigmatic context. To say that he "didn't force classical reverberations" (qtd. in Bruckner 399) is to say that they entered naturally into the poem. One might argue that the work of, say, Pound or Eliot forces such reverberations, whereas the paradigm epicists, such as Virgil, do not "stretch to make associations" (qtd. in Bruckner 399). The point, again, seems to be that he is placing himself in the definitive or paradigm set, above the mere belated followers of Homer, Virgil, Dante, and Milton.

Of course, I am not the first person to question Walcott's assertions here. Many critics have rightly ignored Walcott's claims. Hamner, for example, stresses that, in *Omeros,* "Walcott undertakes nothing less than a modern adaptation of the time-honored genre of the epic" ("Introduction" 10)—not just an adaptation of Homer. On the next page, he goes further and characterizes the poem as "a re-writing of tradition" (11), a point developed with insight and erudition by Farrell. In keeping with this, Hamner ends *Epic of the Dispossessed* by asserting that, "In spite of Walcott's disclaimers, *Omeros* is not only a credible extension of the world's store of epics, it also enriches that venerable genre and exposes unexpected, rarely used resources." Thus, it "deserves to be compared" with works by Homer, Virgil, Dante, and so on (166).

In sum, as Hamner's concluding assertion suggests, Walcott's relation to metropolitan tradition is an attempt to go beyond what might be called "great normalcy"—the usual apex of achievement for contemporary writers from any group—and make himself, instead, exemplary of that tradition, in the way Homer, Virgil, Dante, and Milton are. But, again, the issue is more than individual. If successful, this achievement would implicitly put Afro-Caribbean society on a par with Greek, Roman, Italian, and English society, and Afro-Caribbean writers on a par with those of Europe. Walcott pursues this simultaneously personal and political task by seeking to become a master or exemplar of the master or exemplary genre of the metropolitan tradition.

If I am correct in framing Walcott's project in this way, then some standard ways of discussing the poem appear to be at least partially misguided. Much critical discussion of the poem concerns whether we are to take the Homeric parallels as ennobling their Caribbean subjects or as parodying the European models. Thus Breslin discusses how almost all Homeric "parallels come under skeptical attack" (246). But, at the same time, Breslin notes that "The obsessive proliferation of Homeric comparisons might be seen as a lingering wound of colonized consciousness, motivated by an insecure longing to claim the founding authority of the European canon" (266). Or, as Thieme puts it, the Homeric parallel "inevitably suggests at least a residual sense of need for classical validation" (155). Breslin concludes that the poem combines two contradictory tendencies—one "invested in Homeric analogy," another committed to a "critique of its own analogical method" (272). I do not at all wish to deny that there are contradictory tendencies in any author's aims and practices. It is rare that any of us is fully consistent in our goals or beliefs. Indeed, cognitively, it is well established that even the most apparently univocal outputs may derive from highly ambivalent inputs and processes (see, for example, Ito and Cacioppo 69). However, in this case, the discussion seems to be proceeding along the wrong lines. A writer's relation to literary traditions is not, in general, parallel with an activist's relation to political parties. It is not—at least not primarily, and certainly not solely—a matter of taking a political stand on a program.

Specifically, if we understand Walcott's project as one of establishing his work as exemplary within the reference set for epic, we ask different questions of the work and isolate different patterns. For example, we expect just the sort of ambivalence that we find in Walcott—partial diminution of comparison works (such as *The Iliad*) along with admiration. The diminution is part of what one would expect of any author trying to establish his/her place among revered precursors. Insofar as Walcott ironizes some Homeric parallel, the function is to place his work in the same category, but then simultaneously to differentiate it. After all, he would not be in the same reference set if he merely repeated Homer. Conversely, the admiration is not some surrender to the authority of colonial culture. It is the acceptance of those works as suitable peers. Insofar as it is political, it is not self-abnegation by an Afro-Caribbean writer. Rather, it is an elevation of the Afro-Caribbean writer. Put differently, in placing his poem in a set of paradigm works, Walcott cannot denigrate those works entirely. He must ironize them to some degree, thereby establishing his uniqueness. But if he were to deny their literary stature, he would diminish the value of his own project. It would be equivalent to saying "Homer is overrated. There is nothing special about *The Iliad*. And my poem is in the same class as his." Thus, what appears to be self-contradiction, given standard approaches to the poem, becomes entirely comprehensible and consistent in this context.

But that is not the only difference. If Walcott's main project is one of outdoing a tradition, as represented by paradigm works in the paradigm genre, then the center of Walcott's relation shifts from self-conscious allusion to a more integrated literary practice. Critics treating Walcott's relation to epic have focused primarily on the explicit connections to which Walcott draws our attention by naming them. Moreover, they have focused largely on Homer, with relatively little reference to other epicists. The present account turns our attention toward the often implicit integration of narrative and character structures from a range of paradigm epic works. Thus it leads us to consider the way in which scenes, events, or personal relations derive from and call for comparison with scenes, events, and personal relations, not only in Homer, but in Virgil, Dante, and Milton.

Of course, I am not saying that Walcott was fully aware of this project. Except in the simplest acts, we never fully articulate and theorize our goals. Writing an epic poem is not one of those simplest acts. But we do have a sense of whether or not we are accomplishing our goal. We do one thing after another, groping toward some vague, ill-formulated end. We are disappointed by each attempt, saying "No, that's not it; that's not right." Until we actually *discover* what we were aiming for. The point holds for such banal matters as how one dresses on a given evening and for such important matters as what one does for a living. It certainly holds for writing a poem. This is one of the reasons that introspection is so unreliable. We are only partially aware of even our motivating purposes. Walcott was certainly self-conscious about his project in part. But he was almost as certainly unselfconscious about it in part as well. All that is important for my purposes is that he was able to judge, while writing and revising, whether or not he was fulfilling this partially implicit and unarticulated project.

In any case, when undertaking such a project self-consciously or unselfconsciously—a project where one seeks to make a work exemplary for a genre—an author necessarily begins with a broad schema of the genre in question. Such a schema gives standard requirements for the form. In the case of epic, we are dealing first of all with an extended narrative in verse. But the precise structure of the narrative, the nature of the verse, and other particular matters, are not covered in the schema. For reasons discussed in chapter 1, these are likely to be borrowed from prototypes and from paradigmatic instances or, in our cogntivist terminology, paradigmatic "exempla." Here Walcott draws, predictably, on the five major epics of the European tradition—*The Iliad, The Odyssey, The Aeneid, The Divine Comedy,* and *Paradise Lost.* These serve to provide him with more specific elements for form, plot, character, and so forth.

Of course, Walcott is not the first writer to have undertaken this sort of project. Indeed, he had a particular model in mind—James Joyce. Joyce's *Ulysses* is clearly a work of outdoing in just this sense. It too is a revision of the epic tradition, systematically incorporating and revising both the *Odyssey* and *Paradise Lost,* and including significant elements of Dante and Virgil as well (see Reynolds and Schork). Moreover, one of its chapters, "Oxen of the Sun," comprises a series of imitations that take the reader through the history of English prose style. It is a technical tour de force in part designed to show Joyce's unparalleled mastery of the English language—his exemplary status, indeed, preeminence. Thus, Joyce's novel serves as an exemplum of exactly the task Walcott is undertaking. This gives Joyce's work a special status with respect to Walcott's project. *Ulysses* is a sort of second-order exemplum for Walcott. It not only guides his epic creation as such—a first-order function it shares with the *Iliad,* and others. It simultaneously guides his perception and use of those first-order exempla, his encoding, selection, abstraction, and specification of those paradigm precursors. Joyce's work probably would not have assumed this central cognitive status if it did not have deep emotional significance for Walcott as well. Unsurprisingly, then, Walcott identified with Joyce and Joyce's fictional alter-ego, Stephen, from an early age. King explains that "During 1948 Walcott read James Joyce's *Portrait of the Artist* and *Ulysses.* He wanted to be Stephen Dedalus" (52). Indeed, "He felt Irish. . . . He felt like Joyce" (53).

I will discuss Walcott's use of each of these authors in turn. However, before going on to this, it is important to treat one other reason for Walcott's choice of epic as his genre here, and one other aspect of his outdoing of the tradition—an outdoing that, in this case, relates directly to the issue of biased intergroup comparison. Epic, as is well known, is often a genre of national self-definition and can provide a sort of imaginative center for a nation. This can be true in different ways. Virgil's epic recounts the origin of Rome, and thus is a foundational national epic in the details of its story. Homer's *Iliad,* the explicit model for Walcott's poem, operates similarly in treating part of a major military victory for a united Greek army. *The Odyssey* does not recount a story of this sort. Nonetheless, along with the *Iliad,* it has had a central place in Greek culture and has served as a common reference point for a Greek sense of identity—both modern national identity, and the earlier, prenational identity that led the Greeks to distinguish sharply between themselves and the *barbaroi.* Dante's poem is less obviously national in character, but it established the Italian vernacular as a literary language, and thus effectively founded Italian literature. Moreover, this was not accidental. Dante had earlier defended Italian as a literary language in his treatise *De Vulgari Eloquentia.* Milton's poem too lacks obvious nationalistic connections, but it was certainly central to the English sense of cultural pride. Moreover, as many critics have noted, the poem does in fact deal indirectly with the political events that guided much of Milton's life (see, for example, chapter 29 of Hill). It is, then, in many ways, a complex, ambivalent, epic of the English nation (if not, precisely, an allegory in the narrow sense [see Hill 342–43]). Finally, many lesser epics are as explicit in their nationalist purposes as the *Aeneid.*

This generic function of epic is clearly well suited to the postcolonization poet who is writing at a time when his/her nation is in the process of self-definition, a time when the imagination of the nation is in its early stages. In keeping with this, Walcott takes up the epic form to fashion a national allegory of his native St. Lucia, which achieved independence from England only in 1979, presumably not long before Walcott began writing the poem, which was published in 1990. This is, then, an outdoing of the metropolitan tradition which has a national goal as well. Walcott not only places his own work in the context of the paradigm epicists of the metropolitan tradition, he simultaneously places the small Afro-Caribbean nation of St. Lucia among the paradigm states of the metropolitan tradition. Walcott refers directly to these paradigm states: "the empires: London, Rome, Greece" (*Omeros* 196). He places himself in the company of the great poets from each state—Milton, Virgil, Homer. At the same time, he places St. Lucia in the company of the empires themselves. Indeed, in examining a colony rather than an empire, he in some ways elevates St. Lucia above London, Rome, and Greece, for he makes it a nation, equal in human importance, but not a perpetrator of oppression and cruelty.

THE NATION AND THE EPIC

More exactly, Walcott takes up the common form of national allegory in which the nation is represented by a woman, and two political or other tendencies vying for the nation are presented as her suitors. The woman, in this case, is Helen. It was a fortunate coincidence for Walcott that "Helen" was one name of his island, as well as the name of Menelaus's wife, the object of the Trojan war—a coincidence that eased his use of the *Iliad* for this national allegory. Walcott stresses the point, knowing that it would be unfamiliar to most readers: "the island was once / named Helen; its Homeric association // rose like smoke from a siege" (31). It is worth noting that the connection is also brought out in the St. Lucian national anthem, which refers to St. Lucia as "Helen of the West," and describes her, like Helen, as the most beautiful woman—"Fairest . . . of all the earth."

In this allegory, Helen ambiguously represents St. Lucia as a physical place, St. Lucia as a political entity, and St. Lucia as a people. Walcott repeatedly draws these connections more or less straightforwardly. For example, in the fifth chapter of book one, he refers to the independence of former colonies of Britain, clearly linking Helen with the new nation of St. Lucia: "the Raj, / whose ebbing surf lifted the coastlines of nations // as lacy as Helen's shift" (30). Later, he states the identification explicitly: "the island was Helen" (103). The point is suggested more subtly in Helen's "yellow dress" with a "black V of . . . velvet" (29), for the flag of St. Lucia has a black "V" (upside down) and a yellow triangle at its center. It is clearly not accidental that the White couple sees her as having acquired this dress/national flag by "theft" (62), while Helen insists that it was given to her and is legally hers (64)—the typical difference in opinion between the colonizer and the colonized regarding independence. In either case, "that dress / had an empire's tag on it" (64). The new nation is always in part fabricated by the colonizer—the land is divided by the colonizer, the government defined, the economy structured. The flag of St. Lucia always bears the tag, "Made in Great Britain."

The two suitors are not, as one might expect, named Menelaus and Paris. Walcott does not choose the lovers of Spartan Helen to supply the names here. Rather, he chooses the two great fighters around whom Homer's epic centers—Hector and Achilles (here in its French form of "Achille"). Also fortunately for this allegorical structure, St. Lucia seems to have been fought over by two groups from even before the colonial period. First, there was the conflict between the Aruacs and the Caribs, then the Caribs and the Europeans. Then there were the battles between the British and the French, who passed the island back and forth some fourteen times before it was permanently ceded to Britain in 1815 (one of the crucial battles, the "Battle of the Saints," is treated in the poem). A postcolonial development of this conflict over St. Lucia came in the elections leading to and following independence. In Walcott's retelling of these elections, the "United Force" tried to offer an alternative to this dualism *"two parties, one Greek and the other Trojan, / both fighting for Helen"* (107), but this third party failed in its effort (109).

Most importantly, Hector and Achille represent two possible paths for the cultural future of St. Lucia today. Hector gives up his fishing in order to drive a passenger-van. Representing the crazed pace of modernization and Americanization threatening the Caribbean in recent years (a point noted by Terada [199]), Hector's van moves through the island at breakneck speeds, eventually crashing and leaving Hector dead. Achille, in contrast, continues with his traditional fishing profession. Indeed, he delves even further into his

African roots, taking an oneiric trip back to Africa at the time when his ancestors were abducted into slavery. The allegorical significance of this is straightforward. In Walcott's view, the Americanizing tendency, represented by Hector, is virtual suicide for the Caribbean. In contrast, a commitment to traditional occupations, with a concomitant concern for Afro-Caribbean history and the roots of Afro-Caribbean culture, will lead to strength, health, confidence, and fulfillment. Eventually, this tendency will win the hearts and minds of St. Lucia, just as Achille eventually wins Helen back from Hector.

In keeping with the allegorical significance of Hector, Helen is represented as often engaged in a sort of "whoring" behavior. Allegorically, St. Lucia is whoring after the American dollar. "She was selling herself like the island, without / any pain, and the village did not seem to care // that it was dying in its change, the way it whored / away a simple life" (112). The message here is the same as it is in the case of Hector—imitation of American culture leads to death, while life is sustained by Afro-Caribbean tradition. The link is almost explicit on the next page. Achille, or Walcott, recalls "the smell of fresh bread drawn from [the village's] Creole oven," then thinks, "its flour turned into cocaine, its daughters to whores." He thinks of the slogan of Caribbean modernity, a slogan that recalls the dangerous speed of Hector's van: "WE MOVIN', MAN! WE MOVIN'!" only to ask, "but towards what?" (112). Evidently towards the same end that kills Hector. Indeed, the characterization of Helen as a "whore" (115), leaving Achille for Hector (116), coincides with the introduction of Hector's van (116), and thus with his shift from Afro-Caribbean tradition to Americanization. Achille understands Helen's behavior in terms that fit the nation as well. Everything had been reduced to money, he reflects—how could she act any other way? (44).

This is related to Walcott's allegorical portrayal of colonialism—prominently, the slave trade that was an integral part of colonialism in the Americas. Certainly, colonialism is amply represented in literal terms. But the allegorical representation of its effects is perhaps even more important. Colonialism results in an unhealing wound. The basic meaning is straightforward—a physical wound stands for an emotional wound, an injury to one's sense of personal worth, a severing of possibilities for a fulfilling life, a mutilation of hope. Moreover, colonialism leads to this wound not only for the colonized person, but for the colonizer as well. Philoctete suffers from such a wound. But so does Major Plunkett. (On the range of those who suffer from this wound, see Ramazani, "Wound," 412–15.) The wound is, in a sense, what we carry with us of the traumatic, collective past. It is "the wound of history," in Jahan Ramazani's phrase ("Wound" 405)—imperial history in particular. This idea is part of the legacy from *Ulysses*. For Stephen Dedalus, "History . . . is a nightmare from which I am trying to awaken" (2.377). In saying this, Stephen recalls Haines's comment on "The imperial British state" and its treatment of Ireland—"It seems history is to blame" (1.649). For Stephen, imperial history is the sequence of irreversible events that lead to his family's poverty and disintegration, his own physical and moral decay, and the general despair that surrounds him. It is, indeed, a nightmare. In Walcott, this "nightmare" is shifted to a wound—and just as Stephen cannot awaken from the nightmare, this wound cannot be healed, or, rather, cannot be healed until the wounded men return to their roots in African tradition.

The first image of wounding, in Book I, chapter I, recalls the original moment of Caribbean colonialism—the battle of Europeans against the precolonial inhabitants—and discusses a "wound" produced by the killing of their gods (5). In the next chapter, Philoctete is introduced, "The sore on his shin / still unhealed" (9). In the third chapter, Philoctete gives his account of this wound: "He believed the swelling came from the chained ankles / of his grandfathers" (19). At the beginning of the fourth chapter, he curses his fate—being "without roots in this world"—and "sob[s]" (21). He suffers the effects of the wound, including an inability to scream or to speak—an implication of lockjaw, but equally an expression of the voicelessness of ordinary Afro-Caribbean people, a voicelessness Walcott is trying to redress in this poem.[1] Later, Walcott thinks of "slave shacks" (177), compares them to "a running wound" or "the rusty anchor / that scabbed Philoctete's shin" (178). He explains that "history happens" in "baying echoes of brutality, / and terror" (178).

Philoctete's wound is healed by the same sort of return to tradition that characterizes Achille's renewal, and his crucial difference from Hector. Ma Kilman knows the arts of traditional healing. She seeks out a plant from Africa—"A swift had carried the strong seed in its stomach / centuries ago" (238). "She bathed [Philoctete] in the brew of the *root*" (246, emphasis added), finally curing him. In short, it is only the sense of continuity with the African past, a reaching back into the culture, the learning, perhaps even the physical being, of Africa itself that can cure the wounds of colonialism and make whole the hearts of Afro-Caribbean people. It is not, by implication, the modern techniques borrowed from Europe and America, but the traditions of the people. It is not some powder or injection synthesized by American pharmaceutical companies; it is not American money, commercial entertainment, industry, science, or tourism. Rather, it is African "roots"—one's own "roots" in the African past—that heal. The point applies not only to Philoctete and Achille. It applies to all Afro-Caribbeans, including Walcott himself. Speaking of Philoctete, he says, "we shared the one wound, the same cure" (295).

Indeed, it seems to apply even to non-Africans. After his wife dies, Plunkett too visits Ma Kilman; he too reaches out to some original sense of mystery and spiritual wisdom through her. He too achieves a link with Africa, for "That moment bound him for good to another race" (307). As a result, "His wound healed slowly" (309). In this way, Walcott's appeal to African roots seems to share, somewhat paradoxically, Tutuola's universalist impulse (an impulse also shared by Tagore and Ali).

This healing return to the past leads us to the problem of the future and thus to another standard element in national allegory—the representation of the nation's future as a new child, the baby who has just been born or who is still growing in the mother's womb. *Omeros* ends with Helen pregnant, the nation itself pregnant with the new generation, born after independence, raised not in the British empire, but in the new, independent society. In this case, the paternity of the child is ambiguous. The evidence points to Achille, and he is certainly the most important. The new generation, the future of St. Lucia, results primarily from the union of the new nation with the traditional workers, whose culture has grown naturally from their African roots, which they accept and perpetuate. But there are hints of two other fathers as well— Hector, and Plunkett. While this triple paternity does not literally fit pregnancy, it is appropriate to the allegory. For the new generation will have not one but many fathers. Though Walcott clearly wants Achille to be the dominant figure guiding the future of St. Lucia, he also recognizes that the new St. Lucia will necessarily incorporate elements of (largely American) modernization, represented by Hector, and elements of traditional English society, represented by Plunkett. (It is interesting that, despite the great influence of Ireland on his own work, Walcott has made the Irish presence in the Caribbean into a barren woman, who dies before the poem ends, thus contributing nothing to the new nation—though she is perhaps the most sympathetic character in the work.)

Early in the poem, Helen expresses the point about paternity in this way: "I pregnant, / but I don't know for who" (34)—meaning, first of all, "by whom," but also, "for what purpose" or "toward what future." She could have made the same comment at the end, for even there the future remains uncertain. Ma Kilman explains that "Achille want to give [the child], even is Hector's, an African name," a name that links the future of the society back to its roots. But Helen, despite her attachment to Achille, has hardly given up her mimeticism, her Hectorlike pursuit of the modern—ultimately represented by the American dollar. "Helen don't want no African child"—like St. Lucia itself, she wants American "progress." Achille says that he will wait "till the day of christening," but "Helen must learn / where she from" (318).

It is an important, if rather obvious point that the allegorical personifications of St. Lucia and her possible futures are not, at the literal level, celebrated leaders, members of a political, economic, or educational elite. Rather, they are ordinary, working-class people. This is important because part of Walcott's aim in creating this national allegory out of the European epic tradition is to shift heroism from the "masters" to the "servants," to move away from celebrating the dominant class and celebrate instead those who are dominated. In this,

Walcott turns sharply away from Joyce as well. While Joyce certainly had affection and respect for his characters, he did not elevate them to heroic stature. Rather, he treated them as highly ironic versions of their Homeric precedents. Walcott, in contrast, takes the heroism of his characters quite seriously. In speaking of slaves, Walcott writes, "But they crossed, they survived. There is epical splendour" (149). The sentiment drives the whole of his poem. Hamner is right to call *Omeros* an "Epic of the Dispossessed." It is a poem depicting the epical splendor that is found in the lives of poor, Black people on a tiny island. Walcott sees the entire history of these people as a lost epic poem, filled with strength, bravery, and endurance that seem almost superhuman. He looks at the sea—over which the slaves crossed in an Odyssey more painful and more grand than the royal misadventure sung by Homer—and he hears, the "heart-heaving sough," the rhythm, the hush from each line of tides, begun "in Guinea to fountain exhaustion here." All that human greatness, journeying from Africa to the Americas, faded from the world, like exhausted waves breaking against the shore. In this sea, with its ridges of surf like lines of a poem, he recognizes "an epic where every line was erased." It is his task to undo the erasure and write the splendor of those brutalized but enduring men and women. This ocean has "no memory of the wanderings of Gilgamesh" nor of "the *Iliad*" (296). It is not an ocean of kings, but of servants. It is not the Mediterranean, to which European bards turned for inspiration, but a parallel and inverse source, reaching out to Africa.

In connection with this, Walcott stresses that the European epicists are far from unique in their poetic task. The lost epics lamented by Walcott are not merely a matter of great actions that have gone unrecorded. Often, those actions have been sung—or other actions of the same peoples. But these great oral epics have largely been lost.[2] Whether the epics spoke of ordinary people or, as is more likely, their own elite, each society had an epic poet—each tradition had its Homer, as Homer too had his own oral precursors. Thus Walcott places the Native American shaman, the West African griot, the local bard of St. Lucia (Seven Seas), all on a level with Homer. They are all his peers. But they sang poetry that faded into air. Like the ocean, their lines were erased with each passing wave. It is Walcott's task to retrieve a bit of that history too, to preserve the roots, to acknowledge the songs sung by these non-European Homers, and to elevate them into tradition as well.

THE ILIAD

Just as Joyce bases *Ulysses* explicitly on the *Odyssey* but draws on other epics as well, Walcott bases *Omeros* explicitly on the *Iliad*. It is interesting that, while Joyce names his book after the main character in the precursor epic, Walcott names his book after the author. In part, this is related to the purpose of Walcott's epic. Again, Walcott is setting out to place himself in the same reference set as the great epicists of the Western tradition. In naming the poem *Omeros,* Walcott places his own name in direct parallel with that of the founder of the European epic tradition. Most obviously, the cover of the book includes two names and nothing else—"Omeros" and "Derek Walcott." This pairs the two authors, and may even be seen as tracing a sort of arc from the originator to his contemporary inheritor or descendant.

The point is reenforced by the alteration in Homer's name. The poem is not entitled *Homer* or even *Homeros.* It is, rather, *Omeros.* Walcott deletes the rough breathing mark that begins Homer's name in the ancient Greek. This is similar to Joyce's transformation of "Odusseus" (i.e., Odysseus) into "Ulysses," his adoption of the Latin form, rather than the Greek. In doing this, Joyce suggests that *Ulysses* is an historically mediated alteration of the Greek original. The most obvious interpretation of Walcott's "Omeros" is similar. In Modern Greek, the initial fricative, signaled by the rough breathing mark in Homeric Greek, is no longer pronounced. For this reason, in Modern Greek, the name "Homeros" becomes "Omeros." In choosing the Modern Greek version, Walcott implies that this poem is an alteration of Homer's work, specifically a modernization, a change parallel to that in the name. Perhaps he is even implying that he himself is this new, modern Homer (i.e. "Omeros"), the new Homer who, in modernizing the *Iliad,* transforms it from a story about the heroism of the oppressor to a story about the heroism of the oppressed.

On the other hand, when speaking about Homer in interviews and in the poem itself, Walcott seems to imply that "Omeros" is the correct, ancient version of the name. His informant says "O-meros. . . . That's what we call him in Greek" (14). She does not say, "in modern Greek." Indeed, Walcott sometimes implies that "Homer" is an ethnocentric version of the poet's name—"Homer and Virg are New England farmers" (14). (For a thoughtful discussion of Walcott's views on the name "Omeros," see Dougherty.) This too would fit his project, if we simply assume that he takes oppressed people to have been the true heroes all along. Lefkowitz argues, quite plausibly, that Walcott's Homer is an "everyman's Homer," inspired by an "ancient legend," according to which "Homer came from a humble background and had a hard and lonely life" (400). The poem, like the title, would be a sort of restoration of something misunderstood or misrepresented. In this way, the title still implies a deviation, though not a deviation from Homer per se. Rather, it implies a deviation from Homer *as he has been understood.* This clearly fits with the introduction of Omeros in chapter 38. There, Omeros is not the grand bard of European imagination. Rather, he is an ordinary bum, covered with "grit" and birdshit (193), "scrofulous," wearing a "black greatcoat" like some character out of Beckett. His nose is "bulbed," his face "cragged," his beard wild and white as "foam" on the sea (193). He cannot afford a belt, but uses instead a bit of rope. His manuscript of the *Odyssey* is "turned-down" (194)—which is to say, both dog-eared and rejected by publishers, who have no interest in such stuff. He is kicked away by a "church-warden" (194). Walcott's point here seems to be similar to a commonplace about Jesus—a commonplace partially illustrated in Walcott's earlier *Dream on Monkey Mountain*: If Jesus were to return today, nobody would recognize him, and the Christians would be the first to reject him. Walcott implies that, if Homer were to return today, nobody would recognize him, and the upholders of European culture would be the first to reject him.

In this way, it does not really matter whether Walcott understood the evolution of the Greek language or not. Either way, the interpretation is much the same. He is altering the traditional view of Homer, changing him from a poet of nobility into a poet of the poor. This is also consistent with Walcott's repeated re-creations of the Omeros figure. Again, Walcott represents every society as having its bard, the blind poet who witnesses and memorializes all the suffering of his people. Thus we have the griot in Africa recording the misery of the slave trade and the "white-eyed Omeros" of Native America (216) recording the horrors of American genocide. St. Lucia itself has an Omeros—Seven Seas, another blind seer of the common people. In each of these cases, the bard sings the heroism of those brutalized by colonialism—much as Walcott, a second bard for St. Lucia, undertakes to do with Hector and Achille. It does not really matter whether these bards—and Walcott himself—are an alteration of Homer or a repetition and recovery of Homer. What is important is that Walcott is using the structure of Homer's works—and the works of his followers in the European epic tradition—to engage in just this bardic elevation of the oppressed.

As we shall see, Walcot makes considerable use of both Homeric epics. However, the use of the *Iliad* is more systematic—unsurprisingly, as it is more explicit as well. Walcott obviously draws the names of the major Afro-Caribbean protagonists from this poem. Achille is the great hero; Hector is his noble but defeated enemy; Helen is the prize over which they fight, a morally ambiguous character—a great beauty, but fickle. As Homer's Helen begins with Menelaus, shifts to Paris, then returns to Menelaus after Paris's death, Walcott's Helen begins with Achille, moves to Hector, then returns "home" to Achille (267) after Hector's death. Walcott shifts from Menelaus to Achille and Paris to Hector, presumably to have the two sides represented by their major warriors, not by the inconsequential husband and lover of Homer's epic. This is clearly more fitting for his heroic elevation of Afro-Caribbean people, and his political allegory as well.

As I have been stressing the heroism of Walcott's characters and the heroic nature of his project, it is important to note that some critics have taken precisely the opposite view of the poem. For example, Sidney Burris maintains that Walcott "often sets up an obvious parallel between one of his characters and its Homeric equivalent only to punctuate it with a kind of slapstick disregard" (560–61). It is true that there are ironic elements in the poem. However, these are far from central, and far from slapstick. Consider, for example, the image of Achille's heel—an obvious candidate for analysis as "slapstick." In the very first chapter, the narrator tells us that Achille "saw the swift/crossing the cloud-surf, a small thing, far from its home." Immediately after this, Achille finds that he is caught and cannot move forward. "A thorn vine gripped/his heel" (6). It may seem at first that this is an ironic reference to Achilles' heel—especially as "He tugged it free" (6). But, later, Walcott makes clear that the swift is an image for the African diaspora. Its long journey from home is a symbol of the long journey of Achille's ancestors, when they were brought as slaves to the island. This already suggests what the "Achilles' heel" might mean in this context. The image of the heel caught in a vine recurs twenty-six chapters later, where it becomes clear. Achille has traveled back to Africa in a dream. He sees his ancestral village—its ordinary life. Then he sees his forebears rounded up to be sold as slaves. He witnesses that primal scene, that Fall, that expulsion from Eden—as it will appear in the Miltonic parallel. He thinks "I can deliver/all of them by hiding . . . then I could/change their whole future" (148). But he cannot change this nightmare of history. Just as he tries, "a cord/of thorned vine looped his tendon, encircling the heel/with its own piercing chain" (148). The Achilles' heel of Achille is the chain of slavery. It is history, like Philoctete's wound. It is the Fall from Edenic Africa. On the very next page, Walcott writes of the slaves: "But they crossed, they survived. There is the epical splendour" (149). This is anything but slapstick.

The image of Achille dancing in women's clothing is similar. It appears to be an ironic revision of the story that Achilles' mother tried to keep him away from the Trojan war by disguising him as a girl. And there is certainly something comic in the image of Achille as one of "the androgynous/warriors" (276). But there is seriousness and pathos just below the surface. Achilles' heel was vulnerable because the entire rest of his body was not. His mother, Thetis, daughter of the sea, had protected him—except for that one vulnerable spot. Thetis is like Mother Africa. The Afro-Caribbean people are her children—and also the descendants of the sea, like Achilles, like Thetis. The Mother gave them strength and skill and tradition, but she could not protect them against that one weak point, the chain around the heel. So, too, she tried to conceal them, hide them from the soldiers who—like the Greek army heading for Troy—wished to take them across the sea to a foreign land where they would die. In both cases, the disguise did not work, the mother's protection failed. In the case of Achille, this protection was tradition, a shared cultural practice, remembered and commemorated every year in the New World by slaves trying to recreate a lost home: "Achille explained that he and Philo had done this / every Boxing Day, and not because of Christmas, // but for something older; something that he had seen / in Africa, when his name had followed a swift" (275). It is no accident that, when the dance ends and he collects the money for the dancers, "Philoctete sat down. Then he wept" (277).

Philoctete himself fits this heroic elevation as well. He is based on the character of Philoctetes, whom the Greeks abandoned on a deserted island, because he had been bitten by a serpent and his wound would not heal. As we have already seen, in Walcott's poem, that wound is an outward sign of an inner hurt, a cancer eating at the soul of a people sold into slavery, far from home, separated from their families and friends on a strange island. Philoctetes is eventually cured by Machaon, the son of Asclepius, God of Healing. (On the story of Philoctetes, see Harvey.) Philoctete too is cured by Ma Kilman. She is not the child of Asclepius, but she is a descendant of the healers of Africa: "All the unburied gods, for three deep centuries dead, / but from whose lineage, as if her veins were their roots, / her arms ululated, uplifting the branches / of a tree carried across the Atlantic that shoots / fresh leaves" (242–43). In doing this, she not only cures a bodily wound, but the spiritual ulcer it symbolizes: "the wound . . . its rage / festering for centuries" (244). Again, she does this by rediscovering Africa, tradition, a link with a severed past—roots: "the corolla / closed its thorns like the sea-egg. What else did it cure?" (247). Oddly, Ma Kilman's cure of Philoctete is one of Burris's primary examples of Walcott's "slapstick" (561).

THE ODYSSEY

Walcott's use of the *Odyssey* is less systematic. This poem does not serve so much as a broad structure for organizing the story of *Omeros*. Rather, it appears to serve primarily as a sort of repository of symbols, a store from which Walcott can draw useful images and metaphors, applying them to different characters and situations as the need arises.

Perhaps the most obvious image of this sort is that of Odysseus himself, who serves as an epical exemplum of someone who has been displaced from home, someone who longs to return, to cross the sea back to the place where he/she belongs, but is blocked at every turn. This is most obviously the condition of all Afro-Caribbean people (cf. Figueroa 209). Thus, St. Lucia with its yellow flag, or Helen in her yellow dress, are like "butterflies . . . in their yellow odysseys" (170).

When Achille returns to his people, it is a version of Odysseus' homecoming—"This was the shout on which each odyssey pivots, / that silent cry for a reef, or familiar bird" (159). A dream of Africa, it is a version of Odysseus's "dream of Ithaca" that Walcott mentions later in the poem; "Island after island passing. Still we ain't home" (203). Just as Odysseus sees his beloved plagued by armed suitors, so too does Achille see his people plagued by armed slave traders. The difference is that Achille cannot join with his son, or with any other relative, to kill the suitors, to save his home and wife, but must watch them dragged off to live a history of exile, an unending odyssey, unable to return home, to pass again the degrees of longitude that separate Africa and America, to go in reverse, to achieve that homecoming where the "parallel / is crossed, and cancels the line of master and slave" (159).

Walcott too is Odysseus, doubly exiled—first from Africa, then from St. Lucia: "I thought of Helen / as my island lost in the haze, and I was sure / I'd never see her again" (222); though he is referring to Helen herself in this passage, the implication of Odysseuslike exile from the island she represents is clear. In the next section, he recalls this theme, and looks at the curtains billowing in the wind "like a sail towards Ithaca" (223). Indeed, throughout the poem, Walcott is on an Odysseuslike journey around the world. Appropriately, when he meets Omeros, he thinks "of all my traveling" (282).

But Afro-Caribbean people are not the only ones who seek a home they cannot find. Europeans too have been displaced. They too are like wandering Odysseus. Maud longs for Ireland, but she and Plunkett cannot afford the passage: "Maud marked their routes: / the cost of a second-class berth from Portugal / to Southampton, then Dublin, but the cheapest rates / staggered Dennis" (122). Plunkett himself, "that khaki Ulysses" (263), still carrying the wound of war, remembers his youthful idea of "a masochistic odyssey through the Empire" (90). In the literal sense, he never made this trip. But, in another way, his entire life has been just such a masochistic odyssey through the Empire.

The Cyclops provides another recurrent image for Walcott—in this case, an image of destruction. It is nature that devastates the islands in the form of a "Cyclone, howling because one of the lances / of a flinging palm has narrowly grazed his one eye" (51). It is the history of Anglo-French colonial war, seen "through the Cyclops eye of the gliding glass" (102). It is the second degradation of St. Lucia—now freed from British colonialism, the island has been subjected to the more insidious colonialism of American culture, with its hoards of vulgar tourists clicking snapshots through the single eye of a photographic lens, eating up the local culture. Indeed, this is the enemy that Achille must fight, as if he were Odysseus: "Achille would howl / at their clacking cameras, and hurl an imagined lance! // It was the scream of a warrior losing his only soul / to the click of a Cyclops" (299)—a synecdoche: the soul of the island and its people are lost, not to the camera per se, but to the culture of the American dollar, with its "development" and tourism.

The scar of Odysseus plays a role as well. Indeed, it is a primary source for the image of the wound throughout Walcott's poem. This is particularly clear in the scene when Philoctete's wound is healed, closing into a scar (4). Ma Kilman heals Philoctete's wound by bathing him and the scene recalls the famous recognition of Odysseus's scar (cf. Dougherty 341)—for Homer introduces the scar when Odysseus is being bathed by his nurse, Eurykleia. Indeed, the links between these scenes go deeper. Odysseus has just returned, at last, to Ithaca. As we have already seen, Philoctete's cure is, similarly, a sort of return home. He does not literally return to Africa. But he is cured by the revival of his African heritage. Moreover, Ma Kilman represents a clear parallel to Eurykleia, who nursed Odysseus in his youth, just as the tradition represented by Ma Kilman nursed, not only Philoctete, but all Afro-Caribbean peoples in their (historical) youth.

The appearance of the poet in his own poem owes at least something to the appearance of "the inspired singer/Demodokos" in the *Odyssey* (8.43–44), no doubt the most famous instance of this sort in Western literary history. This is also, and perhaps more significantly, the source for our image of the blind bard: "the excellent singer / whom the Muse had loved greatly, and gave him both good and evil. / She reft him of his eyes, but she gave him the sweet singing / art" (8.62–65)—the model for Walcott's West African griot, the "white-eyed storyteller" who recounted "the tribe's triumphal sorrow" (139), as well as the "white-eyed Omeros, motionless" (216) and alone after the massacre of Native Americans, and Seven Seas. In each case, the bard sings the sorrows of war—destruction, the loss of human lives. In the *Odyssey*, Demodokos's tale is so sorrowful that brave Odysseus can barely control his weeping (see 8.83–89). The stories of the griot and the shaman—stories of colonial history—are, if anything, more tragic still.

It is worth remarking on one particular point in Walcott's characterization of his blind bards. Why are the griot and the shaman both "white-eyed"? They are white-eyed not only because they are blind, but because the horror that has blinded them is the horror of European brutality. Thus the American Omeros sings that his people have grown "tired . . . of fighting the claws of the White Bear, / dripping red beads on the snow." In their defeat, he laments, "Whiteness was everywhere" (217). The "disease" that "obliterated [Seven Seas'] vision" (12) is much the same—a variation on the wound eating into Philoctete's leg: a colonial history so horrible it blinds those who witness it. Walcott extends this image of blindness to St. Lucy, the "blind saint," patroness of the island. This fits as well, for she too was a victim of imperial violence—the legend being that "her eyes were put out" by the Roman emperor Diocletian (Thurston and Attwater 549). Indeed, in the course of the poem, she is implicitly linked with the blind bards, Walcott's versions of Demodokos for the colonized. Referring to Seven Seas, and Seven Seas' assertion that Achille is in Africa searching for "his name and his soul," Philoctete thinks, "What else was left to believe / but miracles? Whose vision except a blind man's, / or a blind saint's, her name as bright as the island's?" (154).

Finally, Walcott makes repeated use of the image of Circe transforming Odysseus's men into swine. At a personal level, it is an image for any sort of unthinking gluttony or lust. At a social level, it represents cupidity that leads nations to violence. Some instances are trivial: Plunkett tries to take a loaf of bread from the package before they reach home. Maud slaps his knee and names his condition: "Pig" (259). This is a transformation due to gluttony. Lust is more common. Walcott is transformed into a swine by desire for his enchanting Circe (155), just as Helen, with her "eyes calm as Circe" reduces Plunkett to porcine stupidity "when he came into the bedroom from the pig-farm" (96). But even here the metamorphosis is more general than mere sexual power wielded by one person over another. Plunkett immediately identifies this "lust" as "History's appeal" (97). In this way, Walcott combines the image of Circe with the broad structure of the story of Helen to yield an account of history as the recurrent narrative of lust. Lust of Menelaus and Paris for Helen, lust of slave traders and plantation owners for wealth, lust of the British and the French for the island of St. Lucia. Thinking of the battles for his island, and thinking of his ache for Helen, Plunkett reflects that "History saw them as pigs," because "History was Circe" (64). A cynical version of Marx: history is driven, not by structures of political economy, but by simple hunger for possession—of bread, of persons, of land, of position.

THE AENEID

Though one might not expect it to be the case, the presence of Virgil in Walcott's poem is considerable. When one recalls the historical orientation of Virgil's epic, however, this becomes less surprising. The *Aeneid* tells the story of the founding of Rome by Trojan exiles. But it does not tell this story as the triumph of, say, the Middle East over the West, what we might now think of as Turkey over Greece. Rather, it gives the background to the rise of Rome over Carthage, and thus, by implication, of Europe over Africa. In the first book of the poem, Virgil explains that Juno "loved Carthage best of all cities in the world" and had "set her heart on making it a capital city governing all the earth" (27). But her plans were foiled by "another breed of men, tracing descent from the blood of Troy" who "would breed a warrior nation, haughty, and sovereign over wide realms; and their onset would bring destruction to Africa" (27–28; *"excidio Libyae"* in the Latin [I.22]). The point is not as objectionable as might at first appear. Virgil did not, after all, envision the slave trade, and the colonization of Africa, centuries later. Moreover, the *Aeneid* is a poem that expresses the despair and hope of any people defeated by a colonial army. The Trojans in this poem are more in the position of Walcott's Afro-Caribbeans than of their European rulers. Panthus, fleeing the devastation wrought by the Greek army, holds in his arms the "sacred vessels and figures of his defeated gods" and laments in words that apply almost equally to Native American or African society, words that could have been spoken, with slight changes, by the griot or the shaman after their own defeat and misery, holding the broken images of their own desecrated shrines: "The last day has come for our Dardan land. This is the hour which no effort of ours can alter. We Trojans are no more: no more is Ilium; no more the splendour of Teucrian glory. All now belongs to Argos" (60–61).

This combination of contradictory parallels and precedents made the *Aeneid* perhaps the one poem it was imperative for Walcott to outdo. For it is a poem about the defeat of Africa and, at the same time, it is a poem about the splendor of those who survive colonial defeat and exile. In this context, it is unsurprising that one of the points Walcott takes over from Virgil is the prophecy of greatness that will reverse the initial loss. Indeed, within Virgil's poem, this prophecy of Trojan resurgence is bound up with the prophecy regarding Carthage—that "their onset would bring destruction to Africa." Historically, this destruction had already advanced considerably by Virgil's time: Carthage had been burned a century earlier, and Virgil began writing his epic shortly after the annexation of Egypt in 31 B.C.E. But, in Walcott's poem, we see another defeat of Africa, and we see it from the other side, just as we see the Trojans in Ilium. In a sense, Walcott shifts the Virgilian point of view from Trojan to African, as Virgil shifted the Homeric point of view from Greek to Trojan—both being cases of systematic transformation within a reference set.

More exactly, Walcott's use of the *Aeneid* focuses on one section, that stretching from Aeneas's encounter with the Sibyl through his meeting with his father—book 6, the visit to the underworld. Walcott uses this as a primary model for Achille's return to Africa and consequent meeting with his African ancestors. At the beginning of this book, Aeneas seeks out the Cumaean Sibyl, a prophetess associated with Apollo, the god of healing. She explains to Aeneas that, if he wishes to enter the underworld, he must acquire the Golden Bough. He is led to the Golden Bough by a pair of doves. In Walcott, these reappear as a single swift that leads Achille to Africa (130–31)—Achille, "another Aeneas," as Walcott calls him (301). The doves in Virgil are recognized by Aeneas as "his own mother's birds" (153). Similarly, the swift is presented throughout Walcott's poem as the bird, not of an Achille's individual mother, but of Achille's ancestral mother, the mother of all Afro-Caribbean peoples—Mother Africa. The doves lead Aeneas up the lake entrance to the land of the dead, just as the swift leads Achille across the ocean to Africa.

After acquiring the Golden Bough, Aeneas returns with the Sibyl, now crossing the river Lethe—Achille too has to enter a river (133)—before passing through the various places of the dead and entering Elysium, an idyllic land where he meets his father, just as Achille meets his father in the idyllic African village. Of course, this is not Achille's immediate progenitor, but rather the father of his people, an ancestor who crossed the ocean in a slave ship and founded the lineage in a new place. But Walcott refers to him, in parallel with Aeneas's father Anchises, as Achille's father.

When they meet, Aeneas tries to embrace his father, but the latter is a mere shade, and Aeneas cannot hold him in his arms. In Virgil, the pathos of this scene is first of all the pathos of a son losing the father whom he loves dearly. "Three times he tried to cast his arms about his father's neck; but three times the clasp was vain and the wraith escaped his hands, like airy winds" (168). The image of the father as an insubstantial shade recurs in Walcott. But here the pathos is the pathos of an entire culture that has been lost, and generations upon generations that have died in exile—all those ancestors, like blind Anchises, borne from his burning home upon Aeneas's back and fated to die on a distant island (Sicily, a parallel to St. Lucia). Afolabe, wraithlike forefather, reminds Achille that he has lost the ancestral past, saying, "if you're content with not knowing what our names mean,// then I am not Afolabe, your father, and you look through/ my body as the light looks through a leaf. I am not here/ or a shadow. And you, nameless son, are only the ghost/ of a name" (138–39). The point of Afolabe's speech is that Achille can seek to reclaim this past, to find his roots, or he can accept forced alienation from his ancestors and their traditions. In this sense, it is up to him, whether he can or cannot embrace his father. Indeed, if Achille does not embrace this past, he too becomes a mere shadow, less even than a shadow, "the ghost/ of a name."

Achille's eyes fill with tears, and in his eyes "the past was reflected/ as well as the future" (139)—for him, as for Virgil, the experience is "prediction and memory" (144). Then Afolabe expresses sorrow over his son's loss (139). This too takes up a scene from Virgil, with tragic irony. Anchises expresses great relief that Aeneas has not been lost. There was one danger he dreaded particularly: "How I feared . . . that the royal power of Africa might do some hurt to you!" (168). Later, Anchises announces, "Come, I shall now explain to you your whole destiny. I shall make clear by my words what glory shall in time to come fall to the progeny of Dardanus, and what manner of men will be your descendants of Italian birth, souls of renown now awaiting life" (170). Like Aeneas, Achille, when he looked at the men and women around him, "foresaw their future" and "knew nothing could change it" (146). But he does not look forward to the triumphal prophecy of Anchises. Rather, the future remembered by Achille is the future characterized by Virgil at the outset of his poem: "destruction to Africa" (Virgil 28). The pathos of Walcott's scene is great enough on its own. It is only heightened when one recognizes the source in Virgil.

However, this is not the only meeting between father and son in the poem, and not the only prophecy. Walcott too meets his father or, rather, his father's ghost. Here the prophecy is more like that of Anchises. First, placing the scene in the underworld, Walcott's father describes the "inferno" of slave women, and of poor women after them, carrying a "hundredweight basket" of coal (74). Then, he prophesies: "you will achieve that height/. . . in couplets lift your pages//higher than infernal anthracite." In other words, just as those women ascend the mountain, engaged in their back-breaking labor, Walcott will achieve similar heights in poetry. While they are subjected to the hell of "infernal anthracite," he will represent that hell in poetry. It is important that Walcott's father sees Walcott as achieving just "that height" scaled by the women. The poet, though more honored, is not better for doing cleaner work. Indeed, Walcott's poetry is possible precisely because these women did this work and survived. Their silent, unrecorded valor allowed him to grow up as he did, learn the epic tradition and at the same time witness the misery and heroism of ordinary people. Speaking of the laboring women, Walcott's father tells him, their "multiplying feet made your first rhymes" (75)—their feet trudging up and down the mountain are what allowed Walcott to make poetic feet, just as their experience of hell allowed him to write hell. He concludes, "your duty/. . . is the chance you now have, to give those feet a voice" (75–76), to make their epical struggle into poetry. Walcott's poetic redemption of these Afro-Caribbean women parallels the task of Virgil himself with respect to his Trojan forebears, memorializing their heroic struggle to achieve new nationhood after devastating colonial defeat and exile. Of course, here too there is a difference for, again, Walcott celebrates ordinary people, not an aristocratic elite destined to be colonialists in their turn.

A more minor echo of the *Aeneid,* book six, may be found in the burial of Hector. Misenus was Trojan Hector's companion. When Hector died, Misenus traveled with Aeneas. But, in time, "he fell into utter folly" (152; *"demens"* [VI.172]), challenging the gods to a contest in music, and Triton drowned him. Aeneas's crew builds a funeral pyre "on the shore" (153). Then, "where the pyre had been, Aeneas the True built a barrow of massive size, on which he set the implements which Misenus had used, his oar and his trumpet" (154). Walcott's Hector too goes somewhat mad, and races his van "as if driven by furies" (231). He is buried "near the sea" (232). Like Aeneas with Misenus, Achille lays "the oar" on Hector's grave, saying, "Mate, this is your spear" (233). The parallel serves to maintain the heroism and excellence of Hector's character, despite the madness—and the associated repudiation of his African heritage—that lead to his premature death.

Walcott also makes extensive use of the figure of the Sibyl, not as a narrative sequence, but as a symbol for the conservation of ancient knowledge, especially knowledge of healing. Thus, he characterizes Ma Kilman's cure of Philoctete as "a sibylline cure" (235), and later he refers to her as "the furious sibyl" (237), which is to say, the Sibyl filled with the furies—for, when the Cumaean Sybil was possessed by Apollo, god of healing, she "ran furious riot in the cave" (Virgil 149), the "vast cavern" that was her home (147). Later, Walcott elaborates on the image, restoring the detail of the cave and characterizing Ma Kilman as "The wild, wire-haired . . . caverned prophetess" (243), who, "in agony, bayed / up at the lights" (244). The image of wild hair—repeated on the next page—is taken from the Sibyl's first experience of possession by Apollo: "suddenly her countenance and her colour changed and her hair fell in disarray" (Virgil 148). Her baying derives from the Sibyl's prophecy, in which, Virgil tells us, "the cavern made her voice a roar" (150); the Latin, *"remugit,"* "bellowed back," implies an animal sound, precisely as in Walcott. In the following pages, Walcott develops the link further. Ma Kilman screams and the sound comes "from the black original cave / of the sibyl's mouth." And he identifies this "obeah-woman," this woman expert in the medicine and magic of her African ancestors, as "the sibyl . . . the spidery sibyl / hanging in a sack from the cave at Cumae" (245—though this specific image is from Petronius, not Virgil).

But why has Walcott drawn this link? There are two reasons. The first is to connect the demeaned Afro-Caribbean tradition with the exalted but fundamentally similar Greco-Roman tradition—to tie the reviled Obeah woman with the revered Sibyl, to give the Obeah woman that stature, to put her in the same category, the same reference set. The second purpose concerns the way in which Ma Kilman heals Philoctete. Again, the cure is a return to the ancestral roots. Ma Kilman uses a physical plant, but the plant operates symbolically to cure a psychological wound. What the Cumaean Sibyl does with Aeneas is similar—she points him toward a physical plant, the Golden Bough, that will allow him to enter into the land of the dead, to rejoin his ancestors, and to gain strength from his father in order to build a new life in a foreign land.

Clearly, the sort of healing art employed by Ma Kilman is not something solely African—if it were, Walcott could hardly identify Ma Kilman with the Cumaean Sibyl. Rather, for Walcott, this is a universal art (perhaps akin to poetry in that respect). However, it seems that, in Walcott's view, the mystical source of sibylline knowledge has been lost to Europe and is now found only in African tradition, a tradition that preserves a sense of origin once common to all humankind. If so, this clarifies why, toward the end of the poem, Plunkett visits Ma Kilman, "the sibyl" (306), and why, after this visit, as we have already noted, "His wound healed slowly" (309). Moreover, linked with

Mother Africa himself, his own lingering, colonial racism dissipates; "he began to speak to the workmen / not as boys who worked with him, till every name // somehow sounded different" (309).

THE DIVINE COMEDY

The most obvious way in which Walcott draws on the *The Divine Comedy* is in the verse. Following Dante, he has chosen to do his epic in *terza rima*. Perhaps more importantly, however, he uses the image of Dante's Inferno for the general situation of Afro-Caribbean laborers, still living the legacy of slavery. For example, his father tells him: "Hell was built on those hills. In that country of coal / without fire, that inferno the same colour / as their skins and shadows, every labouring soul // climbed with her hundredweight basket." The work, like the labors of Sisyphus in Hades (see the *Odyssey* XI, 593–600), was "endless repetition as they climbed the / infernal anthracite hills" and it "showed you hell, early" (74). Walcott's father not only refers directly to "Hell" and "the infernal," his description recalls Dante's entrance to Hell, when he sees the middling spirits, neither bad nor good, an unending line, naked, lamenting (III.22–65). To make the point clearer—that Hell is here, the result of colonialism and slavery—Walcott recalls his father's friend whose "paradise / is a phantom Africa" (72). Just as the Inferno is real labor in this material world derived from slavery, the Paradiso is a mere dream—a dream of the home before slavery, thus Hell, began. Indeed, in Dante, these undone spirits in their endless line go unrecorded, unheard, precisely like the coal-bearers of St. Lucia: *"Fama di loro il mondo esser non lassa"*; "Report of them the world permitteth none" (III.49). As Walcott's father puts it, "they climb, and no one knows them" (75). This, again, names Walcott's poetic task, to give those nameless carriers report, fame. Walcott's father speaks of the carriers' feet upon the hillside, then, as we have already noted, prophecies and enjoins his son's poetic future: "give those feet a voice" (76). The attitude reverses that of Dante, who has little sympathy with these undone men and women.

Perhaps Walcott's most complex use of the *Divine Comedy* concerns that poem's explicit treatment of literary tradition and precursorship. Dante's relation to Virgil as his guide through Hell serves as a model for Walcott's own relation to Joyce. Just as Dante greets Virgil as "my Master" (I.85), Walcott hails Joyce as "our age's Omeros, undimmed Master" (200). More importantly, that relation serves as a prototype for his encounter with Omeros late in the poem, and their descent into the volcano of St. Lucia, which is portrayed as a descent into Hell. In this section of the poem, Walcott relies particularly on Dante's *Malebolge* or "Evil Pockets" of Hell, especially canto 21, the hell of "Barrators and Peculators who made a traffic of public offices" (Binyon 110) and canto 32, the hell of those who "betrayed their country" (Binyon 170). Here, Walcott draws on Dante for Satanic images of the politicians who are selling his island to the economic and cultural imperialists of the United States. Specifically, St. Lucia is a volcanic island—or, rather, a volcanic "island paradise," as the tourist phrase has it. It is one of the island paradises of the Caribbean, and thus one of the places that can be sold to tourists—or, equivalently, prostituted to American money. When Walcott writes that "we smelt the foul sulphur of hell in paradise" (289), he is referring to "the Soufriere or sulphureous mountain" in which "are to be seen several cauldrons in a perpetual state of ebullition" (Davy 270, 271). But, at the same time, he is suggesting that the very advertisement of his country as a (tourist) paradise is what allows him to smell Hell, what allows him to sense the nearness of the Malebolge, with its barrators, peculators, and betrayers.

As Dante met Virgil, who would guide him through the Inferno, Walcott now has met his own guide for a trip to Hell—a guide, who, in a common sort of dream equivalence, is alternately Seven Seas and Omeros. The entire sequence is, in fact, a dream, and ends with the line "I woke to hear blackbirds bickering at breakfast" (294). First he is taken by the "charred ferryman"— charred because he is "black as the coal/ on which the women climbed" (287), but also because he is an Afro-Caribbean Charon, who ferries the dead and has "eyes of glowing coal" (Dante III.110). In the parallel scene of the *Inferno*, before he leaves with Virgil and Charon, Dante reads a sign above the entrance to Hell. It begins, "THROUGH ME THE WAY IS TO THE CITY OF WOE"; its conclusion is the famous, "RELINQUISH ALL HOPE, YE WHO ENTER HERE" (3.1, 9). Walcott too comes upon a sign at the entrance to his Inferno. But this sign reads "Messrs. Bennett and Ward" (289). As Davy records, these were "two enterprising gentlemen" who undertook "the process of collecting" and exporting sulphur from Soufrière (270n.). In short, where Dante finds a sign of absolute suffering and despair, Walcott finds a sign of colonialist economic exploitation of the natural resources of a colony. The implication is that they are equivalent.

After this, "the blind guide led" Walcott to the "foul sulphur of hell." Here they witness "the lava of the Malebolge" where, like Dante's barrators and peculators and betrayers, they find "traitors // who, in elected office, saw the land as views / for hotels" (289). Walcott lists a sampling of "souls who had sold out their race" (289)—for instance, "One had rented the sea // to offshore trawlers, whose nets, if hoisted, would show / for thrice the length of its coast" (290). The perturbations of their bodies are Dantean too: "another thief / turned his black head like a ball in a casino" (290). Here, Walcott refers in particular to the corrupt developers of St. Lucia who set up gambling establishments. They are assimilated to the sorcerers and diviners of Malebolge—appropriately, for, like diviners, their entire business is based on getting people to believe that they can see the future and defeat chance. In Dante, it is just these men who have "turned" their "head[s] like a ball in a casino." Specifically, "Each appeared strangely to be wrenched awry / Between the upper chest and lower face. / For toward the reins the chin was screwed" (20.11–13).

Subsequently, Walcott extends these infernal images to explain his own epic ambition. He looks into "one pit" where he finds "the poets." The poets are "selfish phantoms" who "smiled at their similes" and were "condemned in their pit to weep at their own pages." "And that was where I had come from," Walcott confesses. He suffered the most grievous of sins, "Pride . . . Elevating myself" and thus, like Satan expelled from Heaven, he "kept falling"—even if it was poetic pride, "Pride in my craft," not Satanic pride, self-elevation above God. But he is suddenly saved by Omeros, who "gripped / my hand" and drew him "away from that crowd," out of "that backbiting circle, mockers and self-loved" (293).

This draws on an earlier section of Dante. Virgil, in the opening Canto of the *Inferno,* saved Dante from *"a Leopard (Lust) . . . a Lion (Pride), and a She-Wolf (Avarice)"* (Binyon 3; see also Musa 8, who notes that this interpretation of the three beasts is common, but not at all undisputed). Omeros plays a similar role with Walcott. Specifically, Omeros has already rescued Walcott from his obsession with a "girl," and thus lust. Earlier, Omeros told him "Love is good, but the love of your own people is // greater." Walcott responded, "Yes. . . . That's why I walk behind you" (284)—which is to say, why he "follows" Omeros as a poet. Similarly, after his rescue by Virgil, Dante explains, "Then [Virgil] moved onward: and I went behind" (1.136). As we have already seen, Omeros pulls Walcott from the pit of "Pride" (293), thus saving him from Dante's lion as well. The place of the she-wolf is less clear. Perhaps the "backbiting" of this "circle"—Walcott's Dantean term—suggests avarice as its motive, thus completing the triad. In any case, the implication of the whole scene is that Omeros freed Walcott from the self-obsessions of lyric poetry and thereby allowed him to take up the more consequential and grander design of epic. Specifically, Omeros freed Walcott from personal pride and lust, allowing him to take up national pride and love of a people instead.

PARADISE LOST

Up to now, we have focused on the main narrative of the poem, involving Achille, Hector, and Helen, and on the autobiographical sections. But there is another narrative sequence as well, involving Plunkett, Maud, and Helen. This is less heroically epical than the main narrative, which is appropriate, given Walcott's epic aims; there is, after all, no great need to elevate Europeans to epic stature. But there are still important epic elements in this sequence.

These are drawn from two primary sources—Milton and Joyce. As to the former, Walcott takes up *Paradise Lost* to present Plunkett as Adam, apparently seduced by a Satanlike Helen, with Maud portrayed as a sort of idealized Eve—part Eve, part Mary, "second Eve"—longing for a lost Eden, and continually trying to re-create it.

History, again, is lust and the destruction that follows, most obviously in the endless series of colonialisms memorialized in the epic tradition. What lies outside history is Eden, the time "Before the snake. Without all the sin," as Maud explains "paradise" (63). If history is a battlefield—or, more generally, the sprawling, violent space of conquest and domination—then what lies outside the battlefield is the garden. Aptly, Maud "preferred gardens to empires" (254). Her garden is indeed a prelapsarian place, filled with "angelic lilies" and "seraphic lace" (62). This sort of nature, she whispers, "It's like Adam and Eve all over" (63). Moreover, "Maud / was an adamant Eve" (90), not an Eve who could be swayed by folly or serpents, but solid as stone, unwavering—Eve as Milton's God would have liked her, truly "sufficient to have stood" and, "though free to fall" (Milton, *Paradise Lost* 3.99), unfalling.

But it seems that every time Plunkett emerges "out of Maud's garden," he is "condemned to see" Helen (62). Once, he asks, "What did she want? For History to exorcise her / theft of the yellow frock?" (62). The reference to exorcism suggests Helen's Satanic character. The reference to history makes clear the opposition between her and Maud—she is lust that drives humankind to possess; Maud is the eternal, unhistoried love of prelapsarian nature. At one point, this is explicit. As we have already noted, Plunkett comes upon Helen one day when he is returning "from the pig-farm." Her "eyes" are "calm as Circe"—signs of lust and history. What we did not note before is that Helen's "fist" was "closed like a snake's head"; she moved "with serpentine leisure"; the bracelet she handled "coiled like a snake . . . hissing" (96). Thinking of her, Plunkett imagines that he "can pervert God's grace" (96) and "dare His indignation / at a second Eden with its golden apple" (97).

Needless to say, this is not the most progressive scenario—identifying the Black servant with Satan. But Walcott immediately turns this image around. Plunkett tries to tell himself that he does not desire Helen: "My thoughts are pure. / They're meant to help her people, ignorant and poor" (97). Here, the allegorical significance surfaces. Helen is no Satan, seducing Adam. Rather, Adam/Plunkett/Britain begins by lusting after Helen—woman or island— then repudiates that lust, and claims that the colony and its people constitute a Satanic seductress, that their own mission of conquest and possession is a benevolent, "civilizing" mission. When Plunkett tells himself that his intentions are altruistic, the bracelet, that had "coiled like a snake" (96), replies: "But these, smiled the bracelet, are the vows of empire" (97). Indeed, "in the lust you deny, all History's appeal / lies" (97). This—history, the lust for empire—

is the "original error" (97) or original sin—and like the other original sin, it is inherited by all humankind. Later, Walcott takes up the image of the fall again—and that fall is explicitly colonialism, now clearly identified as the original sin that darkens the souls of all those born from Adam and Eve, the original sin that drove men and women to exile from Edenic Africa. Thus, like a stain on the human soul, passed from parent to child—with one exception only, Mary, conceived immaculate—"all colonies inherit their empire's sin" (208). In this context, it is no doubt relevant that Maud, the Irish figure, is the one most closely linked with the immaculate virgin—though she bears no child, produces no redeemer.

Indeed, the wound that pervades Walcott's poem is precisely this original sin as it is carried on in the individual soul. In this way, the effects of Milton's poem extend well beyond the subplot of Plunkett and Maud. At one point, Walcott speaks of sexual love as leading to "the bride-sleep that soothed Adam in paradise, / before it gaped into a wound, like Philoctete" (42). In Eden, desire had a purity that led to calm. But after the Fall, after the start of History, that desire turned to a destructive lust—empire, and all the wounds that it inflicts. The point is clarified in the subsequent characterization of Philoctete's cure. Once he connects himself again with his "roots," with his ancient heritage, and feels the traditional medicine—or, equivalently, the medicine of tradition—"drag / the slime from his shame" (247), once he frees himself from that wound, that shame of the original sin, he is suddenly "Adam." And the yard in which the cure has taken place is "Eden." And it is no longer the late period of history, long after the Fall, for the "light" that surrounds him is "the first day's" (248). In short, in being cured of his wound, Philoctete returns to Eden before the Fall—he returns to the time before colonialism, the time before History.

Of course, Philoctete does not literally return to Africa—and that makes the "return" in a way all the more Miltonic. Milton stressed that Hell was not a place, but a condition of mind. That is why Satan can never leave Hell: "within him Hell / He brings, and round about him, nor from Hell / One step no more than from himself can fly" (*Paradise Lost* 4.20–22). Or, as Satan put it, "The mind is its own place, and in itself / Can make a Heav'n of Hell, a Hell of Heav'n" (1.254–55). Indeed, Walcott appears to allude to these very statements. He is visiting Vallombrosa, one of Milton's residences, memorialized by Wordsworth. He finds himself "lost" (172) and reflects on his own house, with its "lost garden." He then considers the house as if it were Hell and he were Milton's Satan: "I do not live in you, I bear / my house inside me, everywhere" (174). The same general point could be made about Eden—and is made, if less explicitly, by Milton. When Adam and Eve are expelled from Eden, this is only an outward manifestation of the inner loss they have already suffered. Philoctete's bath in the curative medicine of Africa is a sort of baptism that frees him from the original sin or wound of empire, of history, frees him to feel that where he is, whichever way he goes, is the Garden of Paradise. Earlier, Walcott recognized, but failed to experience, the same sort of thing, when he came to a garden with his father—perhaps his father's afterworld, heaven, Eden—and realized that it was "a paradise I had to believe to enter" (71). The idea may begin to suggest how Ma Kilman cures not only Philoctete, but Plunkett also.

ULYSSES

As we have already noted, *Ulysses* provided Walcott with a second-order model for his epic project. In other words, Joyce's novel served as the prime exemplum for Walcott's engagement with the epic tradition. This is true most obviously in the general sense that Joyce's "mythic method," as Eliot called it ("Ulysses" 27), his decision to structure the contemporary events in a colony by reference to the plot of a Homeric epic, provided Walcott with the basic premise of *Omeros.* Of course, Walcott did not repeat Joyce's exact use of this method. Rather, he abstracted and respecified, in this case through consistent displacements within a reference set, as discussed earlier. These displacements include the shift from the *Odyssey* to the *Iliad,* from prose to verse, and, most importantly, from (roughly) mock epic—in the sense that the characters are ironized and deflated—to (roughly) heroic epic. Such changes not only reflect a desire to be different from the precursor. They also manifest a distinct literary goal of elevating ordinary colonized people to heroic stature.

Less obviously, perhaps, Walcott also takes up Joyce's related emphasis on cycles, his portrayal of history as repeating itself in a series of often detailed recurrences. This idea is most obvious in *Finnegans Wake,* where Joyce draws explicitly on a Viconian conception of history. But it is at the basis of *Ulysses* as well. It is what allows Joyce to portray Bloom as a modern Odysseus, Molly as Penelope, Stephen as Telemachus. Walcott, if anything, extends Joyce's practice, for he identifies Achilles, Hector, and Helen, not only with his three main characters, but equally with the Native Americans and Europeans battling over the island, the French and English at war over the island, the rival electoral parties of independent St. Lucia—indeed, with an endless series of historical, especially colonial, lusts and their consequences. This is crucial because it provides perhaps the fundamental methodological principle of the poem. It allows the lining-up of the great epics and their integration into a national allegory of St. Lucia that, at the same time, expands into an allegory of all colonized places. Early in the poem, Walcott articulates the point: "As in your day, so with ours, Omeros, / as it is with islands and men" (33). And, near the end, shortly before Walcott finds himself rescued from narcissistic lyricism by Omeros, Seven Seas (another Homer) tells him "This is like Troy/all over" (288).

These are, in part, the reasons Walcott addresses Joyce as "undimmed Master" (200)—for it was Joyce who provided Walcott with the basic epic design of *Omeros* and gave him a paradigm case for evaluating his own execution of that design. Again, Joyce here plays Virgil to Walcott's Dante. When Walcott says that "Joyce/led us all" (201), he makes Joyce's Virgilian role almost explicit. Indeed, when Walcott is "saved" by Omeros later in the poem, perhaps he is not saved only by Argive Homer. Walcott has told us that Joyce is "our age's Omeros" (200). If so, then the Omeros that rescues Walcott today should be that modern Omeros, Joyce. In addition, Joyce is a more obvious candidate for the job. *Ulysses* is well known as a work that escapes from the sort of narcissistic, self-indulgent lyricism one might have expected from Joyce's near self-portrait in Stephen—precisely the danger from which Omeros saves Walcott. At the very least, Joyce enters here in guiding Walcott's relation to and understanding of Homer. That is part of what it means for *Ulysses* to serve as a second-order model for Walcott's project.

In keeping with Joyce's role as mediator between Walcott and the broader tradition, it is unsurprising that many of the characters exhibit Joycean traits along with traits of their epic forebears. There is a touch of Bloom in Achille. Terada notes their shared "pacifism" and "humility" (187). Perhaps more strikingly, Achille's nostalgia for an Africa he never knew recalls Bloom's thoughts of Israel. There is a hint of Bloom's rival, Blazes Boylan, in fiery Hector. There is an element of Molly—sexual, seductive, Moorish—in Helen. Indeed, at one point, Helen is linked with Penelope, Molly's prototype in *The Odyssey*—"Not Helen now, but Penelope" (153); the link is, in general, as fitting to one as it is to the other. There are still more elements of schoolmaster Deasy in Plunkett. Plunkett too is a loyalist, but also a St. Lucian—as he emphasizes to Hector: "I haven't spent/damned near twenty years on this godforsaken rock/to be cursed like a tourist" (256)—just as Deasy is both a unionist and an Irishman. Plunkett has the same amateur relation to history that Deasy has to veterinary medicine, and a similar tone in speech. He even taught; Walcott remembers: "he'd led us in Kipling's requiem" (269). Bloom too contributes to Plunkett, most importantly in his lack of a son.

In keeping with this connection between Plunkett and Bloom, Maud is closely linked with Molly. Indeed, Maud is the character most intimately bound to a Joycean model, though there is a significant, systematic transformation of this exemplum, a shift in the reference set—or, rather, several shifts. Some are minor. For example, Maud is a pianist, whereas Molly is a singer; "Maud" is not a name drawn from Ireland's greatest novelist, Joyce, but from Ireland's greatest poet, Yeats—Maud Gonne being his life's love and the inspiration for many of his poems. However, at least one such transformation is very consequential. Maud is precisely the sort of faithful "Penelope" that Molly never can be. In part, this is because Molly lost her first love—a young British soldier who died in war, Lieutenant Stanley G. Gardner (18.389): "Gardner going to south Africa where those Boers killed him with their war and fever" (18.867–68). Plunkett is, in a sense, the beloved soldier that Molly lost. Maud has been more fortunate than her predecessor.

The memory of Gardner—mixed with memories of another soldier, Mulvey, and of Bloom—is developed in Molly's final monologue, which also enters into Walcott's poem. Specifically, Molly recalls a scene "over the firtree cove a wild place I suppose it must be the highest rock in existence . . . the ships out far" (18.790–91, 794). She recalls masturbating Mulvey (18.809, 818), "the day before he left" for the war (18.80–81). Walcott shifts the monologue from Molly to Plunkett. But the scene—a cliff above the water, a soldier with his girl before setting off to war—remains the same, or nearly so. The style too is the same, with its piling up of dependent clauses deferring the full stop to make a single flowing sentence, the fluid rush of memory and speech: "All her county shone in her face when the power / was cut, and the wick in the lamp would leap, as live / as the russet glints of her proud hair when she wore // it long and spread it over the wild grass to give / all that a girl could, with the camouflaged troop-ships / below them in the roadstead, with gulls buzzing the cliff // and screeching above us when she parted both lips / and searched for his soul with her tongue, her wild grey eyes / as flecked with light as the sea" (304–305). The kiss recalls the famous moment of the seedcake in Molly's monologue, the kiss with which the monologue culminates: "I gave him the bit of seedcake out of my mouth . . . after that long kiss I near lost my breath" (18.1574–76). Finally, just as he reverses the point of view, from the woman to the man, Walcott also reverses the agent and the recipient of the masturbation—unacted, in this case: "she was urging // me to go in . . . with my fingers . . . she steered my hand through the froth of her underwear" (305), but "I couldn't" (305).

Maud's death involves a further connection with *Ulysses* as well. Indeed, the shifts from Molly's character to Maud's are in part enabled by this second use of Joyce. For Maud has two precursors in *Ulysses*—Molly and May Dedalus, Stephen's mother. Maud's death from cancer is in part based on the death of Stephen's mother, also from cancer. The "covered keys of the shawled piano she'd never play again" (261) recall Stephen's memories of playing the piano for his mother (1.249–51). The clumps of things and memories that surround Maud's death (261–63) recall the memorabilia found by Stephen in his dead mother's drawer: "Her secrets: old featherfans, tasselled dancecards, powdered with musk, a gaud of amber beads" (1.255–56). Just after the death, Walcott tells us "There was Plunkett in my father, much as there was / my mother in Maud." He then goes on to identify his father with "Ulysses" and himself with "Telemachus," which is to say, Stephen Dedalus (263). Maud is, by implication, linked with Stephen's mother.

There are narrower ties as well. The notion that Achille "had been his own father and his own son" (275) is a heroic version of Stephen's mocking theory of Shakespeare and Hamlet. As Buck Mulligan puts it, "He proves by algebra that Hamlet's grandson is Shakespeare's grandfather and that he himself is the ghost of his own father." Haines responds by pointing at Stephen and asking, "He himself?" (1.555–58). Similarly, Walcott's lament over the cultural destruction produced by slavery—"Now each man was a nation / in himself" (150)—takes up and renders heroic Bloom's statements about nationhood. At a point when his own nationality is at issue because of his companions' anti-Semitism, Bloom is asked to define a nation. "A nation," he responds, "is the same people living in the same place." He is immediately mocked by a barfly with the statement, "if that's so I'm a nation for I'm living in the same place for the past five years." Less in response to this mockery than in remembrance of his own Jewish people—for his Jewishness is precisely what allows the mockery—Bloom alters his definition, "or also living in different places." "That covers my case, says Joe" (12.1422–25, 1428–29). There is also the emphasis on the Sibyl figure, who appears not only in Virgil, but in Joyce.

There are stylistic links between the works as well, along with many specific allusions, phrases and images used less systematically. The question-and-answer format of Walcott's 38.3 seems in part based on the question-and-answer format of Joyce's "Ithaca" chapter. This link is particularly likely as the immediately following section (39.1) begins the treatment of Ireland and Joyce. The shift to dialogue in 35.3 imitates Joyce's "Circe" chapter in both style and substance; the format is the same and the visual impression is unmistakably Joycean. Moreover, the substance of the scene involves the meeting of Achille and the spirit of his father, just as "Circe" involves the meeting of Bloom with the ghost of his father. Indeed, here we see a good example of Walcott reading a classical author through Joyce—a further complication of his relation to European literary tradition. In this scene, Walcott revises Aeneas's meeting with Anchises through Bloom's meeting with Virag. Though, here too, there is a shift from Joyce, the same systematic shift we have seen before—from mock epic to heroic epic.

Finally, this parallel with the "Circe" episode suggests one further instance of Walcott "reading through" Joyce to the paradigm epics of Europe, in this case an instance of symbolism rather than plot. This episode of *Ulysses* revises the story of Circe into a story of prostitution and lust. In Joyce's version, men are transformed into pigs in their drunken visit to a brothel. It is precisely this Joycean transformation that Walcott takes up and transforms again, generalizing the lust and making it politically consequential—making it into lust for possession of the land, for Helen as the island. He also revises the prostitution of individual women into the prostitution of the nation by politicians who lust for money or power. These changes are consistent with the general transformation from mock epic to heroic epic.

EPIC REVISITED

Clearly, Walcott has taken up the European epic tradition, placing himself not only in its main stream, but directly in the company of its paradigm practitioners. He even characterizes himself as saved from inferior poetry by Homer. At the beginning of the poem, he invokes Homer almost as a muse: "O open this day with the conch's moan, Omeros. . . . Only in you . . . can I catch the noise / of the surf lines . . . our epic horizon" (12–13). This is not to say that he accepts the European epic tradition as it has been used. In Georgia, driving past Athens, Sparta, Troy, he thinks "how Greek" the "evil of slavery" was made by these connections. Later he reflects on how "in tense / Southern towns and plantations" the inheritors of Greco-Roman tradition "killed / the slaves" after giving them "Roman names" (206). Yet, despite this, he still thinks of plantations as peopled by "Hectors and Achilleses" (177), epic heroes unsung, or sung only by bards whose words were not recorded, and whose lines of verse faded like the sough of the sea. At one point, Walcott questions his entire epic project: "When would the sails drop // from my eyes, when would I not hear the Trojan War / in two fishermen cursing in Ma Kilman's shop? / . . . When would it stop, / the echo in the throat, insisting, 'Omeros'" (271). In effect, he is interrogating himself—should he not rid himself of this entire tradition, repudiate it, or "write back" in defiance only? This question has been stressed by many interpreters of the poem, anxious to find in Walcott a highly vexed and even antagonistic relation to metropolitan tradition. But, as Figueroa has noted (206), he answers his own questions, and the answer is *no:* "it was mine to make what I wanted of it" (272). He can elevate the unsung Hectors and Achilleses, rediscover "epic splendour" where it has been occluded, place himself and his fellow Afro-Caribbean people within that tradition, even establishing them as paradigms of that tradition. In this way, he can reconfigure the tradition.

As Eliot stressed, however it developed historically, a tradition faces us as a contemporary system, as a whole, in which each part affects the way we understand all the others. Walcott's presence in the reference set that defines the epic tradition alters all other works in that tradition as they face us, just as Joyce's presence alters them. In this way, Walcott's poem opens up new possibilities for both extending and understanding the metropolitan epic tradition, possibilities that, perhaps, can help us turn from celebrating the colonizer to celebrating the colonized. As we have just noted, almost at the start of the poem, Walcott links the beginning of this tradition, Homer, with "the noise of the surf lines" that are equally "the opening . . . of our epic horizon" (13). The ending of the poem implicitly recurs to this image, suggesting a continual renewal and re-creation of epic poetry: "When he left the beach the sea was still going on" (325). The line refers to Achille, and to the future of St. Lucia, but it could refer equally to Walcott himself and to the future of an epic tradition that will be transformed, inevitably and continually. As such, it suggests an ongoing project that affects not only our thought about poetry but our thought about the world, a project of redefining our cognitive exempla, reconstituting our reference sets, remaking our traditions, a project advanced in part by adding *Omeros* to *The Odyssey,* St. Lucia to Greece, and Achille to Achilles.

Chapter Six

Indigenous Tradition and the Individual Talent

Agha Shahid Ali, Laila/Majnoon, and the Ghazal

Walcott set out, again, to overcome or outdo a tradition that had been employed to denigrate the cultures of colonized peoples and to stifle their aspirations to nationhood. In doing this, he took up the epic genre, the genre of nationhood, and shifted the subject from the colonizing country to the colonized country, from the colonizing "race" to the colonized people. He followed through the epic tradition, using scenes, characters, events, and structures from each major epic writer and revising them for his own purposes. In Walcott, as in Joyce before him, this appears to have been a highly deliberate process. In other words, Walcott self-consciously sought to isolate and refashion selected parts of the epic tradition. In this sense, Walcott did not precisely write within the epic tradition. He sought to be read within that tradition. He sought to be understood as creating poetry of similar form and comparable quality to that of the paradigm epicists. His receipt of the Nobel Prize suggests that he succeeded. But his calculated attitude toward that tradition makes his writing, in a sense, "external" rather than "internal" to it. I do not mean this as a criticism. It is merely a descriptive statement, and may apply equally to the paradigm epicists.

But not all uses of a genre are so self-conscious. What, then, makes writing more internal to a tradition? We can understand the issue in this way.

Tradition involves a complex of motifs, ideas, images, forms, rhetorical strategies, and so on. These have become adequately familiar to some body of readers so as to guide their understanding of and response to works in that tradition. Among these readers are authors who have internalized the motifs, etc., in such a way as to enable their own unselfconscious composition of new works. We might consider language by way of comparison. Individual speech is particular, unique, different. As Chomsky has emphasized, virtually all ordinary language use is "creative"; "in normal speech one does not merely repeat what one has heard but produces new linguistic forms—often new in one's experience or even in the history of the language—and there are no limits to such innovation" (*Language* 5). For example, the overwhelming majority of sentences in this book are not sentences that I have heard or read before. But, in order to write any of these sentences, I need to have a language—a set of abstract rules, lexical items, and the like, that provide a systematic link between ideas and utterances. Without a structured lexicon, I cannot use the word "dog" to refer to a dog. Without principles of morphology, I cannot use the sound [z] to mark plural, as in "dogs." Without rules of syntax, I cannot distinguish between "Dogs frighten the Smith brothers" and "The Smith brothers frighten dogs." Moreover, these rules interact in such complex ways that I cannot, for the most part, be manipulating them consciously. If I am fluent in a language, I do not think "Okay, now how do I mark a plural?" Rather, I have internalized the rule for marking plurals and do it automatically. Put more technically, one could say that I have a *procedural* schema for the formation of plurals—even though I may not have a *representational* schema for plural formation. (For a general discussion of the cognitive issues involved in what I am calling "procedural schemas," see chapter 9 of Johnson-Laird on "production memory" and "production rules.") The distinction between these types of schema is crucial for understanding literary identity and an author's relation to tradition. It is nicely illustrated by the difference between Walcott's relation to the epic and Ali's relation to the ghazal.

LANGUAGE AND TRADITION

A representational schema is, again, a hierarchized structure of information regarding an object's properties and relations. The representational schema of a bicycle includes such conceptual and perceptual features as having two wheels, pedals, a handle bar, and so on, all of which fit together in a certain way and function in a certain way. In contrast, procedural schemas are structures that guide our activity. My procedural schema for riding a bicycle is what allows me to ride a bicycle. For the most part, procedural schemas operate unconsciously. I do not think, "Now I press down on the pedal with one foot, while leaning slightly in the opposite direction." I just "enact" the procedural schema. Indeed, procedural schemas are notoriously inaccessible to introspection. When people are asked to describe tying their shoelaces or some other simple, routine task, they come nowhere near giving an accurate description— even though they could easily show someone how to tie shoelaces, even though they could "run" the procedural schema, slowing it down, pausing and repeating subschemas. Our procedural schemas usually incorporate representational schemas (or some other representational structures). For example, to tie shoelaces you need to be able to recognize shoelaces to begin with. Such representational schemas are more readily open to introspection, though even this introspection is less perfect than we typically imagine.

Aspects of our command of a language can be understood in these terms, as just noted. However, there are some significant differences between language and most other systems incorporating procedural and representational schemas. Most importantly for our purposes, both the representational and procedural portions of a language must be shared by some community or they are useless, as Wittgenstein famously argued. If Smith is the only one who speaks a certain language—the only one who has internalized a particular system of representational and procedural schemas—he/she cannot communicate with anyone, no matter how articulate his/her utterances may be within that system. This is not typically the case. For example, if the art of diamond cutting has been lost, and I am the only one who has the relevant procedural schemas, that in no way inhibits my ability to cut diamonds.

A tradition, as I am using the term here, is akin to a language in this respect. A literary tradition is what enables a writer to create a new literary utterance, and to do so in such a way that a readership will be able to understand and respond to it. For example, it provides a writer with a set of resonant images—images that are, in part, made resonant by the tradition itself, whether these are the images of the Petrarchan love poem, the haiku, or the Tamil war lyric. It provides a broader vocabulary as well, a set of forms, a complex of techniques, and so on. One writes within that tradition insofar as one has "internalized" those forms, etc.; that is, technically, insofar as they have become part of procedural schemas. One is drawing on images from within a tradition insofar as those images are incorporated into one's internalized procedural schemas for scene construction, analogy, and the like.

More exactly, composing a literary work involves a number of stages, with a complex of procedural schemas operating at each stage. Different procedural schemas may have different levels of activation at different stages. For example, there is usually a period of preparation for a work. In this period, the author does his/her normal activities, but may be unusually sensitive to particular aspects of his/her daily experience, things that could provide appropriate specifications for literary structures in the new work. Thus an author at this stage may find his/her attention focused on particular scenes, faces, bits of overheard dialogue, or whatever. When concentrating on these scenes, etc., he/she has activated some sort of observation procedure. In the right conditions (given the right probes or triggers), such a procedure—previously operating in the background—is fully activated and brought to the foreground. Thus an unusual appearance, gesture, personal background, or anything else may trigger the observation procedure, though at this point even the author may not understand why this occurs. We referred to something of this sort in discussing Desai. In the period when Desai was preparing to write *Baumgartner's Bombay,* she may have found herself paying particular attention to news reports on unsanitary conditions in shanty towns around Bombay or observing European backpackers with special concentration. At this point, she need not have had any clear idea of how she was going to use these observations. Indeed, the observations were helping to form her sense of what the novel would be, as they were encoded and stored through the activation of procedural schemas.

When actually writing, the author recruits a range of procedures, which run in parallel, though again with different degrees of activation. Thus an author has schemas for the construction of characters, scenes, events, forms, and the like. The formal schemas (e.g., for iambic pentameter) may be running simultaneously with the scene-construction schemas. Moreover, some schemas recruit other schemas to their own purposes. For example, the event-construction schemas would presumably incorporate scene-construction sub-schemas. I speak of "formal schemas," "event-construction schemas," and so forth, in the plural as authors have a range of procedural schemas for each category or task. These schemas are probably organized in loose typologies. For scene construction, these might include schemas for garden scenes, forest scenes, lake scenes, river scenes, urban scenes, suburban scenes. Moreover, there are further schemas—metaschemas, so to speak—that select and coordinate constituent-construction schemas (e.g., scene-construction schemas). For example, romantic love as a topic might lead to the lexical activation of some schemas for event construction, some entries for scene construction, and so on. Of several active entries, the author may choose one or another, applying further schemas (e.g., for abstraction and respecification) in order to vary the features supplied by the entries initially. Thus Samuel Beckett may take "romantic love" as a topic. This activates, say, "garden" and "beautiful, young woman." He then transforms these within a reference set, moving to the opposite and yielding a love story about a young man and an ugly old woman in a garbage dump.

As we have already noted, procedural schemas often incorporate representational schemas. They also incorporate prototypes and exempla. Indeed, to a great extent, these structures are the part of a tradition shared by authors and readers. For both authors and readers, the representational structures serve to fill in details, expand connections, provide emotional resonances that go beyond the direct statements of the literary work. They are crucial to an author in anticipating readers' responses. For example, representational schemas involve ideas about cause and effect. To take a very simple illustration, in a number of traditions of love poetry, separation from the beloved gives rise to specific sorts of sickness on the part of the lover. Portraying a character as sick in those ways communicates to a reader in the tradition that this character is separated from his/her beloved. This is true even when no love theme has yet been introduced. Prototypes include such things as standard characters and standard situations. Thus, the prototypical ghazal includes a prototypical shaikh character who represents oppressive orthodoxy and prototypical lovers in conflict with the shaikh. Thus the introduction of an elder in a ghazal immediately triggers the expectation that he will interfere with the lovers. Indeed, this is one of the reasons why the couplets of a ghazal may be detached easily from their encompassing poems. The expectations are so well guided by prototypes that a listener can infer a larger narrative from very little information. Finally, any tradition also includes a series of particularly salient exempla—instances of character, situation, or scene that are particularly effective or particularly admired. The story of Laila and Majnoon, especially in the version of Nizami, functions in this way in the ghazal tradition. Thus a writer representing lovers may use scenes from Nizami as an implicit basis for evaluating his/her own love scenes, judging their likely effect, determining if they are finished or require further work.

Clearly, these representational structures would be useless if they were not integrated into procedural schemas. This is as true for readers as it is for authors. Readers too have procedural schemas—for reading, interpreting, even for responding emotionally to a work. Actually, these schemas are shared by authors and readers, for authors are, after all, readers as well. Indeed, these responsive schemas are crucial to the author as an author, most obviously in the process of revision. Authors are different from readers in having some further, productive schemas as well. Or, rather, everyone has responsive and productive schemas. Everyone can imagine scenes, draw analogies, speak in regulated rhythms, and so on. But authors have a broader, more complex, more finely differentiated, and more readily manipulable set of productive schemas. To write or read within a tradition is, then, to have a set of shared representational schemas, prototypes, and exempla in one's lexicon, organized into relevant domains (e.g., by genre), accessible by relevant probes for integration into fluent procedural schemas for reception and production (with successful authors distinguished in part by the detail, extent, and flexibility of their productive schemas).

The lexical accessibility of these structures is important and should be underscored. One reads or writes within a tradition not simply when one has certain schemas, etc., hidden away in one's lexicon, but when they are activated appropriately. Put differently, reading or writing within a tradition involves not only the content of lexical items, but the larger lexical structure as well. The internal lexicon is not like a printed dictionary or encyclopedia. It is not fixed in a single order—alphabetical or otherwise. Put differently, when I scan my internal lexicon for words, images, or ideas, I do not always start with the same words—"aardvark," "abacus," and so on. Rather, the order of scanning is determined by context. If the context is legal interpretation, I will use and recognize uncommon legal terms more quickly than if the context is grocery shopping. (The difference is not typically perceptible in ordinary conversation, but is well attested in psychological research. For discussion, see Garman 292–96 and John Holland et al. 56–58.) As is well known, a literary tradition provides a series of word and image preferences—in the ghazal, these would include, for example, "desert," "wine," and "goblet." Writing within a tradition involves the spontaneous re-ordering of one's lexical access such that the preferred words, images, and so on, are "on top," more readily accessed than alternatives. Note that this does not mean an author actually uses those expected words, images, or whatever. It merely means that they are readily cued—perhaps to create expectation, irony, humor, or some other effect. Consider prototypes. If one expects an interfering shaikh when reading a ghazal, then one will respond differently if the male elder ends up helping the lovers, or being one of the lovers. That shift in a reader's response (absent from the response of someone lacking the initial expectation) is often crucial to understanding and appreciating a work.

I have been emphasizing the implicit cognitive processes that operate in creating a literary work. Needless to say, there are explicit, self-conscious processes as well. Again, most aspects of writing within a tradition are unself-conscious. Indeed, writers can only articulate a very small percentage of the processes they follow. Nonetheless, some aspects of a tradition are not only contingently self-conscious, they just cannot be proceduralized (i.e., internalized as procedural schemas). For example, it seems unlikely that one could internalize certain aspects of European epic structure, such as its preference for twelve or twenty-four books. The problem here is that one cannot operate such a procedural schema. It would take too long. More exactly, there appear to be constraints on the "running time" for procedural schemas, constraints that are simply part of our cognitive structure. For this reason, lyric poetry provides the best examples of proceduralization, and thus of writing within a tradition, in the technical sense. While an author necessarily runs many procedural schemas in the course of writing an epic, novel, or drama, lyric poetry presents the clearest illustrations of genre-specific internalization, simply because of its limited length. This is perhaps the reason that lyric poetry has been the paradigm genre of "expressivist" poetics—not only in the West, but elsewhere as well, as Earl

Miner has pointed out (see, for example, 85). The unreflective ease of running procedural schemas is likely to make the lyric at least appear more spontaneous, more directly derived from one's feelings and experiences.

Of course, lyric poems are not simple, direct expressions—even of productive procedural schemas. For example, lyric poems may be extensively revised. But, of course, revision itself is a matter of running procedural schemas. Moreover, the crucial factor here is probably not how long it takes to write a poem—after all, the composition of a brief lyric might take months. Rather, it is probably a matter of whether or not one can run the procedural schemas at each revision. With a short lyric, one can run procedural schemas repeatedly while revising the poem in its entirety, something that is not possible with epics, novels, or most dramas. In these cases, procedural schemas can be run only for sections and are more likely to require self-conscious adjustment relative to representational schemas, such as the twelve or twenty-four book preference.

For the most part, what we have said about writing (or reading) within a tradition fits well with our opening analogy of language use—even down to the combination of implicit and explicit procedures. However, the analogy between language and literary tradition is not perfect—and not only because literary works are themselves products of language. Perhaps most significantly, important literary schemas alter far more readily and far more often than linguistic rules. Moreover, literary schemas are never as strict as linguistic rules. There is always more room for innovation around literary principles than around linguistic principles. It is always easier to change patterns of imagery than rules of pluralization. In part, this is the result of the different ways in which such principles operate in literary and linguistic production and reception. The difference here is related to the common linguistic distinction between rules that are obligatory and rules that are optional. Pluralization is, for the most part, obligatory. With only a few, lexically marked exceptions, one has no choice but to mark plurals by adding an alveolar fricative to the end of the word; one has no choice but to add a mid central vowel after sibilants, and to make that alveolar fricative voiced when following a voiced sound and voiceless when following a voiceless sound (e.g., the plural marker for "cat" is [s]; for "dog," [z]; for "bush," [əz]). In contrast, various rules governing contraction or the simplification of consonant clusters are optional—we can say either "cannot" or "can't"; we can say either "sandwich" or "samwich." Obviously, there are contexts in which one or the other form is "obligatory" in the sense of "proper." But they are never obligatory in the relevant linguistic sense. One could say that the internalized principles of a literary tradition are typically optional, not obligatory.

In part because literary principles are rarely obligatory, literature also allows for a greater multiplication of principles. We cannot incorporate different rules for plural formation into English, since the current rules are obligatory. In contrast, we can easily incorporate new verse forms. In this way, literary traditions allow greater latitude for both innovation and borrowing. This is perhaps particularly striking in cross-language/cross-tradition syntheses. It is, in fact, an enabling condition for syncretism. I cannot choose to incorporate morphological principles from Kinyarwanda into English, despite the fact that they are both based on universal linguistic principles. On the other hand, I will almost certainly be able to incorporate imagery or character types from Kinyarwanda poetry into English poetry.

In short, it is a simple matter for an author to write in one literary tradition, while incorporating elements from another literary tradition. This is particularly likely in contemporary postcolonization literature, for the development of colonialism has produced a situation in which readers in indigenous traditions have also internalized metropolitan traditions. On the other hand, even this situation is complex and manifests the cognitive subtleties of literary tradition. European literary works have often been brought to the colony and incorporated into the reading habits of indigenous peoples by way of indigenous traditions. For example, many Indian readers come to understand Shakespeare's romances not in relation to Roman New Comedy or the Greek prose romance, but in relation to classical Sanskrit romantic tragi-comedy. (Of course, other Indian readers do just the opposite, reading Shakespeare first and subsequently seeing Sanskrit dramas as Shakespearean—or never reading Sanskrit drama at all, as Chinweizu, Jemie, and Madubuike emphasize.) In this way, part of the metropolitan tradition is, in effect, assimilated into indigenous tradition, at least by many readers. At the same time, European modernism involved a continuing incorporation of non-European cultural traditions, largely due to the globalization of culture through colonialism. This work then enters the colonies already including elements of indigenous tradition—and it introduces elements of those traditions to metropolitan readers as well.

In keeping with this, Agha Shahid Ali's "From Another Desert" certainly has elements of a European modernist poem.[1] It shows a particularly strong influence from T. S. Eliot. The case is illustrative. Ali's use of Eliot is, of course, in part, a matter of personal taste—an appreciation of Eliot's talents with words and images. But it is more than that. First, Ali drew on Eliot because Eliot had already been made, in effect, part of indigenous tradition. Ahmed Ali, in his *The Golden Tradition*, more than once links Eliot with the great nineteenth-century master of the ghazal, Mirza Ghalib. He refers to "Eliot's *Prufrock*" as "so close to the ghazal in attitude" (14), and quotes the opening of "The Waste Land" as akin to the ghazal (13–14). This sort of association makes Eliot an obvious metropolitan source for the extension of the ghazal tradition into English. Moreover, Ali clearly felt a deep affinity with

Eliot's view of, precisely, literary identity and literary tradition. Ali published one book of literary criticism, *T. S. Eliot as Editor*. In this book, Ali is concerned primarily with Eliot's emphasis on the writer's place in tradition, his emphasis on tradition as a living part of the present and as the medium in which a writer finds his/her own individuality (2, 148). This interest is unsurprising, for Ali's own relation to the ghazal tradition could be characterized in much the same way. Moreover, for both Eliot and Ali, this relation to tradition should not be understood too narrowly. Thus Ali stresses Eliot's opposition to national or racial insularity in literature, and quotes Eliot on the importance of literary interaction among "every race or nation" (55)—a principle also directly relevant to Ali's insistence on relating his work to both the Urdu and the English traditions (see, for example, his discussion of this in "Introduction" xi). In keeping with this, Ali refers to Eliot's "The Waste Land" in particular as a poem that "changed the course of English—and world—poetry" (1). As we shall see, "The Waste Land" figures importantly in "From Another Desert."

However, to identify the poem with European modernism, to place it first of all within that tradition, would be mistaken. In this poem, Ali is writing primarily within an indigenous tradition. Ali himself suggests this relation in the introduction to his translations of Faiz, perhaps the greatest modern writer in the Urdu ghazal tradition, where he notes that he "must have begun to internalize Faiz from a very young age" (ix). In "From Another Desert," Ali exhibits this internalization of the ghazal tradition. He is, in effect, thinking this poem—along with the experiences and histories it represents—through that tradition. In other words, the poem is most appropriately seen as located within the tradition of the Persian/Urdu ghazal. It is not a response to that tradition, nor an attempt to preserve or outdo it. The poem is directly part of that (ongoing) tradition. At the same time, it varies that tradition by incorporating elements of European literature, especially modernist elements which lend themselves particularly well to this sort of cross-tradition synthesis—and which allow readers with a European literary background to gain readier access to the poem.

More technically, when writing, Ali runs the procedures he has internalized from the ghazal tradition. But, of course, all such procedures from all traditions continually face the author with choices—choices of selection, specification, order. As with language, these schemas cannot fully specify what a poet writes; if they did, every ghazal would be the same. Moreover, as we have been emphasizing, literary procedural schemas incorporate far more optional principles and far fewer obligatory principles than linguistic procedural schemas. Faced with these options—for specification, and so on—along with the always available options for feature transferal and systematic transformation within a reference set, Ali prominently relies on structures drawn from

European modernism, along with his own experiences, to complete and "concretize" his poem. (Obviously, there are other sources for this completion and concretization as well—other literary works, works of history and politics, aspects of popular culture. However, these are, I believe far less significant for this poem.)

Having discussed Ali's relation to Eliot, we should briefly consider his use of autobiographical material before going on to treat the ghazal tradition itself. In fact, Ali's incorporation of personal experience into the ghazal tradition is arguably the most important aspect of his development of this tradition. The very individuality of what a poet has done and undergone serves to extend, respecify, and thus rehumanize a literary tradition. On the one hand, this experience, as expressed in "From Another Desert," is shaped by the tradition. On the other hand, that experience reconnects the tradition to real life.

As this last point suggests, to say that writing within a tradition is different from "outdoing" a tradition is not to say that the former does not involve the revision of tradition. Even a simple utterance in an ordinary conversation—if it is to have force and value—must in some way go beyond or appear to go beyond what has already been said. Indeed, the risk of tradition is that it will grow brittle, shrivel into a lifeless carapace or skeleton of stiff, fossilized rules or conventions, that it will become doctrine. This is most obviously true for religious tradition, with its hierarchies of authority and the imbrication of faith and politics. Indeed, this rigidification of religious tradition is a standard motif of the ghazal tradition itself. But this procedural sclerosis is also a threat to poetic traditions. A poetic tradition too can easily become a fixed set of prescriptive norms, generating standardized bits of verse, like widgets from a factory.

The most obvious way of opposing this sort of rigidification is simply the particularization of tradition to a poet's life, thought, and feeling. That is what I refer to when I say that individual experience "rehumanizes" tradition. Indeed, in reintegrating tradition with his/her own experiential world, a poetically successful writer simultaneously reintegrates that tradition with the experiential world of readers—who may easily become numbed to the mere repetition of standardized motifs and structures without this continual, variable, individualized reparticularization.

In keeping with this, the ghazal has been repeatedly reworked by linking its topics and images with issues and experiences of current emotional importance for its writers—including issues and experiences of great political consequence, such as those arising out of colonialism. Thus Ali refashions the motif of a lost love and the associated, largely metaphorical motif of exile into a treatment of his longing for his homeland while living in literal exile. In doing this, Ali invests the ghazal with feeling, concreteness, and lived concern that embody, but also transform conventional practices of the tradition. Moreover, in doing this, he addresses a topic that is far from idiosyncratic, for exile is a tragically common experience today, when historically unprecedented numbers of people have been displaced from their homes either due to threat of arms or due to economic necessity. In specifying the tradition in this way, then, Ali has humanized the tradition, not only by imbuing it with his own individual feeling, but also by expanding its scope to a pressing modern problem with deep emotional importance for many people.

Of course, one difficulty with the postcolonization use of complex and multiple traditions is that the traditions themselves are often not shared by readers, even when the human experiences incorporated into those traditions are shared. The result is misunderstanding and a lack of full appreciation. Needless to say, this is not something new to postcolonization writers. It is common to all writers who innovate in all traditions. Indeed, one might rephrase the earlier point about the life of tradition by saying that new authors must continually alter the tradition so that there is a degree of misfit between the work and its readers. A tradition stagnates when each new poem fits neatly into the receptive schemas of readers. At the same time, as writers such as Jauss have emphasized, the misfit cannot be too great, for the new work is then likely to be dismissed and forgotten, whatever its intrinsic value. The problem seems to be particularly acute for postcolonization writers as there are so many distinct traditions at stake, and so many diverse understandings of those traditions. Of course, this is good news for literary critics in that one main function of literary criticism is providing readers the schemas, prototypes, and exempla they need to understand the new work. It is also one reason why it is so important for critics of postcolonization literature to develop a fuller, more detailed, and more nuanced understanding of literary traditions in this field.

ALI AND THE GHAZAL

The ghazal is first of all a poetic form—roughly, a sequence of couplets, with each line the same syllabic length, and a rhyme scheme of AA, BA, CA, and so on. The ghazal developed over more than a millennium from Arabic poets, through such Persian masters as Rumi (thirteenth century), to the great South Asian writers—Mir (eighteenth century), Ghalib (nineteenth century), Iqbal (early twentieth century), Faiz (middle twentieth century), and so on. In this time, the genre began to manifest characteristic semantic and narrative features as well—standard dramatis personae, recurring motifs, common image patterns. Thematically, ghazals focus most often on unrequited love. In a partially implicit narrative, the lover struggles to be united with the beloved, but a rigid and intolerant society prevents this. The most famous story of this sort, a story central to the ghazal tradition, is that of Laila and Majnoon. They loved one another deeply, but Laila's father refused to allow their marriage. Majnoon retreated to the desert and became a great poet, continually mourning his separation from Laila.

While this is obviously a love story—one of the most widely read and influential in the history of the world—it was almost from the beginning understood as a religious allegory as well, most often a Sufi allegory. Indeed, Sufism became a strong presence in the ghazal tradition generally. Sufism is the mystical branch of Islam. Levy explains that the "central idea" of Sufism is "the Oneness of the universe" (94). For Sufis, the goal of religious aspiration is not conformity to law or acceptance of doctrine, but the experience of unity with Allāh. This unity cannot be expressed literally, due to "the inadequacies of human language" (95). As a result, Sufis have frequently taken up poetry for their teachings. In that poetry, "Sufi symbolism turns about the pivotal points of Love" (96), with human love serving to suggest the unutterable experience of divine love. As Lichtenstadter puts it, "Only immersion of one's whole being in the all-embracing Being of God" could satisfy Sufi aspirations. Sufis "called the means" to this goal, "Love" and "they called God" the "Beloved" (83). In keeping with this, perhaps the most common interpretation of the story of Laila and Majnoon, and of related stories of unrequited love, is as an allegory for the Sufi mystic who seeks union with God, a union prevented by material life, as the union of Laila and Majnoon is prevented by worldly contingency.[2] In this account, Majnoon's desert is the wasteland of earthly existence, the barren place of separation from God. Finally, the Sufi aspirant achieves union with God only in death, just as the separated lovers meet only after death (see Nizami, canto 54).

The lover's confinement to the desert is related to two other motifs, both of which take up the religious theme—exile and imprisonment. Majnoon is in effect exiled from his beloved. Ghalib refers to himself as "Exiled from home" (in Ahmed Ali 235). Iqbal explains that, in life, "exile" is our "portion" (1.677). The image of imprisonment is also common. Mir writes, "I heard the lamentation of the prisoner in his cage—/ It was *my* heart that ached, and . . . was held captive there" (in Russell, *Anthology*, 147). In Nizami, Majnoon presents himself as "manacled" and Laila characterizes herself as a "prisoner" (123; see also 127, 149, 152). Both motifs are standardly taken as images of the mystic's separation from God—exiled from his/her divine home, imprisoned in the material world.

Subsequently, the ghazal, and the Laila/Majnoon story, developed other allegorical resonances as well. In the eighteenth and nineteenth centuries, the ghazal was used to express "social and political awareness" (Ahmed Ali 21) and to criticize British colonialism. For example, the standard figure of the unscrupulous rival "came to refer to the British" (20). This made the beloved (e.g., Laila) into the homeland. The lovers' struggles to be united became an allegory for struggles against foreign domination of the homeland. In the twentieth century, writers such as Faiz took up the ghazal structure to criticize postindependence governments. Thus Faiz represented and criticized the new nation of Pakistan as a cruel beloved—a beloved with whom the poet would seek union, but who behaves like a tyrant. This development is particularly important because Faiz is perhaps Ali's single greatest influence. Ali translated a volume of Faiz's poetry into English and wrote a lengthy poem on Faiz— "Homage to Faiz Ahmed Faiz." Indeed, in that poem, Ali recounts precisely this development of the ghazal tradition: "you . . . redefined the cruel/beloved, that figure who already was Friend, Woman, God," explaining, "In your hands // she was Revolution" (35). Moreover, Faiz took up the image of separation as prison and made that central to his poetry. Indeed, Faiz was himself imprisoned for his opposition to the Pakistani government. It is in part because of Faiz that Ali refers to "the cry of gods/and prisoners" at the beginning of "From Another Desert," and, at the end, places Majnoon in a prison. Finally, Faiz spent many years in exile due to his political beliefs. Ali felt a particularly close affinity with this aspect of Faiz's life, and said that, in translating Faiz's poems, "I touched my own exile" (36).

These transformations from religious to political allegory fit with another aspect of the ghazal tradition. The material world is not the only obstacle for the lovers. Social structure and convention are equally inhibiting. Most important, in this tradition, is rigid and oppressive Islamic orthodoxy. The worst enemy of the lover, the worst enemy of the Sufi mystic, is the Islamic legalist. In the ghazal tradition, "The true lover of the Divine Beloved is the implacable foe of the *shaikh*," the religious "elder" of "moral authority." This pharisaical character and his rigid traditionalism are "assailed with every weapon of ridicule and invective that the poet can command" (Russell, *Pursuit*, 38). Faiz took up this aspect of the tradition to criticize oppressive aspects of the Pakistani government, most often aspects justified by reference to Islam. In his "Homage," Ali explains that Faiz was exiled "from Pakistan, from / the laws of home which said: the hands / of thieves will be surgically/amputated" (34). Ali here refers to the institution of Islamic law by Zia ul-Haq after 1979. As Weiss notes, the most severe punishments of the Islamic penal code, "hudud" punishments, address "crimes . . . against God's commands" (3). These include the crime of theft: "The punishment for a first offense is amputation of the right hand . . . ; for a second offense, it is amputation of the left foot" (14).

Ali continues this reorientation and reparticularization of the tradition by taking up the ghazal to treat his own exile from Kashmir and to criticize a rigid, legalistic form of Islam that, he seems to imply, is partially responsible for that exile.

"FROM ANOTHER DESERT"

Ali's fifth book of poetry, *A Nostalgist's Map of America,* is largely a meditation on personal loss—the loss of home in exile, and the loss of one particular person. In this collection, the person is named "Phil." I suspect this is the real name of someone Ali loved. But I doubt that he would have used the name if it did not have a broader significance as well, for "Phil" means "Love." Thus, *Phil* is both a particular individual and a general beloved. As this suggests, the collection is not limited to narrowly personal lament. Most significantly, it includes broad social concerns as well. Indeed, some poems anticipate the focus of his next volume, *The Country without a Post Office,* which centers on the violence that has rent Kashmir in recent years. Ali relates such contemporary political issues both to his own experience and to a much longer history of Muslim/Hindu relations in Kashmir, a history that was once exemplary for its intercommunal harmony (see Nehru vii–viii). In this way, Ali locates his own personal feelings and relations squarely within an encompassing, contemporary politics as well as a long social history.

"From Another Desert" develops these concerns in specific relation to the structures and practices of the ghazal. The title itself, with its prominent image of the desert in which the poet is located and from which he is writing, already suggests the ghazal tradition, and, in the context of that tradition, indicates that the poet is longing for a union which he cannot achieve (i.e., someone reading this poem from within the tradition spontaneously fills this in from the prototype). The directly following epigraph from Ghalib reenforces this implication. It refers to "Footprints" in the "desert" (63). As Mustaq Kapadwala pointed out to me, this suggests that Ali is walking in the footsteps of Ghalib, and other writers of ghazals, extending back to Majnoon—even if he is doing so from another desert. Indeed, "another" in the title could mean a "further" desert, as well as a "different" desert. Thus Ali's sojourn takes place in "yet another" desert, a desert in addition to those deserts we have met with in the poems of Ghalib and other writers of the ghazal. Moreover, the footprints Ali is following are "Footprints of blood," indicating both life and suffering—a constant conjunction in the tradition of the ghazal, for, in this tradition, material life, exile from the beloved, is necessarily a matter of suffering.

Unsurprisingly, the first line of Ali's poem is "Cries Majnoon" (65). "Cries" here means both "weeps" and "calls out," which is to say, calls out the story of his despair and love. The legendary Majnoon stands at the beginning of the ghazal tradition. He is the prototypical lover, soul in exile, and poet who sings his sorrows into verse. Here, when Majnoon cries out, weeping, in couplets written by Ali, Ali implicitly identifies himself with this originary poet of the Arabic/Persian/Urdu tradition, and with his suffering, just as he suggested his identification with Ghalib through the epigraph.

The next lines take up the standard motif of this sorrow, why Majnoon cries: "Beloved / you are not here" (65). Readers of Ali know that his own exile from Kashmir is a recurrent motif in his poems. Thus, we may suspect right from the outset that the beloved is Kashmir, or India, in addition to one particular person—Phil, or perhaps someone earlier, someone in India, such as Sunil from the poem, "I Dream It Is Afternoon When I Return to Delhi." Moreover, the collection makes clear that Ali lived for many years in Arizona and presumably wrote "From Another Desert" in that place. In this way, the poet is literally in "another" desert. It is not the Arabian desert of Majnoon, but a desert in the United States, a desert with specific implications of postcolonization exile and homelessness—and, of course, a desert that, along with these implications, extends and reparticularizes the standard ghazal image of separation.

But this is not all. Given the broader tradition, we might also suspect that the beloved is not only a person and a place, but God, and an imagination of society. The connection with religion is made explicit a few lines later, when Ali refers to "the cry of gods" (65). But the reference is odd. Why "gods," not "God"? It is an image more appropriate to Hinduism than Islam. In part, this relates to the fact that Indic Sufism was influenced by Hinduism, specifically the Vedantic doctrine that the individual soul *(atman)* is identical with Absolute Godhead *(brahman),* while the appearance of difference between them is illusory. The Hindu/Sufi link extends back to Arabia. Chaitanya points out that the ninth-century Sufi writer Abū Yazīd was the first to declare openly his belief in monism (113)—the view that "Not only is there no god but God, but there is no being but God" (111). There is "impressive evidence" that "Yazid was influenced" by Vedantism. The connection became stronger and more elaborate in India itself. This was particularly true of the Chishtiyyah brotherhood, a sect of Sufis who adopted "a number of Hindu customs and ceremonials," including specific practices of yoga (Waines 149). In keeping with these religious interrelations, Ahmed Ali stresses that both "the Koran" and "Vedantic beliefs and Hindu philosophy" "enriched the ghazal and gave it a distinctive universality" (9). This begins to give us a hint as to the particular sorrow at issue in Ali's poem.

It is at this point that Ali begins to draw on Eliot, though he continues to do so within the context of the ghazal tradition. The fourth and fifth lines are "It is a strange spring / rivers lined with skeletons" (65). These lines already suggest Eliot's Waste Land in general, which begins in a waterless springtime (see 66; the point is developed over several stanzas). In addition, the line recalls the theme of the first canto of *The Waste Land,* the dead men who lost their bones in that poem (57; see also the subsequent references to bones in this poem [60] and in "Ash Wednesday" [87]). Ali follows these lines ("It is a strange spring / rivers lined with skeletons") with wind images that are also close to Eliot: "Wings beat / in the cages // letting the wind hear its own restlessness" (65). These are reminiscent of Eliot's "the empty chapel, only the wind's home" (68), and, even more so, "These wings are no longer wings to fly / But merely vans to beat the air" from "Ash Wednesday" (86). Ali's next canto begins with reference to "the grief of broken stone," another Eliotlike image, recalling the "stone images" and "prayers to broken stone" in "The Hollow Men" (80, 81) as well as the "heap of broken images" (53) in *The Waste Land*.

Eliot uses these as images of a meaningless modern existence, a modern existence deprived of the higher significance of faith, lacking genuine religious feeling and inspiration. Ali uses them similarly, but also links them with the general narrative structure of the ghazal tradition, and with the motif of exile. This barren spring is "strange," not only because it is peculiar—a spring of drought and death. It is also "strange" in being foreign, alien—springtime in a strange place, transformed into a waste land because of its foreignness. The rivers lined with skeletons not only recall death in what should be a season of new life. They also suggest some destruction in the past that remains with us. These are not decaying corpses, but skeletons—what remains for years, even centuries, once flesh has dissolved. These skeletons are like some dreadful and cruel history, the effects of which continue to haunt the present.

The wings beating in the cages are most obviously an image of the soul, a soul imprisoned—in the material world, in social convention, most of all in the constraints of a society based on legalistic and destructive religion (again, reading in the tradition, one immediately expects this from the relevant prototypes). This entrapment of the "wings" is precisely what fills "the wind" with "restlessness." For here the wind cannot serve as medium for flight, transporting the bird into the skies, the soul to God, the lover to his beloved. That is why the sound of these wings is the very sound of the wind's restlessness and the very sound, Ali writes, of his own "agony" (65).

Ali further clarifies the nature of this prison, desert, waste land, when he describes a ruin of broken stone "among the ghosts of saints and poets" where "the gods have lost their vermilion marks" (66). Here, we begin to discern more precisely what Ali has in mind. It is a destructive history that leads to the present—in this case, the desecration of Hindu temples, which occurred periodically throughout India during Muslim rule. The allusion has a more specific and direct relevance as well, for the saints and poets to whom Ali refers are the Kashmiri writers of Muslim and Hindu mystical poetry. These writers are a central part of the literary tradition on which Ali is drawing. In *The Country without a Post Office*, Ali emphasizes the historical and poetic significance of Kashmiri poet-saints from both communities. One important point about the Hindu and Sufi mystics of Kashmir is that they saw each other as saints, not as heretics. For example, there are legends current in Kashmir that the Sufi saint Hamdani was the only man that the Hindu mystic and poet Lallesvari admired. In "I Dream I Am the Only Passenger on Flight 423 to Srinagar," Ali names Noor-ud-Din, a Muslim, the "true heir" of Lallesvari, "blessed" by her (33). Indeed, some Muslim writers have gone so far as to see Lallesvari as, in effect, Muslim (see Mohammad Khan 70–79), thereby fusing the two traditions in her mysticism. In this way, the mention of saints and poets suggests a condition, not merely of religious toleration, but of profound spiritual interaction, in which understanding, admiration, and learning crossed communal lines, for these saints and poets saw those lines as mere superficial distinctions. The overall implication may be that the intolerant Islam of the iconoclasts has littered history with skeletons, that it has destroyed the mutual admiration and mutual study of Hindus and Muslims. This mutual admiration and study had been deeply beneficial to both communities, fostering in their finest poet-saints a sense that they were all speaking of and working toward the same unutterable, perfect union—though they referred to this in different, equally inadequate terms.

These lines are followed by an elaboration of the same theme: "No priest comforts their loneliness / in the courtyard of these ruins" (66). The Hindu priests have fled from the iconoclasts. None remains to give solace to the broken images of gods, or, more importantly, to the ghosts of saints and poets, whose memory haunts the desolated place. Ali goes on to describe the grass growing over a "wrecked temple," to which "a god returns" (66), now a sort of absolute mendicant, his misery generalized to that of all the world, as he "extends the earth / like begging bowl" (67). Among other things, this suggests that destructive intolerance is global, not confined to one nation or period. The third canto repeats the image of temple desecration: "Each statue will be broken." When the gods return, "they'll pick / up their severed arms // and depart" (68). Severing the limbs of statues was one common method of destroying idols.

For someone such as Ali, raised in Islam, but clearly striving for a union of Muslim and Hindu, these images serve to express a sense that a vibrant form of spirituality and a sacralization of the place itself—India in general, Kashmir in particular—have been lost. A deeply valuable synthesis of these two great religions has been replaced by communalism, hate, and a false, legalistic form of Islam. This is where Eliot fits in. In Eliot's most famous poem, the condition of modern humanity is a condition of living in a waste land—a sort of variation on the desert of the ghazal tradition. Moreover, this exile in a waste land is caused by a form of religious alienation, though not the traditional isolation of man from God in the material world, or not that only. It is in part the more modern loss of the sense of the sacred itself, the loss of even the tradition that turns one's aspirations to God. In the case of Muslim India, Ali implies, this loss is due, at least in part, to the substitution of a dead, legalistic, communalist form of Islam—a skeleton—for the living, open, intercommunal spiritualism of the Sufis, the form of Islam that seeks to set the soul free from its cage to fly on the wind into the heavens, into union with God.

Other poems indicate that this mutual alienation of Hindu and Muslim is bound up with more personal alienations as well. For example, a later poem, "Farewell," is "a plaintive love letter from a Kashmiri Muslim to a Kashmiri Pandit" (Ali, *The Country* 93). In "I Dream It Is Afternoon When I Return to Delhi," which movingly expresses Ali's experience of exile, his oneiric return to Delhi centers around an imaginary reunion with a young Hindu man named "Sunil." The beloved sought by Ali is certainly his homeland, or, rather, his homeland as it might be, as it was, perhaps, at the time of Hamdan, Noor-ud-Din, and Lallesvari—his homeland as a place of Hindu/Muslim brotherhood and sisterhood, and thus a place of genuine spirituality. But the beloved is also a particular person, a Hindu, inaccessible in part due to the separation of these communities. Thus, Ali tells us, the temples of which he is speaking are not only houses of worship. Rather, he tells us, "the heart is a temple" (68), and thus the heart itself is what has been and is desecrated. Ali's own heart, the heart that should be joined with the beloved—Kashmir or India, or some particular Love—is now a temple where Ali finds, not the holy, living experience, the true beloved, but only a "broken" statue with "severed arms."

This puts us in a position to understand an earlier line more fully. As we have already noted, the cry of Majnoon is paired with "the cry of gods"—for it is the communalistic "killing" of the gods, and thus the destruction of the Hindu/Muslim sense of unity, that, at least in part, caused Ali's own suffering. But the full phrase is "the cry of gods / and prisoners" (65). Who, then, are these prisoners? Given what we have been saying, one would expect the prisoners to be anyone who does not conform to the narrow dictates of the shaikh, anyone who does not follow the legalistic doctrines of orthodox Islam. In the twelfth canto, the point is made explicit when Ali writes: "Ambushed in century after century by the police of God / the broken Ishmaels cry out in the blazing noons . . . again declared madmen by the government of Sorrow"—"Majnoon" means, roughly, "madman"—"Majnoon also among them" (80). Ali, it seems, is exiled due to the same intolerant religion that imprisons so many people, and keeps many others wandering amid skeletons in a land barren of the communal peace that they desire. Ali's exile, then, is both personal memory and history, individual life recapitulating and exemplifying the broader tragedies of society, with its endless cycles of human exile: "There again is memory / at my doorstep— // jasmine crushed under / departing feet" (69).

Also in keeping with the ghazal tradition, however, Ali indicates that this sort of authoritarianism and cruelty are not true Islam, but a perversion of Muslim principles. Indeed, he indicates this in the very passage we just quoted. For the police bear down on "broken Ishmaels" who "cry out" like Majnoon, like all the poets, like Ali himself. It is crucial that these are Ishmaels, for Ishmael is the ancestral root of the Arabs. In this way, the attack by the "police of God" is directly an attack upon the sources of Islam itself—for it is an attack on Ishmael, the progenitor who, in Muslim tradition, inherited from Abraham the covenant with God (see the *Qur'ān* 2:122–25 and Maulana Ali 53–54n.168).

Indeed, the scene recalls the most famous moment in Ishmael's life. In Muslim tradition, Abraham was called upon to sacrifice his son Ishmael, not Isaac. When informed of this, Ishmael, surrendering himself entirely to God's will, said "O my father, do as thou art commanded" (*Qur'ān* 37:102). But, of course, God called out that Ishmael was not to be sacrificed, and that no one else was to be sacrificed either. In part, the point of the story is that both Abraham and Ishmael had the absolute devotion to God necessary to fulfill the covenant. But the point of the story is equally that the true God does not demand such sacrifices (see Maulana Ali 861n.2117). In relation to this, the actions of the "police of God" indicate that they have failed to heed God's message. Directly contrary to God's pronouncement, they "break" Ishmael and everyone like him—which is presumably to say all those who have truly inherited the covenant of God. They not only violate the general injunction against sacrifice, they sacrifice precisely those who carry God's promise to humankind. In contrast, these latter-day Ishmaels do not deviate from the behavior of their original, and thus do not deviate from the origins of Islam, because they "cry out . . . welcoming the knives" (80). They, like the first Ishmael, are willing to sacrifice themselves to whatever "trial" they may be subjected, for they know all trials are sent by God (cf. the *Qur'ān* 37:106). All this indicates once again that "there is no justice," as Ali puts it in canto 9 (77)—and, indeed, no true *Islamic* justice—in the "police of God."

In this context, the word "broken" is particularly significant, for it tells us two things. First, these Ishmaels have been brutalized, battered until their will to live is lost, until they accept death, not only from devotion to God, but also from deep despair, the same sort of despair that causes Majnoon to cry out and, later, wish for death (71). Second, as already noted, Ishmael is the ancestral representative of the covenant with God. Indeed, in some interpretations, he does not inherit the covenant from Abraham, but is a part of the covenant from its inception (see Maulana Ali 53n.168). In this way, an attack on Ishmael is an attack on that covenant with God. To say that Ishmael is broken, is to say that the covenant with God has been broken as well—and both are broken by the police of God.

Finally, it is important to note that Ishmael was, in effect, exiled, like Majnoon, or like Ali. In the case of Ishmael, this exile was part of a divine plan, leading ultimately to the birth of the Prophet and the beginning of Islam as a distinct, organized religion (see Maulana Ali 503–504n.1319 and 53–54n.168). Thus it is an exile with a spiritual conclusion. This further serves to link Ishmael with the exiled lover of the ghazal tradition, and to oppose both to the police of God.

This is not to say that Islam—or, rather, what passes for Islam—is the only religion criticized in this poem. The "police of God" are sent out by various denominations. In canto 12, where he introduces the police of God, Ali presents Majnoon digging "graves in the desert // crying out for his dead Laila." Majnoon's beloved has been killed, and Majnoon too, like Ishmael, has been "broken." What has broken Majnoon is another set of ruins, another set of broken stones, like the shattered temples of the Hindus. But this time it is "the ruins of Jerusalem or Beirut // or another rival to the garden of paradise" (80). Here, Ali broadens his critique to the other major monotheisms derived from the Middle East. The ruins of Beirut are, most importantly, the ruins left by the 1982 Israeli invasion. The city was devastated, in the way scattered temples were laid waste by iconoclasts. For example, "An American nurse working in Beirut . . . reported that Israel 'dropped bombs on everything, including hospitals, orphanages and, in one case, a school bus carrying 35 young schoolgirls who were traveling on an open road'" (Chomsky, *Fateful* 226); "A UN report estimated 13,500 severely damaged houses in West Beirut alone, thousands elsewhere, not counting the Palestinian camps (which are— or were—in fact towns)" (223). In addition, in that invasion, the allies of the Israelis were the right-wing Lebanese Christians. Thus both Judaism and Christianity are implicated here. Indeed, it was these Christians who were directly responsible for the brutal massacres at Sabra and Shatila (see Chomsky, *Fateful* 364–75). The reference to Jerusalem could allude to any number of conflicts, extending back from the current crisis to the crusades or even earlier. The historical depth of the problem, indicated right at the outset in the image of skeletons, recurs with the description of Majnoon in relation to "the ruins of Jerusalem or Beirut": "where his heart broke and broke centuries ago" (80). The repetition suggests that the breaking occurred both recently and in the distant past—in short, throughout history, which is a history of religious intolerance and cruelty.

Indeed, the pattern extends back further still. For Jerusalem and Beirut are themselves linked with "another rival to the garden of paradise." Just as Ali writes from "another" desert, implying that this loss of the beloved—in all its meanings—is continually repeated in different places at different times, so too is this destruction of an Edenic condition continually repeated in different places at different times. There is always some loss comparable to the Fall of humankind; the loss of Hindu/Muslim community—represented by Hamdan, Noor-ud-Din, and Lallesvari—is just one case of this type. These gardens of paradise engage rivalry, and thus destruction, because the conquering peoples see them as Edenic. The Turko-Afghan Muslims come to India, or the Crusaders to Jerusalem, in order to wrest that "Eden" from its possessors. To take one example, Wolpert explains that Mahmud of Ghazni invaded India "for plunder" and "for the promise of paradise" (107). Moreover, when members of one religious group seize this garden of paradise, they typically subject it to their particular form of worship, their particular ritual, their particular legal code, independent of the beliefs and customs maintained by the inhabitants. Indeed, the conquering religion routinely excludes all others, characterizes all others as false and blasphemous, and thus makes it imperative that these other religions be destroyed and their people converted or punished for their heretical impiety. Wolpert notes that Mahmud "smash[ed] countless Hindu temple idols, which he viewed with Islamic iconoclastic fervor as abominations to Allah" and, according to a chronicler, in one day killed "more than fifty thousand Hindus" (107).

In this way, it is important that Ali refers to the police of *God* (singular), giving further resonance to the opening image of the cry of *gods* (plural). As Daniélou has noted, a particular sort of religious dogmatism is a much greater risk for monotheists than for polytheists; "in monotheist creeds, we find . . . so little place for tolerance, so little respect for modes of thought, or worship, or behavior different from the 'norm'" (10). There is a broad tendency for polytheism to be incorporative and monotheism to be exclusionary. Polytheistic religions tend to allow different people their own deities, and to include those deities in an expanded pantheon.[3] Mysticism has the same sort of incorporative tendency, even when monotheistic, as in Sufi Islam, for it sees different "gods" as different names for one God, who is not owned by any one faith nor defined by any single creed, who, indeed, necessarily exceeds all faiths and creeds. In contrast with these tendencies, standard monotheisms are rigid in defining religious truth as singular, as their own particular and narrowly specified doctrine. Thus, it is monotheism that sends out the police to control doctrinal error, to wipe out heresy, to shatter gods, to break Ishmaels and their divine covenants.

Despite significant references to Christianity and Judaism, however, the focus of the poem is clearly on Islam. Again, the breaking of Ishmael implies that current Islamic orthodoxy does not represent genuine Islam, Islam in its original impulses. Elsewhere in the poem, Ali hints at a history to this alteration of Islam. In canto 7, the speaker asks, "Who now weeps / at the crossroads." The image of the crossroads recalls the speaker's exile, the point at which he took the way from home and toward the desert. But it also recalls a point in the past when things could have been different, when, perhaps, history as a whole could have gone in another direction. The mourner "remembers the directions / that led so soon // to betrayal" (73). What is this betrayal? Certainly, betrayal is always a concern in ghazals of love. However, in connection with

Islamic legalism, with the breaking of Ishmaels, and with the earliness of the betrayal ("so soon"), the speaker seems to allude to a particular series of events that split the Muslim community only decades after the Prophet's death. I am referring to the mistreatment of Muḥammad's son-in-law 'Alī and, even more, the murder of 'Alī's son, al-Ḥusayn. The latter in particular precipitated the split between the Sunnī and Shī'ah sects of Islam and is seen by Shī'ah Muslims as the definitive early betrayal of the founding principles of Islam. (Ali identifies himself as Shī'ah on the first page of *Ravishing DisUnities*.)

Specifically, Shī'ah Muslims—a roughly 10 percent minority within Islam—believe that Muḥammad chose and announced 'Alī as the one who should guide the Muslim community. After Muḥammad's death, three other companions of the Prophet preceded 'Alī as Khalīfah, leader of the community. In the Shī'ah view, this was an illegitimate usurpation. Worse still, even as Khalīfah, 'Alī had to face open revolt including "betrayal from among his own supporters." Ultimately, he was assassinated. The conflict surrounding 'Alī's succession was repeated with his son, al-Ḥusayn. In this case, the conflict culminated in a battle at Karbalā', where, "Facing overwhelming odds, al-Husayn and most of his small party . . . were slain" by the army of the new Khalīfah, Yazīd (Waines 159). The martyrdom of al-Ḥusayn is recalled by Shī'ahs through ten days of mourning every year, including a passion play in which participants flagellate themselves. Agha Shahid Ali addresses this commemoration in a later poem where he explains, "We're cut to the brains. . . . We mourn the martyrs of Karbala, our skins torn with chains" (*Country* 84).

Of course, in "From Another Desert"—as in Shī'ah thought—the significance of these tragic events is broader than some conflict over succession to leadership. The betrayals of 'Alī and al-Ḥusayn constitute a betrayal of Islam as a whole. More broadly still, they instance a betrayal of human feeling and moral principle by those with "eclipses / hidden in their eyes" and those "folding . . . their wallets" (73), which is to say, hypocritical and greedy religious authorities—precisely those represented by the shaikh in the ghazal tradition. Perhaps more importantly, this moment is an exemplary betrayal in the poem, for the battles surrounding succession after Muḥammad, battles that engulfed 'Alī and 'Alī's son, are early instances of internal dissension and mutual acrimony arising within a community that once lived in harmony. Just as the union of Sufi and Hindu mystics in Kashmir degenerated into communalism, so too did the common society of Muslims degenerate into factionalism and civil conflict, into betrayal of 'Alī and al-Ḥusayn, into hatred and war. Indeed, Kashmir was not untouched by this division within Islam. Rafiqi explains that Kashmir has been "torn by Shi'i-Sunni conflicts" (96). Indeed, some Sunnī writers in Kashmir argued that "the Shi'is are heretics . . . and therefore their wanton destruction is lawful" (221).

Canto 9 continues these general themes, considering the political and imperial development of Islam, and its connection with related betrayals. Specifically, Ali discusses two paintings, "Persian miniature[s]" (75). The first concerns Majnoon's separation from his father. The second concerns "A royal hunt" in which "the world goes on/without" Majnoon. The theme of religious persecution and the betrayal of Islamic principle is clearly indicated in the latter, through the image of "Prince Jehangir // soon to be Emperor of Hindustan" (76). Jehangir took his name, meaning "World Seizer" (Wolpert 134), after he rebelled against his father Akbar, evidently poisoned him (Wolpert 134), and took over his kingdom. When paired with Ishmael, this image is even more powerful. While Ishmael was willing to die so that his father could fulfill God's will, Jehangir killed his own father in order to achieve worldly ambition. Where God explicitly forbade Abraham from sacrificing Ishmael even for religious purposes, Jehangir murdered his own father for secular ambitions. The image of the hunt is particularly relevant here because, as a young man, Jehangir (then named Salim) had lived a dissolute life. After an initial rebellion against Akbar, he seemed to reform. However, Lal writes that "he soon reverted" to drunkenness and lechery, as well as "long spells of hunting to satisfy his lust to kill" (57)—a prelude to his renewed rebellion.

This is a particularly apt historical example, for Akbar was a Chishtiyyah Sufi, who drew extensively on Hinduism in his own mystical beliefs (Wolpert 132), and more generally sought to learn from and synthesize various religions (132; for a fuller discussion, see chapter 10 of Rizvi). Waines explains that Akbar brought "Muslims of differing religious standpoints, Hindus, Christians, Jains, Zoroastrians, and Jews" to his "House of Worship" for religious discussions and debates (190) and "emphasized the truth to be found in all faiths" (191). Malik discusses "Akbar's close association with Hindu *yogis*" (25). Though he probably overstates the case, de Souza goes so far as to claim that Akbar was "impressed more by Hinduism, Jainism and Zoroastrianism than by the theological intolerance of Islam and Christianity" (112). In short, Akbar provided the possibility of Hindu/Muslim unity. After a period of communal antagonism and oppression, his rule might have brought Hindus and Muslims together into a community of mystical belief, like that shared by the poet-saints of Kashmir. But he, and the entire history he represented, was betrayed. His assassination was another Edenic loss. As Lal explains, Jahangir needed allies to defeat his father. Unsurprisingly, "The chief among them were the Sayeds of Burha, an influential and powerful clan opposed to Akbar's policies of tolerance and liberalism. They struck a deal with Salim." In exchange for their support, Salim/Jahangir "was to protect orthodox Islam and give no quarter to its enemies" (60).[4]

The conjunction of Majnoon's father and Jehangir serves to reenforce these points, in part by contrasting Majnoon with Jehangir, both directly and

through the imagery of the paintings: Majnoon's father "rest[ing] his head on
an uncut sapphire" and Jehangir with "Ruby buttons glisten[ing] on his
coat/drops of blood" (76). Though Majnoon caused his father great sorrow,
Nizami stresses the love Majnoon bore both his parents, and carefully portrays
his anguish at their deaths (see, for example, 32 and 101)—the only anguish
that could distract him from his brooding over separation from Laila. This
canto of Ali's poem is thus designed to call up these images and contrasts in
the reader's mind without explicitly stating them—images readily available to
anyone who reads Ali from within the ghazal tradition. Just to be clear, however, Ali includes a judgment on this entire state of affairs: "Oh
Majnoon/there is no justice," and goes on to note that Jehangir "will not dis-
mount/in your wilderness" (77). Jehangir will not sacrifice the world to love
an ideal. He will go on to seize the world, to murder his father, to betray the
promise of communal harmony in India. He will not live in the desert of
Sufistic longing. And his father, who felt that longing, will not rest his head
upon a sapphire—precious and blue as the heavens, and once thought to calm
the maddened mind ("Gem Superstitions"). Rather, Akbar's blood will spat-
ter Jehangir's clothing—and his vast decorations of wealth, the bloodlike
rubies glistening on his coat, will be allowed only by that murder.

Ali returns us to the present with the motif of prison, developed in cantos ten and eleven. Canto ten begins mythically, "In prison Majnoon weeps for
Satan" (78). In the one prose passage of the poem, Ali briefly retells the story
of Iblis, an angel who refused to worship man and was, for that reason, condemned to Hell by his Beloved—God (*Qur'ān* 7:11–18). There is an implication that the speaker's situation is parallel to that of Iblis, that he loved his
home, as Iblis loved God, and because of this love the speaker refused to worship something merely human, for which reason he was exiled. Though this
image seems to pit the lover against God, it in fact links him/her deeply with
God. From the perspective of the Sufi mystic, it is precisely the sectarian and
legalistic shaikh who demands that all men and women bow down and worship mere human forms—legal proscriptions, outward signs of piety, the letter of the law overseen by the police of God. The true lover of God, the mystic who seeks absolute union with the divine, refuses to worship mere form.

Majnoon's apparent or outward impiety—and its relation to a true, inner
piety—is a recurrent motif in the ghazal tradition. For example, at one point
in Nizami's poem, Majnoon's well-meaning father takes him to the sacred
Ka'bah in Mecca. This is related to "the final and most complex ritual duty"
of Islam (Waines 91)—the *ḥajj* or pilgrimage to Mecca. To fulfill this obligation, the pilgrim not only visits the city, but enters "the sanctuary of the
Ka'bah," circumambulates the Ka'bah, and follows other traditional practices
(Waines 92). As they stand "in the shadow and protection of the Holiest of
Holies" (26), Majnoon's father urges Majnoon to beg that God relieve him of

the madness of love, so that Majnoon can lead a normal life, following the normal conventions—thus living in the sensual pleasure of a rich man, focusing his mind on power and material gain. Though well meaning, the entire journey is a spiritual error. First, he has brought Majnoon to the central holy place, and to a central holy object—as if one physical space or one thing could be holier than anything else, in a universe pervaded by God's spirit. Moreover, he has asked Majnoon in effect to worship the life of material opulence that characterizes men of his station, to worship, not man per se, but mere human forms of life, to substitute these for his consuming love of Laila, which, again, represents his consuming love of God. But Majnoon refuses. Indeed, he calls upon God to increase his love, and increase his madness. From the perspective of the shaikh, Majnoon is a demon, an Iblis. But from the perspective of the Sufi, he is a poet-saint who refuses to lie down and worship a false god. As Waines explains, "from the Sufi vantage point, each of the obligatory rituals of the faith is valid owing to its inward purpose and meaning," and only because of that. "Al-Hujwiri comments, for example, that pilgrimage *(hajj)* is an act of self-mortification whose true object is not to visit the Ka'bah in Mecca but to contemplate Allah" (140–41). In the mystical interpretation of the story, that is precisely the point Majnoon enacts.

Indeed, this returns us to Islamic iconoclasm. The implication of this teaching—and thus of Ali's canto in this context—is that the sort of religion that demands worship of mere human convention is a type of idolatry. The religion of the shaikh, the police of God, the government of Sorrow, is a religion that tries to confine God to a finite form, made and perpetuated by humans, a religion that says God is this one set of practices and ideas only, not anything else. It is then a violation of the principles that underlie Islamic iconoclasm—this suggests a particular hypocrisy in the iconoclasm perpetrated against Hindu temples and shows again the degree to which legalistic and destructive leaders have betrayed Islam's foundational commitments.

Of course, Ali's allusions here are not merely mythological, but historical and personal as well. "Iblis" clearly refers to those modern writers—prominently Faiz—who refused to worship the human forms of Islamic government, enforced by the police of God, and were in consequence imprisoned or exiled. Indeed, in this and the following section, Ali seems to have Faiz particularly in mind. One could say that Faiz loved Pakistan so much that he refused to worship the mere human forms instituted by its cruel government, a sort of contemporary inheritor of such rulers as Jehangir. For this refusal, he was imprisoned, and exiled. Indeed, at some level, it seems that Majnoon weeping for Satan is Ali weeping for Faiz, and recognizing their kinship. The subsequent reference to Beirut, where Faiz was exiled, gives further weight to this connection. Of course, the image is clearly more general than Faiz. It applies to a wide range of poets who rebelled against the shaikh, in his various historical forms. Nonetheless, Faiz is a prime example of the type, an Iblis, a Majnoon, an Ishmael, an exemplum of the character Ali wishes to celebrate and mourn in this poem.

This is all a part of the ghazal tradition. However, there is also a metropolitan element—Romantic Satanism, the celebration of Satan's refusal to submit to divine will, and the linking of this refusal with political defiance and with the rebellious stance of the poet. This fits well with the general concerns of the poem. Moreover, it is drawn from a "subaltern" aspect of metropolitan literature. Not that the literature in question was written by minorities or women—it wasn't, for the most part. But it was vehemently oppositional, critical of standard practices and standard beliefs, and, in some cases, even explicitly revolutionary. In other words, it was directly relevant to the particular subaltern stance of Faiz, with his beloved, the new society—or "Revolution," as Ali put it ("Homage" 35).

On the other hand, even this use of metropolitan tradition is "indigenized." The hero is changed from Satan to Iblis, and the act of defiance is a refusal to honor man, linked with the general Islamic principle of prohibiting the identification of God with any mere human form. Moreover, there are precedents for some of this in the ghazal tradition itself. Nizami repeatedly has characters refer to Majnoon as a demon (see, for example, 48, 51, 66)—though this is most often due to his madness or "possession," and is certainly not celebratory in the manner of the Romantics. Perhaps more significantly, Nizami and others draw on the imagery of Hell to represent the lover's suffering in separation from the beloved, which itself represents the mystic's suffering in separation from God (see, for example, Nizami 93, 123). In this way, the most devoted and pious mystic may also be the person deepest in Hell. In his important long poem *Javid-Nama*, Muhammad Iqbal develops these ideas in connection with Iblis. When Iblis expresses his misery over separation from God, Iqbal writes, "how blessed the soul that can feel anguish!" (l.2506). It is only a short step from this to Ali's linking of Majnoon with Iblis.

In any case, after treating the police of God in canto twelve, Ali begins the concluding canto (thirteen) with what appears to be a classic Sufi statement: "The self is lost, erased at this moment" (*The Belovéd Witness* 64).[5] In Sufism, that moment is, of course, just when the self is lost *in God*, when the lover and beloved are, at last, united. Unfortunately, that moment never comes in life. It comes only in death—hence, the immediately following question, "When, at last, that hour comes, who will lead me / through the catacombs to the swordsman's arms?" Before he goes to the executioner, the speaker wonders if his escort will "bring a message / from her eyes" ("From Another Desert" 81). Here Ali alludes to the recurring concern of Nizami's Majnoon, and Laila. Whenever either one meets a visitor, he/she asks for a message from the other. Here, the speaker wonders what message will be brought from his beloved—person or homeland—when he approaches death. Having asked this, Ali retreats immediately from this future execution to the present—the time of current exile, the time of writing letters home, and receiving letters. In Nizami's poem, the lovers do manage to exchange letters briefly. So, Ali, modernizing the story slightly, turns next to "envelopes": "Tonight the air is many envelopes / again. Tell her to open them at once // and find hurried notes about my longing / for wings" (81–82). Wings, to fly free from the cage of canto one, in which they beat the restless air and echoed the speaker's agony of separation. Wings to fly back home, to fly heavenward, to reach Allāh. But he will have wings only when he has died, only when he has left the cage of human form and become pure soul. Indeed, even here, a question remains. If he dies and becomes a winged angel, will he be a spirit like Gibreel, beloved by God, living in eternal joy, or will he remain Iblis, damned to an eternal exile for his love, and his refusal to submit to human forms? In short, who is right, the mystic, or the shaikh?

The poem ends in a passage that is likely to seem enigmatic to any reader unfamiliar with the ghazal tradition and Nizami's great, canonical poem. The lover in a ghazal often has a good friend who serves as confidant and supporter (Russell, *Pursuit,* 44). Here Ali introduces such a figure, evidently identifying him with the escort to the executioner—an apt identification, since both are intermediaries in his union with Laila. The speaker addresses this confidant, telling him what to say to the beloved "when that hour comes," that is, at his death. The message is bare and enigmatic: "Speak, simply, of the air" (82). What does this message mean?

Majnoon has already said that "the air is many envelopes." This tells us that the air is the vehicle for a message from the speaker to the beloved. But the image, and its significance, are not confined to this internal reference. They derive, in part, from Laila's and Majnoon's use of the wind as a messenger in Nizami's poem. Early in that work, Majnoon gives "a message" for Laila "to the east wind." He asks it to "caress her hair and whisper in her ear," and requests that it have her "send him a breath of air" in return "as a sign" that she is thinking of him (12). Later, "If a gust of wind sweeps by," Majnoon "believes" it to be "from her and he thinks he can inhale her scent. He recites his poems, hoping that the wind . . . will carry them along to his beloved" (48; see also 91)—an image that gains plausibility as one recalls the allegorical connection between the beloved and God. Indeed, the air does bring to Laila the poems composed by Majnoon, for they are sung by "every passer-by" (40), and Laila herself composes poems, which "she wrote down on little scraps of paper" and "entrusted . . . to the wind" (40–41). These too reach Majnoon, for, ultimately, "there was no veil which could hide his beloved" from Majnoon (41). The wind is what lifts that veil.

To speak simply of the air is, then, to speak of or even to bring Majnoon's poetry to his beloved, the poetry that communicates his love and suffering, the poetry that represents his soul, longing for wings. It is also to hint that she should send her poetry to him as well. This poetry—his or hers—is the song mentioned a few lines earlier, when Laila "gaz[es] // at a dream in which the ghosts of prisoners / are shaking the bars till iron softens // into a song" (81). The iron can soften into song, the prisoners can escape the prison, precisely because they are now "ghosts," released from the dungeon of life into death—perhaps at last to reach the beloved. Or can they escape? The image is not as unequivocal as it might seem. First, it is a mere dream. Second, it recalls "the ghosts of saints and poets" who still haunt the "broken stone" of the temples (66). Clearly, death does not inevitably lead to union. Indeed, this image of dead and wandering spirits—suggested by repetition of the word "ghosts"—may indicate that the apparent optimism of the final lines is misplaced, ironic, false, that the poet will never be united with the beloved. Perhaps his poetry will be passed on. But he will not gain his wings and fly to her on the air, drawn by her songs. Instead, he will wander in dead places, haunting a waste land of skeletons and severed arms, a different and, now, eternal desert.

The poem ends in a deep and troubling uncertainty. Again, the speaker awaits "a message from her eyes" (81). It could resolve these ambiguities. However, we may already have heard the message that Majnoon will receive, after death, from his beloved. At the end of the sixth canto, Ali speaks of "answers" that come "from everywhere." They are, he explains, brought by "Silence" as it "continue[s] to echo" (72). But this too is uncertain. Does it mean that Silence will yield finally to a positive answer or that, as an echo (an echo necessarily of nothing), Silence is an endlessly repeated lack of an answer—or that it is an answer, but an answer of Nothing, an absolute and definitive denial of union with the beloved?

FROM THE TEXT TO THE WORLD

Faced with the insistent ambiguity at the end of Ali's poem, a critic might respond in different ways. Two such responses are particularly relevant here. On the one hand, the Silence of the Beloved leads us back to the literary tradition, to the motifs of the ghazal, to the metaphors of the Sufi mystics, to the exemplary poets filled with hope and despair. Sufism does not involve a merely vague longing for divine union. There is a Sufi *path*, a set of stages that one works through to achieve the goal. A crucial part of that path is the moment of stifling spiritual darkness, a moment when, far from achieving union, one receives no answer to one's harrowing spiritual doubts and one feels nothing but absolute isolation and despondency (see, for example, Attar 221–22)—a despondency that we as readers could not understand outside that tradition. This backward turn to tradition is, of course, what I have been emphasizing, not only for Ali, but for a wide range of postcolonial works.

The other way a critic could turn at the end of such a poem is toward the social and political conditions that surround our reading. Unfortunately, this approach too seems to point toward despair. The Chishtiyyah brotherhood of Sufis, the brotherhood that drew so directly on Hindu practices and that found an exemplary advocate in Akbar, derives its name from "a local association . . . from the town of Chisht in modern Afghanistan" (Waines 149). Though Ali's poem was written years ago, its insistence on betrayal only acquires further resonance from this accidental link. The connection with Afghanistan recalls the narrowness and brutality of the Taliban regime, so far from the syncretistic open-mindedness of Chishtiyyah humanism. It also recalls the U.S. bombing of Afghanistan, which is going on even as I write these words—bombing supported by God Himself, according to George W. Bush. Both remind us of traditions, and the ways in which traditions become narrowed into xenophobia and cruelty. The ghazal tradition stood against the rigidity and authoritarianism that has in recent years been manifest by the Taliban. But it stood against this rigidity on behalf of an absolute spiritual unity, not a national interest that will punish the victims of the oppressive shaikh more than the shaikh himself. Like many works of art, "From Another Desert" extends out from its origins to encompass conditions that arose only after it was written. In this case, it calls to mind a whole nation, first "Ambushed . . . by the police of God," then crushed under "the stones rained down on them . . . by the government of Sorrow" (80), a people who must all too clearly "remember the directions / that led so soon / to betrayal" (73).

"We Are All Africans"

The Universal Privacy of Tradition

Understanding history helps teach us who we are and why. But a full understanding of our collective history requires a critique of its Eurocentric biases. Afrocentricity is one angle of that critique. We all can gain perspective from its insights. After all, as the recent findings of molecular genetics have revealed, we are all Africans.
—Salim Muwakkil (21)

In the preceding pages, I have referred to such entities as European tradition, Hindu tradition, and so forth. In many ways, this is misleading. By stressing the existence of subversive components in these traditions, and by pointing to cases of corrective revision within a single tradition, I have indicated that traditions are far from unitary. But it may still seem that traditions, however torn by differences, still have a sort of objective, semi-Platonic existence that there really is a "European tradition" or a "Hindu tradition," even if it is a tradition with "subaltern strains." Moreover, it may seem that the conflicting components of a tradition are limited in number and political function—a matter of class, caste, gender, and a few other parameters. In fact, I do not believe any of these things. Rather, I believe that "tradition" is nothing more than a convenient way of referring to patterns across individual ideas, feelings, and behaviors that exhibit many degrees and kinds of similarity and difference.

As we have already noted, theoretical linguists largely follow Noam Chomsky in denying that language exists, except as an abstraction from individual grammars. In other words, my internal lexicon, principles of syntax, and other components of grammar, exist; your internal principles of syntax, etc., exist, and so on for every individual speaker. All these individual grammars share a range of principles, called "universals." Many of them share more specific properties as well. For example, my grammar and yours and those of many other people—most of the people living in North America, the British Isles, Australia, New Zealand—share a very large number of properties. They share so many properties at such a degree of specificity that we can all readily comprehend one another when we speak, each tacitly following his/her individual grammar. We refer to those shared properties as "English." However, English does not have any existence apart from those individual grammars, along with the grammars of our ancestors and other people whom we include in the same category. Indeed, we might have grouped people differently; we might have set up different boundaries for English. Using the term "superlanguage" to refer to a supposed supra-idiolectal, autonomous, Platonic language, Chomsky argues that "speakers of what is loosely called English do not have partial knowledge of some English superlanguage, but rather have knowledge of systems that are similar but in part conflict." He goes on to ask: "How broadly should the 'superlanguage' German extend? To Dutch? If not, why not, since it will presumably cover dialects that differ from one another more or less in the same way some of them differ from Dutch" (Rules 118). When we decide that Dutch is one language and German another, we do so, not for scientific reasons, but for "sociopolitical and normative" reasons (*Language and Problems* 37).

My view of tradition and culture is identical with this view of language. Tradition does not exist apart from individual ideas and expectations, beliefs, habits, and so on. "English," "Yoruba," or "European" tradition is simply an abstraction from individual conceptions, actions, and expectations. Indeed, I can see no way of making sense of the notion of Yoruba tradition or European tradition as anything else. All the arguments presented against the existence of an autonomous or Platonic language, independent of idiolects, apply with equal force to traditions. (As I have discussed these arguments at length elsewhere, I will not repeat them here; see chapter 2 of *On Interpretation*.) Thus "English tradition" or "Yoruba tradition" is an abstraction in precisely the same way that "English language" or "Yoruba language" is an abstraction. Moreover, it too is a sociopolitical abstraction. The isolation of such traditions is based on grouping people in particular ways due to political structures and political interests. To take a simple example, we refer to "Yoruba," "Fon," and "Igbo" traditions or cultures, even though the customs of some Yoruba are closer to the Fon, those of some Igbo closer to the Yoruba. In technical terms, we segment practical identities not only by reference to practical fit or shared competence, but also—and crucially—by reference to categorial identities.

This idiolectal view of tradition has a number of consequences. One of these is particularly relevant to our consideration of the multiple and complex ways in which authors from colonized groups respond to traditions after colonization. I refer to this as "common cultural ownership." It is the view that no tradition or culture is the special property of a particular ethnic or racial group. Rather, every tradition belongs only to humanity. It is collectively owned. This socialistic conception of tradition is not strictly entailed by an idiolectal view. But idiolectalism of this sort does undermine the usual reasons for seeing culture as bound to an ethnic or racial group. For one thing, tradition is not a uniform existent thing that can be appropriated by any group. Again, it has no Platonic autonomy, no ideal existence. It is a diversity of practices, ideas, and the like, and nothing more. In keeping with this, there is no strict rule to say that one view or practice is part of "the tradition" and another is not. Again, like language, strict divisions between traditions have only a sociopolitical basis. Outside the political uses to which group definition is put, there is only an issue of overlapping idiolects—can two or more people understand one another, debate their differences, work together toward common goals, and so on?

In an idiolectal view, even when a certain group genuinely shares many ideas, practices, and so on—thus, a tradition—the connection between that group and that tradition is purely contingent. To take a simple example, it is entirely a matter of accident that one person greets acquaintances by pressing his/her palms together and nodding, while another person extends his/her arm to shake hands. One's links with a tradition are as contingent, as nonethnic, as one's links with a language. A monoglot English speaker of French ancestry is an English speaker; insofar as we can categorize people by language categories, such a person has no claim to the "French" category. Similarly, an African, raised in France, speaking only French, is, by that fact, part of the French language community, not part of the Wolof language community. The same principle holds for tradition. Yoruba or European tradition does not exist apart from those who are able to interact in certain ways. Once someone begins to interact in those ways, once someone has the relevant competence, he/she is as much a member of Yoruba or European culture as anyone else. There cannot be any issue here of prior ownership. Again, there is no objective entity to own, no Platonic Tradition. There is only the set of expectations, skills, beliefs, ideas, in my mind, or in yours. In this way, a question of cultural ownership cannot arise. For surely each of us has a right to his/her own expectations, skills, beliefs, and ideas.

Indeed, the point is even sharper with tradition and culture than with language. A Vedāntist may have beliefs that are substantially identical with those of a Sufi mystic, and almost entirely incompatible with those of many Rāma devotees. Why, then, is it so likely that the Vedāntist will categorize him/herself and the Rāma devotee as "Hindu," while labeling the Sufi a "Muslim"? If tradition is seen as an autonomous entity—especially one linked to a racial/ethnic group, which itself has broad supra-individual reality—then this identification perhaps makes sense. But once one eliminates the idea of a supra-individual culture or tradition, once one sees culture and tradition as sets of partially overlapping but partially divergent individual idiolects (beliefs, skills, etc.), then the reason for privileging such categories as "Hindu" and "Muslim" disappears. Moreover, the entire argument applies *pari passu* to the racial and ethnic groups themselves. For they too exist only as individuals, who could be gathered and categorized in many different ways.

This suggests the real reason for our standard assumptions about tradition and ethnicity—as in the privileging of "Hindu" and "Muslim" in the case just mentioned. These assumptions and this privileging are the result of the functionalizing—indeed, essentializing—of the partially arbitrary categories of attributed identity. Individuals come to be linked definitively with certain groups and certain groups come to be linked definitively with certain traditions only because certain categories (e.g., "Hindu," "Muslim," "European") have developed important social functions—most often, because they operate crucially in the formation of social hierarchies. The Vedāntist categorizes him/herself as "Hindu" along with the Rāma devotee, while separating the Sufi as "Muslim"—rather than joining with the Sufi as, say, "mystic" and separating the devotee as "devotional"—because "Hindu" and "Muslim" are socially functional, whereas "mystic" and "devotional" are not.

Of course, one could try to salvage the notion of ethnicity by an appeal to ancestry. One might say, for example, that Irish people have a special connection to one another, and to Irish tradition, because of shared ancestry. But this too will not work. First, it remains impossible to salvage the notion of "Irish tradition" itself. It remains a concept without a referent. It is a useful abstraction, but it is, at best, akin to a statistical concept, such as the "average American family" with its impossible fraction of a child. There are only real American families, with whole numbers of children. Similarly, there are only cultural idiolects. The second problem with an ancestry-based approach is that it makes no more sense to link tradition with ancestry than it does to link language with ancestry. For the connection to make sense, it would require a biological propensity, some tie between the tradition or language and the gene pool, perhaps. But there is no such propensity. I have no biological predisposition toward Irish language. I have no biological affiliation with Irish tradition or culture—with ancient Druidism or modern Catholicism. If I write verse, my ancestry does not predispose me toward the poetic genre of the *aisling* rather than the sonnet. My grandfather was an Irish speaker and a nationalist revolutionary. He fought in the Anglo-Irish war and was "court-martialed . . . for levying war on the British forces and for being in possession of firearms" (Browne 162). After being amnestied, he served in the Irish parliament for most of his adult life. But this gives me no more connection with the Irish language and no greater claim on Irish tradition and culture—religious, artistic, and so forth—than the grandchildren of the English counterinsurgency police who arrested him, or than a descendent of Cromwell or Milton or anyone who sought to destroy Irish people, their practices and ideas. With regard to common practices, beliefs, ideas—as with regard to syntax or morphology—we are all equal, and free from ancestral guilt, or privilege.

We are misled into thinking that ancestry gives us special connections and special claims in part due to the unfortunate metaphor of "roots." We refer to ancestry as "roots" and then see the soil nourishing those roots as the ancestral culture. But we are not plants. We are human beings. We do not have roots—nor do we lack them. It is true that many people today feel that they are cut off, rootless, that they need a tradition to ground them and give them security. That is one reason people turn to ethnicity—to find a sense of belonging. But what people lack is a sense of community, right now. The particular practices and ideas of one's great-grandparents have no special bearing on this dilemma. The ease of shared beliefs and the comfort of shared acts may be missing, but this ease and comfort are not tied to one particular set of such beliefs and acts, inherited like eye color.

Indeed, the whole notion of definitive ancestry here is untenable as well. It involves an intellectually arbitrary delimitation of one's "heritage" at a particular historical stage. Consider my case. First, I know nothing about it prior to my great-grandparents, and only two of them. Thus I have some sort of knowledge about eight of my forebears. But since the time of Cromwell, I've probably had something on the order of a thousand ancestors. How confident should I be that these ancestors were all "Irish"? More importantly, even if they were, how did they come to be defined as Irish? It seems reasonable to assume that my ancestors, like everyone's ancestors, began in Africa. At some point, they left and went to central Eurasia. Some from that group went to Persia or India. My forebears evidently migrated west on the European continent, eventually coming to Ireland. My more recent ascendants continued this westward journey to North America. Thus, to define my ethnicity as Irish is to exclude a large number of my ancestors. It is to assume that there is some point at which the geographical location and practices of my ancestors count as definitive, while other points do not count. What makes the period in Ireland definitive, rather than the more recent period in America, or the Western continental period, or the central Eurasian period, or the original, African period? Like all the other divisions we have been discussing, not only "ethnicity," but even "ethnic ancestry" is a political category, not a scientific one. It is like "language," "tradition," and "culture." Its divisions are a matter of social function only.

All this applies to literary traditions just as much as it applies to religious or social traditions. Of course, mentioning literary traditions reminds us that many of these traditions are based on texts. Though this complicates the situation, it does not fundamentally alter it. Specifically, in text-based traditions, there are, so to speak, two levels of idiolectalization—one, the sort we have been discussing, the other bearing on the texts that are considered part of a tradition. More exactly, literary tradition involves a canon. This appears to be objective, something transcending idiolect. But, first of all, the very idea of the canon is idiolectal—a function of what individual readers read, what individual critics interpret, what individual literary historians conceive of as the canon. Second, even when the canon itself is shared (i.e., even when our idiolects commonly overlap on this topic), the resultant body of texts affects us only through our interpretations of their meanings. The impact of texts, even sacred texts, on living tradition is not the product of "the texts themselves." Rather, it results from what we make of those texts. It results, not from the real object, but from the "intentional" object, as Phenomenologists say, the object as we construe it. Clearly, this intentional object, this construal, is not autonomous or Platonic. Our interpretations are as individual and idiolectal as language.

Thus, like culture and language—like all tradition—literary tradition is ultimately private. It too cannot be bound to any particular group. This opens all literature to all individuals, to all writers and critics, for explication or imitation, for outdoing or writing back, for preservation or extension or canonical restructuring. Or, rather, it provides a theoretical justification for the opening that has already occurred among postcolonization writers.

In the preceding chapters, I have of course focused on the communal coherence that extends across sets of idiolects, the shared practices and ideas that we may reasonably identify as a tradition, even while recognizing the partial nature of this tradition and its internal diversity. Clearly, this sort of analysis is crucial, especially for readers who do not share the relevant competences with the author (e.g., those who do not share a knowledge of the *Rāmāyaṇa* and the varieties of dharma with Tagore). Yet the individual particularity of all culture suggests that such interpretation, however important, may at times be deeply misleading as well. In this way, the privacy of tradition indicates something very strange—that nontraditional and even antitraditional interpretations may be extremely valuable. It indicates that, in some cases, our best understanding of a work will come from interpretations that blatantly flout the practical literary and cultural identities in which the work in question is most obviously located. Specifically, if tradition is only a set of partially overlapping but partially contradictory attitudes, ideas, practices, and the like, then every individual will have some attitudes, ideas, practices, that do not fit those of the group. Empirically, this is obvious to everyone about his/her own group. We all know that virtually no one fully fits into the "mainstream." And our general view of poets is that they fit even less well than everyone else. It is only when we turn to other groups that we fail to understand this. This is part of a general human tendency to view members of out-groups "as relatively less complex, less variable, and less individuated" than members of in-groups (Duckitt 81). But, of course, no group is less complex than any other group of the same general type.

The diversity within both in-groups and out-groups is not merely a matter of individual variation within narrow parameters set by an overarching tradition or culture. Acknowledging this diversity is more than recognizing that authors may criticize or disagree with their own traditions; it is more than noting that they might write back or discover subaltern tendencies. To understand the depth of this diversity, we need to distinguish not only idiolectal tradition and tradition as an abstraction from idiolect. We need to distinguish what might be called "official tradition," tradition as it is widely understood. Consider an extreme example. Europeans have commonly conceived of European tradition as based on reason, the European narrative tradition as based on tightly Aristotelian plot structure, and so on. In contrast, they have tended to think of Indian tradition as intuitive, with its narratives lacking rigorous Aristotelian structure. This view has been accepted by many Indians as well. But, in fact, there is no reason to believe that it accurately characterizes these traditions. Quite the contrary, in fact. It simply does not appear to be the case that European tradition, understood as an abstraction from idiolects, actually has the properties commonly attributed to it. The same holds for Indian tradition. For this reason, we risk severely misinterpreting a literary work any time we approach it via official tradition, taking up presumptively common principles of a tradition—even when an author has located his/her work in that tradition, even when the author self-consciously shares the official view of that tradition.

This arises as a problem because, when we study tradition—or when we generalize from our experience of tradition—official tradition is often most salient and most "authoritative." This results from the fact that official tradition adheres to identity categories and thus it is most fully elaborated and recorded. It is also the most fully interested, for it is ideologically functional. On the other hand, the problem does not arise only for cases of sheer propaganda. It arises even in cases where official depictions of culture and tradition are largely accurate. More exactly, we all have various and unique ideas, perceptions, and so on. These do not always fit official scripts, and we are not always able to articulate them, either to ourselves or to anyone else. Indeed, we may not even recognize these ideas self-consciously. However, an author will almost invariably embody some such unselfconscious idiosyncracies in his/her literary works. Thus it may be that reading even, for example, a self-consciously, self-assertively Christian author through accepted ideas of Christian ethics will misrepresent that author's ethical responses, as embodied in his/her characters and their actions. It may be that the particular moral complexities of Shakespeare's *Troilus and Cressida*, say, are more fully illuminated by Confucian ethics than by Aristotelian or Christian principles. It may be that a European play is more fittingly analyzed in terms of Sanskrit aesthetic theory than in terms of mimesis. The point is familiar to Marxist critics. As Georg Lukács argued, following Engels, sometimes a professedly bourgeois author manifests a proletarian view in his/her writings (see Lukács 40). To interpret such a writer in terms of bourgeois ideas, rather than Marxist ideas, would lead to misinterpretation. What Lukács noted about class applies equally to cultural and literary traditions.

In this way, the diversity of tradition and the diversity of responses to tradition turn out to be still more extensive and radical. Not only is tradition idiolectal and universal (i.e., not bound to any particular group), individual works are open to—indeed, they often require—analysis in relation to "alien" traditions, traditions of which the author may have been entirely unaware. (This is, of course, in addition to analysis via the familiar or proximate traditions.) And this is not in any way confined to postcolonization literature. The radical multiplicity of tradition and of interpretation hold across the board. The distinctive feature of postcolonization literature in this regard is simply that the political and cultural conflicts surrounding colonization have rendered this multiplicity unusually explicit. In this sense, postcolonization literature is not only an intrinsically valuable object of study, it may also be a particularly illuminating object for the examination and understanding of tradition more generally, for it foregrounds complexities that are hidden in less obviously transnational and cross-cultural literatures.

In sum, the relation of postcolonization literature to literary tradition is neither simple nor univocal. For instance, we have seen that postcolonization writers do not necessarily write back to the metropolis, nor are they always successful in undermining metropolitan ideology when they do write back. Sometimes postcolonization authors fit well into an indigenous tradition; sometimes they write back to indigenous tradition; sometimes they segment the indigenous or metropolitan tradition and choose a subaltern element; sometimes they accept or even extend colonialist attitudes and ideas—and that is only a fraction of the possibilities. The relations between an individual work and the various disunified traditions that precede and enable it are multiple and variable, and, if we are to understand the new work, it is necessary to understand these relations. In the preceding chapters, I have set out theoretical treatments of some of these different relations. In this afterword, I have sought to present a theoretical account of their multiplicity and variability per se. I have also sought to expose some further implications of this multiplicity and variability. The result is not paradoxical, but it is so at odds with current thinking in literature that it is bound to appear paradoxical. For the conclusion of this argument is that cultural study is deeply important, as important as any culturalist has ever claimed. Yet culture and tradition do not exist in any of the usual senses. Stranger still, no literary work is bound to any one culture or tradition. We and all our works are, actually or potentially, part of every tradition. Or, what comes to the same thing, we are part of one tradition only, the tradition defined by the one identity category that is not simply political, the one ancestral division that is intellectually binding, that of our common human origin—the group identity named by Salim Muwakkil when he explained that "we are all Africans."

INTRODUCTION. DECOLONIZING CULTURAL IDENTITY

1. A complete treatment of categorial identification after colonization would take into account other cultures as well—for example, the cultures of other colonies, or even rival metropolitan cultures. Thus Irish categorial identifications after colonialism often involved significant relations to Indian and French culture. However, the home culture and the colonizer's culture are by far the most important. I will confine the discussion to these.

2. There are other options as well. Thus a reactionary traditionalist might maximize the difference between traditions or a mimeticist might overstress the aspects of metropolitan culture that appear to have facilitated its domination. However, these do not seem to be as common, at least in literature.

3. Though I do not treat syncretism extensitvely, I do consider it briefly in each of the three chapters treating indigenous tradition. I have not devoted a separate chapter to syncretism for the simple reason that, in order to treat the synthesis of traditions, one must first have a good sense of the component traditions themselves and the author's response to those traditions. In saying this, I don't mean to imply that explorations of syncretism have no value unless they are preceded by detailed work on separate traditions. For example, Jahan Ramazani's *Hybrid Muse* is an excellent study that focuses on syncretism. However, the strength of Ramazani's book lies in its sensitive readings of individual poems and its relation of these readings to broad issues of cultural syncretism. Ramazani does make occasional reference to the intermingling of literary traditions. But these are not points that he develops in interpretive or theoretical detail. I take it that this is precisely because detailed interpretive and theoretical analysis of the poets' relations to their distinct precursor literary traditions has not yet been done.

4. And of some indigenous reactions against indigenous reactions—as when some Indian writers denigrate Sanskrit study because other Indian writers have tried to use Sanskrit study for oppressive and communalist (e.g., anti-Muslim) ends. To my mind,

this is no less a reactionary position than the fundamentalism it opposes. Indeed, like other forms of reaction, this is often stereotypical and bound up with colonialism. For instance, a common element of opposition to Sanskrit is anti-Brahminism, blaming a very small, birth-defined group, Brahmins, for the evils of Hinduism—the caste system, etc. This assumes that other high castes had nothing to do with caste oppression, that Brahmins are and were uniformly socially dominant (on destitution among Brahmins, see Sarkar "Middle-Class" 253), and so on. Moreover, as Sarkar notes, anti-Brahminism was fostered by some British scholars and officials during the colonial period ("Middle-Class" 266).

CHAPTER ONE. IDEOLOGICAL AMBIGUITIES OF "WRITING BACK"

1. For ease of exposition, I am simplifying the notion of schemas here; for a fuller discussion, see, John Holland et al. 12–21, or, for a treatment with more direct bearing on literary interpretation, see chapters 6–8 of Bordwell; on the relation between schemas and perception, memory, etc., see Edward Smith 34–35.

2. On prototypes, see Johnson-Laird and Wason 342, Estes 9, John Holland et al. 182–83. On the cognitive importance of instances—what I am calling "exempla"—see Nisbett and Ross 15; on the relation between exempla, prototypes, and schemas, see Ortony, Clore, and Collins 159. Shanks argues that prototypes may be nothing more than a broad range of exempla; even if this is the case, the distinction remains, for there is still a difference between the cognitive use of a single instance and the cognitive use of a range of exempla, which collectively yield the same complex of default properties as would define a distinct prototype. A good overview of the research on exempla—termed "exemplars" in this case—may be found in Hampton 94–96.

3. There is no firm agreement on whether all this should be thought of as forming a single lexicon, or as divided into distinct but interrelated systems—primarily dictionary/encyclopedia, on the one hand, and a personal archive or "episodic memory" (see Schacter 17, 134–35), on the other. Here and throughout, I assume a single mental structure, but nothing in the analysis rests on this assumption. The only important point is that the different types of information are mutually accessible and operate jointly in the processes we will be examining. For a detailed, lucid introduction to the mental lexicon, see Aitchison.

4. As far as I can tell, the connection of Desai's novel with *Heart of Darkness* has not been touched on in previous criticism. Moreover, the related ideological issues have not been seriously taken up. In part, this is due to the fact that, thus far, there has been relatively little criticism published on the novel. A number of works on Desai (e.g., those of Singh and Pathania) more or less ignore it. Those which do treat the novel, on the other hand, tend to do so in terms of broad, ahistorical themes, with little mention of precursors or even the colonial situation. (I am not criticizing this work, merely noting its limited relevance to the project at hand.) For example, Khanna discusses the development of Baumgartner's character, stressing his "sensitive heart" and "thinking mind" (110). Solanki, Sharma, and Dash each focus on Baumgartner as an isolated and

alienated individual, with Solanki emphasizing "the existential viewpoint" (65), Sharma discussing Baumgartner's "mother-fixation" (140), and Dash treating "the apathetic and malignant influence of the city" (38). Gopal similarly claims that the novel "has for its theme . . . tension between the individual and the social forces" (59). Afzal-Khan places the novel in a broadly post-colonial context, but concentrates her specific analysis on "the conflict between the mythic and the realistic impulses" (93). Newman is a partial exception to this in treating "Orientalist romance" (41) and other colonial themes, and in noting some very plausible links between *Baumgartner's Bombay* and *A Passage to India*. Nonetheless, the focus of her analysis—which takes up both Baumgartner's relation to his mother and the issue of realism and myth—is clearly quite different from that of the present study.

5. There are also some very specific echoes of phrasing and incident—such as Desai's use of the Conradian epithet "sepulchral" (163), Marlow's well-known phrase for the Belgian capital being "the sepulchral city" (72), or her image of Baumgartner's feet soaking in blood (179), which recalls Marlow standing in "a pool of blood" that made him "morbidly anxious to change [his] shoes and socks" (47).

6. Conrad does ultimately relate the two women in a nondichotomous way. Indeed, the African woman may well come across somewhat better. However, the point here is not to determine a correct interpretation of Conrad. Rather, it is to examine the effect of Conrad's work—as implicitly understood by Desai—on Desai's novel.

CHAPTER TWO. RAISING INDIGENOUS PRECURSORS, REIMAGINING SOCIAL IDEALS

1. Tagore had made use of the *Rāmāyaṇa* for political purposes more than once prior to *The Home and the World*. In his 1895 essay "The Five Elements: A Novel Ramayana," he revised and allegorized the story to criticize part of Hindu tradition. Roughly a decade later, he took up the epic again in *"The Ramayana."* Written shortly before the action of *The Home and the World*, the essay manifests Tagore's nationalistic orientation at the time. This makes the poem a particularly apt model for his highly critical treatment of nationalism in the 1916 novel. (Tagore was briefly swept up in the nationalistic fervor portrayed in the novel. By 1907—the time of the riots presented in the novel—he had withdrawn from the movement. By 1910, "he told his son . . . that he felt ashamed of his drum-beating in 1905" [Dutta and Robinson 149].)

2. This is at least in part the result of lexical ordering. The lexicon does not have a fixed order, but alters with changing circumstances, making some entries more readily accessible in certain conditions, thus more likely to be activated, and others less accessible, thus less likely to be activated. To take a simple example, entries such as "dharma" are more readily accessible to someone engaged in a discussion of Hinduism than to someone playing soccer or listening to a financial report. On the nature of lexical orderings and their relation to lexical access, see Kenneth Forster.

3. In saying this, I am disagreeing with a part of Ashis Nandy's important analysis of Tagore. According to Nandy, Tagore saw the violence of nationalist leaders as drawn

from the colonizer and as inconsistent with indigenous tradition (*Illegitimacy* 26). Certainly, Tagore saw this violence as violating some aspects of Hindu tradition—those codified in universal dharma. But he undoubtedly saw them as conforming to other aspects of Hindu tradition—those codified in kṣatriyadharma. There is nothing at all specifically European about the tactics employed by Sandip. They are, in fact, the standard political methods set forth in Kauṭilya's *Arthaśāstra*, Nārāyaṇa's *Hitopadeśa*, and other handbooks of success in political life, and they are, again, pervasive in the *Rāmāyaṇa*.

4. Readers familiar with Mahāyāna Buddhism will recognize that Tagore is drawing on this tradition as well. Unfortunately, one cannot treat every component of influence in a single essay.

5. As Fredric Jameson has noted, national allegory is particularly common in colonies struggling for nationhood and in recently independent nations. Indeed, at least two other works examined in this volume—Walcott's *Omeros* and Ali's "From Another Desert"—have elements of national allegory. Jameson no doubt overstated the case in insisting that "all third-world texts" are of this sort, as Ahmad and others have argued [see chapter 3 of Ahmad]. But it is nonetheless true that attention to potentially allegorical elements in postcolonization works is often illuminating, and not infrequently essential for even basic interpretation—a point that should be unsurprising, given the historical circumstances just mentioned.

6. In the Bengali original, there are two characters of this sort, one of which is dropped in translation (see Nandy *Illegitimacy* 11). It is unclear why this has occurred. In any case, having two jealous widows in the household at the outset arguably fits the *Rāmāyaṇa* parallel more exactly, for the exile of Rāma is devised by two jealous women, Kaikeyī and her maid-servant, Mantharā.

7. After writing this chapter, I was pleased to discover that Cynthia Leenerts notes some of these character parallels, in a very different interpretive context. I should note that the *Rāmāyaṇa* is not the only precolonial, South Asian source for Tagore's characterizations here. For other influences on his treatment of Bimala in particular, see Koljian.

8. The links just discussed suggest the inadequacy, or at least incompleteness, of some common views about Bimala—for example, that she represents a failed "synthesis of private virtue and public life" (Mitra 255), manifests the author's presumptions about "essential female nature" (255), and is symptomatic of Tagore's growing conservatism (258). There are conservative elements in the novel, certainly. And there are suggestions of gender essentialism. But it should be clear that the character of Bimala is deeper psychologically, and more politically complex, than these observations suggest. Even more positive interpretations of Bimala tend to understand the value and social implications of this character in limited terms. For example, Majumdar writes that "For the first time in the history of Bengali . . . literature a lady of aristocratic family came forward to record minutely the details of her psychological conflicts between the loyalty to her idealistic husband and strong attraction for his flamboyant friend" (248). This is certainly important and Majumdar is right to stress the point. However, to understand just what Tagore is saying even on this topic one needs to recognize the resonances of the novel that go well beyond straightforward social realism.

CHAPTER THREE. SUBALTERN MYTHS DRAWN FROM THE COLONIZER

1. Though the point is clear in *Dream*, Walcott developed the theme even more explicitly in connection with a proposed screenplay, "Vangelo Nero," shortly after writing *Dream*. As King summarizes, Walcott's Christ was "a revolutionary martyr with a spiritual vision. Where the Jews suffered under the Romans, the Africans suffer under imperialism. In our age the whites are Romans, the Jews are black" (287–88).

2. A few critics have noted this link in passing, but the detailed use of Christianity in the play seems to have been ignored. In part, this is due to the focus of critics on specifically Afro-Caribbean elements in the play. For example, Thieme stresses the "quest for a Caribbean aesthetic" (74) and Bobb focuses particularly on vodoun. Both are certainly important. Indeed, Afro-Caribbean religion was the focus of my own earlier treatment of the play (chapter 2 of *Colonialism*). The two are, of course, not mutually exclusive. For example, Burnett places particular emphasis on the plurality of mythic sources drawn on by Walcott throughout his work (see chapter 4 of *Derek Walcott*). Nonetheless, the lack of any serious treatment of Christian elements in Dream indicates again that the sense of literary tradition in postcolonization literary study, and the understanding of different authors' diverse relations to tradition, is excessively limited.

3. This ambivalence is discussed in much of the limited criticism on the play; see, for example, Breiner 79, Nelson 55, Lloyd Brown 196, and Taylor 204.

4. The point has been stressed by many critics. See Taylor 204, Lloyd Brown 197, Samad 19, Olaniyan 164, Urbach 581, and Breslin 153–55.

CHAPTER FOUR. PRESERVING THE VOICE OF ANCESTORS

1. There may also be a bilingual pun here. Again, the animal in dispute is an *emon*, or in a more precise transcription system, *ẹmọ̀*. Palm wine, the object of greed in the other frame narrative, is *ẹmu* (see *Dictionary of the Yoruba Language* 78). Likewise, there may be a bilingual pun in the second story of the frame narrative, where the drinkard uses an egg (Yoruba "ẹyin") to relieve the famine (Yoruba "ìyan"). A full discussion of the linguistic complexity of the text and its relation to readers who are Yoruba speakers, as well as readers who are not Yoruba speakers, would have to treat such issues.

CHAPTER FIVE. OUTDOING THE COLONIZER

1. Of course, literary clichés notwithstanding, he is not, in fact, letting ordinary Afro-Caribbeans speak. He doesn't need to. They have been speaking all along (whether or not the powerful have been listening). Instead, he is speaking for ordinary Afro-Caribbeans—a potentially problematic enterprise, but one he undertakes with respect and with genuine effort at empathic identification.

2. Largely, but not entirely. Indeed, a good deal of African epic remains, and has even appeared in English translation. See, for example, Johnson, Hale, and Belcher.

CHAPTER SIX. INDIGENOUS TRADITION AND THE INDIVIDUAL TALENT

1. Unlike the writers discussed in the preceding chapters, Ali may not be familiar to most readers. Until his premature death in 2002, he was arguably the most important poet from South Asia writing in English. (Despite this, there is relatively little published criticism of his work. For approaches that differ from the present study, see Needham and my *Philosophical*.) Born in New Delhi, Ali was raised in Kashmir, the one Muslim majority state in India. After studying at the universities of Kashmir and Delhi, he came to the United States, where he did a Ph.D. This led to the publication of a scholarly work on T. S. Eliot, who remained a significant influence on Ali's work. Ali published seven books of new poetry, a volume of selected poems, an anthology of ghazals by other authors, and a translation of selected poems by the important Urdu poet Faiz Ahmed Faiz.

2. On allegorical interpretations of Nizami, see Gohrab; Talattof and Clinton 7; and Azada 18 and citations. On allegory in other rewritings of the story, see Talattof 68–69 and Kalpakli and Andrews 34.

3. Of course, this is not absolute. The Bharatiya Janata Party and its various Hindu fundamentalist components are doing their best to make Hinduism as intolerant as any of the monotheisms just mentioned. Moreover, there are other problems with polytheism—for example, a tendency toward internal hierarchies, such as caste. Finally, this does not mean that political leaders in a largely polytheistic society will follow more benevolent policies, internally or externally. The point is tragically clear from India's brutal military policies in Kashmir in recent years.

4. It is worth noting that Ali's emphasis on Sufism as a unifying force in India is not idiosyncratic. Engineer argues that, in the past, Sufi doctrines were "instrumental in promoting communal harmony" ("Sufism" 70) and could bear on current conflicts as well. The point is echoed by writers such as Uttam and Rasheeduddin Khan. Khizer goes so far as to argue that "If the national integration is to be achieved, we need to revive the spirit of Sufism" (123).

5. Here I use the revised version of "From Another Desert" included in *The Belovéd Witness*, rather than the earlier version in *Nostalgist's Map*.

Glossary of Selected Theoretical Concepts

Abstraction, the most basic mode of altering a precursor work, and one presupposed in all other alterations. It consists in drawing on the precursor work, not in its details, but only in some more general way—from plot structure to character typology to preferences in diction.

Actional presuppositions, any assumptions shared by two or more people governing mutual or cooperative action; for example, one standard actional presupposition is that, if you pass me something, you will not let go until you believe I have grasped the thing being passed.

Alienating hybridity, a form of categorial identity in which one implicitly or explicitly affirms a synthesis of cultures, but finds oneself practically disconnected from both traditions in the relevant areas.

Assimilation, a form of categorial identity in which one implicitly or explicitly affirms one's relation to metropolitan tradition, and finds oneself practically integrated into (i.e., competent in) that tradition.

Attentional focus, whatever occupies one's consciousness directly at any given moment; for example, a sentence as one is uttering it.

Authorial idiolectal tradition, the set of conscious and nonconscious beliefs, affinities, competencies, etc., that constitute a particular author's understanding of tradition; equivalently, the set of lexical entries linked in an author's idiolect in the domain of a tradition—Christian tradition, epic tradition, or whatever. In the case of literature, this would include the author's partially tacit conception of what works constitute the common literary canon, his/her implicit interpretation of particular canonical works, his/her representational and procedural schemas for traditional genres, his/her idea of which works fall into common reference sets, and so on.

Basic domain terms, those lexical items in a domain that serve to define other lexical items in the same domain; for example, "hot" and "cold" in the domain of temperature—as opposed to "frigid," "searing," etc.

Bitraditional, having internalized two traditions, which is to say, sharing competence with the relevant groups for two traditions.

Canon, in literature, the set of works generally accepted as part of a given tradition. The notion of the canon is narrower than that of *domain,* but broader than that of *reference set.* For example, the domain of epic would in principle include every epic ever written in a given tradition; the reference set would include only the paradigm epics; the canon would include the paradigms plus those epics which, though non-paradigmatic, continue to be read and studied.

Caste dharma, in Sanskrit ethical theory, the ethical duties and social obligations that derive from the caste into which one is born. The duties of a priest/teacher are not those of a warrior/ruler, merchant/cultivator, or servant.

Categorial identity, one's self-concept, defined initially not by introspection, but by social attribution according to gender, family, race, ethnicity, and so on. These categories are organized into a hierarchy such that the putatively more important or definitive categories are highest. This hierarchy is a function of the degree to which particular categories are socially essentialized or functionalized. Equivalently, categorial identity is one's lexical entry for oneself. As such, it involves an extensional component and a semantic component. The extensional component merely indicates who falls into the category. This part of an identity category is the basis of in-group/out-group definition. Thus it is functionally primary. However, it is semantically vacuous. In other words, in-group/out-group divisions are produced even by explicitly arbitrary assignment of people to groups. The semantic component includes a prototype-based definition of group members with a strong normative component (i.e., it defines "good instances" of the group—for example, what it means to be "typically Irish" or "authentically African"). In *Colonialism and Cultural Identity,* I have referred to this as "reflective identity." Categorial identity is particularly to be distinguished from situational identification and practical identity.

Category relevance, the bearing of an identity property on some judgment or action. This bearing may be logical/empirical or social/functional. For example, sex categories are logically and empirically relevant to reproduction, but to little else. However, they are socially functional and thus have nonlogical, nonempirical bearing on a wide range of other actions and judgments (e.g., in employment).

Character, see "Literary character."

Cognitive monitoring, a process in which one focuses attention on the components of an action (including a mental action, such as empathic response) and thereby encodes those components to an unusual degree. The encoded information is compared to a goal or ideal at each step and corrected accordingly. Cognitive monitoring is a primary way in which categorial identification leads to changes in practical identity. The identity category provides the ideal which serves to guide and reorient practice.

Common cultural ownership, the view that all individuals are equal in their propensity toward, affinity for, and claim on any set of cultural practices, beliefs, etc.; put differently, no culture is the property of a particular ethnic group. In the version of this view presented in the afterword, it is bound up with the argument that neither cultures nor ethnic groups exist except as political constructs.

Communicative presuppositions, any definitional, empirical, or other information required for understanding a particular communicative intent, tacitly assumed to be shared by those communicating. For example, if I am speaking to a colleague in literature, I can presuppose that "trochee" does not have to be defined, or that I do not have to explain that there has been controversy over canon formation in the academy. These are part of shared conversational presuppositions. If I am speaking with my parents, these conversational presuppositions change.

Competence, a term borrowed from Chomskyan linguistics, where it refers to a speaker's/hearer's state after acquiring a grammar in line with that of his/her community. Here, it is used more generally to refer to any practical identity that is functionally integrated with that of the relevant community. This integration includes grammar, as well as larger practices and presuppositions of discourse, physical actions (even such simple actions as knowing how to shake hands and with whom), etc.

Concretization, a term from the Phenomenological literary theory of Roman Ingarden. Ingarden notes that any literary work is necessarily incomplete in many specifics. The reader has to supply those specifics when constituting scenes, characters, and so forth. Ingarden refers to this supplying of particulars as "concretization."

Constitution, a Phenomenological term, referring to the process by which one synthesizes various partial experiences of an object, event, person, or whatever, into an intentional object. For example, I read a few sentences about a character's appearance; later, I read about his/her utterances; later, I read about his/her actions. I do not keep these different bits of information entirely separate. Rather, I synthesize them, bring them together into a coherent imagination of the character. This imagination includes underlying principles which I infer to explain the character's behavior, etc.

Constituent-construction schemas, procedural schemas for composing parts or aspects of a literary work—scenes, characters, events, and so on.

Corrective revision, sometimes called "writing back," a form of negative modeling in which an author from a subaltern group sets out to rewrite a canonical precursor work in such a way as to correct what he/she perceives to be a bias in that precursor work. For example, in *Water with Berries*, George Lamming sets out to correct what he sees as colonialism in Shakespeare's *The Tempest*. Though typically viewed as politically progressive, I argue that corrective revision often repeats the oppressive ideology it is designed to oppose. The degree to which this occurs is a function of several variables, including the extent of the modeling, that is, whether it is general or detailed; the pairing of the elements—for instance, whether the new author pairs subalterns with subalterns or switches the roles, placing the dominant group in the stereotyped position; the ideological complexity of the precursor work; and the degree to which the new author sees the precursor as ideologically pernicious—in general, the more racism or sexism the new author sees in the precursor, the more likely it is that racist or sexist elements will find their way into the new work.

Countertraditional interpretation, interpretation that examines a work in relation to some tradition other than those familiar to and directly influential for the work's author. No individual fully conforms to any given tradition. Interpreting a work within an author's most familiar or immediate tradition is likely to render salient just those points where the author was most closely connected with that tradition, positively or negatively. Such interpretation is likely to occlude aspects of the work that deviate more subtly and unselfconsciously from the familiar tradition. Countertraditional interpretation serves as a crucial corrective to this bias.

Default hierarchy, the structure of a lexical entry such that some features—the defaults—are standard and thus accessed automatically, while other, alternative features are accessed only in special circumstances. In other words, when accessing a lexical entry, we activate only the standard features or defaults, unless specific information overrides the default. For example, the default hierarchy for "man" would include "two arms." This could be overridden by explicit statement, "Smith lost his right arm in an accident," or context, such as an amputation ward.

Discourse community, any group that shares a higher degree of lexical overlap than standard in a given society; such groups would include professions in which technical vocabulary is shared, families in which particular memories are shared, and so on.

Domain, a set of lexical entries linked together by some principle. This principle may be isolated explicitly and stored in a permanent lexical entry or it may be articulated ad hoc (on ad hoc formations, see Barsalou). For example, "Monday," "Tuesday," and so forth, form the domain "Weekdays."

Encoding, the process of selecting, structuring, and storing experience as cognitive information. We constantly encounter a vast array of information. We notice only certain aspects of this. Moreover, we implicitly structure those aspects that we do notice; we fill in perceptual details or conceptual relations. Thus what we store in memory has been selected and given a preliminary cognitive organization. In the present context, it is important to note that, in reading, we encode only certain aspects of literary works or literary traditions.

Essentialized categories, see "Socially essentialized categories."

Ethical mechanism, the cross-culturally common view that extraordinary events of great positive or negative consequence, such as famines, require not only a physical, but an ethical explanation, roughly in terms of reward and punishment.

Exemplum, any instance of a lexical category. A particular dog would be an exemplum of the category "dog"; the *Iliad* would be an exemplum of an epic poem.

Experiential reparticularization, see "Reparticularization."

Extension, the set of objects to which a lexical category refers. For example, all dogs form the extension of the category "dog."

Feature, any element included in a lexical entry, from abstract or concrete properties to personal memories.

Feature transferral or combination, the synthesis of features from different precursor works or, more generally, from distinct lexical entries, including those bearing on one's own experience; for example, the formation of a new character based in part on Rāvaṇa, Milton's Satan, and one or more personal acquaintances.

Function, see "Socially functionalized categories."

Gaps, a term used by Wolfgang Iser to refer to the moments when a text frustrates our expectations and the reader must imaginatively supply missing connections.

Generative narratives, in any given culture, the shared stories that serve as prominent models for structuring a wide range of other stories. Most often, these generative narratives are a subset of the foundational myths of a culture—such as the story of Adam and Eve in Judeo-Christian tradition—or, less frequently, a subset of literary paradigms. Note that only a fraction of literary or mythic paradigms serve as common generative narratives within a tradition.

Genre, a literary type defined by abstract schematic principles (e.g., obligatory verse forms), prototypes (e.g., standard characters), exempla (e.g., particular events), domains (defining sets of related or opposed genres), a general lexical ordering that makes some images and vocabulary items unusually accessible, etc.

Hierarchy-disrupting elements of tradition, any ideas or practices in a tradition that currently function to oppose structures of domination within that tradition or that, if invoked and enacted, would serve such a function; for example, antipatriarchal or protosocialist views in Luke's gospel within Christian tradition.

Hierarchy-preserving elements of tradition, any ideas or practices in a tradition that currently function to support structures of domination within that tradition or that, if invoked and enacted, would serve such a function; for example, patriarchal views in Paul's epistles within Christian tradition.

Humanization, an author's reformulation of internalized traditional principles by way of his/her own personal experiences; equivalently, an author's alteration of traditional practices by conscious or unconscious relation to affectively saturated elements of his/her personal archive—for example, the redevelopment of elegaic conventions by reference to an author's own experience of personal loss. Humanization is particularly consequential for literary tradition when it involves a type of personal experience that is common, and yet, in its details, new to the tradition—for example, loss due to the particular sorts of exile that have followed modern colonialism.

Ideology, the sets of socially standard beliefs, goals, attitudes, and so forth, that function to preserve oppressive or exploitative social hierarchies—colonial, patriarchal, or whatever. Colonialist beliefs about the racial inferiority of colonized peoples are a simple and obvious example, serving to justify, and thus continue, colonial domination.

Idiolect, the complex mental system that allows for speech and verbal understanding, the entirely individual set of procedural and representational structures that govern syntax, morphology, phonology, the lexicon, and so on. Chomsky has argued persuasively that national languages, such as English, have no distinct existence, but are rather abstractions from idiolects. I have argued that a directly parallel point holds for literary and cultural traditions, which may therefore be termed "idiolectal," in a slightly extended sense.

In-group, any group defined by a category included in one's categorial identity, especially when there is an opposite category, which defines an out-group; for example, if my categorial identity includes "man," then men are likely to constitute one such in-group, in opposition to women. Much research indicates that there is a general human tendency to evaluate in-group members far more favorably than out-group members and to build individual self-esteem on the basis of in-group dominance.

Intentional object, a Phenomenological phrase referring, roughly, to an object as one conceives of, understands, or imagines it; for example, though *Paradise Lost* as a series of sentences may be the same for, say, Tagore, Walcott, and Joyce, it differs for each author as an intentional object. An author does not respond to a precursor work in itself, but as he/she understands it. Thus it is the intentional object that bears on any response to a precursor, such as corrective revision.

Intercategorial comparison, a comparison of one's in-group with the relevant out-group or, less often, a comparison of oneself with a member of the out-group, understood and evaluated as such; for example, for a woman, a comparison between men and women or a comparison of herself with a man, conceived of specifically as a man.

Internalization of tradition, the incorporation of traditional principles into procedural schemas in one's lexicon. For example, an author has internalized traditional principles in the use of imagery when he/she is able to follow, and vary, those principles spontaneously as he/she writes.

Intracategorial comparison, a comparison of oneself to other people of the same identity category; for example, a man's comparison of himself with other men (in contrast with women).

Kṣatriyadharma, in Sanskrit ethical theory, the ethical and social obligations of kṣatriyas, members of the Hindu warrior/ruler caste. Based on a duty to protect the kingdom and to preserve internal order, kṣatriyadharma allows for—arguably fosters—violence and deceit. It is directly opposed to, and incompatible with, universal dharma.

Lexical access, the full activation of a lexical entry or part of a lexical entry such that it is brought into attentional focus.

Lexical category label (sometimes simply "lexical category"), the word or phrase that names a lexical entry and an associated extension, such as "dog" for the lexical entry *dog* and the set of dogs.

Lexical entry, an item in the mental lexicon, usually (though not always) associated with a single, standard lexical category label; for example, the features associated with the lexical category "dog" or *War and Peace,* along with that category label. The lexical entry typically includes schemas, prototypes, and exempla, ordered into a default hierarchy. It is not confined to definitions, but includes empirical information, relevant personal memories, etc. (Alternatively, it includes definitions and empirical information and is closely linked with a distinct memory system for personal memories.)

Lexical ordering, the sequence in which one can access lexical entries or features in lexical entries. This sequence is in part context dependent. Thus, some vocabulary items, images, procedures, etc., are more accessible in the context of a heroic epic or a romantic sonnet than in ordinary conversation or in discussing a treatise on economics.

Lexical overlap, see "Standard lexical overlap."

Lexicalize, to incorporate into the mental lexicon. A "lexicalized" object or experience—for example, a lexicalized novel—is simply those elements of the object or experience that have been encoded, then stored in the lexicon.

Lexicon, see "Mental lexicon."

Literary character, a hierarchical structure of features in the mental lexicon, including generative principles (such as contextual propensities) that operate to predict behavior, to evaluate the typicality of actions, and so forth. The lexical structure for characters is roughly the same as that for historical persons or personal acquaintances.

Long-term memory, that part of human memory that stores encoded information—word meanings, personal experiences, and so on—for extended periods. Some information never enters long-term memory and is retained only for very short periods. Many writers (e.g., Schacter) distinguish "episodic" long-term memory (i.e., memory of personal experiences) from "semantic" long-term memory (roughly, the lexicon). However, since the two systems are clearly connected even in this account, I have treated them as a single system for ease of exposition.

Mapping, systematic interpretation of one structure of properties and relations by reference to another structure of properties and relations, typically such that the two are matched point for point; for example, in colonial ideology, cultures are sometimes conceptualized by being mapped onto human ages—European culture as adult, Indian as superannuated, African as infantile. Mapping is a form of modeling.

Mental lexicon, the network of lexical entries. These entries are connected to one another by multiple links that allow structured access among related items—for example, among "Homer," "*Odyssey,*" and "*Iliad.*" Moreover, these entries are not in a fixed order, but may be rearranged by context. The lexicon is not confined to definitions, as is a dictionary. Rather, it includes empirical information of the sort found in an encyclopedia, common opinions, ideals, standard uses, a personal archive of memories and associations, etc. (On the relation of personal memories to the lexicon, see "Long-term memory.")

Mimeticism, a form of categorial identity in which one implicitly or explicitly affirms a metropolitan identity, but finds oneself practically disconnected from metropolitan tradition. This disconnection may result from a stereotypical view of metropolitan tradition or the defensive repudiation of some hurtful aspect of that tradition (e.g., anything that is reminiscent of indigenous tradition). These may be called "stereotypical" and "purgative" mimeticism, respectively.

Modeling, the use of one structure to shape one's experience, understanding, interpretation, recreation of something else; for example, one might use a fictional character from a certain ethnic group as a model to understand a real acquaintance from that group, to interpret his/her actions, to infer motives, and so on. Modeling may be positive or negative. Thus one may use a model to understand a new experience by way of comparison or by way of contrast. Finally, modeling may be conscious or unconscious.

Multitraditional, having internalized multiple traditions, which is to say, sharing competence with the relevant groups for the traditions in question.

Obligatory rules, principles that automatically apply in particular contexts, yielding procedures about which the agent has no choice; for example, when I say the plural of a word ending in a voiced consonant, I add [z], not [s], and I am not free to change this rule. This is true in two senses. First, I am usually unable to formulate such rules and thus to make a choice of varying them. Second, even if I do decide to vary such a rule, I fail in my communicative intent as following the rule is a conversational presupposition of my addressees. Thus one might say that rules may be obligatory both individually and socially.

Official tradition, tradition as it is widely interpreted and summarized within a given group, independent of the accuracy of that interpretation and summary. For example, European plot organization is widely viewed as tightly structured in an Aristotelian manner and, as such, opposed to plot organization in Indic literary tradition. Though this opposition does not appear empirically plausible, its broad acceptance has important consequences for common responses to and understandings of these traditions.

Optional rules, principles that an agent is free to employ or not to employ in any given context—for example, rules for contraction (e.g., "It is" to "It's"). To say that a rule is open to choice is not to say that its use is always a matter of choice. Optional rules may and often do go into effect automatically.

Orthodoxy, a form of categorial identity in which one implicitly or explicitly affirms one's relation to an indigenous tradition into which one is practically integrated (i.e., a tradition in which one is competent) either through lived experience or through training or both.

Outdoing the tradition, seeking to establish oneself individually, and one's in-group more generally, in the reference set for some aspect of tradition; for example, in *Omeros* Walcott attempts to establish himself individually and St. Lucians more generally in the reference set for Europhone epic poetry, along with Homer/the Greeks, Virgil/the Romans, and so on.

Out-group, any group defined by a category that is lexically opposed to a category in one's categorial identity; for example, if my categorial identity includes "man," then women are likely to constitute one out-group for me. Much research indicates that there is a general human tendency to evaluate in-group members far more favorably than out-group members and to build individual self-esteem on the basis of in-group dominance.

Paradigms of a tradition, any items—works, authors, genres—considered as establishing the evaluative ideals for any domain within a given tradition; for example, Virgil is a paradigm epic poet, for he, along with Homer, Dante, and a few others, is widely accepted as establishing the highest standards for epic excellence in the European tradition. Equivalently, paradigms are the elements of a reference set.

Personal archive, an individual's experiential memories, which form part of his/her mental lexicon (for example, memories of one's own friends linked to the lexical category "friend"). The personal archive appears to have a significant affective component—for example, involving sorrow associated with memories of personal loss. These memories and emotions are central to the humanization of tradition. (On the relation of experiential memories to the lexicon, see "Long-term memory.")

Platonic, any entity, such as a tradition, that is assumed to have an existence that is neither material nor mental. A Platonic view of language sees it as existing separately from individual idiolects. Just as Chomsky has argued that language has no Platonic existence, I have argued that tradition has no Platonic existence.

Poetic voice, an individual author's distinctive manner of writing, encompassing style, standard themes, organizational principles, etc. Clearly, poetic voice cannot be simply imitative. But it also cannot be entirely idiosyncratic—inaccessible to readers, incomprehensibly distant from any tradition. Thus, the development of poetic voice necessarily involves a personal engagement with shared traditions. Though most often used to refer to purely aesthetic properties of literary works, the idea applies equally to the political and social concerns of a writer's work, as part of his/her encompassing literary accomplishment. This political and social part of poetic voice includes aspects of all the responses to tradition considered in the preceding chapters, such as outdoing and corrective revision.

Politics of Otherness, a form of cognitive monitoring in which one sets out to bias one's evaluations in favor of out-groups and out-group traditions.

Practical identity, one's ordinary, habitual practices or, rather, the set of internalized cognitive structures—procedural schemas—that underlie those practices, along with one's actional and communicative presuppositions regarding others.

Priming, the partial activation of a lexical entry or part of a lexical entry such that it is placed high in the hierarchy for lexical access, but is not in fact accessed; primed entries, especially primed personal memories, may have an important function in the emotional impact of literature, and the priming of literary exempla appears to play a role in the ethical impact of literature.

Probe, any mental content—a word, a perception, a memory, a feeling—that activates related lexical elements. For example, if a poet wishes to write a poem about his/her nation, both "poem" and "nation" may operate as probes giving different levels of activation to different items in his/her lexicon. Both might serve to activate an entry such as "epic," thus giving that entry an unusually high degree of activation.

Procedural schemas, cognitive structures that serve to organize and guide particular types of action, such as tying one's shoes or developing a literary scene. When the structure for a type of action is internalized so that one can perform it unreflectively, then it has become a procedural schema. In literature, gaining fluency or ease in "craft" is a matter of internalizing procedural schemas.

Productive schemas, procedural schemas for composing a literary work.

Proceduralize, internalize a practice as a procedural schema.

Prototype, the most standard case covered by a lexical category; put differently, a schema with all the default values in place, along with some average properties (e.g., the prototype human has two arms and is of roughly average height). In literature, prototypes guide our understanding of authors, periods, genres, and a range of other matters. For example, the prototype European epic has twelve or twenty-four books, begins *in medias res,* and so on. The reader expectations discussed by Hans Robert Jauss and Wolfgang Iser are largely a matter of such literary prototypes. In politics and society, prototypes guide our conception of races, cultures, and so on.

Racial despair, the sense of hopelessness that results from intercategorial comparison in which one judges one's racial in-group to be eternally condemned to an inferior social position. The phrase was coined by Derek Walcott to refer to the despondency felt by Afro-Caribbeans due to racial denigration and deprivation (see "What the Twilight Says" 21).

Reactionary authenticity, a form a categorial identity in which one implicitly or explicitly affirms one's relation to an identity group, but finds oneself disconnected from that group in practical identity. (Reactionary authenticity is roughly equivalent to reactionary traditionalism, but refers to cases, such as sexual orientation, where tradition per se may not be seen as crucial to defining identity.)

Reactionary traditionalism, a form of categorial identity in which one implicitly or explicitly affirms one's relation to indigenous tradition, but finds oneself disconnected from that tradition. This disconnection may result from a stereotypical view of indigenous tradition or from a defensive repudiation of some hurtful aspect of the tradition, especially whatever elements of the tradition one sees as facilitating colonial domination. These may be called "stereotypical" and "purgative" reactionary traditionalism, respectively.

Receptive schemas, procedural schemas for understanding and responding to a literary work.

Reference set, a subset of a lexical domain consisting in the normative paradigms for a tradition from that domain; for example, the reference set for epic in the European tradition would include Homer, Virgil, Dante, and Milton. Reference sets are important for individual self-evaluation and for group evaluation.

Reparticularization, a necessary concomitant of abstraction, in which a new author, having drawn an abstract structure from a precursor work, specifies that structure differently. This specification is typically guided by feature transferral from another precursor work, by the new author's personal experiences (i.e., by feature transferral from the new author's personal archive), or by transformation through a domain or reference set.

Representational schema, a complex of features, organized into a default hierarchy as part of a lexical entry. These features are presumed to match properties in those real objects that constitute the extension of the encompassing lexical category. For example, the representational schema of "human" includes such default features as "has two arms." We assume that these features match properties of real humans, whom we expect to have two arms, unless we are given information to contradict this assumption. Schemas define our most abstract understanding of various literary structures, such as genres; for example, the commonly definitive properties of epic (e.g., "long narrative poem") are part of the schema for epic. Representational schemas are differentiated from procedural schemas, but are necessarily incorporated into procedural schemas, allowing, for example, perceptual identification.

Running time, the time it takes to execute a procedural schema. Though procedural schemas may be repeated in cycles, it appears that the running time of a single procedural schema must be fairly short. For this reason, procedural schemas are unlikely to have much bearing on large structural principles of, say, epic, which are, in consequence, likely to be self-conscious, not proceduralized.

Sādhāraṇadharma (universal dharma), see "Universal dharma."

Saliency, the degree to which a property or relation is likely to trigger encoding (to draw attentional focus, etc.). Saliency is greatly affected by the models with which one approaches an object or situation. For example, reading *The Home and the World* in relation to the *Rāmāyaṇa* renders certain, otherwise minor properties of the novel highly salient, making it much more likely that one will notice and recall these properties.

Second-order structure, a cognitive structure used to guide, organize, regulate, the use of another cognitive structure. For example, Walcott uses James Joyce's *Ulysses* as a second-order model for incorporating and responding to paradigm epics (i.e., for using those epics as first-order models for developing characters, etc., in his own depiction of a colonial island).

Selection principles, principles that allow one to isolate properties and relations from a complex experience. For example, Conrad's account of Africa in *Heart of Darkness* provided Desai with selection principles by which she was able to choose particular events, behaviors, appearances, and so on, from her experience of India, which would otherwise be a chaos of particular, partial, contradictory moments (like anyone's experience of any social life). Selection principles may operate consciously or unconsciously.

Semantic field, see "Domain."

Situational alienation or estrangement, an acute feeling of individual or group difference based on non-sharing of actional or communicative presuppositions, specifically a sense that one's actional or communicative presuppositions with respect to some other person or persons fall below standard lexical overlap.

Situational identification, a feeling of individual or group sameness based on sharing of actional or communicative presuppositions beyond standard lexical overlap.

Socially essentialized categories, categories that apply to persons and that have been functionalized in all or virtually all contexts in a given society and which are therefore of central importance for categorial identity. One's sex is an obvious example, for it has broad bearing on a person's social treatment and professional opportunities.

Socially functionalized categories, categories that apply to persons and that have direct, systematic social consequences in some context. For example, weight has bearing on some professions and on some leisure activities; it therefore counts as functionalized in those contexts. In contrast, having a curled or straight little toe has no such consequences; it is not socially functionalized. In general, socially functionalized categories have greater importance for categorial identity.

Standard lexical overlap, the degree to which one expects one's lexical entries (including procedural and representational structures) to coincide with those of any ordinary person in one's society or in whatever narrower group is contextually relevant (e.g., a professional community); put differently, the degree to which one expects other people to share actional and conversational presuppositions in a given context.

Subaltern group, any group that is systematically disprivileged within a particular social structure, especially by way of a socially essentialized category; for example, women, racial minorities, indigenous peoples in colonies, and so on.

Subaltern traditions, those aspects of any tradition that serve to challenge the disprivilege of subaltern groups, primarily through portraying the viewpoints (experiences, feelings, and so forth) of members of those groups. Most works in any given subaltern tradition were written by members of subaltern groups.

Syncretism, a form of categorial identity in which one implicitly or explicitly affirms a synthetic relation to both traditions in certain respects and where one is in fact practically integrated into both traditions in those respects that bear on the synthesis (e.g., if affirming a synthesis of Indian and European dance, one has competence in both to the degree necessary for producing the synthesis). Alternatively, a form of synthesis-affirming categorial identity in which one has acquired competence in a set of already stable practices in some syncretistic community.

Threshold of distinctiveness, the highest point at which abstraction from a precursor text remains recognizably linked to that particular text. "Conflict over a woman" is an abstraction that fits the *Iliad,* but it fits so many other works that it cannot be considered recognizably linked to the *Iliad.* It has not reached the threshold of distinctiveness for the *Iliad*. Put differently, we could not identify the *Iliad* as the precursor of a more recent work on the basis of this description. This threshold is culturally relative and is in part a function of the cultural prominence of the work in question. Thus "war relating to the abduction of a woman," though quite abstract, may be sufficient for Indians to link this description to the *Rāmāyaṇa* or for Europeans to link it with the *Iliad*.

Threshold of salience, the point at which the link between a new work and a precursor becomes obtrusive, an object of a reader's self-consciousness awareness. When the link between, say, *Omeros* and the *Aeneid* becomes evident to a reader, then it has reached the threshold of salience for that reader. (A link may unconsciously affect our understanding of and response to a work without reaching the threshold of salience.)

Tradition, an abstraction from partially overlapping, but partially contradictory, sets of idiolectal ideas, beliefs, norms, habits, skills, etc.—thus procedural and representational schemas, prototypes, and so on. The overlap of these idiolects results from the multiple networks of interaction among the various "bearers" of the tradition, much as the overlap of idiolects in a language results from the multiple networks of interaction among speakers of that language. This idiolectal overlap of tradition is often associated with a set of artifacts, including texts, though it may be purely oral. Traditions are open to many contradictory delimitations, depending on which set of idiolects one chooses to isolate. No one of these divisions is uniquely correct. Certain divisions come to appear correct only because they are defined by functionalized categories, such as race, religion, or nationality. More exactly, traditions are commonly conceived of as supra-idiolectal or Platonic and as linked in a proprietary fashion with some ethnic or related group that is itself presumed to have a definitive group identity. Thus Irish people might be assumed to have a definitive Irish identity and to have a special claim on Irish tradition. But the tradition has no Platonic existence and the group has no definitive identity. Both are, rather, collections of particulars whose inclusion in a single set is largely the result of contingent political factors. Moreover, the contingently defined groups do not have any special claim on the contingently defined traditions. Rather, traditions, in their multiple forms and variant specifications, are— like the languages they include—common human property.

Transformation through a domain or reference set, the alteration of a precursor work by taking some general principle or principles from the precursor and systematically shifting them from one item to another in the same domain or reference set, as when Walcott, drawing on Joyce, models *Omeros* on the *Iliad* rather than the *Odyssey*, thereby systematically shifting Joyce's method of modeling from one object to the other in the domain "Homeric epic."

Universal dharma, in Sanskrit ethical theory, the ethical obligations that apply to all people at all times. Universal dharma prominently includes two commitments— to truth and to *ahiṃsā*, or nonviolence. It stands in direct contradiction with kṣatriyadharma.

Voice, see "Poetic voice."

Writing back, see "Corrective revision."

Writing within a tradition, writing produced by internalized procedural schemas that manifest principles of plot, character, scene, form, etc., characteristic of works in that tradition (i.e., principles that surpass the threshold of distinctiveness for that tradition). Writing within a tradition is spontaneous in roughly the way fluent language use is spontaneous and is to be distinguished from self-conscious responses to or uses of tradition.

WORKS CITED

Abraham, R. C. *Dictionary of Modern Yoruba*. London: U of London P, 1958.

Achebe, Chinua. *Things Fall Apart: The Story of a Strong Man*. New York: Astor-Honor, 1959.

———. "An Image of Africa." *Massachusetts Review* 18 (1977): 782–94.

Afzal-Khan, Fawzia. *Cultural Imperialism and the Indo-English Novel: Genre and Ideology in R. K. Narayan, Anita Desai, Kamala Markandaya, and Salman Rushdie*. University Park, PA: Pennsylvania State UP, 1993.

Ahmad, Aijaz. *In Theory: Classes, Nations, Literatures*. London: Verso, 1992.

Aitchison, Jean. *Words in the Mind: An Introduction to the Mental Lexicon*. Oxford: Blackwell, 1987.

al-Fārābī. *"Canons of the Art of Poetry."* In Vicente Cantarino. *Arabic Poetics in the Golden Age: Selection of Texts Accompanied by a Preliminary Study*. Leiden: E. J. Brill, 1975: 110–15.

Ali, Agha Shahid. *The Belovéd Witness: Selected Poems*. New Delhi: Viking, 1992.

———. *The Country without a Post Office: Poems*. New York: W. W. Norton, 1997.

———. "Farewell." In *The Country without a Post Office: Poems*. New York: W. W. Norton, 1997: 21–23.

———. "From Another Desert." In *A Nostalgist's Map*: 63–82.

———. "Ghazal." In *The Belovéd Witness*: 71–72.

———. "Homage to Faiz Ahmed Faiz (d. 20 November 1984)." In *The Belovéd Witness*: 34–37.

———. "I Dream I Am the Only Passenger on Flight 423 to Srinagar." In *The Country without a Post Office: Poems*. New York: W. W. Norton, 1997: 30–34.

———. "Introduction." In Faiz: ix–xxvi.

———. *A Nostalgist's Map of America: Poems*. New York: W. W. Norton, 1991.

————, ed. and intro. *Ravishing DisUnities: Real Ghazals in English*. Hanover, NH: UP of New England, 2000.

————. *T. S. Eliot as Editor*. Ann Arbor, MI: UMI Research P, 1986.

Ali, Ahmed, ed. and trans. *The Golden Tradition: An Anthology of Urdu Poetry*. New York: Columbia UP, 1973.

Ali, Maulana Muhammad. *The Holy Qur'ān: Arabic Text, English Translation and Commentary*. Columbus, Ohio: Ahmadiyyah Anjuman Isha'at Islam Lahore, 1995.

Althusser, Louis, and Étienne Balibar. *Reading Capital*. Trans. Ben Brewster. London: Verso, 1979.

Amadi, Elechi. *The Concubine*. London: Heinemann, 1966.

Ashcroft, Bill, Gareth Griffiths, and Helen Tiffin. *The Empire Writes Back: Theory and Practice in Postcolonial Literatures*. London: Routledge, 1989.

Attar, Farid Ud-Din. *The Conference of the Birds*. Trans. Afkham Darbandi and Dick Davis. New York: Penguin, 1984.

Awolalu, J. Omosade. *Yoruba Beliefs and Sacrificial Rites*. Harlow, UK: Longman, 1979.

Azada, R. *Nizami Ganjavi*. Baku: Elm, 1981.

Bakhtin, M. M. *Rabelais and His World*. Trans. Helene Iswolsky. Bloomington: Indiana UP, 1984.

Baron, Reuben, and William Graziano, with the assistance of Charles Stangor. *Social Psychology*. Fort Worth, TX: Holt, Rinehart and Winston, 1991.

Barsalou, Lawrence W. "Ad Hoc Categories." *Memory and Cognition* 11.3 (1983): 211–27.

Bascom, William. *The Yoruba of Southwestern Nigeria*. New York: Holt, Rinehart and Winston, 1969.

Bauckham, Richard. "2 Peter." In Metzger and Coogan: 586–88.

Beier, Ulli, trans. and ed. *Yoruba Poetry: An Anthology of Traditional Poems*. Cambridge: Cambridge UP, 1970.

Beilis, Viktor. "Ghosts, People, and Books of Yorubaland." *Research in African Literatures* 18 (1987): 447–57.

Best, Ernest. "1 Peter." In Metzger and Coogan: 583–86.

Bhabha, Homi. *The Location of Culture*. London: Routledge, 1994.

————, ed. *Nation and Narration*. London: Routledge, 1990.

————. "The Postcolonial Critic: Homi Bhabha Interviewed by David Bennett and Terry Collits." In *Literary India: Comparative Studies in Aesthetics, Colonialism, and Culture*. Ed. Patrick Colm Hogan and Lalita Pandit. Albany: State U of New York P, 1995, 237–53.

Binyon, Lawrence. Arguments to the cantos of *The Divine Comedy*. In Dante.

Bobb, June D. *Beating a Restless Drum: The Poetics of Kamau Brathwaite and Derek Walcott*. Trenton, NJ: Africa World P, 1998.

Boehmer, Elleke. *Colonial and Postcolonial Literature*. New York: Oxford UP, 1995.

Bordwell, David. *Making Meaning: Inference and Rhetoric in the Interpretation of Cinema*. Cambridge: Harvard UP, 1989.

Borthwick, Meredith. *The Changing Role of Women in Bengal 1849–1905*. Princeton: Princeton UP, 1984.

Breiner, Laurence A. "Walcott's Early Drama." In Stewart Brown: 69–81.

Breslin, Paul. *Nobody's Nation: Reading Derek Walcott*. Chicago, IL: U of Chicago P, 2001.

Brown, John Pairman. "Techniques of Imperial Control: The Background of the Gospel Event." In *The Bible and Liberation: Political and Social Hermeneutics*. Ed. Norman K. Gottwald. Maryknoll, NY: Orbis Books, 1983: 357–77.

Brown, Lloyd. "Dreamers and Slaves—The Ethos of Revolution in Walcott and Leroi Jones." In Hamner, *Critical*: 193–201.

Brown, Stewart, ed. *The Art of Derek Walcott*. Glamorgan, Wales: Siren Books, 1991.

Browne, Kevin J. *Eamon de Valera and the Banner County*. Foreword by Thomas P. O'Neill. Dun Laoghaire, Co. Dublin: Glendale P, 1982.

Bruce, F. F. "Acts of the Apostles." In Metzger and Coogan: 6–10.

Bruckner, D. J. R. "A Poem in Homage to an Unwanted Man." In Hamner, *Critical*: 396–99.

Brydon, Diana. "The Thematic Ancestor: Joseph Conrad, Patrick White, and Margaret Atwood." *World Literature Written in English* 24 (1984): 386–97.

Burnett, Paula. *Derek Walcott: Politics and Poetics*. Gainesville: U P of Florida, 2000.

Burris, Sidney. "An Empire of Poetry." *The Southern Review* 27.3 (1991): 558–74.

Bush, President George W. Address to a Joint Session of Congress, 20 September 2001 (transcript). http: // www. cnn.com/2001/US/09/20/gen.bush.transcript

Butler, Judith. "Imitation and Gender Insubordination." In *Inside/Out: Lesbian Theories, Gay Theories*. Ed. Diana Fuss. New York: Routledge, 1991, 13–31.

Cameron, Deborah. *Feminism and Linguistic Theory*. London: Macmillan, 1985.

Cassidy, Richard J. *Jesus, Politics, and Society: A Study of Luke's Gospel*. Maryknoll, NY: Orbis Books, 1973.

Césaire, Aimé. *Une Tempête*. Paris: Éditions du Seuil, 1969.

Chaitanya, Krishna. *A History of Arabic Literature*. New Delhi: Manohar, 1983.

Chandler, Steven R. "Metaphor Comprehension: A Connectionist Approach to Implications for the Mental Lexicon." *Metaphor and Symbolic Activity* 6 (1991): 227–58.

Chinweizu, Onwuchekwa Jemie, and Ihechukwu Madubuike. *Toward the Decoloniza-tion of African Literature: African Fiction and Poetry and Their Critics.* London: Routledge and Kegan Paul, 1980.

Chomsky, Noam. *Aspects of the Theory of Syntax.* Cambridge, MA: MIT P, 1965.

———. *The Fateful Triangle: The United States, Israel and the Palestinians.* Boston: South End P, 1983.

———. *Knowledge of Language: Its Nature, Origin, and Use.* New York: Praeger, 1986

———. *Language and Problems of Knowledge: The Managua Lectures.* Cambridge, MA: MIT P, 1988.

———. *Rules and Representations.* New York: Columbia UP, 1980.

Clarke, William H. *Travels and Explorations in Yorubaland 1854–1858.* Ed. J. A. Alanda. Ibadan: Ibadan UP, 1972.

Cliff, Michelle. *No Telephone to Heaven.* New York: Penguin, 1987.

Coates, John. "The Inward Journey of the Palm-Wine Drinkard." *African Literature Today* 11 (1980): 122–29.

Coburn, Thomas B. *Encountering the Goddess: A Translation of the Devī-Māhātmya and a Study of Its Interpretation.* Albany: State U of New York P, 1991.

Cohen, Joshua, ed. *For Love of Country: Debating the Limits of Patriotism.* Boston: Bea-con P, 1996.

Collins, Harold. *Amos Tutuola.* New York: Twayne, 1969.

Conrad, Joseph. *Heart of Darkness.* Ed. Robert Kimbrough. 2d ed. New York: W. W. Norton, 1971.

Conway, Martin A. *Cognitive Models of Memory.* Cambridge, MA: MIT P, 1997.

Cruse, D. A. *Lexical Semantics.* Cambridge: Cambridge UP, 1986.

Cullmann, Oscar. *Jesus and the Revolutionaries.* Trans. Gareth Putnam. New York: Harper and Row, 1970.

———. *The State in the New Testament.* London: SCM P, 1957.

Curtis, L. P. *Anglo-Saxons and Celts: A Study of Anti-Irish Prejudice in Victorian Eng-land.* Bridgeport, CT: Conference on British Studies at the University of Bridge-port, 1968.

Daniélou, Alain. *The Myths and Gods of India.* Rochester, VT: Inner Traditions Inter-national, 1991.

Dante Alighieri. *The Divine Comedy.* Trans. Laurence Binyon. In *The Portable Dante.* Ed. Paolo Milano. Revised ed. New York: Penguin, 1969.

———. *Inferno* (Italian). In *Dante Alighieri's Divine Comedy, Volume I, Inferno: Italian Text and Verse Translation.* Trans. Mark Musa. Bloomington: Indiana U P, 1996.

Dash, Sandhyarani. *Form and Vision in the Novels of Anita Desai.* New Delhi: Prestige, 1996.

Dathorne, O. R. "Amos Tutuola: The Nightmare of the Tribe." In *Introduction to Nigerian Literature*. Ed. Bruce King. New York: Africana Publishing, 1972.

Davis, Gregson. "'With No Homeric Shadow': The Disavowal of Epic in Derek Walcott's *Omeros*." *South Atlantic Quarterly* 96.2 (1997): 321–33.

Davy, John. *The West Indies Before and Since Slave Emancipation*. London: Frank Cass, 1971 (1854).

de Bary, William Theodore, with Stephen Hay and I. H. Qureshi. *Sources of Indian Tradition*. Vol. 2. New York: Columbia UP, 1958.

Delgado, Richard. "Storytelling for Oppositionists and Others: A Plea for Narrative." *Michigan Law Review* 87 (1989): 2411–41.

Dennett, R. E. *Nigerian Studies or The Religious and Political System of the Yoruba*. London: Frank Cass, 1968 (1910).

Desai, Anita. *Baumgartner's Bombay*. New York: Penguin, 1988.

De Souza, Teotonio. "*Hajj* without Spice? Politics of Religion between Akbar and the Portuguese." In Iqtidar Khan: 106–13.

Dharwadker, Vinay. "Print Culture and Literary Markets in Colonial India." In *Language Machines: Technologies of Literary and Cultural Production*. Ed. Jeffrey Masten, Peter Stallybrass, and Nancy J. Vickers. New York: Routledge, 1997: 108–33.

Dimock, Edward et al. *The Literatures of India: An Introduction*. Chicago: U of Chicago P, 1974.

Dinnage, Rosemary. "Exiles" (Review of *Baumgartner's Bombay*). *New York Review of Books* 36 (1 June 1989): 34–36.

Dougherty, Carol. "Homer after *Omeros:* Reading a H/Omeric Text." *South Atlantic Quarterly* 96.2 (1997): 335–57.

Drewal, Henry, and John Pemberton, with Rowland Abiodun. *Yoruba: Nine Centuries of African Art and Thought*. Ed. Allen Wardwell. New York: Center for African Art, 1989.

Drewal, Margaret Thompson. *Yoruba Ritual: Performers, Play, Agency*. Bloomington: Indiana UP, 1992.

Duckitt, J. H. *The Social Psychology of Prejudice*. New York: Praeger, 1992.

Dutta, Krishna, and Andrew Robinson. *Rabindranath Tagore: The Myriad-Minded Man*. New York: St. Martin's P, 1996.

Edwards, Paul. "The Farm and the Wilderness in Tutuola's *The Palm-Wine Drinkard*." In *Critical Perspectives on Amos Tutuola*. Ed. Bernth Lindfors. Washington: Three Continents Press, 1975: 255–63.

Eisler, Robert. *The Messiah Jesus and John the Baptist*. Trans. Alexander Krappe. London: Methuen, 1931.

Eliot, T. S. *Collected Poems: 1909–1962*. New York: Harcourt, Brace and World, 1970.

———. "Ulysses, Order, and Myth." In *Critical Essays on James Joyce*. Ed. Bernard Benstock. Boston: G. K. Hall, 1985.

Ellis, A. B. *The Yoruba-Speaking Peoples of the Slave Coast of West Africa*. Ooserhout, Netherlands: Anthropological Publications, 1970 (1894).

Emecheta, Buchi. *The Joys of Motherhood*. New York: George Braziller, 1979.

Engineer, Asghar Ali. "Sufism and Communal Harmony." In Engineer, *Sufism:* 160–71.

———, ed. *Sufism and Communal Harmony*. Jaipur: Printwell, 1991.

Estes, W. K. *Classification and Cognition*. Oxford: Oxford UP, 1994.

Faiz, Faiz Ahmed. *The Rebel's Silhouette: Selected Poems*. Trans. Agha Shahid Ali. Revised ed. Amherst: U of Massachusetts P, 1995.

Farrell, Joseph. "Walcott's *Omeros:* The Classical Epic in a Postmodern World." *South Atlantic Quarterly* 96.2 (1997): 247–73.

Figueroa, John. *"Omeros."* In Stewart Brown: 193–213.

Forster, Kenneth I. "Lexical Processing." In *An Invitation to Cognitive Science (Vol. 1): Language*. Ed. Daniel N. Osherson and Howard Lasnik. Cambridge, MA: MIT P, 1990: 95–131.

Foucault, Michel. *The Archaeology of Knowledge and The Discourse on Language*. Trans. A. M. Sheridan Smith. New York: Harper and Row, 1976.

Frye, Northrop. *Anatomy of Criticism: Four Essays*. Princeton, NJ: Princeton UP, 1957.

Gachet, Charles. *A History of the Roman Catholic Church in St. Lucia*. Port of Spain, Trinidad: Key Caribbean Publications, 1975.

Gadamer, Hans-Georg. *Truth and Method*. 2d ed. Trans. Joel Weinsheimer and Donald Marshall. New York: Crossroad, 1989.

Gandhi, Leela. *Postcolonial Theory: A Critical Introduction*. New York: Columbia UP, 1998.

Garman, Michael. *Psycholinguistics*. Cambridge: Cambridge UP, 1990.

Garnham, Alan. "Representing Information in Mental Models." In Conway: 149–72.

Geertz, Clifford. *The Interpretation of Cultures: Selected Essays*. New York: Basic Books, 1973.

"Gem Superstitions." *Compton's Interactive Encyclopedia*. SoftKey Multimedia, 1996.

Gilman, Sander. *The Jew's Body*. New York: Routledge, 1991.

Gohrab, Asghar Abu. "Majnun's Image as a Serpent." In Talattof and Clinton, *Poetry:* 83–95.

Gopal, N. R. *A Critical Study of the Novels of Anita Desai*. New Delhi: Atlantic Publishers, 1995.

Gordon, Leonard. *Bengal: The Nationalist Movement 1876–1940*. New York: Columbia UP, 1974.

Grzimek, Bernhard, ed. *Grzimek's Animal Life Encyclopedia*. New York: Van Nostrand Reinhold, 1975.

Guha, Ranajit. *Dominance without Hegemony: History and Power in Colonial India*. Cambridge, MA: Harvard UP, 1997.

Hallgren, Roland. *The Good Things in Life: A Study of the Traditional Religious Culture of the Yoruba People*. Loberod: Bokforlaget Plus Ultra, 1988.

Hamner, Robert, ed. *Critical Perspectives on Derek Walcott*. Washington: Three Continents P, 1993.

———. *Epic of the Dispossessed: Derek Walcott's Omeros*. Columbia: U of Missouri P, 1997.

———. "Introduction." In Hamner, *Critical*: 1–12.

Hampton, James A. "Psychological Representation of Concepts." In Conway: 81–110.

Harris, Wilson. *Palace of the Peacock*. In *The Guyana Quartet*. London: Faber and Faber, 1985 (1960): 15–117.

Harvey, Sir Paul, ed. *The Oxford Companion to Classical Literature*. New York: Oxford UP, 1984.

Hegel, G. W. F. *Aesthetics: Lectures on Fine Art*. Trans. T. M. Knox. Oxford: Clarendon P, 1975.

Herskovits, Melville J., and Frances S. Herskovits. *Dahomean Narrative: A Cross-Cultural Analysis*. Evanston: Northwestern UP, 1958.

Hibbert, Christopher. *Africa Explored: Europeans in the Dark Continent, 1769–1889*. New York: W. W. Norton, 1983.

Hill, Christopher. *Milton and the English Revolution*. New York: Penguin, 1979.

Hirschfeld, Lawrence A. *Race in the Making: Cognition, Culture, and the Child's Construction of Human Kinds*. Cambridge, MA: MIT P, 1996.

Hoehner, Harold. "Herodian Dynasty." In Metzger and Coogan: 280–84.

Hogan, Patrick Colm. "Beauty, Politics, and Cultural Otherness: The Bias of Literary Difference." In *Literary India: Comparative Studies in Aesthetics, Colonialism, and Culture*. Ed. Hogan and Lalita Pandit. Albany: State U of New York P, 1995: 3–43.

———. *Colonialism and Cultural Identity: Crises of Tradition in the Anglophone Literatures of India, Africa, and the Caribbean*. Albany: State U of New York P, 2000.

———. *The Culture of Conformism: Understanding Social Consent*. Durham, NC: Duke U P, 2001.

———. "The Gender of Tradition: Ideologies of Character in Post-Colonization Anglophone Literature." In *Order and Partialities: Theory, Pedagogy, and the "Postcolonial."* Ed. Kostas Myrsiades and Jerry McGuire. Albany: State U of New York P, 1995: 87–110.

———. "Gora, Jane Austen, and the Slaves of Indigo." In *Rabindranath Tagore: Universality and Tradition*. Ed. Hogan and Lalita Pandit. Cranbury, NJ: Associated U Presses, 2003.

———. *Joyce, Milton, and the Theory of Influence*. Gainesville: UP of Florida, 1995.

———. "Literary Universals." *Poetics Today* 18.2 (1997): 223–49.

———. *The Mind and Its Stories: Narrative Universals and Human Emotion*. Cambridge: Cambridge UP and Paris: Éditions de la Maison des Sciences de l'Homme, 2003.

———. *On Interpretation: Meaning and Inference in Law, Psychoanalysis, and Literature*. Athens: U of Georgia P, 1996.

———. *Philosophical Approaches to the Study of Literature*. Gainesville: UP of Florida, 2000.

Holland, John, Keith Holyoak, Richard Nisbett, and Paul Thagard. *Induction: Processes of Inference, Learning, and Discovery*. Cambridge, MA: MIT P, 1986.

Homer. *The Iliad*. Trans. W. H. D. Rouse. New York: New American Library, 1938.

———. *The Odyssey*. Trans. Richmond Lattimore. New York: Harper and Row, 1965.

Ibn Rushd (Averroes). *Averroes' Middle Commentary on Aristotle's Poetics*. Trans. Charles Butterworth. Princeton: Princeton UP, 1986.

Ibn Sinā (Avicenna). *Avicenna's Commentary on the Poetics of Aristotle: A Critical Study with an Annotated Translation of the Text*. Trans. and ed. Ismail Dahiyat. Leiden: E. J. Brill, 1974.

Idowu, E. Bọlaji. *Olódùmarè: God in Yoruba Belief*. New York: Frederick Praeger, 1963.

Ingarden, Roman. *The Literary Work of Art: An Investigation on the Borderlines of Ontology, Logic, and the Theory of Literature*. Trans. George Grabowicz. Evanston, IL: Northwestern UP, 1973.

Iqbal, Muhammad. *Javid-Nama*. Trans. Arthur J. Arberry. London: George Allen and Unwin, 1966.

Irele, Abiola. *The African Experience in Literature and Ideology*. London: Heinemann, 1981.

Iser, Wolfgang. *The Implied Reader: Patterns of Communication in Prose Fiction from Bunyan to Beckett*. Baltimore, MD: Johns Hopkins UP, 1974.

Ito, Tiffany, and John Cacioppo. "Affect and Attitudes: A Social Neuroscience Approach." In *Handbook of Affect and Social Cognition*. Ed. Joseph Forgas. Mahwah, NJ: Lawrence Erlbaum, 2001: 50–74.

Jameson, Fredric. "Third World Literature in the Era of Multinational Capital." *Social Text* 15 (1986): 65–88.

Jauss, Hans Robert. "Literary History as a Challenge to Literary Theory." *Toward an Aesthetic of Reception*. Trans. Timothy Bahti. Minneapolis: U of Minnesota P, 1982.

Jayadeva. *Love Song of the Dark Lord: Jayadeva's Gītagovinda.* Ed. and trans. Barbara Stoler Miller. New York: Columbia UP, 1977.

Jerusalem Bible. Ed. and trans. Alexander Jones et al. Garden City, NY: Doubleday, 1966.

Johnson, John William, Thomas A. Hale, and Stephen Belcher. *Oral Epics from Africa: Vibrant Voices from a Vast Continent.* Bloomington and Indianapolis: Indiana U P, 1997.

Johnson, Rev. Samuel. *The History of the Yorubas: From the Earliest Times to the Beginning of the British Protectorate.* Ed. O. Johnson. London: Routledge and Kegan Paul, 1921.

Johnson-Laird, P. N. *The Computer and the Mind: An Introduction to Cognitive Science.* Cambridge, MA: Harvard UP, 1988.

————, and P.C. Wason. "Introduction." In *Thinking: Readings in Cognitive Science.* Ed. Johnson-Laird and Wason. Cambridge: Cambridge UP, 1977.

Joseph, Margaret Paul. *Caliban in Exile: The Outsider in Caribbean Fiction.* New York: Greenwood P, 1992.

Josephus. *The Works of Josephus.* New updated ed. Trans. William Whiston. N.c.: Hendrickson, 1987.

Joyce, James. *Ulysses.* Ed. Hans Walter Gabler, with Wolfhard Steppe and Claus Melchior. New York: Vintage, 1986.

Kalpakli, Mehmed, and Walter G. Andrews. "Layla Grows Up: Nizami's *Layla and Majnun* 'in the Turkish Manner.'" In Talattof and Clinton, *Poetry:* 29–49.

Kant, Immanuel. *Critique of Pure Reason.* Trans. Norman Kemp Smith. New York: St. Martin's P, 1965.

Kautilya. *The Arthashastra.* Ed. and trans. L. N. Rangarajan. New Delhi, India: Penguin, 1992.

Khan, Iqtidar Alam, ed. *Akbar and His Age.* New Delhi: Northern Book Centre, 1999.

Khan, Mohammad Ishaq. *Kashmir's Transition to Islam: The Role of Muslim Rishis (Fifteenth to Eighteenth Century).* New Delhi: Manohar, 1994.

Khan, Rasheeduddin. "The Role of Sufism in Building the Values of a Composite Culture of India." In *Contemporary Relevance of Sufism.* Ed. Syeda Saiyidain Hameed. New Delhi: Indian Coucil for Cultural Relations, 1993: 209–41.

Khanna, Shashi. *Human Relationships in Anita Desai's Novels.* New Delhi: Sarup and Sons, 1995.

Khizer, Mirza M. "Sufism and Social Integration." In Engineer, *Sufism:* 102–27.

King, Bruce. *Derek Walcott: A Caribbean Life.* Oxford: Oxford UP, 2000.

Kipling, Rudyard. *Kim.* New York: New American Library, 1984.

Kittay, Eva Feder. *Metaphor: Its Cognitive Force and Linguistic Structure.* Oxford: Clarendon P, 1987.

Knappert, Jan. *Indian Mythology: An Encyclopedia of Myth and Legend*. London: Aquarian P, 1991.

Koljian, Kathleen. "'Durga—for whom I would redden the earth with sacrificial offerings': Mythology, Nationalism, and Patriarchal Ambivalence in *The Home and the World*." In *Rabindranath Tagore: Universality and Tradition*. Ed. Patrick Colm Hogan and Lalita Pandit. Cranbury, NJ: Associated U Presses, 2003.

Kopf, David. *The Brahmo Samaj and the Shaping of the Modern Indian Mind*. Princeton, N.J.: Princeton UP, 1979.

Lakoff, George, and Mark Johnson. *Metaphors We Live By*. Chicago, IL: U of Chicago P, 1980.

————, and Mark Turner. *More than Cool Reason: A Field Guide to Poetic Metaphor*. Chicago, IL: U of Chicago P, 1989.

Lal, Muni. *Jahangir*. Delhi: Vikas, 1983.

Lamming, George. "Caliban Orders History." In *The Pleasures of Exile*: 118–50.

————. "A Monster, A Child, A Slave." In *The Pleasures of Exile*: 95–117.

————. *The Pleasures of Exile*. London: Michael Joseph, 1960.

————. *Water with Berries*. New York: Holt, Rinehart & Winston, 1971.

Leenerts, Cynthia. "Rabindranath Tagore's and Satyajit Ray's 'New Woman': Writing and Rewriting Bimala." In *Rabindranath Tagore: Universality and Tradition*. Ed. Patrick Colm Hogan and Lalita Pandit. Cranbury, NJ: Associated U Presses, 2003.

Lefkowitz, Mary. "Bringing Him Back Alive." In Hamner, *Critical*: 400–403.

Levy, Reuben. *An Introduction to Persian Literature*. New York: Columbia UP, 1969.

Lichtenstadter, Ilse. *Introduction to Classical Arabic Literature, with Selections from Representative Works in English Translation*. New York: Schocken Books, 1976.

Lindfors, Bernth. "Amos Tutuola: Literary Syncretism and the Yoruba Folk Tradition." In *European-Language Writing in Sub-Saharan Africa*. Vol. 2. Ed. Albert S. Gerard. Budapest: Akademiai Kiado, 1986.

————. *Folklore in Nigerian Literature*. New York: Africana Publishing, 1973.

Livingston, James. "Derek Walcott's *Omeros*: Recovering the Mythical." *Journal of Caribbean Studies* 8.3 (1991/1992): 131–40.

Lukács, Georg. *Essays on Realism*. Ed. Rodney Livingstone. Trans. David Fernbach. Cambridge, MA: MIT P, 1981.

Lyons, F. S. L. *Ireland Since the Famine*. Bungay, Suffolk: Fontana, 1973.

Macaulay, Thomas Babington. "Minute on Education." In de Bary: 44–49.

Mack, Maynard et al. *The Norton Anthology of World Masterpieces, Volume 1: Beginnings to 1650*. Expanded ed. New York: W. W. Norton, 1995.

Majumdar, Bimanbehari. *Heroines of Tagore: A Study in the Transformation of Indian Society 1875–1941*. Calcutta: Firma K. L. Mukhopadhyay, 1968.

Malik, Z. U. "The Eighteenth-Century View of Akbar." In Iqtidar Khan: 239–59.

Massey, Lesly F. *Women and the New Testament: An Analysis of Scripture in Light of New Testament Era Culture.* Jefferson, NC: McFarland, 1989.

McClure, Charlotte. "Helen of the 'West Indies': History or Poetry of a Caribbean Realm." *Studies in the Literary Imagination* 26.2 (1993): 7–20.

Metzger, Bruce M., and Michael D. Coogan, eds. *The Oxford Companion to the Bible.* New York: Oxford UP, 1993.

Michaels, Walter Benn. *Our America: Nativism, Modernism, and Pluralism.* Durham, NC: Duke UP, 1995.

Miner, Earl. *Comparative Poetics: An Intercultural Essay on Theories of Literature.* Princeton, NJ: Princeton UP, 1990.

Mill, John Stuart. *On Liberty.* In *Essential Works of John Stuart Mill.* Ed. Max Lerner. New York: Bantam Books, 1971: 253–360.

Milton, John. *Paradise Lost.* In *John Milton: Complete Poems and Major Prose.* Ed. Merritt Hughes. Indianapolis, IN: Odyssey P, 1957.

———. *The Works of John Milton.* Ed. Frank Patterson et al. 18 vols. New York: Columbia UP, 1932.

Mitra, Indrani. "'I Will Make Bimala One with My Country': Gender and Nationalism in Tagore's *The Home and the World.*" *Modern Fiction Studies* 41.2 (1995): 243–64.

Moore, Gerald. "Amos Tutuola: A Nigerian Visionary." In *Critical Perspectives on Amos Tutuola.* Ed. Bernth Lindfors. Washington: Three Continents Press, 1975, 49–57.

Musa, Mark. *Dante Alighieri's Divine Comedy, Volume 2, Inferno: Commentary.* Bloomington: Indiana UP, 1996.

Muwakkil, Salim. "History or Myth? Afrocentricity Is Under Attack But More Influential Than Ever." *In These Times* (29 Nov. 1998): 20–21.

Nair, Supriya. *Caliban's Curse: George Lamming and the Revisioning of History.* Ann Arbor: U of Michigan P, 1996.

Nandy, Ashis. *The Illegitimacy of Nationalism: Rabindranath Tagore and the Politics of Self.* Delhi, India: Oxford UP, 1994.

———. *The Intimate Enemy: Loss and Recovery of Self Under Colonialism.* Delhi, India: Oxford UP, 1983.

Narayan, R. K. *The Ramayana.* New York: Penguin, 1977.

Nārāyaṇa. *Hitopadeśa.* Ed. and trans. M. R. Kale. 6th ed. Delhi, India: Motilal Banarsidass, 1989.

"National Anthem" of St. Lucia. "Nations of the Commonwealth." Http://www.tbc.gov.bc.ca/cwgames/country/StLucia/stlucia2.html.

Needham, Lawrence. "In Pursuit of Evanescence: Agha Shahid Ali's *A Nostalgist's Map of America.*" *Kunapipi* 15.2 (1993): 123–27

———. "'The Sorrows of a Broken Time': Agha Shahid Ali and the Poetry of Loss and Recovery." In *Reworlding: The Literature of the Indian Diaspora*. Westport, CT: Greenwood P, 1992, 63–76.

Nehru, Jawaharlal. "Foreword." In Prithivi Nath Kaul Bamzai. *A History of Kashmir, Political, Social, Cultural: From the Earliest Times to the Present Day*. Delhi: Metropolitan Book, 1962: vii–x.

Nelson, Emmanuel S. "Black America and the Anglophone Afro-Caribbean Literary Consciousness." *Journal of American Culture* 12.4 (1989): 53–58.

Newman, Judie. "History and Letters: Anita Desai's *Baumgartner's Bombay*." *World Literature Written in English* 30.1 (1990): 37–46.

Nisbett, R. E., and L. Ross. *Human Inference: Strategies and Shortcomings of Social Judgment*. Englewood Cliffs, N.J.: Prentice-Hall, 1980.

Nizami. *The Story of Layla and Majnun*. Trans. and ed. Rudolf Gelpke, in collaboration with E. Mattin and G. Hill; final chapter trans. Zia Inayat Khan and Omid Safi. New Lebanon: Omega Publications, 1997.

Nussbaum, Martha C. "Patriotism and Cosmopolitanism." In Cohen: 2–17.

O'Flaherty, Wendy Doniger. "The Clash between Relative and Absolute Duty: The Dharma of Demons." In *The Concept of Duty in South Asia*. Ed. O'Flaherty and J. Duncan M. Derrett. N.c.: South Asia Books, 1978, 96–106.

Ojo, G. J. Afolabi. *Yoruba Culture: A Geographical Analysis*. London: U of Ife and U of London P, 1966.

Ojo, S. Ade. "André Malraux et Sembene Ousmane: Createurs des Romans Proletariens Historiques?" *Peuples Noirs/Peuples Africains* 17 (1980): 117–34.

Olaniyan, Tejumola. "Corporeal/Discursive Bodies and the Subject: *Dream on Monkey Mountain* and the Poetics of Identity." In *Imagination, Emblems and Expressions: Essays on Latin American, Caribbean, and Continental Culture and Identity*. Ed. Helen Ryan-Ranson. Bowling Green, OH: Bowling Green State U Popular P, 1993: 155–71.

Ong, Rev. Walter J. "The Myth of Myth: Dialogue with the Unspoken." In *The Barbarian Within and Other Fugitive Essays and Studies*. New York: Macmillan, 1962: 131–45.

———. *Orality and Literacy: The Technologizing of the Word*. London: Methuen, 1982.

———. "The Writer's Audience Is Always a Fiction." In *Interfaces of the Word: Studies in the Evolution of Consciousness and Culture*. Ithaca, NY: Cornell UP, 1977: 53–81.

Ortony, Andrew. "The Role of Similarity in Similes and Metaphors." In *Metaphor and Thought*. Ed. Andrew Ortony. Cambridge: Cambridge UP, 1993: 342–56.

———, Gerald Clore, and Allan Collins. *The Cognitive Structure of Emotions*. Cambridge: Cambridge UP, 1988.

Pagels, Elaine. *The Origin of Satan*. New York: Vintage, 1995.

Pandit, B. N. *History of Kashmir Saivism*. Srinagar, Kashmir, India: Utpal Publications, 1989.

Pandit, Lalita. "Caste, Race, and Nation: History and Dialectic in Rabindranath Tagore's *Gora*." In *Literary India: Comparative Studies in Aesthetics, Colonialism, and Culture*. Ed. Patrick Colm Hogan and Pandit. Albany: State U of New York P, 1995: 207–33.

Parrinder, Geoffrey. *West African Religion: A Study of the Beliefs and Practices of Akan, Ewe, Yoruba, Ibo, and Kindred Peoples*. London: Epworth, 1961.

Pathania, Usha. *Human Bonds and Bondages: The Fiction of Anita Desai and Kamala Markandaya*. Delhi: Kanishka, 1992.

Pound, Ezra. *Selected Poems of Ezra Pound*. New York: New Directions, 1957.

Quayson, Ato. *Strategic Transformations in Nigerian Writing: Orality and History in the Work of Rev. Samuel Johnson, Amos Tutuola, Wole Soyinka and Ben Okri*. Bloomington: Indiana UP, 1997.

Qur'ān. In Maulana Muhammad Ali.

Radvansky, Gabriel A., and Rose T. Zacks. "The Retrieval of Situation-Specific Information." In Conway: 173–213.

Rafiqi, Abdul Qaiyum. *Sufism in Kashmir from the Fourteenth to the Sixteenth Century*. Varanasi: Bharatiya Publishing, 1972.

Ramanujan, A. K. "Three Hundred *Rāmāyaṇas*: Five Examples and Three Thoughts on Translation." In Richman *Many Rāmāyaṇas*: 22–49.

Rao, Velcheru Narayana. "A *Rāmāyaṇa* of Their Own: Women's Oral Tradition in Telugu." In Richman *Many Rāmāyaṇas*: 114–36.

Ramazani, Jahan. *The Hybrid Muse: Postcolonial Poetry in English*. Chicago, IL: U of Chicago P, 2001.

———. "The Wound of History: Walcott's *Omeros* and the Postcolonial Poetics of Affliction." *PMLA* 112.3 (1997): 405–17.

Ray, Rajat Kanta. *Social Conflict and Political Unrest in Bengal 1875–1927*. Delhi: Oxford UP, 1984.

Reynolds, Mary. *Joyce and Dante: The Shaping Imagination*. Princeton: Princeton UP, 1981.

Rhys, Jean. *Wide Sargasso Sea*. In *The Complete Novels*. Ed. Diana Athill. New York: W.W. Norton: 463–574.

Riches, John. "Essenes." In Metzger and Coogan: 198.

Richman, Paula. "E. V. Ramasami's Reading of the *Rāmāyaṇa*." In Richman *Many Rāmāyaṇas*: 175–201.

———. "Introduction: The Diversity of the *Rāmāyaṇa* Tradition." In Richman *Many Rāmāyaṇas*: 3–21.

————, ed. *Many Rāmāyaṇas: The Diversity of a Narrative Tradition in South Asia.* Berkeley: U of California P, 1991.

Ringe, Sharon H. *Luke.* Louisville, KY: Westminster John Knox P, 1995.

Rizvi, Saiyid Athar Abbas. *Religious and Intellectual History of the Muslims in Akbar's Reign.* New Delhi: Munshiram Manoharlal, 1975.

Rodney, Walter. *How Europe Underdeveloped Africa.* Washington: Howard UP, 1982.

Roland, Joan. *Jews in British India: Identity in a Colonial Era.* Hanover, NH: UP of New England, 1989.

Roscoe, Adrian. *Mother Is Gold: A Study in West African Literature.* Cambridge: Cambridge UP, 1971.

Roumain, Jacques. *Gouverneurs de la Rosée.* Paris: Les Editeurs Français Réunis, 1946.

Rushdie, Salman. *Midnight's Children.* New York: Penguin, 1980.

Russell, Ralph. *An Anthology of Urdu Literature.* Manchester, England: Carcanet, 1999.

————. *The Pursuit of Urdu Literature: A Select History.* London: Zed Books, 1992.

Said, Edward W. *Culture and Imperialism.* New York: Alfred A. Knopf, 1993.

Salo, Kalervo. *Luke's Treatment of the Law: A Redaction-Critical Investigation.* Helsinki: Suomalainen Tiedeakatemia, 1991.

Samad, Daizal R. "Cultural Imperatives in Derek Walcott's *Dream on Monkey Mountain.*" *Commonwealth* 13.2 (1991): 8–21.

Sarkar, Sumit. "'Middle-Class' Consciousness and Patriotic Literature in South Asia." In *A Companion to Postcolonial Studies.* Ed. Henry Schwartz and Sangeeta Ray. Oxford: Blackwell, 2000: 252–68.

————. *The Swadeshi Movement in Bengal 1903–1908.* New Delhi: People's Publishing House, 1973.

Schacter, Daniel L. *Searching for Memory: The Brain, the Mind, and the Past.* New York: Basic Books, 1996.

Schork, R. J. *Latin and Roman Culture in Joyce.* Gainesville: U P of Florida, 1997.

Seely, Clinton. "The Raja's New Clothes: Redressing Rāvaṇa in *Meghanadavadha Kāvya.*" In Richman *Many Rāmāyaṇas:* 137–55.

Shakespeare, William. *The Tempest.* Ed. Louis Wright, with Virginia LaMar. New York: Washington Square P, 1961.

————. *The Tragedy of Othello, the Moor of Venice.* In *The Riverside Shakespeare.* 2d ed. Gen. ed. G. Blakemore Evans. Boston, MA: Houghton Mifflin, 1997.

Shanks, David R. "Representation of Categories and Concepts in Memory." In Conway: 111–46.

Sharma, Kajali. *Symbolism in Anita Desai's Novels.* New Delhi: Abhinav Publications, 1991.

Sidhwa, Bapsi. *The Bride.* New York: St. Martin's P, 1983.

Simpson, George E. *Yoruba Religion and Medicine in Ibadan*. Ibadan: Ibadan UP, 1980.

Singh, Sunaina. *The Novels of Margaret Atwood and Anita Desai: A Comparative Study in Feminist Perspectives*. New Delhi: Creative Books, 1994.

Smith, Edward E. "Categorization." In *An Invitation to Cognitive Science (vol. 3): Thinking*. Ed. Daniel N. Osherson and Edward E. Smith. Cambridge, MA: MIT P, 1990: 33–53.

Smith, Katharine Capshaw. "Narrating History: The Reality of the Internment Camps in Anita Desai's 'Baumgartner's Bombay.'" *Ariel* 28.2 (1997): 141–57.

Snead, James. "European pedigrees/African contagions: nationality, narrative, and communality in Tutuola, Achebe, and Reed." In Bhabha *Nation:* 231–49.

Solanki, Mrinalini. *Anita Desai's Fiction: Patterns of Survival Strategies*. Delhi: Kanishka Publishing, 1992.

Soyinka, Wole. *The Bacchae of Euripides*. In *Collected Plays 1*. Oxford: Oxford UP, 1973: 233–307.

———. *A Dance of the Forests*. In *Collected Plays 1*. Oxford: Oxford UP, 1973: 1–77.

———. *A Play of Giants*. London: Methuen, 1984.

———. *The Strong Breed*. In *Collected Plays 1*. Oxford: Oxford UP, 1973: 113–46.

Spivak, Gayatri Chakravorty. *In Other Worlds: Essays in Cultural Politics*. New York: Routledge, 1988.

Tagore, Rabindranath. "The Five Elements: A Novel Ramayana." Trans. Tista Bagchi. In *Rabindranath Tagore: Selected Writings on Literature and Language*. Ed. Sisir Kumar Das and Sukanta Chaudhuri. New Delhi: Oxford UP, 2001 (1895), 91–94.

———. *The Home and the World*. Trans. Surendranath Tagore. New York: Penguin, 1985 (1916).

———. *Nationalism*. New York: Macmillan, 1917.

———. "The *Ramayana*." Trans. Bhawani-Prasad Chattopadhyay. In *Rabindranath Tagore: Selected Writings on Literature and Language*. Ed. Sisir Kumar Das and Sukanta Chaudhuri. New Delhi: Oxford UP, 2001 (1904), 252–57.

Taiwo, Oladele. *Culture and the Nigerian Novel*. New York: St. Martin's Press, 1976.

Tajfel, H. *Human Groups and Social Categories*. Cambridge: Cambridge UP, 1981.

Talattof, Kamran. "Nizami's Unlikely Heroines: A Study of the Characterizations of Women in Classical Persian Literature." In Talattof and Clinton, *Poetry:* 51–81.

Talattof, Kamran, and Jerome Clinton, "Introduction: Nizami Ganjavi and His Poetry." In Talattof and Clinton, *Poetry:* 1–13.

———, eds. *The Poetry of Nizami Ganjavi: Knowledge, Love, and Rhetoric*. New York: Palgrave, 2000.

Talbot, P. Amaury. *The Peoples of Southern Nigeria*. Vol. 3. London: Frank Cass, 1969 (1926).

Taylor, Patrick. *The Narrative of Liberation: Perspectives on Afro-Caribbean Literature, Popular Culture, and Politics*. Ithaca, NY: Cornell UP, 1989.

Terada, Rei. *Derek Walcott's Poetry: American Mimicry*. Boston: Northeastern UP, 1992.

Thelwell, Michael. "Introduction." In Tutuola, *Palm-Wine,* v–xviii.

Thieme, John. *Derek Walcott*. Manchester: Manchester UP, 1999.

Thurston, Herbert, and Donald Attwater, eds. *Butler's Lives of the Saints*. Vol. 3. Westminster, MD: Christian Classics, 1990.

Tiffin, Helen. "Post-Colonial Literatures and Counter-Discourse." In *The Post-Colonial Studies Reader*. Ed. Bill Ashcrift, Gareth Griffiths, and Helen Tiffin. London: Routledge, 1995: 95–98.

Tulasidasa. *Shriramacharitamanasa (The Holy Lake of the Acts of Rama)*. Trans. R. C. Prasad. Delhi: Motilal Banarsidass, 1990.

Tutuola, Amos. *My Life in the Bush of Ghosts*. In *The Palm-Wine Drinkard and My Life in the Bush of Ghosts*. New York: Grove P, 1994 (1954): 5–174.

——— . *The Palm-Wine Drinkard and His Dead Palm-Wine Tapster in the Dead's Town*. New York: Grove P, 1984 (1953).

Tversky, A. "Features of Similarity." *Psychological Review* 84 (1977): 327–52.

Uhrbach, Jan R. "A Note on Language and Naming in *Dream on Monkey Mountain*." *Callaloo* 9.4 (1986): 578–82.

Uttam, A. J. "Sufism and Communal Harmony in Sindhi Poetry." In Engineer, *Sufism:* 87–97.

Vālmīki. *Srimad Vālmīki Ramayanam*. Trans. N. Raghunathan. 3 vols. Madras: Vighneswara Publishing House, 1981–1982.

Venkatesananda, Swami. *The Concise Rāmāyaṇa of Vālmīki*. Albany: State U of New York P, 1988.

Virgil. *The Aeneid*. Trans. W. F. Jackson Knight. New York: Penguin, 1958.

——— . *Aeneidos*. In *P. Vergili Maronis Opera*. Ed. R. A. B. Mynors. Oxford: Oxford UP, 1972: 103–422.

Waines, David. *An Introduction to Islam*. Cambridge: Cambridge UP, 1995.

Walcott, Derek. *Dream on Monkey Mountain and Other Plays*. New York: Noonday P, 1970.

——— . *Henri Christophe: A Chronicle in Seven Scenes*. Barbados: Advocate Co., 1950.

——— . *The Joker of Seville and O Babylon!: Two Plays*. New York: Farrar, Straus, and Giroux, 1978.

——— . *Omeros*. New York: Farrar, Straus and Giroux, 1990.

——— . *The Sea at Dauphin*. In *Dream:* 41–80.

——— . "What the Twilight Says: An Overture." In *Dream:* 3–40.

Wallerstein, Immanuel. "Neither Patriotism nor Cosmopolitanism." In Cohen: 122–24.

Weiss, Anita M. "The Historical Debate on Islam and the State in South Asia." In *Islamic Reassertion in Pakistan: The Application of Islamic Laws in a Modern State.* Syracuse, NY: Syracuse UP, 1986.

Wittgenstein, Ludwig. *Philosophical Investigations.* 3d Ed. Trans. G. E. M. Anscombe. New York: Macmillan, 1958.

Wolpert, Stanley. *A New History of India.* 4th ed. New York: Oxford UP, 1993.

Woolf, Virginia. *A Room of One's Own.* San Diego, CA: Harcourt Brace Jovanovich, 1957.

Zabus, Chantal. *The African Palimpsest.* Amsterdam: Rodopi, 1991.

INDEX